THE SIXTEENTH
ROUND

Also by Rubin "Hurricane" Carter

Eye of the Hurricane: My Path from Darkness to Freedom

THE SIXTEENTH ROUND

FROM NUMBER 1 CONTENDER TO NUMBER 45472

RUBIN "HURRICANE" CARTER

Lawrence Hill Books

Cover design: Matt Simmons, www.myselfincluded.com
Cover photo: © Bettmann/Corbis

This edition published 2011 by Lawrence Hill Books
An imprint of Chicago Review Press, Incorporated
814 North Franklin Street
Chicago, Illinois 60610
ISBN 978-1-56976-567-8
Printed in the United States of America
15 14 13 12 11

Promised to . . .

Mae Thelma,
who
blessed my life with **Theodora,**
who

together . . .
create the only two reasons why I am
not lying flat on my back, *knocked out cold!*
And . . .
everything else is irrelevant.

Acknowledgments

On this page I would like to mention the least first—the ungodly nemeses in my life who have made it necessary for me to write this book: the corrupt and vindictive officials who played their roles to a T in this tightly woven drama to bury me alive, aided and abetted by laws which simply do not protect the sovereign rights of the individual, as the Bill of Rights requires, but the blatant wrongs of a select few.

This is not to say that no pure gems have passed through this wretched life of mine, because they came in droves, the most important one being Linda Yablonsky, my editor, the beautiful—and sometimes disturbing—woman, who waged an uphill battle in her efforts to make a writer out of a fighter, hoping to show in the final analysis that the *pen* is indeed mightier than the *sword*. But without her nourishing the literary seed, this story might not have been told in this particular medium.

My deepest appreciation is also extended to all those beautiful and courageous people who, at the risk of being incarcerated themselves, still appeared in court to testify in my behalf, stood firm on what they *knew* to be the truth, and suffered miserably for it at the hands of Madam One-Eyed Justice. Those people were Mrs. Catherine McGuire, Mrs. Anna Mapes, Merrit Wimberly, Welton Deary, Edward Allen, Hector Martinez, and John "Bucks" Royster.

I would also like to thank Peter Rush, Ronald Lipton, Frederick Hogan, and Billy Kilroy—four honest police officers—who at one time or another during the past seven years traveled on their own volition to the Rahway State Prison to offer their assistance in the struggle to set me free.

A special accolade goes to Frank Earl Andrews, for his guidance in making *The Sixteenth Round* a reality; to Mrs. Eleanor Howard, for her consistent words of encouragement, which somehow always managed to come when times were bleak; to Dave Anderson of *The New York Times*, whose enlightening articles exposed my fate to the public; and finally, to Richard Solomon—my main kazaam—who at times could be both warm and friendly, yet coldly precise and highly critical, and who always had his mind set toward furthering our common goal—my freedom.

Lastly, I would like to offer my gratitude to all the people—especially those millions of *little ones*—who, despite their Constitutional guarantees, are always subjected to the abuse of the law. Their strength has always been a constant reminder to me that love, compassion, beauty, and hope can still survive, even under this oppression.

For this I thank you one and all.

—RUBIN CARTER

September 1, 1973
Rahway State Prison,
New Jersey

CONTENTS

THE SIXTEENTH
ROUND

THE PRELIMINARY

At about 3:00 a.m. on June 17, 1966, the late-night calm of Paterson, New Jersey, was suddenly shattered by the voices of an angry white mob that had gathered in front of a dilapidated old bar and grill. The crowd furiously pushed and shoved against a cordon of police officers who had surrounded the tired nightspot, trying to get a look at the four bullet-riddled, blood-smeared bodies lying on the floor inside.

Their attention was momentarily diverted as a five-car, siren-screaming cavalcade sped around the corner and screeched to a grinding halt in front of the tavern. Several shotgun-bearing policemen leaped out of their cars and scrambled around a white Dodge that they had just escorted to the scene.

The chattering mob pressed closer as the police forced the two black occupants of the car out onto the street. The two men were confused by the hostile reception the mob gave them, and they had reason to be. I know, because I was one of them.

"Get out of the car!" a bull-faced cop snarled as he pulled open the door. "Stand up against that wall over there, and don't move until I tell youse to!"

Whatever else was wrong, I knew that getting out of that car might prove to be by far the worst thing I could do. "What the hell did you bring us here for, man?" I asked, but the cop just backed away and snaked out his pistol.

"Shut up!" he barked. There was complete silence around us now. Everybody in the street must have heard me when I swallowed. The cop pulled the hammer on his pistol back to full cock. "Just get up against that wall, and shut up!" he growled.

Before I could think of anything more to say, a paddy wagon and several more ambulances added further confusion to the already congested area. I felt myself being roughly searched, along with John Artis, a twenty year old boy who had been riding with me. Then we were pushed into the stinking rear of the paddy wagon and it took off, leaving my car behind.

My mind began racing for an explanation, but I could find none. Things were happening too fast. Before I had grasped the full significance of my predicament, the wagon slid to another halt at Paterson's St. Joseph's Hospital. Surrounded by squads of fully armed cops, we were hustled out of the truck and into an emergency operating room. There, a crew of doctors and nurses were frantically trying to save the life of a balding middle-aged white man. He had been shot in the head. The bullet had made a jagged exit from his left eye.

The room, along with almost everything in it, was all white. Cops dressed in blue, with white faces, crowded around us. Not a black man in the bunch. The sickly odor of ether hung in the air, and the room reeked of dried blood. I hated hospitals. Especially this one.

"Can he talk, Doc?" asked the bull-faced cop who a few minutes earlier had acted like he was Quick-Draw McGraw.

The doctor was clearly irritated by our sudden intrusion into his operating room. He glanced back over his shoulder, giving the cops, and then John and me, an annoyed look. When he spoke, it seemed to be with extreme reluctance.

"Yes, he can talk," he said finally. "But only for a moment." With the aid of one of the nurses, he raised the victim's head. The man was weak, pale, and seemed nearly dead; he had a ragged hole in his face where his left eye had been.

"Can you see clearly, sir?" Quick-Draw asked, absurdly. "Can you make out these two men's faces?"

The wounded man nodded weakly.

"Are these the two men who shot you?"

For what seemed an eternity, the injured man stared at me intently with his one remaining eye, glanced at John, then stared back at me some more. I almost cried with relief when he began to shake his head from side to side.

"But sir!" the cop said urgently. "Are you *sure* these are not the men?"

Then I saw it coming. Everything suddenly fell into place. I realized with a deep-seated uneasiness that if, in fact, two black men had shot this man, then it would make no difference to him that I was short, and the boy with me tall; that I was bald, bearded, and ugly while John Artis had no hair on his face at all; that I was black as virgin soot, and he as yellow as the sun—because to this critically injured man teetering there on the brink of death, all black people would look the same, especially those the cops had brought in.

I stood there watching the tortured expressions of pain wash over the one-eyed man's face, and felt a sharp pang of my own. But unlike his, mine came only with the memory of my past run-ins with the cops, of past incarcerations and hostilities. I closed my eyes and clenched my fists in rage, and at that moment I might indeed have been able to commit murder.

"Dirty sonofabitch!" The words spurted out of me so loudly and suddenly that everybody in the room turned in surprise and stared. "Dirty motherfucker!" I cried out again, and heard the despair in my voice. Dirty motherfucker, I thought. Here I go again.

THE FIRST ROUND

The Beginning

RUBIN, my Christian name, comes from the Book of Genesis, chapter 29, verse 32 of the Holy Scriptures. Other than both of us being black, that's about the only thing the Bible and I ever had in common.

HURRICANE is the professional name that I acquired later on in life. It provides an accurate description of the destructive forces that rage within my soul.

CARTER is the slave name that was given to my forefathers who worked in the cotton fields of Alabama and Georgia, and was passed on to me. The name is like any other—worthless—but it's the one that appears on my birth certificate.

The kindest thing that I can say about my childhood is that I survived it. I was born of devout Christian parents, May 6, 1937, in Delawanna, New Jersey, a small suburb of Clifton in Passaic County. My father, like his father and his eleven brothers, were all God's little children—preachers of the faith. Since I was the youngest of three sons, and neither of my brothers desired to tread on the heels of our religious father, it was always hoped that when I became of age, I would be the one to follow in his footsteps and choose the ministry as my way of life.

Considering that my father was a senior deacon in an impressive Baptist church, and that my family was thought to be somewhat better off than most, I can't really say that I was a victim of circumstance, or that the environment of my early life was unkind to me. I simply didn't have to bear the hardships and miseries that some of my black brothers and sisters living in the ghettos did; trigger mechanisms of violence—such as inadequate supplies of food, clothing, or shelter—were absent. My family didn't have the very best in material advantages, but we always managed to live comfortably.

I don't know at what age one becomes aware of the problems—

or rather, the moral precepts—society lays down for us to live by, but since my earliest recollections are of a time I pressed my nose against an icy window pane to watch the snow falling outside, and of heat, this autobiography begins around the age of five.

This was during the winter of 1942, a cold, bleak period in the United States: Pearl Harbor had just been bombed, and America was at war with two flanking countries at the same time. Fuel and food were being assiduously rationed out, and confrontations across both seas were rampaging furiously. At that time my family consisted of three boys and two girls: Lloyd Junior was the oldest; then came Lillian, James, and myself; then Beverly, the baby.

Our home was in a four-family apartment building in Passaic, and since we didn't enjoy the modern conveniences we have today, our principal fuel was wood or coal. Our friendly heat-maker was a monstrous, fuel-devouring four-plated burner, which we considered ourselves extremely lucky to have; not all families had stoves of this caliber then. Although our coal bill was exceptionally high, the stove was something we cherished.

My mother and father, Bertha and Lloyd, were born and raised in Georgia. On very cold evenings our family would gather around that homely stove and roast peanuts that had been sent to us by relatives still living in the South, while Dad would tell us strange stories about his childhood on the farm.

He would talk about stubborn mules named Sam or Jennie—white mules who wouldn't plow unless you called them "sir." He also told us about the snakes, coach-whipping snakes that could beat a man to death; ghosts that could scare a man to death; and tobacco-chewing crackers whose greatest pastime was tarring niggers, hanging niggers, and just plain killing black folks on some general principle.

Although I didn't understand the reasons for the things the crackers did to the niggers in Dad's stories, I would listen, enthralled, as his voice turned to an emotional whisper and his eyes brightly burned. Taking off my shoes, I would spread my legs out toward the warmth of the stove and allow my mind to race through the Georgia swamps with some big, terror-stricken nigger who had a pack of whooping crackers and howling dogs hot on his trail. Man! I was scared to death just thinking about it. But these were times we all enjoyed, pleasant evenings we always looked forward to.

Each family in our building had equal floor space in the basement for the storage of their coal—providing they had any. Since it was the duty of us boys in the family to replenish the fuel supply whenever we needed it upstairs, one of us would have to go back and forth to the cellar at least four or five times a day.

One day this irritating task fell to Jimmy. With the coal box in the house nearly empty, Jimmy, being very obedient (my father would tear his ass up if he wasn't), hurried to the cellar and was confronted with a neighboring family's son—the dreaded bully of the block—who, to make an already bad situation worse, was stealing our coal.

This young fellow was so bad he was even nicknamed "Bully." With flat African features pasted to a high-ridged head that easily could have belonged to a pancake-faced gorilla, he was short, powerful, shiny black—so black that a blue shadow seemed to lie upon him—and ugly enough to break daylight with his fist.

This lad's home was somewhere in the deep bayou country—Mississippi, I think—and it was very easy to picture him, even at this tender age, walking behind an old gray mule, sniffing farts, or picking cotton. This sucker was out there, and mean as a black bear during mating season.

Jimmy, on the other hand, was not a rough type. He was slender and more inclined to use brains than brawn. (His overt display of intelligence later carried him to bachelor's, master's, and doctor's degrees.) His handsome face, which was usually smiling, marked him as being good-natured and of a pleasant disposition. All in all, Jimmy was meek and kind of humble and, I venture to say, somewhat on the timid side. Physical conflict was not his cup of tea.

Unfortunate as it might have been, this was one confrontation he couldn't avoid: if he didn't get the coal and let the fire in the stove go out, my father would skin his ass alive when he came home from work that night. So it was either an ass-whupping downstairs or an ass-whupping upstairs. Jimmy chose the former, and rightly so.

What went on downstairs he later told us himself. It seemed that when he first stumbled upon Bully stealing our coal it scared him almost to death. He knew he couldn't stop, or beat, this black gorilla, so he decided to try a little cunning, hoping to appease Bully, get our coal, and get the hell out of there.

"Hi, Bully," Jimmy called, with a sheepish grin on his face.

But Bully wasn't going for none of that funny shit. Without

further provocation—other than that of getting caught stealing our coal—he sprang on my brother and unleashed a brutal attack that left Jimmy thoroughly beaten. Jimmy got out of that basement as fast as his little legs could carry him, making it upstairs for safety and assistance. Meanwhile big bad Bully, confident that there was no one to stop him now, returned to pillaging our coal.

Help for little Jimmy was not to be found upstairs. My mother and father had already gone to work, leaving my oldest brother in charge. Lloyd Junior undoubtedly could have taken care of the little hoodlum, had he seen fit, but, from what I saw, he had little inclination to do so and displayed no concern in the matter whatsoever.

This was more than I could bear. Jimmy was hurt, crying something awful. His nose was already swollen, spreading across his face, blood pouring from it constantly. But no one paid any attention to him—no one except me—as he sobbed through his story. Listening, I was confused: this situation was asking too much of my inexperienced mind. My emotions completely overpowered what little sense of reason I had, if indeed I had any at all. Every fiber of my body became taut with the anticipation of what must be done. My only thought was that the Carter family had to be avenged.

I imagine it was because I was immature that the only thoughts that came to me were those of violence. Bully's size and strength, prowess and daring, never entered my mind. Without uttering a word, and before anyone could think to stop me, I bolted down the stairs.

When I reached the cellar, I vaguely made out the outline of Bully's body in the obscurity of the coal bin. His features blended almost perfectly into the blueness of the coal he was stealing—this cat was just that black. Then, as my eyes became accustomed to the darker darkness around him, I realized that my quarry had not yet discovered me. He had his broad back to me and was nonchalantly heaping Lloyd Carter's coal into his bucket.

The element of surprise was in my favor. At that time I didn't know anything about fighting fair; in fact, I didn't know anything about fighting, period. But before my roguish opponent could straighten up and defend himself, I hurled my body into him with all my might, and with a vengeance that shocked even me. I hadn't known I was capable of such feelings.

Bully tripped and went down. I crouched over him, whaling like mad, until he finally managed to fight his way back to his feet. We stood toe to toe, slugging it out, swinging for all we were worth. Then I landed a sizzling haymaker against his bullet head, and he started backing up, with me crowding him, firing on him. The fighting became easier then, and I found I liked it. The more we fought, the better I seemed to get.

A shiver of fierce pleasure ran through me. It was not spiritual, this thing that I felt, but a physical sensation in the pit of my stomach that kept shooting upward through every nerve until I could clamp my teeth on it. Every time Bully made a wrong turn, I was right there to plant my fist in his mouth. After a few minutes of this treatment, the cellar became too hot for Bully to handle, and he made it out the door, smoking.

This was my first experience in fist fighting, and the fruits of my victory were sweet indeed. I could feel the pull of the little muscles interlinked and interchained from my fingertips to the small of my back. I felt the muscles in my legs too, from hip to toe, supporting me as I swayed, tired now. But dammit, I felt *good*. Even though I had come out with a busted lip, I had beaten the big bad block bully—and, man, I was hot-to-trot to fight some more.

Bully, however, must have run straight home to his black mammy. I couldn't begin to guess at the excuse he gave for his appearance, but it must have been a winner. Because the moment my mother and father came home from work that night, they were confronted with Bully's weeping mammy screaming accusations of how unmercifully I had beaten her poor little manchild.

My father entered my bedroom quietly and woke me up. I eased out of bed joyfully, not making a sound, being very careful not to arouse my sleeping brother. I was confident that Daddy was going to lavish royal praises on me for saving his coal, and I was just as anxious to tell him that I knew how to fight. I didn't want Jimmy awake for this, no, sir. I wanted to bask in the sunshine of Daddy's thanksgiving all by myself.

But when I entered the kitchen, my father yoked me with an unfamiliar roughness. He locked my head between his knees, pulled my pajama bottoms off, and whaled on my ass with the cord from the iron. I knew this wasn't for saving his coal. I jerked and sputtered, twisted and stuttered, desperately trying to find out what I had done wrong. But all my inefficient struggles and tears were in vain. I couldn't talk. I had an acute speech impediment at that time and could never say three clear words that made any sense to anyone but me.

But what hurt more than anything else was that my father didn't even try to find out of his little son had been justified in his actions or not. And being the deacon that he was—I suppose—he readily accepted someone else's version because it had come from an adult, and not because it was the truth. He could at least have tried to get my side of the story, I felt, or even my brother's or Lillian's. No. He believed Bully's black picker-headed mammy—and I'll bet she was the one who had sent Bully over in the first place. They surely didn't have any coal for themselves.

That beating is the first I can distinctly remember, and it was one of many just like it that would follow in its wake, some of which, I think, were totally uncalled for. But in my father's eyes they were ratified and sanctioned by the Holy Bible.

Thus began my first real awareness of my existence. I imagine such a blatant event was necessary to prod the faculties of my brain into full consciousness. It seems to me to have been similar to the birth of a baby—that is, to the moment the physician slaps the infant's buttocks and provokes his first sensations, indicating the proper functioning of his respiratory system.

Well, when my father got through with me that night, I couldn't say for sure what it did for my respiratory system, but I knew damn well that it interfered with my system of sitting down for quite some time.

Early the following morning I was awakened with the rest of the kids for school. I was enrolled in the kindergarten of Public School No. 7 and had been there for one half-term. I remember the family being somewhat solemn as we sat down for breakfast that morning, although the table was, as usual, heaped with plenty of succulent goodies to eat: southern-fried ham, eggs and hominy grits, steaming hot biscuits with Argo syrup, and plenty of butter on the side.

Man! Even though my butt was blistered, there was nothing wrong with my stomach, and I was ready to grease. But before anyone dared touch a morsel of food on the table, my father, seated at its head with his eyes closed and his hands folded, began his daily ritual of saying grace. We all had to follow his example.

"Dear Lord," he would reverently begin, "we are thankful for the food which we are about to receive. . . ."

But on that morning I didn't close my eyes. I just sat there looking at my daddy as his voice droned on emotionally, wondering how he could be talking to the Lord in such a convincing manner and know that he had unnecessarily abused me the night before. I couldn't understand it, and I was hurt. Hurt as only a small boy could be when his dad, his idol, has rejected the one contribution he feels he had made to the family—saving their coal.

When school was out that day, Jimmy came to take me home. We all attended the same school, so the task of taking me back and forth fell into the hands of Lloyd, Lillian, and Jimmy. I remember the weather as being very mean that wintry afternoon. It had been snowing exceptionally hard all day, and the snowdrifts were piled high.

As we struggled homeward, Jimmy suddenly clutched his stomach, became violently sick, and fell to the ground, vomiting. The whites of his eyes were the only signs of life I could detect in his dark face, and he trembled as if he were freezing over. This really scared me, and I immediately threw myself to the ground in the snow beside him and grabbed his coat, trying to pull him up.

"Jimmy! Jimmy!" I cried, brushing snow off his face. "Get up! Get up, Jimmy. Jimmy, please get up."

But he didn't seem to hear me. He just lay there, shivering, gagging, and trying to catch his breath. A group of school kids gathered and stood around looking at us like damn fools, but no one offered any help. Eventually someone—an older student, more than likely—told some teachers about what was taking place outside, and they rushed to help my brother. I was kneeling beside him in a snowdrift when they came and threw me aside to get to him.

I don't know why, but somehow I got the impression that they were handling him much too roughly for people trying to help him. This feeling reactivated my newly discovered fighting abilities, and as they struggled to pick Jimmy up, I tore into them for all I was worth, punching, kicking, and biting anything that got in my way.

"Leave my brother alone!" I cried, fighting desperately and feeling that same extraordinary sensation of the previous day welling up in me again. "Leave him alone! Leave him alone!" I fought all the more furiously as they got him up and started for the building.

Somebody grabbed me from behind and held on so I couldn't get away. I stopped struggling and just stood there, crying in frustration, wondering what was happening to my brother. When at last I was set free, I began walking in the direction I thought would take me home. I stumbled blindly, not really knowing where I was going, until a warm arm slithered around my shoulders.

"C'mon, Rubin," a sweet voice whispered. "Jimmy's gonna be all right. C'mon, let's go home."

I stopped and looked up, and there was Lillian with a sad smile on her face. But it was a smile that filled my heart with joy, for I could see the tenderness and affection in her eyes as she hugged me tighter. I leaned closer, feeling the warmth of her arms around my shoulders, and somehow everything seemed to be a little better. We turned around, and she took me home.

That night, when the family had seated itself at supper, Jimmy was still among the missing. As my mother set a steaming plate of collard greens upon the table, I asked her the question that had been bugging me all day. "Ma, wh-whe-wh-whe-where's Jimmy?" I stammered.

"Hush up, Rubin," she scolded fondly, but with sadness in her voice. "Jimmy's going to be all right. We will just have to do without him for a while. But we'll all go to see him pretty soon."

And so we did; the rest of the winter was consumed mainly by going to the hospital to visit him. Jimmy, it turned out, had come down with double pneumonia, and for weeks he was more dead than alive. My mother and father accepted the news, and the expense, like the champs they were.

While Jimmy was a boy he was always the sickly type, susceptible to anything. I can vividly remember the time he caught the measles and deliberately rubbed himself against me so that he could have a playmate while the rest of the kids were in school. When finally we both had the measles, Jimmy laughed like a sonofabitch, happier than a fag in a Turkish bath.

In a time between Jimmy's illnesses, my mother also went to the hospital, and the next time I saw her I had a new sister, named Rosalie. Now that puzzled the hell out of me. I mean, I had always been under the impression that babies were found under cabbage leaves, and this new development seemed mighty strange to me. Here I was with a brand-new baby sister, and, as I knew doggone well, my father didn't have a vegetable garden.

THE SECOND ROUND

The Birth of Vengeance

In the following spring, 1943, my father bought a new house, which naturally aroused much interest in our family. We were all filled with the happy anticipation of moving to a different environment. The menial chores that usually were the cause of bickering among us children we performed quickly, quietly, and with astounding proficiency.

Our new home was located on Twelfth Avenue in Paterson, New Jersey. And to say the least, in comparison with Passaic, the neighborhood looked bad. We had taken it for granted that we would be moving to a locale that would by far surpass the neighborhood we had been living in. The new house was much larger and prettier than our previous one had been, but the streets were dirtier and made of unsightly cobblestones, with twisted trolley tracks cutting through them.

When the family car and the moving van stopped in front of our new home, men, women, and children poured out of the neighboring houses and gathered on the sidewalks, watching our every move. They critically inspected the condition of our car, the style of clothing that we wore, the newness of our furniture—especially the floor-model radio. You can rest assured, they didn't miss much. They were like an audience of convicts watching a nude female perform.

The city itself was divided up into four sections—Up the Hill, Down the Hill, Crosstown, and Bunkerhill—and each sector had multitudes of rough, vicious young gangs controlling it. Our house was situated in the "Up the Hill" section. Each fellow residing in that particular six-block area—between Auburn and Carrol on the north and south, and Godwin and Governor Streets on the east and west—be he black, white, or technicolor, was destined to become a member of a gang called the Apaches. If he didn't belong to the tribe, he ventured outdoors at his own risk.

You couldn't go to school or the playground or even sit on your own front porch without a member of the Apaches trying to get to your black ass, or white ass, as the case might be. It didn't make any difference to them what color it was; if you didn't belong to the Apaches, then you had to be the enemy.

Man, it was like nothing I had even dreamed about before, a terrible, terrible place—not poverty-stricken, but simply one with a rough class of people. I learned sometime later that a white school-teacher had owned our house before my father and had thought it best, in view of the violence surrounding it, to leave. But I found out that, violent and destructive as the neighborhood was, there was one good principle to be learned by all, and it has remained with me throughout my life. This was the acceptance of people, regardless of race, creed, or color. The simple truth was, these distinctions were never evident, and the subject was not discussed. There were no such people in our young lives as Mister Charlie or the Devil—meaning white people—or Aunt Mary and Boy—meaning our mothers and fathers.

Maybe I was foreseeing the future, I don't know, but I made it my business to ask Dad why we had moved to Paterson when our old neighborhood was so much nicer. Now, usually he would have told me to shut up and mind my own business. This time, however, he must have detected a premonition in my voice. He explained that because of the increased size of our family we needed a bigger place to live. And with the purchase of this particular house, he had also bought an ice business to add to the family income.

Well, awright, then, I thought proudly. That makes all the difference in the world. Now we can show these nosy people that we're not trash—the Carter family are business folks.

After we were settled, our new home became a meeting place for young and old alike. I sometimes wondered if its attraction was due to the congenial, Christian disposition that my father made us reflect at all times, or to the fact that we were the first in the neighborhood to own a television set. In any case, everybody was welcome in the Carter house, and everybody came.

To say merely that my father was a good provider would not be doing him justice. His vigor, pride, and dedication to whatever he did—from raising a family of seven to preaching the Gospel on Sunday to slaving on two jobs six days a week—did much more than provide. They brought respect and solidarity to the family.

But it was my mother, dark and beautiful, the strong, silent figure in the family, who exercised a subtle control over all. Out of concern for his health, Mom often begged my father please to slow down before he killed himself. In his own defense on these occasions, Dad would seek comfort by quoting the Holy Scriptures.

"Bert," he would say to her, " 'whatsoever thy hand findeth to do, do it with thy might; for there is no work, nor device, nor knowledge, nor wisdom, in the grave, whither thou goest.' " And he'd keep right on slaving, just as hard as ever.

His work day would begin at five o'clock in the morning, when he picked up his ice from Crosstown and took it to the little icehouse around the corner to store it. Then he would make his rounds. He had to deliver the ice in the early morning, before his customers left for work, or the food they had in their iceboxes would go bad during the day. At three in the afternoon, he would lock up the icehouse and go to work at the Manhattan Rubber Company in Passaic. There he worked an eight-hour shift and returned home, bone-weary, at twelve. He got three or four hours of sleep, and then it started all over again.

It was my mother, finally, who conceived the idea that we boys should take over the management of the icehouse, so that our father could get some rest. At that time Lloyd Junior was fourteen years old, Jimmy was ten, and I was eight. When Mom presented the idea to my father, he grudgingly gave his consent. He did have some doubts about our using his truck to make the deliveries, but, after much thought, agreed to let us have it—with the stipulation that Lloyd Junior be the only one to drive it.

We had already boasted to our schoolmates—and convinced most of them—that we had always been running the business, not our father. So, in order to give truth to our lies, we eagerly grabbed at Mom's proposition.

Since I was unable to carry the heavy blocks of ice up three or four flights of stairs, my job was to cut the ice and service all the first-floor customers. I also had to stand on the running board of the truck and holler, "Ice! Iiiiice man! Get yo' ice while you can!" Then, when customers called to me, I would shout, "Whoooooooa, mule!" Lloyd would stop on a dime and give it nine cents change, jump out of the truck, and then he or Jimmy would take the ice I gave them to the customer.

At times business came so hot and heavy that Lloyd would violate my father's rule and let me drive. When that happened, you can't imagine how proud I felt. No one could tell me that I wasn't as much of a man as the others. Even though I had to sit on two or three pillows to look out the windshield, I was a man.

At the end of the hard day's work, we returned home, bathed, ate our supper, and then joined the rest of the fellows in the neighborhood. As in most clubs or gangs, one had to be fearless, had to thrive on fighting to become a member with any recognition. Because fighting, or going to war, was just like eating and sleeping— it was a necessity. And, to be sure, I had my share of fights. Perhaps I had the shares of some others as well. It seemed as if I was constantly being challenged by members of rival gangs and, more often than not, by the constituents of my own. It was still impossible for me to talk without stuttering. I had to stomp my feet to force the words out of my mouth. And people usually got quite a kick from the way I stammered, but if they made the mistake of laughing out loud, I would fire on them immediately, if not sooner, and try to knock their fool heads clean off.

Before many moons had traversed the skies, my fighting reputation prospered, and I became known as one "good with his hands." I took to fighting like a duck takes to water. Even at my age I could outfight most of the Apaches' members, but those that I couldn't— those that might have whupped me if we tangled—didn't care to chance it. If there just had to be a fight with the Rube, the general feeling went, they made damn sure it was for a good reason, because I fought hard, and I fought to win.

With an overabundance of heart combined with crude skill, I was soon elected to the position of "war counselor." Now this bizarre incumbency was a utopian honor among gang members— and goddamn fools—because the job included choosing the place where a brawl was to be held, the weapons that were to be used, and the time the scramble would take place. But these were only a few obligations of the job. Usually there was a reciprocal declaration of war between rival gangs, and when war was declared, each club dispatched its war counselor to meet and set the rules for the impending conflict. On many occasions, however, the threatened baptism by fire could be averted if the war counselors agreed to fight it out and settle the matter between themselves.

So it shouldn't be too difficult to understand that the war counselor had to be the best, or at least one of the best, fighters in his clan. Too many people were depending on his abilities for him to be any less; he maintained the integrity of the club.

I was proud of my position. It made me feel like a god. In my mind, I vaguely recalled some misbegotten slogan that went "Equality for all under God." I couldn't accept that. What with the position I held, and the gang's dependence upon my fighting skills, I felt uniquely superior. In the Apaches I was, in fact, accepted as a god, and there could be no equality in the world that I lived in—a world of conflict and confusion, where only the strong survived.

We were looked upon as a rough, menacing phalanx, an antisocial mob. To live up to this reputation, I must admit, we performed deeds that one might easily classify as being against the best interests of society. But we were *Apaches*—so we raided the enemies' neighborhoods, fought to a standstill the marauding gangs that violated our territorial boundaries, and pillaged the downtown marketplaces.

One day, while returning home from the movies, we decided to perform a feat of daring. There were about fifteen or twenty Apaches along, since the movie house was situated in enemy territory and we needed a show of force to deter any possible attack. We were approaching a store that had racks and racks of clothing displayed outside on the sidewalk. The object of each Apache was to run past the display, grab as much of the merchandise as he could handle, and then escape without getting caught.

The thought of keeping those clothes never entered my mind. Excitement, and the defiance of society, was our motivation. If, after we had stolen the clothing and made good our getaway, we could have returned it without further ado, we would have done so, gladly. The thrill was in eluding our pursuers, if there were any, and in putting the blame on that territory's own gang.

As one of the fastest runners in our club, I was the second or third to reach the clothing racks. Aided and abetted by the loose shirt I was wearing that day, I crammed it with sweaters and polo shirts until I looked like a top-heavy freak. Then I spun around and ran like hell, heading for the hills.

When I arrived home that midsummer afternoon, my mother and father were not in the house, and when my brothers and sisters spied all those clothes in my possession, they naturally claimed them for themselves. I took great pleasure in being able to give them something—even though that "something" wasn't mine to give. But it filled my heart to see them enjoying themselves, changing from shirt to sweater, back and forth, until they finally got what they wanted and the clothes were divided equally.

When my father came home that evening—I was out with the gang—and saw all his children wearing brand-new top clothes that he hadn't bought, he demanded to know where they had come from. And, being justifiably fearful of the harsh consequences if they were caught in a lie, my brothers and sisters naturally told him that Rubin had brought them home.

I returned later than usual that evening, slipped into the house, and crept upstairs to my bedroom, knowing that it was way past my curfew hour. Mom and Dad slept on the first floor, while we children slept upstairs.

Since each of us had his own room now, I had gotten into the habit of sleeping naked on warm nights. I had just made myself comfortable and was on my way to sleep, when my bedcovers were suddenly snatched off my body.

"Rubin? Wake up, boy!" I heard my father's gruff voice demand. "Where did you get all of these clothes from, huh?"

Slowly, cautiously, I opened my eyes and found my father sitting on the bed. In his huge hands were the shirts that I had gleefully distributed a few short hours before.

"A lady gave them to me, Daddy," I lied instantly, stammering badly, but thankful that my mind could think much quicker than I could speak.

My father stood up and spread the shirts out on the bed. He indicated the price tags. "Now don't lie to me, boy," he said threateningly. "All of these shirts have price tags on them. So tell me why somebody would *give* them to you?"

I'm a dumb sonofabitch, I thought to myself in disgust. Those price tags knocked the wind out of my lie. Why didn't you get rid of those tags, fool? I questioned my limited intellect. And then, though I knew that my father hated liars more than the people in hell wanted ice water, I stubbornly continued my prevarication.

"The woman gave them to me for working for her this afternoon, and she—"

"Awright, boy." My father held up his hands to silence me. "I'm going to buy that story. Now tell me where I can find this lady."

I lay there crouched up in fear, scared to death, and broke out in a cold sweat. I knew from the tone of my father's voice that he knew I was lying, and I knew that my goose was just about cooked. So, attempting to claim whatever leniency I could, I then tried to tell the truth.

"Daddy, I—I—"

"Yup! That's just what I thought!" he exploded with a ferocity that scared me even more. Then he dragged a thick belt from around his waist. "Boy, you've been lying to me all this time. Now I'm going to tear your ass up, and then I'm going to call the police. I won't have a lying thief for a son."

The heavy impact of the leather strap against my naked rump and shoulders produced a sharp sound that could be heard throughout the house. I'll wager my life that the cry I let out could be heard throughout the city. Each time my father lashed down with his cold-blooded belt, a welt the length and breadth of a pocket comb would take its place on my body. Several times, as I struggled to escape the descending whip, his belt would find my face as its target, and it rendered one of my eyes temporarily sightless.

This was by far the worst whupping that I had ever received, and had it not been for my mother, I might have been seriously injured by my father's evangelical rage. Waiting in the bedroom downstairs, my mother had suffered the noise and my increasingly feeble cries for help until she could resist no longer. "Lloyd! Lloyd!" I heard her calling through the mist of pain that racked my body. "Don't hit him anymore. He's had enough."

And the hot belt fell no longer.

I withered there in agony, trying to feel sorry for myself. I attempted to soothe the pain by fanning it, but I couldn't muster up much remorse for my stupidity. I knew that I'd been wrong. Wrong first for stealing the clothes, and then for piling a stupid act on the wrong one, by bringing the clothes home. I should have known that my father wouldn't go for that kind of bullshit, and that I should have told him the truth. I don't know what I was thinking about in the first place.

Twenty or thirty minutes must have passed before I heard someone coming up the stairs again. I had been waiting impatiently for that sound, because it had always been my father's custom to return to the child he had punished and calmly try to reason with him. So before he could reach my door, I hobbled painfully out of bed and opened it up.

Then I almost shitted on myself. Standing on the threshold of my room, almost filling the doorway, was a great big white man. But what really scared the hell out of me was that the man was dressed in a blue uniform, had a silver badge pinned to his chest, and wore an oversized pistol strapped to his waist. And if that doesn't add up to *cop* all over the world, there ain't no niggers in Harlem.

Thinking seriously about it now, it shouldn't have surprised me as much as it did. All that had been necessary for me to remember was that my father didn't pay courtship to lies. If he ever tells you that a mosquito can pull a plow, don't even bother about asking him how—just hook the motherfucker up. That's the type of man my father is.

"Are you Rubin?" the policeman inquired.

"Ye-y-yes, sir," I stammered.

"Then put your clothes on, kid," he ordered, circling the room and picking up the stolen merchandise. "We want to have a talk with you downstairs."

By the time I finished dressing, my surprise had turned to terror. When I finally stumbled down to the first-floor landing, I looked for my father to be waiting there for me—but he was nowhere in sight. The only other person I saw was another cop standing at the front door. He was holding it open.

"Where's his father?" the officer who had followed me down the stairs asked. It was the same question that was running through my mind.

But the waiting cop just clamped his hands to the seat of my britches, and shoved me out the door. "He don't wanna see this punk," he growled, pushing me down the front stairs. "So I'm locking the little nigger up."

I was propelled into the back seat of their patrol car, and then we headed for the police station. En route to headquarters, the cop that had walked me down the stairs spoke to his partner:

"Joe, isn't this the call that we received earlier today about stolen clothes?"

"Yeah, I think so."

"Well, wasn't there supposed to be more of them?"

"The whole damn gang—or so it seemed," the driver acknowledged. "But now that we've got this one, we'll get the rest of the black bastards too. You don't have to worry about that."

The two officers continued their conversation as if I was either deaf or didn't exist at all. They discussed the trouble in the city that various gangs, including the Apaches, caused and what they should do about it. Some of the remedies they suggested were exaggerated to the point of depravity, though I don't know if they were talking so sadistically just for my benefit or not. I do know it scared the hell out of me.

A few minutes later, and after much more conversation, we arrived at Headquarters and I was told to get out. As soon as my feet touched the ground, I had the impulse to run like hell.

As if he had read my mind, one of the cops cautioned me: "Little nigger," he said, "I wish you would run." He stood there patting his holstered pistol. "And I'll put a bullet right in your dead black ass!"

Not even a damn fool, which I wasn't, would have to think much on that statement. So the idea of running immediately evaporated from my mind. I didn't want a bullet in my black ass—or anywhere else for that matter. No, I'd just have to take my chances —if and when any came.

My escorts followed me into the stationhouse and led me up to a desk sergeant who was grinning as if they had just captured Baby Face Nelson. "Sarge," one of them said, "we caught one of the black punks who stole all of those clothes today, sir."

"Well, well, whatcha know 'bout that," the sergeant smirked, not even looking up from his work. "And where might the rest of them be, do you think?"

"Ah—ah—this one's old man turned him in, sir."

"Well, goddammit the hell!" the sergeant shouted, banging his fist on the desk. "There was more than just one of them, you Johnny-fat-ass! You know what I mean?"

"Yes, sir. I know, sir," Johnny-fat-ass responded nervously. "But don't worry, Sarge. We'll make this little bastard talk."

I was standing there with my knees knocking, shaking something awful, and knew that I was in a hell of a fix. Undoubtedly, these people meant business. The officer that had incurred his sergeant's wrath was standing directly behind me, breathing down my neck. If there is anything about that confrontation I'll never forget, it's the terrible odor of his breath. It smelled like wild apeshit. I felt nauseated, sick to my stomach, and I was ready to admit my guilt— anything—just so he would get out from behind me. I tried to move away, but he clamped his hand tighter around my neck and bent forward with a sickly grin on his pasty face.

"Ain't you gonna tell us what we want to know, little bitty black boy?" he sneered.

"Ye-ye-yes, sir," I sputtered, and at that moment meant every word.

Then I was hustled upstairs to the detective bureau and placed in a small room without windows.

"Sit your ass down right there, boy," the cop ordered, shoving a chair at me. "And when we come back I want the truth and nothing but the truth—or I'm going to use this on your ass. You understand me, boy?" He showed me his blackjack and grinned like a cannibal.

"Ye-yes, sir," I replied humbly. The two of them left the room and locked the door behind them.

Well, Rube, I thought, discouraged as I looked around the dismal little room, you've got your butt caught in a sling now and your gang's not here to help you out. In fact, the only way that you can get out of this mess is to tell the cops what they want to know.

Hell no, I'm not going to do that, I admonished myself. I'm not going to cop out first. But if things started getting too rough . . . well, what could I say? I only knew that I didn't want to get hurt any more because of some clothes that I couldn't use anyhow. My father had hurt me enough.

The little room that I was in was sparsely furnished. There was a broken and battered table, and the one chair that I was sitting in. The ceiling was so dirty and cracked that it looked like a detail map of Africa. The four paint-hungry walls were defaced with huge pockmarks, and my impressionable nine-year-old mind could almost visualize the many busted heads that might have contributed to the mutilation. But more than anything else, I worried that my own head would soon make some new additions to it.

Finally the door was unlocked and in walked the cop called Joe, the fat sucker who smelled like wild apeshit. "Awright, kid. I'm ready now," he said, sitting down on the table. "All you got to do is tell me who was with you, and give me their addresses. Then we'll take you home. After all, I don't think it was entirely your fault."

I looked up at the roly-poly officer in confusion. His considerate tone of voice was not what I had expected, but it did ease my troubled mind. Well, all right then, I sighed in relief. This is more like it. Now if I can just bullshit this fat chump for a little while longer, I thought to myself, I might get out of here without being hurt, and without squealing on the other fellows. My thoughts began to skyrocket as I tried to get a plausible story together. Lying my little ass off.

"Well, sir," I began, stammering just a little bit more than was necessary. The cop removed a pencil and pad from his shirt pocket. "As I was coming home from the movies today, I saw some boys stealing clothes from this store. But," I pleaded, "I had nothing to do with it, sir."

The officer sitting there on that table in front of me didn't move, he just sat there looking at me. He hadn't even moved to record anything that I'd said so far. With an exasperated sigh, he returned the notebook to his pocket and stood up.

"Yeah, and then what happened, kid," he inquired softly, giving me the distinct impression that he was really believing what I was saying. "Go on with your story. I'm listening. Keep talking."

Mistaking the man's sympathetic tone of voice for authentic gullibility, I added insult to injury and kept right on lying.

"As I was saying, sir, I was on my way home, and when I turned the corner, I found a bag of shirts lying in the street—the same ones that my father gave to you. I didn't mean any harm, sir," I began sniffling, trying to clinch my story with his pity.

"Why you lying black bastard!" the cop exploded savagely, smashing me in the face with one hand and then the other. "Look over there, you punk sonofabitch!" the man screamed, pointing to the door. "Do you see that looking glass hanging there? Well, that's what you call a two-way mirror. And standing on the other side of that mirror, looking in here right now, is the owner of the store that you niggers robbed. He has identified you as being one of the first to pilfer his goods. Now whatcha got to say about that, you lying bastard?" He slobbered from his mouth.

"But—but—but—" I stammered.

"Don't lie to me anymore, nigger," the cop threatened viciously. "Or I'll knock you off that goddamn stool."

"But—I—I—" and then a blue and yellow explosion erupted in my head. The blow hurt bright red, and then amber, and the impact went mushy inside my head, swelling up black and taking everything over. I found myself lying on the floor with the cop's foot pressing down on my head.

"I ought to stomp your fucking brains out," he snarled down at me, using his foot to bash my face against the floor again and again. "You didn't think we knew about that old lady you punks knocked down while stealing those clothes, did you?"

I tried to dissolve my body, melt into the floor to escape the wicked punishment of his foot before the fool could hurt me anymore. I didn't know anything about a woman being knocked down, and no one had mentioned it to me—or at least, I couldn't remember it.

But one thing was vividly clear: knocking me down and stomping my head into the floor did not serve the purpose for which it was intended. Any kind of word, harsh or sympathetic, would have been far more effective than what this cop was doing.

This man scared me, and it was during this instant that vengeance —stripped naked and real—claimed me as its victim and I felt the first tremors of a fiery passion engulf my body. It was not a pleasant feeling. It was a terrifying one that I did not fully understand, but it so dominated the moment that I willingly trusted my life to its sole discretion.

I looked up at the fat man hovering above me now with a brand-new weapon—hatred, and I knew in my heart of hearts that I wasn't going to tell this motherfucker a goddamned thing. From this point on, I decided, no man—I mean *no* man—would ever again put his hands on me in anger and be around tomorrow to talk about it. This included anybody and everybody, be they black, white, or technicolor; my father, a preacher, or the police.

I got myself together, up off the floor, and stood there glowering at the fat cop. I watched as he wiped the sweat from his face with a filthy brown handkerchief he had just blown his nasty nose into.

"Awright, punk," he barked, "let's get down to business now. I want the names and addresses of those other bastards, and I want them *now*." But only silence greeted his demand.

He immediately lost his temper again. His eyes burning bright with anger and disbelief, the man stepped forward and raised his hand to hit me again.

"Why you dirty sonofabitch, you!" he shouted, moving closer. "Don't you hear me talking to you, boy?" I backed up a step and crouched.

"D-don-do-don't hi—don't hit me no more, man," I warned, my voice barely above a whisper, my body tense and coiled. I was ready to spring at him at the slightest provocation, regardless of the consequences.

The warning in my voice arrested the man's hand on its downward arc, and I could detect a slight flicker of amazement invade his eyes. I could almost hear him ask himself, "What the hell is this?"

Just in the nick of time, the door creaked open and in walked the cop's partner.

"You all set to go, Joe?" he asked, locking the door behind him.

"No, not yet, Mike," his partner answered vaguely, still looking at me very peculiarly. "But you know something? I've got a strange feeling about this guy."

"Whatcha mean—a strange feeling, Joe?"

"Awwwww, shit! Skip it," the fat cop said, sounding a little bit disgusted with himself. "Just find out what are we going to do with this guy. Because he's not telling us nothing."

The larger of the two cops looked at his partner as if he had suddenly lost his cotton-picking mind.

"Whatcha mean he's not gonna tell us anything?" he asked. "What are you—"

"Jesus fuckin' Christ already, Mike!" the fat cop shouted at his buddy, his face turning beet-red. "Just do what I asked you to do, okay?"

Whereupon Mike, stunned and bewildered, turned and left the room.

When the door was closed and locked again, Joe and I went on glaring at each other from opposite ends of the table. Finally, when the quiet in the room had become almost unbearable for me, he broke the silence.

"Want a smoke, kid?" he asked.

"N-n-no, sir."

"Look, relax, kid," the officer consoled. "Everything's going to be all right now."

I looked at the man appreciatively, wanting to thank him for leaving me alone. I wanted to tell him how glad I felt, but I couldn't speak to save my life. I had always been told that as I became older, my speech would eventually straighten itself out, but it did not happen that way with me. Any effort I made to talk made my speech worse, and therefore my habit was to speak as little as possible. My reply to most questions was either yes or no.

I then began to realize why this cop was beating on me. Since one of my eyes had already been completely closed by my father's belt when he first saw me, the man probably thought that if my own father didn't give a damn about me, why should he? I realized that if I was to have any protection at all, I would have to provide it for myself. But I had been hurt by adults enough on this day to last me forever, and if I could possibly help it, it would never happen to me again.

When Joe had finished his cigarette, his road partner returned from his errand.

"Joe, the captain said to take him home now, and to tell his parents to report with him to the Child Guidance Bureau tomorrow at ten o'clock."

"Okay, Mike. And thanks," Joe replied. He turned to me. "Let's go, kid. You're going home."

My mother was waiting for us when we arrived back at the house, and opened the door before the policeman had a chance to knock.

"Mrs. Carter?" the officer inquired. "May we speak to your husband, please?"

My mother invited them in and left them in the living room with my father, who had been sitting there reading the evening paper. She took me into the kitchen and fed me the supper I had missed earlier that night. On the way to the kitchen, I had to pass my father in conference with the two cops, and I prayed that he would say something to me then. But he acted as if I didn't exist, and that hurt more than anything else.

"Goddamn!" I wanted to cry out. "I didn't kill anybody. All I did was steal some clothes."

The following day I was placed on two years' probation for petty larceny. I stood there and listened to the probation officer righteously proclaim that because my father had turned me in, "Justice had been tempered with mercy." But the dumb sonofabitch didn't mention that if it hadn't been for my father in the first place, I wouldn't have been on probation at all.

THE THIRD ROUND

A Fight for Life

As we Apaches grew older, our activities didn't change much, except that our doings became more adult. So, in the next three years, I became involved with the police on two or three other occasions—but now they kept their hands to themselves. Because I was ready, I was willing, and, goddammit, I didn't give a fuck!

My education suffered similar changes when I was about eleven and was sent to a disciplinary school, which only added fuel to my already simmering fires. This school had all the hard-to-handle juveniles in the city. All the teachers were men, and only the strong survived. An instructor's only means of discipline was physical force, and you better believe that he had to be very careful with it. Because authority meant nothing to us boys, and a good fight was appreciated by all.

Whenever the weather permitted, swimming led the agenda as our gang's favorite pastime, and we used the local river branches and sumpholes for our bare-assed beaches. There was one sump-hole that we patronized more than any of the others, one that all the gangs in town considered neutral territory.

The gangs' governing bodies had agreed that there could never be any justifiable reason to violate this swimming hole's neutrality. To do so was looked upon as an act worse than treason. It was the only place in Paterson—or in all of Passaic County, for that matter —where all club members were on neutral ground.

We called the place "Tubbs"—a reference to its size and shape. Relatively speaking, Tubbs was no larger than an ordinary bath-tub, but hardly pure enough to bathe in. The filthy water in which we luxuriated was about five or six feet deep, complicated by a deadly whirlpool where a small waterfall began. More than one boy had lost his life in these muddy waters, but Tubbs was our

Mecca in the summertime, the only one we had, and we loved every stinking nasty inch of it.

On one weekend day in June, with Paterson withering under its first heat wave of the summer, we Apaches were sweltering in the heat of our chicken-coop clubhouse, undecided as to what kind of deviltry we could get into. Someone suggested we go swimming, and we all agreed.

By the time we had hiked across town and reached the swimming hole, it was late afternoon and Tubbs was pretty crowded. It seemed that many of the clubs had had the same thought we had—it was just that hot. All our rivals were there: the Cherokees, the Optimists, the Gaylords, the Mohawks, the Outlaws.

Even allowing for the official neutrality of the territory, there was very little intermingling between us. But the rules required greetings and salutations, and these we extended to each member of the other clubs, according to his rank and reputation.

"Hi, Rube!" hollered Tiny Tim, the six-foot war counselor of the Mohawks.

"Hi, Tiny," I answered.

"Hey, Silent Knight!" the president of the Gaylords yelled from the water, using the nickname they sometimes called me. "C'mon in, man, and let's see who can get closest to the waterfalls without going over. Okay?"

I stood there facing the water for about five minutes while I tried to answer the challenge, to tell the guy he had a deal. But all I could do was stutter and stomp my foot, then sputter and stomp some more. I spun around when I heard what I thought was mocking laughter coming from behind me.

"S-som-something fun-fun-funny to you, man?" I challenged Lurkie White, the dreaded warlord of the Cherokees.

"Naw, I wasn't laughing at you, Rube," he said with a note of sincerity. His dark, handsomely chiseled face lit up in a wide, shit-eating grin. "But if and when I do laugh at you, buddy, I'll do it to your face and not behind your back. Can you dig it?"

I gave him a piercing stare for a few seconds, trying to ferret out a deceptive look, smile, or anything that might show me he was making jokes at my expense. When I had satisfied myself that he was not, I replied, "S-sol-solid, jack. Just c-c-come ahead whenever you're ready."

When the others realized that Lurkie and I weren't going to fight and disturb the tranquility of this sacred hollow, the tension eased and my words settled the air like a spray of water on a dusty street. It was well known that if ever two people despised each other, here we were, face to face—the two most treacherous warloads in Paterson.

All of central Passaic County remembered the chaotic state of affairs that had once existed between the Cherokees and the Apaches. It had become a legend that was still told over counsel fires, but it was a period of bloodletting that the two opposing factions did not care to revive.

The war had been instigated primarily by the foolish act of an overly courageous Apache, a dumb sonofabitch who was caught in Cherokee territory by himself. Needless to say, they hung some mean sport right on his black ass, which could only have been expected. But the vicious amputation of the fellow's left ear and the branding of a letter "C" on his forehead was, we felt, going too far. It was the work of a sadistic monster—Lurkie. Even though it had been our boy's own fault for getting caught in restricted territory, he was still an Apache, and therefore entitled to his pound of flesh in revenge. Immediately there was a declaration of war. Word was sent to the Cherokees. Lurkie and I met to discuss the terms under which the war would be fought. Then the war began.

I won't go into the gory details of that brawl now, because someone might get the impression he was reading a report of the 1953 African uprising in Kenya. We fought harder, or at least as hard, as Jomo Kenyatta and his Mau Maus fought when they battled Britain for their independence. Suffice it to say that we scuffled for weeks upon torturous weeks, and a good many people were critically wounded.

Finally, in an act spawned by desperation, the two governing bodies called a meeting and sat down at the negotiating table. They agreed that if the warfare was allowed to continue any longer, there wouldn't be enough able-bodied men left uninjured to make up one gang, much less two. Therefore it was suggested and readily agreed upon that the two warlords would fight it out to settle the matter. And may the best man win.

The following morning Lurkie and I met on our way to school. The Cherokee war counselor was not a large fellow. One could even say that we were exact replicas of each other, both equally short and stocky, though his shoulders were much wider than mine, and I had not been gifted with his handsome facial features. But Lurkie wasn't much of a talker, and I couldn't talk at all, so we started fighting right away. The moment we squared off and hooked up, I knew that I had more hell on my hands than I'd ever had before.

Lurkie turned into a savage monster. We fought in the street like wild cats and dogs for about an hour and a half before we were stopped by a passing police car. But as soon as the twelve o'clock lunch whistle blared, we were at it again. This time we fought our way home, ate lunch, and battled our way back to school. When class was through for the day, we rumbled some more. Man, by this time I was getting pretty tired of fighting. But the honor of the Apaches was at stake, and I had to fight; so fight I did.

Eventually, anything can cease to hold one's interest, and our fight was no exception. After days of savage brawling at the rate of four times a day, the battle was called to a halt and considered a draw. Each club was satisfied with the results, and I was satisfied just to have the fighting stopped.

Since nothing had really been proved by our brutal confrontations, there always remained an uneasy truce between the Cherokees and us. The more Lurkie and I ran across each other, the worse the situation became. It was a simple matter of who could beat whom. We both wanted to know but were reluctant to take the necessary steps to find out.

Now Tubbs was situated in a small valley surrounded by medium-sized mountains, with the renowned Passaic Waterfalls on one side of it, and a chain of dye factories staggered along the other. To enter or leave the place, it was necessary to travel a narrow footpath that led into the mountains, over the waterfalls, and out to the streets. This was the only way in, or out.

When we had deliriously swum away a good part of what remained of the day and it started getting cool, we dressed quickly for the long trip back home. My mind had by this time wandered far away. I was totally relaxed, snug, and at peace with the world.

"Hey, Rube!" a familiar voice called, startling me out of my reverie. "Look at that bum stretched out there in the grass," the boy laughed. "Man, that cat is really tore down."

I turned my head and looked over in the direction that the boy was pointing, and sure enough, there was a white man lying in the grass. He didn't look like the common hobo that I was familiar with, nor did he appear especially drunk. He was medium-built, ruddy complexioned, and seemed to be in his early thirties. While he may have had a few drinks up under his belt, I knew he couldn't be as drunk as he was pretending. As we stood there looking at the man rolling on the ground, he imitated an exaggerated stagger and pulled himself to his feet.

"Hey, c'mere, fellows!" he invited, pretentiously slurring his words. "Ya' wanna see some'hing?" he called. He held out his arm to reveal a gold wristwatch, and steadily advanced on us. "Don't be afraid," he soothed. "I'm not going to hurt you."

As he wobbled closer, he took off the watch and tried to give it to one of the boys. I felt a sharp twinge of foreboding.

"Le-l-let's go, fellows," I said, pushing the boys ahead of me. I shoved them down the path where the rest of the gang had disappeared five minutes before. "C'mon, let's get out of here!" I said more forcefully, realizing that this man had purposely waited until the others had gone before stopping the last ones in line—us.

Now the man appeared to be sober. Anticipating our move, he jumped in front of us to block the path.

"Hold on there, Moonshine!" he sneered sarcastically, removing his wedding band and holding it out for me. "Here, I've got something for you, too." He threw the ring, and hit me in the chest with it.

Now my premonition had developed into fear. I shouldered the boys in front of me, trying to push them past the roadblock, and barked at them in the most menacing tone I could muster. "A-al-all right, yo-yo-you guys!" I sputtered. "Le-le-let's—"

Once again my inability to speak without stuttering foiled my plans. The man grabbed one of the boys around the waist and dropped to his knees, pleading, "No! Please! You stay here with me, darling. Let the others go if they want to."

That was the straw that broke the camel's back. Something was terribly wrong with this fool. He must be crazy or something, I thought. He wasn't drunk at all. The boy struggled furiously in the man's clutches, trying desperately to free himself. Then he shouted out in alarm, "Hey! Whatcha trying to do, man?"

"Oh, c'mon, sugar," the man whimpered miserably, fumbling with the struggling boy's belt. "Be good to mama, darling, and I'll let you keep the watch."

"Look out, motherfucker!" the frightened boy screamed, punching the man in the face. "Turn me loose, man! Turn me loose!"

But the white man suddenly picked the boy up and threw him viciously to the ground, straddled him and tried to pull his pants down.

"Why you black bastard, you," he growled spitefully. "Now I'm going to take some."

I could feel fear and anger erupt within my body, the anger dominating the fear as the man's malicious words echoed through my mind. He had used the word black as though it was something nasty. A stinking motherfucker who was trying to force us into an indecent act had the nerve to call us "black" with the implication that we were nasty, because of our blackness.

I reached down and picked up a large soda bottle that was lying at my feet. I yelled a warning to the man to let my friend go, but the slobbering punk clung tenaciously to the boy's waist. Realizing that the man wasn't listening to anything I'd said, I reared back and threw the bottle with all my might. I wanted to bust that sissy wide open, and prayed my aim would be true.

The airborne bottle streaked through the summer air, twisting and sparkling, caught in the ebbing rays of the fading sun. *Ka-thunk!* It splattered against the man's head, and he toppled slowly to the ground, blood gushing from his wound.

"Run! Run!" I shouted in alarm, as the man groggily regained his feet. But my partners needed no second invitation; they ran like reindeers.

In my concern for them, however, I had somehow neglected to protect number one, and now I found myself dangling in mid-air. He had grabbed me by the neck and thighs, and was holding me up over his head.

"Ah-haaaaaa, you black bastard, you!" the man's bloodied face laughed up at me. "I got you! I got you now, and I'm going to throw your nasty ass over that cliff." And with that he started walking toward the Passaic Waterfalls, twenty or thirty feet away.

I begged and pleaded, I kicked and hollered, fighting desperately to break away. But the man was too strong for me. I cried and begged some more, but nothing seemed to affect him. I looked down, panic-stricken, as we neared the edge of the cliff. My eyes fell on the bloody gash in the man's head, and for some reason it reminded me of the scout knife in my pocket. Since I had my hands free, I reached in my pocket and got my knife.

"You bet-bet-better pu-put me down, man!" I warned him when we were about two or three steps away from the cliff's edge.

"Shut up, you no-talking sonofabitch," he snarled at me, now standing on the very edge of the cliff, "because tomorrow there'll be one less nigger in this world. You!"

I cannot record precisely the thoughts that went through my mind then. Time and other, similar circumstances, have withered my recollection. But this man frightened me, scared me like that cop had on my first arrest, and I wasn't about to let him hurt me if I could help it. I took my knife and tried to break it off in his head.

"Owwwwww, you stabbed me!" he shrieked, throwing me to the ground and kicking me in the stomach. "Awwwwwww, you've got it coming now, boy." He charged at me as I struggled to my feet, the knife still clutched in my hand.

Here was a situation in dire need of a diversion. If there was a God, now was the time for him to show Himself. Here I was, faced with defending myself against a degenerate old man. Or, to satisfy the skeptic, here was a gentleman protecting his valuables from the clutches of a young thug. Whichever version the reader cares to assume for his own personal satisfaction doesn't matter to me.

In any case, my struggles to regain my footing quickly resulted in getting my legs tangled up, and I fell back to the ground. The man, in the momentum of his charge, tripped over me and fell to the ground too. As he fell, he grabbed onto my legs.

"Awwwwwww, I got you now, boy!" he said with satisfaction.

"Pl-plea-plea-please, mister!" I begged, frustrated with my speech, tears flooding my eyes. "Ple-plea-please, lemme 'lone."

"Oh, nooooo, you sweet little bastard, you," the man slurred, gleaming wickedly. "No, no, boy. You cut me. Now I've got to show you who's boss."

Apparently the man forgot, or simply chose to disregard, the knife I had in my hand. He knelt before me, blood streaming down his face. My mouth opened and closed silently, trying to form the words that were in my mind but would not come to my lips. Then he threw himself on me with a grimace of delight, moaning, groaning, and blissful.

"Ahhhhhh, sugar-baby," he whispered in a tone of ecstasy, his arms encircling my neck, his scratchy beard massaging my face. "Mmmmm, this feels good," he was saying when I drove my knife in his side.

"Uhupppppp!" he grunted with pain, his eyes snapping open in surprise. Blood spurted from his lips, and I drove my knife again and again into his ribs. Then he jerked and sagged heavily on top of me.

I pushed him off and got on top of him, but still he struggled. My mind was shouting, "I told you not to scare me, mister! I told you not to scare me!" And each time this thought flashed through me, I plunged the knife into his heaving chest again.

Then a convulsive shudder racked his body, and his eyes fluttered open. A long, wheezing, gurgling sound escaped his lips, and the man struggled no more. I peered at the chalk-white face beneath me; sightless eyes stared back. An electrical charge shot through my body, and my hands began to quiver and shake uncontrollably.

I leaped off the man, the knife slipping from my limp fingers, and sank to the ground. "Oh, my God," I remember saying, tears streaming down my face. My hands were covered with blood. "Oh, my God," I thought. "What have I done?"

I didn't know if he was dead or alive (the latter, it turned out), but I knew I had to get out of there. A steel band that seemed to be embracing my chest had reduced my breathing to short gasps. The cool breeze no longer stirred, and the birds that had been chirping a few minutes earlier were now gone. The warm sun had long since faded, and everything was dark and quiet. Quiet as death.

"Get yourself together, fool!" some still-rational segment of my mind demanded. "Get yourself together and get out of here." As if this urgent petition had been directed to my feet, rather than to my head, I found myself racing down the pathway towards the street.

"Wait! Wait a minute, fool," that same voice reasoned. "Where's your knife, dummy? Go back and get your knife, fool! Get your knife," it demanded. Reluctantly, I went back and got the knife, then continued on my way.

It was twilight when I got back to my neighborhood that evening. I had no thought of searching out the gang. I was troubled, confused, and scared—so scared that I went straight home, up the stairs, and got right into bed. Lying there in the dark, I still trembled with fear.

When I didn't show for supper, my mother came upstairs to see what was wrong with me. "Rubin?" she called softly, coming towards the bed where I stayed huddled beneath the covers, alternately sweating and shivering. "What's wrong, baby?" she asked, sitting down and placing her hand on my forehead to see if I had a temperature. "You don't look too good. How do you feel?" she asked gravely. Her beautiful brown eyes radiated love.

Immediately I became a captive of her concern, and all my afflictions of the day returned to haunt me with a mulish perversity.

"Oh, Momma, Momma!" I cried, falling into her arms and hugging her tightly, laying my head on her breast.

"Now, now, Rubin." She stroked my head soothingly, and gently began rocking me. "Tell Mama what's wrong with her little man," she said apprehensively. She knew that if I was crying, something unusual had to have happened.

But I couldn't have told her what was wrong even if I'd wanted to. There was no way in the world she could have understood it. I didn't understand it myself. But I knew that if I broke down and told her what I had done, she would tell my father, and he would call the police. So I just lay there in her arms, secured and comforted by her mere nearness. Sometime after that, I fell asleep.

That night, or in the early morning hours, I was suddenly awakened by a bright light shining in my eyes. My bed was soaking wet, and the room was brilliantly lit by lights that couldn't possibly have come from the lone bulb of my small lamp. Loud clanging noises seemed to perforate my ears and surround me. 1 looked for its source.

Across the room, on the walls, I saw people. Little people with hoods covering their faces as they raced up and down the wallpaper. I began laughing. Laughing hysterically.

Then I saw a slew of funny little policemen driving great big motorcycles, chasing the hooded men all over the walls. The crooks, whom I assumed the hooded men to be, were themselves riding in an oversized automobile, driving it recklessly all over the place to escape the long arm of the law.

This mockery of my senses made me laugh harder and harder. I couldn't have stopped for all the tea in China. I laughed and laughed. I cried and cried. Sharp pains began shooting through my stomach, hurting me something awful. I couldn't catch my breath, and it seemed that I was on the verge of passing out. But I couldn't stop laughing.

"Ma! Ma! Look, Ma!" I laughed, convulsed with pain. I picked my mother's face out of the many gathered in my room. "See the little men, Ma! See the men!" I cried, laughing harder and harder.

"Stand in front of him, Mrs. Carter," a strange voice ordered. "Block the walls so that he can't see."

Obeying, my mother sat down and pulled me gently, but persuasively, into her arms, and pressed my face against her bosom. But it didn't matter, I could see right through her.

"Look, Ma, look!" I demanded, my voice a little muffled by her body. "Can't you see them, Ma? Can't you see?" I laughed until excruciating pains choked me, and doubled me up.

"Get that blanket and put it over his head," the strange voice spoke again. As I broke away from my mother, painful spasms racked my body, but tears of laughter still streamed down my face.

Then two men entered my view, picked up a blanket and held it up to block the walls.

"Help, Ma! Mama, help!" I screamed, struggling to get off the bed, trying to see around the blanket. "Don't l-le-let them do that! I can't see! I can't see the little men!" I cried, fighting furiously to keep the two men from covering my head.

Then something that felt like a sharp needle pricked me in the butt—and that's all I remember.

When I regained consciousness, or whatever it was, two full days had passed. Days of which I knew nothing. Long dreary hours filled with work and worry for my beautiful mother, who slept not and ate not, but endured a full-course meal of trepidation.

I had been downed by a disease that had no name, but one that had carried my temperature up to a deadly hundred-and-six. The doctor, whose strange voice I had heard in the room that night, had placed me on the critical list, and thought I'd die by morning. Fate, however, had intervened. And, as in Rocky Graziano's life story, maybe, just maybe, Somebody Up There liked me, too.

A few days later, however, I was well enough to return to school, the episode at Tubbs all but forgotten. Walking to school with several club members, I noticed no change in their normal demeanor. No one mentioned Tubbs. But before we reached our destination, I received word from a passing teacher that I was wanted in the main office. There a secretary informed the principal that I had arrived, and told me to have a seat. It wasn't long before he appeared in his doorway.

"Come in here, Rubin," he motioned, his perpetual grin on his face. (He always looked like the cat that had just eaten the proverbial canary.) "Gentlemen, this is Rubin Carter," he announced, nodding for me to take a chair at a table where two other men were already sitting. "Rubin, these men are from Police Headquarters," the principal went on. "They would like to speak with you."

There had been no need for the principal to tell me who these men were or where they had come from. I knew from the giddy-up they were cops. Shit, even at my age cops looked like something other than human, and these two misfits were no exception.

The one sitting closest to me had a shiny bald head, and his hawk nose sat between pure blue eyes that appeared blank. He sat very erect, which gave me the impression that he was tall, and while his shiny head made him look hideous, his features were not ugly—only sharp and harsh, like a man who didn't take any shit.

The other "gentleman," as the principal had called him, was a short, fat, sloppy individual of questionable gender. In his fat face, shadowed by black and gray whiskers, his tiny eyes were spiritless holes between which was a thin, pale nose that expanded to wings as broad as the thick lips beneath it. His double chin was surrounded by shadowy wads of dirty flesh.

"Awright, punk!" he snarled. He picked a booger out of his nose and added it to the other stains on his suit. "We want the truth, and if you—"

"Now, hold on, gentlemen," the principal interrupted. "That tone of voice, and its implied threats, will not be tolerated in this office."

The cop's face turned crimson under his dirty beard, and he looked to his partner for help. No help was on the way.

"In that case, sir," the cop said meekly, "can we take him with us?"

"Yes, I think you'd better," the principal snapped. "And while you're doing that, I will notify his parents." He was picking up the telephone as they led me out the door in handcuffs.

When we arrived at Headquarters ten or fifteen minutes later, I was locked in a cell that had a long slat hanging from the wall for a bed. The cell was the old-fashioned kind, with bars so close together that I couldn't pass my hand between them. It had no toilet.

After I'd been there alone for a couple of hours, the two policemen returned and locked themselves in with me. They ordered me to tell them about the man at Tubbs, and I, of course, replied that I didn't know anything about a man at Tubbs, and hadn't been there for quite some time.

"Look, wise guy!" the fat man bellowed, pacing up and down

the floor. "We know you were at Tubbs last week, and we know who was with you, too. So you better believe that we know what happened also. Why don't you just tell us about it and get it off your chest."

Silence.

The bald-headed detective pulled up a chair then and spoke for the first time.

"Rubin?" he addressed me in a mild tone that belied his awesome appearance. "He's telling you the truth, son. We have three signed statements against you already. Did you think that those other punks were going to take the weight by themselves?" he asked.

Silence.

"Big Bad John," the one who had started the questioning, couldn't take my tight-lipped attitude, and he advanced threateningly, cursing and shouting profanities. "Goddammit, boy! You'll talk! You'll talk, you dirty sonofabitch. You'll be making speeches when I get through with your black ass!"

The other policeman jumped up and wrestled with his partner for a minute or two, pleading for time to talk to me while the other waited outside, where he could cool off. Big Bad John agreed, but as he was going out the door, he just had to leave a warning.

"Okay. Okay. I'll leave already," he told his partner, "but if this little nigger hasn't talked by the time that I come back in here, it's gonna be me and his black ass!" Then he slammed the door shut.

"Don't mind him, Rubin," the remaining officer excused his fat buddy, not knowing—or maybe he did—that I didn't mind the threats, because if that man had put his hands on me, he would have had to kill me right then, to protect himself. "He's just an old-fashioned hothead," the bald-headed officer was saying, "but he didn't mean any harm." Then the man opened up a briefcase and removed some papers from it.

"Here, Carter," he said, handing me three sheets of the paper. "I'll show you I've been leveling with you. I mean, about those statements I mentioned."

After I read and re-read the statements over and over again, I gave them back to the detective.

"Where are these guys at now?" I asked.

"Oh, they're home, of course. I told you they wouldn't take any of the weight."

"Well, what's going to happen to me?"

"Well, to be truthful with you, Rubin, we want to hear your side of the story. Because, judging from the condition that man was in, we don't think it could have been done by you alone. So we want what really happened, you understand what I mean?"

Solutions began to materialize in my mind. In the incriminating statements the other fellows had made, they had admitted to being at Tubbs on the day in question, and to having run away when I told them to. This in itself was not too damaging to me. But the statements went further to say that a few days prior to my arrest, one of the boy's parents had caught him wearing a gold wristwatch. His mother, indoctrinated like my father with Christian dogma, questioned him and wanted to know where he had gotten the watch from. When he couldn't give her a plausible answer, she turned the watch over to the police with the explanation that he had found it. That wasn't too bad either. But when the police found the man's name engraved on the back of the watch, and his wife identified it as being her anniversary gift to him, the cops picked the boy up for questioning. As he was unaware of what had taken place after he had escaped, he told the police where he had gotten the watch, and who was with him. When the other two fellows were picked up, they told the same story. There wasn't the slightest discrepancy. So they were freed, and I was arrested.

What could I say? This was it. I was caught dead to rights, so to speak, by these three statements.

"Where is the knife that you used, Rubin?" the officer asked, interrupting my thoughts.

"I don't know," I said. "I broke it up and threw it in the river."

"But where?" the cop urged. "Where did you throw it? What part of the river?"

The man's persistence kindled a flame of anger in me, and the impulse to end it all right there.

"Man, you better leave me alone," I warned him. "I told you. I broke it up and threw it in the river."

"Okay," he said, and went for the cell door. "But I think it would be wise for you to give us a statement, Rubin. If for nothing else, at least to protect yourself, son. Because if you don't, nobody else will."

I thought about that for a long moment or two, then shook my head. I didn't want to make any statements.

"Well, is there anything else you would like to tell me before I leave?" he inquired.

Silence.

"All right, Carter. I won't press you anymore," he said, unlocking the door. "Can I get you a soda, or something?"

Silence.

Then he was gone.

As the cell door closed and was locked again, I wondered what would happen to me next. What would they do to me? Maybe they'll give me probation, I decided foolishly, and without much hope. Or maybe they'll let me go home?

"All right, Rubin, it's time to go," the cop said, startling me as he unlocked the cell door and put the keys in his pocket.

"Home?" I asked, hoping it was true.

With a faint note of compassion in his voice, the cop answered, "Yes. Come along, son. You're going to a new home."

Hope Dell, my new home, was a diagnostic center for juvenile delinquents, a way station for the transgressor headed for his inevitable day in court. Situated in the hills of northern Passaic County, it was a combination old folks' home and home for wayward children. The grounds were beautiful, the air fresh and clean. The food was not only delicious but plentiful—cake and ice cream every day. Were it not for my troubles with the law, I would have given anything to live peaceably in that paradise forever.

I was escorted to Hope Dell by the police, taken to the Youth Department there, and introduced to the man and woman in charge. They were a middle-aged couple, as I remember them, and the woman was rather attractive—a dark-eyed brunette who wore her long hair Veronica Lake-style, and had a figure one would have to call voluptuous. Her voice was always affectionate.

Her husband, on the other hand, was a different proposition. He was a great big sucker with the look of an athlete gone to fat: his broad shoulders looked like young mountains, he had a chin like a sledge hammer, a cauliflowered ear, and scar tissue over his eyes. His black hair was peppered with gray, his eyes dark, but bright. Someone had broken his nose earlier in life, and others had obviously been pounding away at it ever since. All bore witness to an unsatisfactory ring career.

If any fellows came to Hope Dell with the idea of being bad characters, it quickly disappeared at the sight of this man. At your arrival, he would make it abundantly clear that he was the boss; that you had been sent there because you couldn't seem to get along out in the streets, and not to be his master. By the time he was finished running down his riot act, any thought of disobeying him had been abandoned. But, all in all, he and his wife were very fair-minded people; after being at Hope Dell for a while, the man's bark became far worse than his bite.

When I had been a resident of the community for four or five days, I met with a pleasant surprise—the black bastard who had put me there, the boy whose God-loving mammy had caught him with the watch. He had brought the other two boys with him. I felt sorry for them, but not for him.

Many nights had passed during which I lay awake wondering why that fool had kept that watch. What had he been thinking about? Didn't he realize that sooner or later someone would see him wearing it and would want to know where he had gotten it from? He knew damn well he had no business with an expensive watch—or any watch, for that matter—and to say that he had found it was just plain goddamn stupid. But I was glad that he was here. I wanted to have a fist-to-face talk with that dumb sonofa-bitch.

I spent two or three weeks in Hope Dell. During that time, my mother and father came to see me three or four times a week. They wanted to know, naturally, why I did what I had done. I tried to tell them as simply as I could, but I could see they didn't believe me. They didn't believe that a white man would try to force their young one into performing an unnatural act. They just couldn't conceive of the situation with their ole-time religious mentalities. It was equally impossible for me to understand their attitude. In their eyes, I was wrong—dead wrong. But in my heart I felt that I was right. I knew that if the same thing ever happened to one of my future children—color, ethics, religion, and the law be damned—I would do the same thing again with no regrets.

In court, the judge asked each of us to tell him what had happened. Each of the other three boys tried to explain what he thought had taken place, and I accepted the responsibility for it all. I explained to the judge that it was my fault, not theirs, but the man wasn't going for that. The police had filed a report saying that one person alone could not have done what was done to that man; Carter had to have had some help.

The victim—the police said—had been a pillar of society, a man active in his community, an individual for whom the welfare and rights of others had always come first. The police report read something like this: "Rubin Carter is an antisocial person, and if something is not done with him very soon, he will ultimately become a dangerous man later on in life." It said a lot of other things too, prefabricated lies to tear me down and make it appear that I had forced my boys to commit the crime.

The judge sat high above us, his black robe rippling in the breeze of a huge fan. "These hoodlum cutthroats in this city are a menace to our society," he said, as I remember it, "and must be stopped at any cost." He glared from behind his horn-rimmed glasses. "Therefore, it is my duty to sentence you three boys"—he pointed to those beside me—"to the State Home for Boys for nine months, at which time, if your records are clean, you will be subject to recall. And I hope this teaches you to pick better friends the next time."

Then he cleared his throat, and took a long drink of ice water, as though his lips had become parched from his condemning speech. Then he turned his frigid eyes on me.

"As for you, Rubin Carter, I only wish you were older so I could send you to State Prison—where you obviously belong—and where they have cages for animals like you. As I read your school report,* I can see that everything these police officers have said about you is true. Why, just look at yourself glaring at me now! You act as if you want to kill me, too."

He paused dramatically then, and cleared his throat again. "You seem to have a mean streak clear through you, and it's getting to be impossible to control. Well, sir," he went on, "I'm going to send you to a place that has adequate facilities to accommodate you. I sentence you, Rubin Carter, to Jamesburg State Home for Boys, as of this day until you are twenty-one years of age. So be it."

There was utter silence in the courtroom. The only sound I was aware of was the deep throbbing of blood in my ears. My mother grasped my hand tightly and cried. I was numb with shock. Until I am twenty-one years old? I thought. Goddamn! That was ten years away. Ten long years. A lifetime.

I looked over at the other fellows standing there with their parents, tears flooding their eyes, and I felt miserable, wishing that I could cry too. But there were no tears in me. I could accept that I had done wrong in the eyes of the law, but it had been my fault, my

---

* This had been provided by the disciplinary school which I attended.

wrongdoing, and not the others'. I was furious with this hypocritical judge and all of his white authority.

I knew this Janus-faced cracker had to have heard the truth of each one of our unrehearsed versions of what happened, had to have realized that, in our youth, we were completely ignorant of homosexuality and of people who catered to those desires, because the police had made damn sure that we didn't get together to talk it over until that moment in court. They knew the man was a homosexual, because it was not the first time this depraved individual had been involved with young boys. It seemed he had an unerring propensity for tender black meat, and outside the courtroom we heard the cops laughing about how his love affairs at Tubbs had finally caught up with him. But when they came before the judge, the police never even mentioned it. Instead, we were made out to be "hoodlum cutthroats," a story the judge accepted without question.

The man lived, but I wondered what would have happened if he had thrown me off that cliff. Other than my dying, of course, what would have been the role of this backsliding jurist then? Though many years have passed since that incident, the answer is more vivid today than I ever could have expressed it at that time: that judge would have given that faggot a gold medal, and made up a tear-jerking drama about us niggers attacking him, saying that he was well within his rights—protecting himself against harm. "After all," he would have said complacently, "he only killed a nigger. And all of them are expendable."

But back then, needless to say, I didn't know what I know now, and it disturbed me no end to have this white man sitting up there on a bench cloaked in self-righteousness and condemn me for adhering to the first law of nature—self-preservation—when he himself had put the lap on the crime by letting the police cover up the known perversion of that eminent faggot.

He managed to find a law to justify what the police were doing because we were black, and therefore prejudged guilty, and, as they put it, "a menace to [their] society." When these white bureaucrats looked at me, they saw a horror that they themselves had created, compelling them to remove me from their sight.

THE FOURTH ROUND

Hell Hath No Fury Like
the State Home's Scorn

On that same afternoon the sheriff and his deputies delivered me, handcuffed, shackled, and bound up like an animal, to my comeuppance in southern New Jersey—to the Jamesburg State Home for Boys.

This institution was a gigantic operation, state-owned property stretching out for miles all around it. Everything needed for its survival was produced right there on its own grounds. It had farms, dairies, truck gardens, workshops, tailor shops, commissaries, and bakeshops, providing all the necessary merchandise one would find in a small town. It was a city within a city, a world within a world, a diabolical place of horror that I would be forever sorry to have known existed.

Jamesburg, with a beautiful parade ground at its core, looked to be like an exquisite college campus or a military school. The three-story red brick buildings that we lived in, called "cottages," were systematically strung out adjacent to the parade field. Each barrack housed fifty to sixty inmates, assigned there according to their age, size, and color. Segregation was strictly enforced.

On the third floor of each building was an apartment for the man and woman in charge of the cottage, known as the cottage mother and father. On the second floor were a library, a television room, and a long dormitory where everybody slept. Downstairs in the basement, which was where an inmate spent most of his time, were footlockers for clothing, the recreation room, the toilet, and showers.

Every cottage was identical. Identical, that is, except for the people. Cottages Two, Six, Seven, and Eight were Black Only; Three, Four, Eleven, and Twelve White Only. The two remaining cottages—One, the honor cottage, and Five, the kitchen detail— were the only mixed houses on the grounds.

On our arrival at the State Home for Boys, my three companions and I were delivered to the Main Building to receive our state numbers, then escorted to the Reception Cottage for thirty days' orientation. We were turned over to the cottage father, a Mr. Grey, who had a strong stench of whiskey around him as he stumbled through us in a rambling inspection. He fingered us like one would examine cattle, feeling here and pinching there. Once he had completed the inspection to his satisfaction, he ordered us to join the twenty or thirty other black inmates who were standing at the back of the room at attention, stiff as boards, while the white inmates in the cottage sat around playing cards, laughing and joking and making fun of the "coons," as Mr. Grey called us.

This officer was a sho'nuff cracker: tall, southern, and dissipated, "gotch-eyed," and drunk as a coot. His small, frittered-away face might have been smooth some four or five days before, but now it was peppered with black and gray whiskers. And every time he opened his nasty mouth to speak, the twangs of Georgia, Mississippi, and Alabama would leap out on his drawling tongue.

He hated niggers. That black inmates stood at attention, I soon found out, was considered the status quo in his cottage. There would be days upon days when we would have to do this just for the hell of it, for the amusement of Mr. Grey and the white inmates. If by chance one of us became ill, or just couldn't stand any longer and fell to the floor—which happened on a number of occasions—Mr. Grey would stomp him almost to death until he had recovered and could resume his place in the ranks.

The dormitory itself was just one long room with army-type cots sporadically spaced across the floor. There were no beams or pillars, so if a person stood in the doorway of the room, he would be able to see everyone at the same time. But Mr. Grey had segregated the room in such a way that all of us black inmates had to sleep in one tiny corner at the back, while the white boys slept in luxurious space at the front.

There were fifty to sixty new inmates, or "fish," as we were called, in Reception when I got there, and as circumstance would have it, there were more black inmates than white. It was physically impossible to cram all of us into that one tiny corner, but Mr. Grey didn't care. He simply would not permit a black inmate to bed down in the white section. If there were no beds to be had in our microscopic corner, our best bet was to sleep on the floor, because if Mr. Grey ever caught one of us trying to integrate his dormitory, he would hang that black ass from the nearest tree.

We would get up at six o'clock in the morning to dress, and then have to stand in line at attention until seven thirty, breakfast time. Then we would goose-step across campus to the mess hall and eat. Or, I should say, try to eat. The food was pathetic. Even the pigs were fed store-bought grain—the swine wouldn't eat the shit they served us. Every morning of every day, seven days a week, one would have to evict the "cock-a-roaches," bedbugs, caterpillars, and various other kinds of insects he might find in his food. The inmates of this institution being inordinately devilish, the oatmeal which was our daily breakfast was made into a training ground for all the waterbugs, beetles, ants, and any other grain-eating thing that the inmates could find to keep as a pet.

But whenever an inmate found any of this animal-matter in his food and was dumb enough to tell the police about it, the response would most likely be a crisp "Whatcha complaining about, you goddamn dizzy dip, you? You're getting more meat than the rest of them are, aren't you? Sit down and shut up!"

As I would soon discover, it was here in this scum-laden mess hall that the spirit of self-preservation would emerge in all its splendid brutality. If we wanted to eat our bare essentials free of insects, nails, and other rot, we were forced to hurt somebody, instill the fear of God in the kitchen personnel, just so the food would be treated with some hygienic consciousness.

Though their crimes ranged from playing hookey to manslaughter, many of the boys I was in with should never have been sent to Jamesburg. They had been plucked from their homes for vague reasons and thrust into an atmosphere more vicious than the slums they left could ever be. Eight-year-old kids became the prey of fifteen-year-old killers, rapists, and boys for whom crime had become the only way of life—tough kids who respected nothing but brute force, and didn't give a damn about authority. They knew they weren't being confined for rehabilitation—that was a big joke in the New Jersey jails—and most of these fellows were parole violators, just marking time and waiting for their transfers to other, similar hellholes of degradation.

Through my everyday dealings with them, it wasn't long before it became apparent that I had gained the admiration of the majority, and I found myself enjoying the same popularity I once had among the Apaches. There was nothing mysterious or supernatural about my leadership ability, and I will always believe it was only a consolation prize for being shortchanged in the speech department. Whatever the reason, when anyone had a problem of some sort, he would usually come to me for a solution. And I, not knowing what else to do, would try to help him as best I could.

Also, a truce surprisingly developed between Mr. Grey and myself. From my looks and my hostile attitude, no doubt, I had let the man know that I didn't particularly like what he was doing to the black population, and furthermore, I made it clear in no uncertain terms that I was not about to accept his bullshit myself. None of this was said with words, but he must have understood me, because he left me alone.

Because of these two things, my popularity and my understanding with Mr. Grey, I was made "line sergeant" of Reception Cottage, a promotion that made me stand out like a sore thumb.

Jamesburg was not only built like a military school, but its inmates functioned as if they were in one as well. We marched everywhere we went in close-order drills, at times even carrying wooden rifles in parades. Each cottage had two line sergeants—the two toughest boys—and these line sergeants unquestionably enforced the cottage's rules. So when I became line sergeant of Reception, the only cottage that had never had one before, everybody wanted to know who I was, what I was, and how "good" I was. At fist fighting, they meant.

With the added responsibilities of this new role, my thirty days in Reception passed quickly, and before I knew it, my quarantine period was over. My three companions were transferred to Cottage Seven, the younger boys' barracks, and one of them later became a member of the "Original Ham-Boners," who managed to put in an appearance on Ted Mack's Amateur Hour. I was transferred to Cottage Eight.

When I arrived at my new quarters, the rest of the inmates were out working. I was told to remain within the compound until they returned. I wandered aimlessly about the grounds surrounding the building, fear creeping up on me like a dark serpent. I wondered how these people would react to me, a newcomer. I was wondering if they—

The twelve o'clock work-in whistle interrupted my thoughts, and I returned to the cottage, waiting anxiously for my brother-prisoners to arrive. It wasn't long before I heard them coming.

"Hup, ho, thrup, fo' . . . hup, ho, thrup, fo', hey left, riiiiight, left! Straighten, you dumb motherfuckers, straighten up!" a youthful voice blared out with authority. "Straighten up and move it out!"

I could hear their marching long before I was able to see them. The measured tread of their feet was very loud, though not unharmonious, just blustering and continuous. Like a well put together machine. When they finally came into my view, I saw four columns of quick-stepping youngsters being driven by the crisp commands of two line sergeants strutting beside them like peacocks.

I stood there with my mouth hanging open. Their unity was the most beautiful thing I had ever seen. It grabbed me, so intrigued me, that I failed to hear Mr. Willis, the cottage father, stroll up behind me.

"Can you march like that, Carter?" he asked, nodding toward the group.

"No, I-I-I—" don't think so, I started to say, before his stern voice wedged in and cut me off.

"*Sir*, boy! When you answer me, you say 'sir!' Do you understand me?"

"Y-ye-yes, sir!" I answered as quickly as I could, but stammering as badly as ever. "I-I for-forgot, sir!"

But the man had turned around to watch the marchers, and somewhat less severely he replied, "Well, don't you forget again, fellow, and we'll get along just fine." Then he called to one of the line sergeants, "Awright, Little A, bring them on in and let's go to chow!"

"Yessir!" was the snappy reply. A few more crisp commands, and the cottage came marching home.

When all the boys had been assembled at the cottage, we went downstairs and sat on our footlockers; that is, everybody but the two line sergeants. One of them stood on his locker across the room from me, looking mean as hell, while the other one strutted back and forth like a bantam rooster patrolling the barnyard.

The boy on the locker was a short, dark, husky lad who answered to the name of Little A. He had all the features of the classical African, from the heavily muscled body to the thick lips, wiry hair, and widespread nose. His brown eyes were two startling dark pools of malignant fire which, if one were to look directly into them, would seem to become the mouth of giant twin flesh-eaters. Two dark holes of unbridled hatred they were, hair-triggered and ready to explode into a bloody vendetta against all mankind.

The other line sergeant, Chink by name, was a slight, fair-complexioned boy whose thin, upturned lips made him look as if he always had a sarcastic smirk plastered on his face. His slinky eyes, like an Oriental's, gave him his name.

Chink was a parole violator, and had been at Jamesburg three or four times before. Now the authorities were only waiting until he was old enough to send him to a penitentiary. Meanwhile, he was as treacherous as a Georgia mule, outrageous and malicious in his dealings with the other inmates, and deadly as the bubonic plague. He wasn't wrapped too tight, either.

He would only fight fair when it was an absolute necessity. Though he was a helluva brawler, he always maintained a select group of seven or eight fair-to-middling warriors to guard his wretched ass anyway—perhaps because the two line sergeants did not particularly care for each other, and only went through peaceful motions out of constraint.

"Fall out for chow!" the cottage father's voice boomed from upstairs. "Clear the basement! Clear the basement!"

The basement was cleared.

Outside on the sidewalk, the ranks quickly formed according to height, with the shortest inmates up front. When it was done, the lines resembled a human pyramid—four perfect steps of black heads going upward, and not a one out of place. I had learned how to march during my thirty days in Reception Cottage, but I realized that I wasn't good enough to step with these veterans yet. I didn't want to make them look bad—nor make a damn fool of myself—so I asked the line sergeant if I could march at the end of the line. Permission was granted.

En route to the mess hall, I really tried to keep in step, but it was soon clear to me, and probably to everybody else as well, that this was a physical impossibility: sixty inmates, operating as a single body, were executing so many different moves so rapidly that I wasn't sure if I was coming or going.

Completely frustrated by the time the command of "Double-to-the-rear, march!" was given, I found my stupid ass marching alone one way, and the rest of the group going the other. Very embarrassed, I turned around and caught up with them, then stood off to the side and watched.

"Get your black ass back in that line, punk!" a voice demanded from behind me. "Who'n the fuck do you think you are, eh?"

I wheeled around and found Chink standing there.

"Didn't you hear what I said, motherfucker?" he roared belligerently. "Get your black butt back in that line before I break my foot off in it!" There being little room for reply, I got back in the ranks.

Now Brother Chink had been chanting the cadences all this time, and I guess my inability to stay in step made him feel good, because he started calling them as rapidly as he could, trying to keep me confused. He succeeded—most thoroughly.

We arrived at the mess hall a few minutes later. Even there we were compelled to stand at attention, ramrod straight, until we received our food and could sit down to eat. As I stood there, rigid as petrified wood, Chink sashayed up to me with a sarcastic smirk glued on his lips.

"What's the matter, sucker?" he sneered. "Can't you stay in step with the rest of us?" Then he spun around and walked away.

After the gangrenous fodder that constituted our lunch had been consumed—or thrown away—we regrouped outside and began our journey back. This time my inability to march in time with the rest of the fellows irked Chink to no end. "Goddamn, man!" He shook his head disgustedly, as if I were a hopeless case. "I don't know what I'm going to do with you, you little worthless nigger! But I think that we better have a little talk in my office when we get back to the cottage, okay?" Not waiting for me to answer, he strutted off again.

When we returned to the cottage, everybody went downstairs and stood on their lockers instead of sitting down. As usual, the cottage father was nowhere in sight. The feeling in the room was unusually tense and expectant, as if something peculiar were about to happen. I sensed sneaky eyes on me, but I couldn't be sure.

Chink, meanwhile, was actively employed at his locker, taking off his shirt and slipping on a pair of skintight gloves. Then he moved out into the center of the room with a piece of paper in his hands.

"Awright, you miserable cocksuckers!" he announced. "The names that I call, line up in front of my office door: Miller, Tree-Top, Walker, and my good buddy, Missus Carter."

When I heard my name, I looked around for an office of some sort, but couldn't find any. "Line up at his office door," I muttered to myself. "Man, I don't see no office down here." But I saw it a moment later, when three boys stepped down off their lockers and stood, one behind the other, all facing the bathroom door.

I stood there looking at them for a good while, wondering why anybody would want to talk with me in there, and then became aware that everybody else was looking at me. I shrugged my shoulders, got down from the footlocker, and went to stand behind the last boy in line.

There were two doorways into Chink's "office." The one on the right led into the shower room, and the other—the door that we were facing—led to the washbasins and toilets. When Chink was satisfied that he had everybody's attention, and that we, his subjects, were as humble as we ought to be, he pranced past us with a dramatic display of arrogance and went into his office. Then he called out in a loud clear voice, "Come in and see daddy, Brother Miller!"

Suddenly, a familiar sensation of tingling ants began stealing over me, the same jittery feeling of fierce pleasure that always seems to come to me before a fight. I wanted to look into the bathroom to see what was going on, but the line had formed to the side of the doorway, blocking my view.

It was only a few seconds after the first boy had gone into the bathroom that I heard the distinctive sound of a fist colliding against meat, and immediately following that, the dull thump of a heavy object collapsing to the floor.

"What da fuck!" I exclaimed, refusing to believe I had heard what I heard. Then my eyes focused on the boy standing in front of me. He was trembling violently, and his pants legs were soaked— soaking wet from having pissed on himself. I could see that fear had collared him, the kind of deep-belly fear that makes a person do things he wouldn't normally do. I just couldn't believe it.

I stepped out of line and looked inside the bathroom. I saw Chink first. Following his downcast eyes, I saw the boy named Miller stretched out on the shithouse floor, cold as a cucumber. He was breathing heavily, a frothy saliva spilling out of his lifeless lips. His left foot was twitching spasmodically. His pupils played hide-'n'-seek in the sockets of his eyes.

"Whatcha doing in here, punk!" Chink demanded, reeling around. "Get your black ass outta here, nigger. Your turn is coming soon enough!"

"Sh-sh-sh-shitttt!" I sneered at him in contempt, turning around and going back to my locker. "You'll kiss my black ass, you yellow motherfucker! That's what you'll do for me!"

Now the adrenaline was flowing rapidly through my body, transforming my heart into a savagely pounding drum that threatened to demolish my chest. I felt light-headed and ferociously alive. My mind clicked, seeing everything, missing nothing, just as it always does whenever danger is near. What's wrong with these goddamn people? I asked myself. Have they lost their motherfucking minds? Do that fool think that I'm going to let him do that to me? I wondered. If that wooden-headed nigger even makes me *think* he's going to hurt me, I'll kill him so quick that he'll stink standing up! That was the way I felt.

I sat there flabbergasted, watching the other two boys go meekly into the bathroom to get knocked dead and come out staggering with their lips busted, eyes swollen shut, and looking like goddamn fools. I still couldn't believe it. This was too much for me. Man, I told myself, if that yellow nigger even dreams about treating me like that, he'd better wake up and beg my pardon, immediately.

"Awright, Boston Blackie," Chink stepped out of the bathroom and pointed to me. "Let's go. You're next!"

My heart began racing even faster, but I rose sluggishly to my feet. I moved towards him submissively, sniffling like I was really scared.

"Ple-plea-plcase, Mi-mister Chink," I whimpered. "I-I didn't do noth-nothing." Chink looked at me scornfully, a malicious grin stealing across his face. This ugly nigger's a punk, I imagined he was thinking. Contempt was written all over him.

"Just trot your narrow ass into my office, mama!" he barked at me, both hands on his hips. He stepped aside to let me pass. "Just come on here to daddy," he said, "and then we'll talk about it, baby."

"Oh, plea-please, Mister Chink," I begged and pleaded, shuffling slowly until I was standing in front of him. Then I fired on his dumb-ass—"cocked a Sunday" (a sneak punch) on him!

Chink's slanty eyes bulged out in surprise. Fear twisted his face. He realized, too late, that he had made a mistake. He shrieked in alarm, looking at me openmouthed, not even aware that he was falling already, and that was the last thing he saw for some time. My fist crashed against his chin a second time before he fell and stretched him out senseless on the floor. He made the same sound I had heard coming from the bathroom a few minutes earlier.

Down, down, down he fell, flat on his treacherous ass. His head smacked loudly against the cement floor. Then his legs started quivering. For a brief moment the basement was cloaked in a velvety silence, but then it erupted in astonishment as everybody pressed around the unconscious body, watching Chink's legs continue their spasms for some two or three minutes more, when he regained full consciousness.

"Whew!" he exclaimed, sitting up and shaking his head. One of his lieutenants reached down and helped him to his feet.

"What happened, man?" Chink asked.

Before the boy could answer, Little A, who was still standing on his locker across the room, satisfied Chink's curiosity. "You finally got popped, you dumb motherfucker, that's what happened!" Little A grinned. "I told you that somebody was gonna get your ass one of these days. And now you got it. How does that grab you? You wanna talk to somebody else in your office?"

Chink was still groggy. He stood there shaking his head incredulously as Little A's words finally penetrated his befuddled mind. Then he looked at me in amazement.

"You cocked a Sunday on *me*, nigger?" His eyes flashed with new anger. "Do you realize that I'm gonna take your motherfucking life for that? Boy, do you understand that I'm going to kill you—*dead!*"

"W-we-we'll die *together*, motherfucker!" I stammered, "You're the one who started this shit, not me."

"Yeah, and I'm the one who's gonna finish it, too!" he growled, his boys crowding around him. "Because tonight, after chow, me and you got the floor, you bad little nigger, you!"

The room was now so still that I could hear passionate breathing all around me. Then a voice rang out from across the room. "Well, whatever it's gonna be, Chink!" warned Little A, "it's going to be a fair one between you and him, or I'll be in it too. You can bet your butt on that!"

Little A's intrusion seemed to madden Chink more than my knocking him down had. His eyes suddenly turned yellow with fury.

"Black nigger!" he spat viciously back at Little A. "Who'n the name of God do you think you are? What makes you think that

I give a fuck about you—or the horse you came to town on? Big nigger, I wantcha to take this little nigger's place! That's exactly what I wantcha to do! And you can take it *now* if you want to! Unless you're just talking out your ass, because your mouth is full of shit!"

"Fall out for work!" the cottage father's voice boomed from upstairs. "Clear the basement! Clear the basement!"

The basement was cleared.

I was rushed outside in the embroiled wake of the other hustling inmates, the fight postponed for the moment. I didn't have a steady job as yet, so once outside, I was ordered to mow the lawn of the baseball diamond. As I began cutting the grass, the work took on a new dimension, a salve for my troubled soul.

There was no denying that I had my butt caught in a sling again, and if I couldn't think of a practicable way of getting it unslung, it was going to get launched into space. The more I thought about this hazardous situation, the worse it got; the worse it got, the faster the grass flew. After a while, grass was flying every which-a-way.

I was so absorbed in the turmoil of my situation that the work-in whistle blew before I had realized it was so late. After I cleaned my cutting tools and returned them to the machine shed, I went inside and downstairs to the basement, where I flipped on the lights.

Mr. Willis's voice startled me from across the room. "Cut those lights off, Carter. It helps keep it cool down here."

Whew! My heart was pounding. I thought that one of these treacherous niggers had crept down here and was laying for me. But I got myself together and switched off the lights. Then, still shaking a little, I went to the water cooler and got a drink.

"I've been sitting here at the window watching you, Carter," Willis said. "And from what I just saw, work is not a stranger to you. I like that. But I also know that you had a fight with my line sergeant this afternoon, and I don't like that worth a damn! So what have you got to say for yourself, mister?"

What have I got to say? Boy! If only I could have talked without stuttering, I would've goddamn-sure told him what I had to say. I would have asked him where the hell was *he* at when all that shit was going on? He seemed to know so doggone much about it, why didn't he stop it before it happened? He had to know that his precious line sergeant had been knocking these kids' brains out every day; why hadn't he put an end to it? What did I have to say? I probably would have cussed his lazy ass out, but I couldn't talk. So I just stood there, and said nothing.

When Willis realized that I wasn't going to answer him, he continued talking as if he had never asked the question.

"Are you going to fight him again, Carter?" he asked. A worried frown creased his brow. "Because if you are," he went on, "in all fairness to you I think I'd better warn you about something. *Are* you going to fight him?"

Still I was silent.

He shifted and lit up another cigarette. "Chink's a worthless, good-for-nothing scoundrel," Willis said thoughtfully, as if picturing the boy in his mind, "but he does take good care of this cottage. However, I don't want to see him hurt any more of you people, and that's why I'm telling you to be very careful, to watch yourself. Because he's a dangerous person. He'll try to hurt you if he can." And with that he got up and left.

A few minutes later, the work details returned to the cottage in a mood of noticeable anticipation. They were traveling under the auspices of a small, bifocaled, underweight officer who, in keeping with his well-established routine, scurried upstairs upon entering the building, turned on the television set, pulled up his favorite chair, and sat his stinking ass down. I'll call him Mr. Lightfoot.

To try to describe Mr. Lightfoot with any authenticity would be time and energy dedicated to a worthless cause, because this man was a pampered and spoiled thirty-three-year-old sissy whose momma—with whom he still lived, and probably always would—had protected him from the world all of his natural life. A young man in the prime of his years, he was too helpless to hold down a job anywhere but at this cesspool. If one can picture such a person, he would see our Mr. Lightfoot in totality.

Before anything untoward could develop in the basement, the chow whistle blew, and sixty famished inmates bolted for the mess hall—and the mess. But when we returned, the sixty energetic juveniles sitting in the room created a vibrant air of restraint. To my ears, the mere shuffling of restless feet were like small explosions, and the careful shifting of impatient bodies built to an uproar. Cottage Eight was uptight. Everybody was waiting for the inevitable.

Ordinarily, upon returning from the evening mess, we would

scrub floors, grab a quick shower, and shoot upstairs to catch *The Lone Ranger*. Tonight this custom was completely abandoned, for tonight reputations, integrities, and honors were hanging in the balance. Tonight, if Chink didn't carry out his threat to retaliate in the most devastating manner, his fame would suffer in the critical eyes of his quick-to-condemn fellows. Because of the many inmates he had hurt in the past, he would be putting his life in immediate danger. The nature of the wolfpack promised that when the leader fell, fifty-nine savages would fly at his throat and rip it to shreds, making him meal for the multitude. Such was the dog-eat-dog life at Jamesburg. And the last dog took the bone.

"Awright, you punk motherfuckers!" Chink cried out defiantly. "Let's get this shit on the road!" His warriors crowded around him, smiling.

"Talk about it, baby!" they chorused. "We're ready to hump!"

We had all been waiting for this, but were playing pass the money, so Chink's voice caught us off guard. The moment I heard it I jumped up in self-defense, though neither Chink nor his boys gave the slighest indication that they knew I was even in the room. They all just stood together in the middle of the floor and stared intensely in one direction—straight at Little A—all cotton-picking seven of them.

"Little A?" Chink summoned his adversary politely. "This is something that me and you should have done a long time ago. You know what I mean?" he asked. "Because I really never dug you— and I know damn well that you don't dig me either. Am I right?" Little A nodded his woolly head in agreement.

"Yup, you got that right, sucker," he said with contempt. "But it wasn't *my* fault. Because I always wanted to dig you—and plant you too, you punk motherfucker! Six feet under!"

"That's exactly what I'm talking about!" Chink said, pulling on his skintight gloves. "So let's me and you settle this shit once and for all. Because I don't want you getting into my business from now on. So come on down here and meet your master."

Little A's dark eyes had subtly undergone a swift transformation from deep black to fiery red. He stood there quivering, anger making his temples throb. "You must be out of your mammy-jammy mind!" he growled. "I'm not going to fight all of you pussies at one time. You must think I'm a goddamn fool, or something! But you fight me alone, motherfucker, just me and you, and I'll put something real and horrible on your stinking ass. I betcha that!"

"I don't need no help, you monkey-looking sonofabitch!" Chink roared back, motioning his fellows away. "Just come on down here and put your ass where your mouth is, punk! Then we'll see what's jumping off. Come on down here!"

Little A stepped down off his locker. He reached into his back pocket and slipped on a pair of gloves that were similar to Chink's. Then, without uttering another word, the two warriors met. They clashed head-on in the middle of the floor, barefoot and naked from the waist up.

In direct contrast to Little A's short and heavily muscled body, Chink's torso was whipcord lean, smooth and graceful as a ballet dancer. They circled one another, guardedly at first, with a finesse that would have made Joe Louis blush. Bobbing, then weaving, feinting with tricky head and body movements, they each tried to lure the other into making his fatal mistake.

"Pop him, Chink!" shouted one of his admirers every now and then.

"Watch out for that locker behind you, baby!" another would caution, as the boys glided skillfully in and out, patiently waiting for an opening. When both of them began to sweat in earnest, we knew the feeling-out phase had come to its end. The boys were settling down to do some serious thumping. And swifter than a striking rattler, Chink smashed across a sizzling right-hand that landed high on his opponent's darting, cobra-like head.

"Ooooooooh, shit!" a spectator moaned, as Little A barely managed to slide his head out of the way. But with a determination that refused to die, and the dexterity of a coiled viper, Chink leaped in again, nailing his stocky opponent with a bone-crunching left hook that knocked a crown of perspiration from Little A's pain-distorted face. And down he went, flat on his back.

"Stomp the motherfucker, Chink!" one of his bloodthirsty mob demanded from the corner. "Stomp the nigger! Stomp him!"

Feeling confident that a fair-and-square victory was now just within grasp, Chink, surprisingly, didn't press his strong advantage. He danced away beautifully, exhibiting some of Sugar Ray Robinson's mastery, and then backed up, smiling. He knew who was the boss.

"Get up, you bad motherfucker!" Chink beamed down on his fallen foe. "I haven't even begun to fight yet," he said. "And there you are, laying on the floor, trying to go to sleep already! Get up from there, you black bastard!"

"Whoooooeeie!" one of his followers shouted joyfully. "Talk your talk and walk your walk, Chink, baby! And the next time he falls do the 'Bill Robinson' on his ass! You just bought the nigger, baby, now sell him back to his black mammy!"

The basement roared with laughter.

Now wobbling and struggling mightily, Little A stumbled to his ramshackle feet. Blood was streaming from his badly bruised nose. His eyes were glazed and cloudy, and he shook his head like a stunned bull, trying to clear the cobwebs from his mind. Then, tucking his chin carefully between the hillocks of his well-muscled shoulders, he started forward. Shuffling in circles, he flatfootedly tried to trap his fleet-of-foot opponent.

Suddenly, he bobbed, weaved, shifted his pattern and nailed Chink with two, three jolting left jabs. Then, very masterfully switching to circling tactics, Little A popped him with three more stiff jabs that slipped through Chink's guard and bloodied his nose. Little A was battling desperately now, trying not to make the same mistake that had prompted his first trip to the hard cement floor. It looked like he was back in the fight.

Chink's killer-instinct, however, thought different. It was not going to stand still for Chink's own laying back. Waiting for a mistake to come from the now invading Little A, Chink's pugilistic reflexes were telling him that the fight was still his, if he would only make one more vicious and vehement attack. He took the advice. Chink danced in, raining lefts and rights through Little A's thick-armed defense. Some reached their intended target with chilling accuracy, while others were ingeniously parried.

"Atta boy, Chink!" his mob encouraged, sensing that the end was near. "Finish him now, baby!" they cried, as Little A retreated and covered up for dear life. "Finish him now! Finish him now!" they chanted.

But their leader needed no encouragement. His ferocious assault seemed to me to border at the brink of insanity. Its numbing effect was, at any rate, clearly visible, as Little A staggered in apparent calamity. He floundered from locker to locker, trying to evade the sniping artistry of Chink's deadly power. Inadvertently, he stumbled into the corner where Chink's bloodthirsty cheering section was straining at the leash

"Get back out there and fight, you black sonofabitch!" one of the horde snarled, pushing the dazed boy away. He punctuated the demand by kicking Little A in the ass. Whirling around, Little A slammed a bone-mashing fist straight to the face of the boy who had kicked him. The blow struck the culprit right in his nasty mouth, shattering his teeth and turning loose a torrent of thick blood and splintered fangs. Then, like man-eating piranhas seeking fresh blood, the entire mob pounced on Little A. Chink joined in on the slaughter.

For a long precious moment, I sat there stupefied. Everything had happened so lightning-fast that it took a full minute or two for my eyes to believe what they were seeing. Now Little A was down again, flat on his back, struggling helplessly, being trampled by Chink's white-livered niggers' shameless stomping.

Finally it dawned on me what was taking place. What in the hell am I sitting here for? I berated myself. This was *my* fight, not his, but here I sat watching him getting whupped for me! Get yourself together, Carter! I kicked my own self in the ass. And get your black butt out there and help that boy!

As my feet pounded across the floor to the combat zone, one of Little A's attackers looked up and spied my smoke. But when he opened up his mouth to sound the alarm, his piercing shriek was abruptly choked off as my fist crashed against his unprotected chin. He toppled to the floor, cold as an Eskimo's nose in Alaska.

My unexpected intrusion was devastating in its immediate results: I was able to down one, then two more of the coldblooded punks still trampling Little A. But when the rest of the crew became aware that I was visiting chaos and systematic elimination upon their ranks with my bushwhacking tactics, they forgot about Little A, and unleashed their hateful vengeance on me.

Googobs of uncontrolled fists began flying every which-a-way, and very soon I found myself fighting with every ounce of uncultivated savagery that I could muster up and press into service. As the battle began to lengthen, however, it became obvious that I was fighting too many people at one time.

"Whap!" My fist would dart out and stagger one of the invaders.

"Whop!—Bop!—Bam!—Bam!—Bam!" came the retaliating reply, and I was hit from five directions at once.

"Crash!" I would fire back in desperation, and another one would hit the floor, but four more would immediately take his place.

Whew!

There was no doubt about it, this fight was too much for me to handle alone. I had bitten off more than I could ever hope to chew. My arms felt weighted down with lead that refused to move. My lungs seemed to have collapsed. I felt the chill fingers of cold fear begin to crawl into my mind. I was scared. I knew that if I ever stopped fighting, or was knocked down, that I would be dead in a matter of minutes. I also knew that I couldn't continue fighting much longer.

Little by little, the smothering force of the battle seemed to lessen; it took on a whole new perspective. Half the weight had been lifted from my shoulders, and I could breathe again. "Thank God!" I sighed gratefully, firing on another sucker. I was swinging at anything that moved. "Thank God!" I said again.

When finally I gained a brief moment of respite in the brawl, I glanced out the corner of my eyes and found Little A standing with his back to mine, fighting like a wild demon. And from that moment on, we dished out as good as we got. In fact, we dished out exactly what we got, and ladled out hot knuckles for dessert.

By this time Little A had somehow recovered from the ill effects of his earlier trompings and, back-to-back, we made an ideal combination. We were dominating the fight at every turn, and, not thinking clearly, I turned my back to the enemy. I was trying to climb up on the locker behind me, so I could dive off into the crowd below. But somebody caught me, and, grabbing hold of the collar of my shirt, slung me to the floor.

Flat on my back, I tried to avoid a hard-toed brogan that was rocketing my way. I could see the black shoe coming at me from the moment it was drawn, but I couldn't get out of the way. The paralyzing impact snapped my head down and to the side, smashing my face against the cement.

"Oh, my God!" I screamed, waves of dizzying pain exploding and twisting in my guts. "Goddamn!" I cried. They done kicked my eye out, I thought. I began seeing deep red, then green, then amber, and then blackness welled up and tried to take over. I fought to escape the black emptiness coming across my vision, and all the while a terrified voice was screaming in my ear.

"Get up, fool! Get up, goddammit!" the voice demanded. "Get up before they stomp you to death! Get up, boy!"

Frantically, I called on all the strength that I possessed, and then braced my hands against the floor. Totally blinded, but painfully aware of life, my instincts told me to get up, grab onto the first person that I could touch, and hold on for dear life.

I pushed myself to my feet, with my arms stretched out, and was hammered unmercifully about the face until I was able to make contact with a struggling body. Fate was playing Russian roulette with my life. I had grabbed Chink. My arms were wrapped around his lean and willowy waist, and when I discovered who it was I had seized, I wasn't about to turn him aloose. He twisted and turned, raking his heels up and down my shins, trying to shake himself free in a hopeless struggle.

Finally, a ray of light filtered its way through to my uninjured eye, and as my sight returned, I reached the conclusion that I had had enough. Fuck this knock-down, drag-out shit, I snorted to myself. I'm going to end all of this mess right now! I released my life line and headed for a utility closet just as fast as I could get there. Fast as I was, Little A was right there beside me, and together we grabbed two baseball bats and came out smoking.

We must have looked like two husky black savages when we thundered back out of that closet, swinging those mutilating bats and screaming the piercing war cry of the African Zulu. Both of our bodies were battered, soaked by sweat and streaked with blood, and dressed only in the tattered remains of clothing which hung off of us in torn shreds. The right side of my face was blown up like a purplish-black balloon. Little A's head was split open from the crown almost to his eyes, and his blood gushed all over the place. He had lumps the size of dirty golf balls twisting his features and making them gruesome.

When those fifty-eight juveniles saw us coming, they panicked, and bolted for the stairway, climbing over each other's backs in their desperate fight to reach the door and safety. Boys that were knocked down in the cyclone scuffle were crushed and trampled by the stampeding force of the mob behind. In the midst of it all, to make matters worse, a shrill voice screamed in mortal fear, "Help! Mr. Lightfoot, help! Help! Mr. Lightfoot, help!"

The soul-rending plea did not reach the absent ears, however; Mr. Lightfoot was gone. As soon as he had recognized the loud and continuous scuffling in the basement for what it really was, he had wisely decided the best place for him would be outdoors, and he got his ass in the wind—only to have the rest of the inmates coming hot on his heels shortly thereafter.

Then only Little A and I were left in the building.

As the heat of combat slowly subsided within me, it was replaced by an eerie coldness, a sense of futility. I stood still, feeling addlepated, wondering what was happening to me. I looked at the heavy bat that I still had clutched in my hand. I shook my head in bewilderment. I had never acted like this before. But then I had never been in jail before, either.

I gazed at my companion beside me. He looked as though he had just swallowed three or four fire-eyed dragons. "God-god-goddamn, man!" I sputtered and pointed to his face. "You look like hell!"

"Shit!" he grimaced with pain, trying to smile. "You don't look like no Don Juan your goddamn self!"

We went into the bathroom and I looked in the mirror. "Wow!" I exclaimed involuntarily, as a distorted and unfamiliar face glared back at me through one eye. "Goddamn," I muttered to myself, flabbergasted. "I'm ruint. My poor face will never straighten out." Then Little A's bloodshot eyes attracted my attention. Looking at him, my good humor faded. Something else was wrong, for his face had taken on a solemn expression.

"Rube, ole buddy-buddy," he said seriously, extending his hand. "I'm really proud to meetcha, man. You're all right. But don't get too comfortable down here, because the shit hasn't even started yet."

"Hasn't started yet!" I exclaimed. "Whatcha talking about?"

"Well," he said, going to the washbowl, splashing cold water on his battered face, "by this time, Rube, Mr. Lightfoot has already gone to the Main Building. And God knows what he told them people. But, anyway," he explained, "he won't come back in here until the headwhuppers arrive. And then, little buddy, if we're not really careful . . . we just might get hurt."

I looked at him as if he were crazy. "*Might* get hurt?" I felt exasperated. What the hell did he think I was feeling now, if I wasn't hurt already? And who did he say was going to do it? "Headwhuppers!" I exclaimed absently, never having heard the word before. "What is that?"

Little A stopped what he was doing and looked at me meaningfully for a second or two, a naked expression of disbelief further distorting his mangled face. "Are you for real, man?" he challenged me, as if it could not be possible that I didn't know what he was talking about. "Haven't you ever been in jail before?"

"No, this is my first time."

"Well, then I can dig it," he said, as if that explained everything. "But headwhuppers ain't that!" he went on to say. "What I mean is, headwhuppers are people—cops. The goon squad of this institution who will come here now and try to bump us off, if they can."

"With their hands?" I asked, incredulous.

"Hmph!" Little A snorted derisively. "I only wish they would! Because then we might have a chance. But no," he said. "These dirty motherfuckers carry blackjacks!"

Here Come the Headwhuppers!

Headwhuppers! Blackjacks! Cops! Goddamn, I thought, getting scared all over again. Would I ever stop getting into trouble? It seemed like I had leaped out of the proverbial frying pan and into the gaping jaws of eternal damnation. I sneaked a look at Little A, trying to see how he was accepting the head-whuppers, but he was washing his face and I couldn't see his expression. "Oh, well," I shrugged my shoulders resignedly and went over to a washbasin to splash water on my face. If he can take what's coming, I decided, then dammit-the-hell, so can I.

My eye was woefully sealed by swollen, purplish skin, and the cool water burned the bruised surface like molten lava—but damn, it really felt good. Soothing as the water was, however, it didn't prevent my mind from returning to thoughts of the notorious head-whuppers. "When will they get here, Little A?" I inquired, hoping he wouldn't hear the trembling in my voice.

"Who?" he asked absently, turning away from the mirror. "Oh! You mean the headwhuppers!" he said, as if he had forgotten about them. "They'll be here soon enough without you worrying about them. So just be cool."

"But we haven't done anything to them!" I protested. "Why would they want to hurt us?"

Little A paused, squinted at me for a long moment, then answered with the profound realization that I hadn't fully comprehended what was taking place. "It's not that we've done anything to them, little brother," he said, almost to himself. "But you're new here, so they'll want to teach you a painful lesson for future reference, and, at the same time, remind me of what I should have known. You understand what I'm talking about?"

Before I could sputter an answer, the telephone upstairs began ringing shrilly, almost jumping off the hook. Little A spun around. "Listen! Listen!" he whispered excitedly, looking like Gunga Din with his hand cupped over his ear. "Here they come!" he said emphatically. "Here they come!"

I peeked out of the bathroom expecting to see Gargantua and his bald-headed mammy standing out there in the middle of the floor. But I didn't see anybody. "Where? Where?" I whispered, breathless, looking all around.

"Goddamn, man!" Little A exploded. "You can't be that fuckin' dumb! Listen, man! Just listen!"

Then I heard it, the sound of automobiles screeching to a halt outside the building, and the angry voices of several men as they approached the cottage.

"By Gawd!" a deep voice with a southern drawl boomed. "Where're the black sons-a-bitches?"

"In—in the cottage, sir," Mr. Lightfoot answered meekly.

"Well, gawddammit, man!" the southern voice retaliated. "Don't just stand there with your gawddamn finger stuck up your stinking ass! Open the fucking door so we can get at 'em!" it cried. "What the hell are you waiting for—the Marines?"

By this time the marauding headwhuppers had stationed themselves at the front entrance, and I could hear someone fumbling with a key to unlock the door. I was surprised at the way I felt. I should have been scared shitless, but I wasn't. I felt downright calm about the whole thing. But that alone should have scared me, if nothing else.

"Here they come, baby boy," Little A cautioned me grimly. He handed me a baseball bat. "Now just be cool," he said. "And do what I do. And everything will be all right. Okay?" he asked.

I nodded and took the weapon; what else could I have done? I was forced to face reality. This whole situation reeked of disaster, and judging from the angry voices I heard coming from the men outside, my troubles seemed destined to get still worse. I must protect Rubin at any cost, I told myself. That was the only thing that mattered to me—self-protection.

Then came the sound of many angry feet pounding the stairway like a buffalo stampede. But when the men came into the room, I counted only five of them. The first was a hard-eyed, redneck cracker who was sweating like he had just run thirty miles. A huge sonofabitch, he was six-foot-six, weighed in at about three hundred pounds, and didn't have a discernible ounce of fat on his body— except between his two piggish ears. He looked plain unfriendly. I found out later that his only real asset was his hatred of all black people. A vicious mean streak had kept him actively employed at this concentration camp for the past ten years, during which time he performed all the dirty details and used his muscle whenever called upon to do so. Like he was doing right now.

"Awright, gawddammit!" Gargantua's mammy growled. He appeared to be the group's spokesman. "Put them fucking bats down and let's go," he ordered.

"Go where?" queried Little A.

The officer exploded. "What did you say, boy?" He raised his blackjack and moved toward us. "Nigger!" he screamed. "You don't question me! Just who in the gawddamn hell do ya'll think ya'll talking to, huh?" He moved in closer.

Little A and I backed up a step and separated. We had our weapons raised and ready, which stopped the big man dead in his tracks. I could see understanding creep into his eyes: he knew we were for real. And to attack us with his small brigade would be like sending a black man like me to court to look for some justice: There was simply no way of knowing exactly what the outcome would be, if indeed, he came back out at all.

Gargantua glared at us for a minute or two, then his face turned beet-red and he backed up to where the other officers were standing. "Ah-haaaaa!" he said nervously, trying to save some face. "You two coons want to go the hard way, huh?" He smiled at the other men. "Well, by Gawd, that's okie-dokie with me. It's your bacon fat in the fire, by Jesus, not mine." He turned his back to us with contempt, and spoke to one of his men. "Phil, go upstairs and call Main Building, will ya? Tell 'em to send me some more men over here—that we're having a mite bit of trouble with these niggers. And make it quick, okay?"

The man nodded and ran up the stairs.

Now this was too goddamn much for me. I was worried enough about the five crackers already there, and this fool was calling for ten or fifteen more. Kiss my ass! Come *on*, Little A, I wanted to shout. Let's give up now! Let's give up before those other cops get here and beat our brains out! Fortunately, Little A had been thinking very much along the same lines, but his greater experience had given him more sway.

"Come on, Rube!" he whispered. "We got to get that fool before he calls Main Building, because if we don't," he said decisively, "there'll be too many of them for us to fight later on."

I looked at him like he had just lost his mind. But he hadn't asked for my opinion. What he said was final, and he wasn't going to wait around for any of my insignificant bullshit. So Little A made his move, and with my bat, I brought up the rear.

"Watch out! Watch out!" an officer screeched. He was surprised that we would be attacking them, instead of the other way around, but by the time his alarm penetrated the minds of his confused comrades, we were in the midst of them and pushing our way through to the stairs. We raced up the narrow passageway and arrived on the first-floor landing.

"Stay here, Rube!" Little A shouted back, pointing to the stairs. "Keep those guys down there," he said, "I'm going to get the man at the phone." And he ran on up the next flight of stairs.

I spun around and stood there with my baseball bat, looking down at the men in the basement. They couldn't all come up the stairway at one time—it was too narrow for that—and I knew that if they tried, I could bust one or two of them in the head before they were halfway. Then I heard scuffling sounds coming from up above.

"Ouch! Don't hit me!" a voice squealed. "Please don't hit me," it begged pathetically. "I haven't called anybody yet."

"Then put that damn phone down!" Little A growled. "And get your stinking ass back downstairs!"

"Yes, sir!" The man gave in willingly. He slammed the phone back into its cradle and ran down the stairs. I stepped aside and let him pass. His face was ashen. Little A had confiscated the man's blackjack, and now he stood beside me with his bat in one hand, and the blackjack in the other.

"Get on down those stairs!" he ordered, smacking the man on his ass with his own club. "And you better touch nary a step all the way down, either!" The officer jumped so he didn't touch any. Little A and me laughed like hell.

Our moment of joy was very short-lived, however. I knew we were going to get the shitty end of the stick. The five men tucked away in the basement were but a flimsy indication of the vast law-and-order structure that we were opposing. Eventually, we would be overwhelmed.

The only thing we could hope for in this scrimmage was to make damn sure that we didn't get hurt. *If* we had to fight these people at all. If that became the case, then our next problem would be to minimize their number as much as we could. Since we were stationed in the doorway upstairs, no one could come or go except through us. There would be, at least, no reinforcements for the men down in the basement.

"You stay here, little brother!" Little A said, snapping me to attention. "I'm going back upstairs to look around. I wanna make sure nobody is creeping up on us." Then he disappeared up the stairs again.

The men in the basement were huddled in a corner, talking amongst themselves. I couldn't hear their conversation, but judging from the angry buzz of their voices and the violent gesticulations they directed towards one another, I assumed they were in disagreement. Finally, Gargantua separated himself from the rest of the group and approached the stairwell. "Say there, youngster?" he called up to me as politely as you please, peaches and cream dripping from his lips. "What's your name, son?"

I just looked at him.

"Look, my boy, we don't want any more trouble, and I'm sure you don't, either," he said. "Now, if you'll just give me your bat and let me come upstairs, I'll conveniently forget about your part in this matter. How about that?" he asked hopefully.

The sphinx-like silence with which I greeted his proposal was loud enough to send him off into a roaring tantrum. He began stomping back and forth across the floor, raving like a maniac, hurling curses and violent threats of brutal mutilation up at me. "Why you . . . black, bullet-headed, sonofabitch, you," he drawled, savoring each succulent vernacularism on his tongue. The peaches and cream had turned to shit. "I'll get you, you little bastard, you! And when I do, I'll personally bust your fuckin' head!" He raised his club. His anger was so blinding that he stumbled into a nearby school desk and bumped his knee. "Owwwww! Gawddammit!" he howled painfully. Whirling around, he smashed his blackjack across the staid offender.

Crash!! The desk fell to the floor, split in two.

Silence. The big man just stood there and looked at the desk, shocked by his own violence. But he was no fool. He realized this savage display of strength just might be his ticket to freedom.

"See that, nigger!" he shouted. "Did you see that?" He kicked the splintered halves of the desk against the wall. "That's gonna be your head, you little black sonofabitch! Because I'm coming up those stairs right now!" He started up, and I started down, fully prepared to stop him at any cost.

"Hold it, Rube! Hold it, man!" Little A called. "Here comes the superintendent! Now maybe we got a chance. We can talk to him, but you better keep those guys down there anyway, while I go see the man."

When the group downstairs heard that the superintendent was on his way, they grabbed their blackjacks and made a last-ditch effort to break out of their confining cavity. Step by step they crept up the narrow stairway, one behind the other. When the first one came within range of my bat, I drew back to cut loose on him.

"Look out!" he screamed, and unceremoniously wrestled his way back to safety.

"What's wrong with you, gawddammit!" Gargantua's jeering voice said from below. "You scared to go up there or something?" he asked. "Somebody's got to go, you know."

"Then, goddammit-the-hell!" another voice barked resentfully. "You take your bad-ass self up there, because I'll be goddamned if *I'm* going!"

"Shit!" came the reply. "You must be a gawddamn fool! I ain't about to let that crazy nigger hit me with that fuckin' bat!" They all burst out laughing.

But it wasn't funny to me. Their actions only confirmed my fast-growing suspicion that I had been committed to an insane asylum, not a jail. I just didn't know what to make of these people. Everybody at Jamesburg was acting as if he were crazy—and now I was doing it, too. Goddamn! I was so absorbed in my thoughts of the strange proclivities of these unusual people that I failed to hear Little A and the superintendent coming in behind me.

"Stand aside, son!" An enormous weight grasped my shoulders and moved me out of the way. "Come out from down there, you men!" he scolded them. "Take your blackjacks and get out of here, right now!" A few seconds later, five men and four blackjacks sheepishly filed out the door.

If it had seemed to me that the whole world was made up of big people, Mr. Moore, our superintendent, was the biggest I had seen yet. He casually strolled up the stairs into the television room, pulled up a chair, and sat his huge frame down.

"Well now, fellas," he said, looking at us with eyes of clear light blue, "how about telling the old man what this was all about?"

Little A stepped forward immediately to take the blame. "I had

a fight, sir!" he began very fast, "but then seven guys jumped me
and were doing me under." He punctuated his words with action.
"But my little buddy here came to my rescue, and then we beat the
shit out of them! And then—"

"Whoa on there!" Mr. Moore interrupted. A pleasant smile
brightened his face. "From the looks of both of you," he said, "I
would guess that you got the shit beat out of *you!*"

"No, sir! That's not true, sir!" Little A shook his head. "We *won*
the fight! You should see the other guys," he added meaningfully,
"but we didn't hurt anybody else, and we wasn't going to fight your
officers either!" he lied. "We were just holding them off until we
could get some help, sir."

The superintendent didn't say anything. He just leaned back
comfortably in his chair and looked at us thoughtfully. A disturbed, V-shaped frown hovered over his eyes. A muscle in his jaw
rippled. He looked mad, but when he spoke, his voice did not
betray anger.

"What's your name, son?" he asked me.

"C-Carter, sir! R-Rub-Rubin Carter."

"Well, Rube," he said, smoothly altering my name to what I
liked being called, "go outside and get Mr. Lightfoot in here for
me—on the double, now!" I was gone before his last word was
out.

The rest of the inmates were all clustered around Mr. Lightfoot,
talking excitedly, but when I reached them they fell silent. My
passage through the crowd created a tangible electricity in the air,
like that of an impending thunderstorm. I could feel it, and I took
pleasure in it. Tired and beaten as I was, it brought me to life
again. I told Mr. Lightfoot what Mr. Moore had said, and sissy-
like, he scampered away.

The inmates pressed around me like vultures, pleading with me
to provide them with shreds of vicious gossip. Unaccustomed to
talking as I was, I couldn't begin to answer their questions, so I
kept my mouth shut, frowning upon my inability to talk, and
pushed my way out. But they didn't understand my reasons for
keeping silent, and interpreted it for themselves as a sure sign of
strength, a badge of lawlessness—which was the only thing they
understood. As I pushed my way through the mob, maybe a little
more roughly than I should have, their comments followed in my
wake: "Man, did you see that mean motherfucker look at me!"
exclaimed one inmate to another.

"Yeah! But did you see that nigger's eyes!"

"Man!" another inmate said with respect. "I ain't gonna never have no trouble with that sonofabitch if I can help it! Did you see the way he was downing those guys?" He sounded incredulous. "Goddamn!" he went on. "That's a hard-hitting young boy!"

As I heard these remarks, a tingling sensation gripped my heart. I complimented myself on having shown these people that I could fight—and I liked doing it, besides. Now, maybe, I thought, these people would have to accept me, or at least leave me alone—the latter being preferable.

When I returned to the cottage, Little A was standing outside the door leading into the room where the superintendent and Mr. Lightfoot were holding their conference. Their voices were too muffled for me to distinguish their words.

"What's going on in there?" I asked Little A.

"I don't know," he answered, shrugging. "But from the way it sounds, I think the man's digging in Lightfoot's ass!" He smiled.

"Well if the man's doing that to *him*," I asked, picking up on the jailhouse jargon, "what's he going to do to *us*?"

"I don't know that either," he said. "But we'll soon find out, won't we?"

The wait, while tedious, was not very long. Mr. Lightfoot came out a few minutes later, and Mr. Moore called us in. "Sit down, fellas," he said soberly, indicating two chairs in front of him. "I've just had a talk with Mr. Lightfoot, as you know," he said, "and I'm of the opinion that this little episode didn't turn out as badly as it could have—namely with you fighting my officers." He cleared his throat.

"Here at Jamesburg, Rube and Alfred [Little A], there are three sides to every story: your side, the officer's side, and my side, which, of course, is the right side. Now, speaking very frankly, I like your side best this time, and for that reason I'm going to forget this incident. In the future, however, neither of you had better forget that when my officers tell you to do something, you better hop to it, and hop to it damn quick! Am I making myself clear?"

"Yes, sir!" Little A and I responded together, grateful to be out from under the hammer. But it was too late, I was hooked. In Jamesburg I had saddled a monster, and he who rides upon the back of a man-eating tiger, dares not dismount.

THE SIXTH ROUND

The Death of a Young Soul

Following the superintendent's departure, the cottage's volcanic atmosphere returned to some semblance of normality. Those of us who had participated in the fight received the necessary medical treatment, and after returning from the hospital, we went downstairs to take our showers.

As I started to undress, still apprehensive and uncertain about what I should expect from the young hellions around me, I kept my eye glued to Chink and the rest of his boys. One eye was all I had. From its corner, I spied the dastardly brogan I had seen earlier, a split second before it had crashed into and mangled my other eye. The shoes were distinguishable because they were black, as opposed to the state-issued brown ones the rest of us wore.

Immediately, my heart began to race with a renewed vengeance, and I knew I would have to fight again or pass out from acute frustration. Almost blinded by my emotions, I stumbled over to Little A and whispered this information in his ear.

"That's Sconion-Eyed Jones!" he whispered back. "A treacherous sonofabitch! What do you want to do about it?"

"I know what I'm going to do!" I told him bitterly. "I'm going to kick his goddamn eye out, that's what I'm going to do!" Then I went back to my locker and put on my shoes.

Sconion-Eyed Jones stood six feet tall and dwarfed the rest of us by at least six inches. A rangy, light-skinned fellow, he had sharply slanted eyes that always seemed to be watering—which was the reason for his name.

Once I had laced up my boots and gotten myself together, I went out and stood in the middle of the floor, hotter than a bushel of motherfuckers. "You, there—monkey!" I glared at Sconion-Eyed Jones, and pointed my finger at him. "Yo-yo-you're the nigger who stomped me!" I accused. "Now, come on out here on the floor, you dirty moth-mo-moth-motherfucker! Come on out here, and let's me and you start from the giddy-up!"

I was stuttering so badly that before I could suitably challenge the towering Jones, Chink had interfered.

"Now just a cotton-picking minute!" he grumbled, letting me know that he was still boss. "How do you know that he was the one who stomped you? How do you know it wasn't me, or one of the others?"

Smoke jumped straight from my head, and I blew my cool. "Why you stinking, low-life motherfucker!" I sneered venomously, not stuttering anymore. "Man, if I just *thought* you were the one! If I just thought *you* were the one I would be hopping around on one leg right now," I told him, "because the other one would be planted so far up in your stinking ass that the hospital would have had to cut it clean off to get it out!"

Chink knew I meant it too, so he didn't push it any further. Instead, he turned to his boy and started coaching him. "Awright, Sconion, baby," he said, urging him on, "he's all yours now! But take your time and watch yourself, because the little nigger hits harder than a Mississippi mule kicking downhill, backwards!"

"Ohhhh, that's awright with me!" Sconion boasted, strutting forward and moving out to the center of the floor. "Fuck the little nigger! He's going to wish that I kicked *both* of his goddamn eyes out!" he stated emphatically. " 'Cause I've got something for all you hard-hitting motherfuckers!" With a burst of speed, his right hand dipped and flashed into his pocket and whipped out a long, razor-sharp shiv.

Chink gasped in astonishment, and unconsciously moved towards him. "What da hell!" he mumbled, still moving, but he stopped dead in his tracks when Sconion wheeled around and thrust the knife in his direction.

"Back up, Chink!" he warned. "I told you I had something for all of you hard-hitting motherfuckers. And now I'm going to cut this nigger too short to shit! When I get through with his hard-hitting ass, he'll have to reach *up* to tie his own goddamn shoes!"

I stared at him in disbelief, almost paralyzed with fear. A sickening wave of terror chilled my blood and froze me in my place. I became frightfully aware of my wretched condition: with only one eye working properly, and it half closed, the probable outcome of this fight became obvious. But, as it turned out, I didn't have too much time to think about it. Sconion-Eyed leaped right in and started raking at me with his blade.

His watery eyes, now pinpoints of hatred, scared me all over again, but I instinctively backpedaled out of range. Moving quickly and carefully, making sure I stayed away from the dangerous corners, I circled the room looking for a weapon. I tried to work my way around to the utility closet, to get to my baseball bat again, but Sconion was having none of that. He kept me well away from the closet, and continued to stalk me slowly, cautiously, his glazed eyes fixed upon my face. The only thing I could lay my hands on was an old ragged coat, and I grabbed that up and held it bunched in one hand.

With each step Sconion-Eyes took, he switched his knife from hand to hand. Then suddenly, without a hint of warning, he lunged in again. Hooking, jabbing, slashing at my stomach. There seemed to be a kind of effervescence about him, as if he had eaten fire. His eyes were slits of amalgamated hatred, but his movements were slow—much slower than before. His actions now, it seemed to me, were somehow exaggerated and relaxed, more lazy than harmful.

He smiled, and backed away. Then, he started in again. But now I was ready for him. I timed his motion and grabbed his arm, then groaned in excruciating pain as a deep piercing tongue of flame ripped through my side and let me know I'd been had, tricked into grabbing the wrong arm. Before he could stab me again, I latched on to the right arm, and with all the strength that I had, forced it up toward my face and sank my teeth in to the bone.

"Oh, my God!" he screamed, like a scared bitch. Blood gushed from his wound, and the knife slipped away from his limp fingers. But his God couldn't help him now. My fist shot out in a short swinging arc, colliding with his jawbone with a crunching impact, and down he fell—unconscious before his back hit the floor.

I reached down and picked up the knife, and a wheel of fire scorched my ribs. I moved toward Sconion with the clear intention of slitting his throat. I wanted him to wake up in hell. But just before I could reach his sprawled-out body, the roof fell in. Little A and the rest of the boys wrestled me to the floor and tried to take the knife.

I fought them savagely, hammering away at anything I touched. I thought that everybody had turned against me, and I was trying to break that knife off in somebody's head. But the struggling mass was too much for me. I felt the knife being wrenched from my hand, and at any second I expected it to be plunged into my chest.

The pain I'd felt earlier fled and a mixed media of emotions sliced through my heart.

"Hold him down, man! Hold him, goddammit!" Little A hissed, his voice penetrating my mind and adding fury to my struggle. "Take it easy, Rube!" he said soothingly. "We're not trying to hurt you. We're only trying to help you."

I lay there on the cold floor and gasped for breath. The concrete slowly cooled the heat of combat that raged within me, but as it subsided, something else died, too. I mean, some feeling, some sort of sensibility—call it benevolence for my fellowman—was gone now. Wiped out in the face of this persistent violence, hatred and fear, it was replaced by a seething distrust of everything and everybody, except Rubin Carter.

When finally I pulled myself up off the floor, I realized that I wasn't hurt as badly as I'd thought—although my side continued to burn like Lucifer's candle. The coat I had grabbed while Sconion was stalking me around the room might have been what had saved my life. His knife had hit me only after slicing through its thickness, thus minimizing his thrusting power. For the second time that night, I went to the hospital. When I returned, everybody was fast asleep, and I quickly followed suit.

One hour . . . two hours . . . maybe three hours had passed when I was jerked awake. Fully alert, I sat upright in my bed. My heart was fluttering in a fearful serenade of perturbation, trying to understand what had gotten me so scared. I looked around. Something was tugging at my bedcovers. There, lying on the floor and grinning like a Cheshire cat, his pearly teeth gleaming in the darkness, was Little A. Before I could ask what he was doing there, he motioned for me to be quiet and follow him. I hesitated at first, then eased out of bed and to the floor. Together we belly-slid from bed to bed, moving toward the far corner of the dormitory.

When my eyes became accustomed to the darker darkness beneath the beds, I saw that there were other people squatting down at the opposite end of the room. As we closed in, the fragrant odor of cigarette smoke invaded my nostrils. Smoking was prohibited at Jamesburg.

"Were you sleeping, little fighting man?" Chink questioned with a smile, giving me and Little A a cigarette. His battered face was covered with bruises. Sconion-Eyed Jones was there too, along with a boy called Salty Dog, and another, Boston Beans.

"No, I wasn't asleep," I lied easily, handing him back the weed. "And I don't smoke, either," I said.

This was a strange and unusual group to be clustered in amity beneath this little bed. I mean, there were lumps, bumps, and bruises in evidence everywhere. We were all fucked up. But, be that as it may, there was something about these fellows that stood out and puzzled me no end—their composure. While it was true we were all very young, their posturing reeked of a maturity well beyond their years.

Take Sconion-Eyed Jones, for example. Here was a fourteen-year-old who knew more about handling a knife than Jim Bowie. This boy had been locked up for killing his father—who had killed his mother—and was now a permanent ward of the state until he reached twenty-one. Sconion-Eyed was what we called "a state baby," and his notorious reputation with a knife became a legend in the years to come—until one day he died, burned to a crisp in the electric chair.

As for the rest of the group, while their crimes were not as heinous as that of Sconion-Eyed Jones, they were all mentally abused products of a morally abusing environment, shamelessly vicious, corrupt, and depraved. To make matters worse, these were contagious qualities.

"C'mon, Chink!" Salty Dog complained impatiently after finishing his cigarette. "Shit, man, we've got to go to work this morning, so let's do what we're gonna do if we're gonna do it! It's getting later all the time, you know."

"Yeah, I guess you're right," Chink agreed thoughtfully, knocking the fire off his cigarette. "Okay," he said, "let's make it then." He started creeping back under the beds on his belly, the rest of us following close behind. We had crawled all the way to the other side of the room before Chink reached up and shook someone lying in the bed above.

"Huh!" a startled voice cried out, the bed springs squeaking from his movements.

"Shhhhhhh, be quiet, motherfucker!" Chink cautioned the noise-maker, putting a hand over his mouth. "Ease out of bed and get down here on the floor," he snarled, "and you better not make anymore goddamn noise, either! You hear?" The bed springs squeaked softly one more time, then a small body slipped soundlessly to the floor.

"I'm sorry, Chink," whispered a tiny petrified voice. "I didn't mean to make any noise." It was pathetic. We turned around and crawled back to the smoking corner.

Now I might have been a little more naive than was considered healthy for a Jamesburg youngster at that time, but I'll be goddamned if I was downright stupid! Jamesburg had taught me *something* since I'd been incarcerated there: now I knew what a faggot was when I saw one, and this was what we had in tow—a goddamned faggot, a fuck boy.

Wait a minute. I'll have to retract that statement; it's not entirely the truth. The boy was not a committed homosexual, but he did submit, nonetheless, to what, I think, were the degrading desires of stronger inmates in return for cigarettes, food, and favor. At Jamesburg, it made no difference if one had or didn't have the inclination to become somebody's "wife." If one couldn't protect himself in a sure-fire, devastating manner in a fight, before very long he would find himself switching and "married" to a tougher inmate. So this boy was less a pedigreed faggot than a simple jailhouse punk, which in my estimation is the difference between sugar and shit.

When our group had arrived back at the smoking corner, the cigarettes were lit again and passed around to everybody except the newest member. He was instead ordered to remove his pajamas and lay down on his stomach. Then, one by one, each of my associates mounted the boy-girl's back, grunted for a minute, groaned for another, then shuddered and relaxed.

This was the first time that I had ever witnessed a homosexual act, and, to be truthful, it was neither fascinating nor overly repulsive to me. But it did stink. I looked upon the deed with an attitude of dishonorable indifference: indifference, in that it had no physical effect upon my person; dishonorable in that, if this punk had offered only a molecule, a mere speck—a tiny *smithereen*—of resistance, verbally or otherwise, I would have forced myself to become his ally and be ready to go to war again, if necessary.

But undeclared offers are worthless. When my turn came to take a ride in his saddle, I declined as gracefully as possible. The only person who seemed to be offended was the punk himself, and if he had said anything, I would have broken my foot off in his nasty ass. Nobody else pressed the issue. Then we all went back to bed. Thus ended my first day in Cottage Eight.

THE SEVENTH ROUND

Vindictiveness

That first day's initiation into the regular Jamesburg population quickly made me realize that I was no longer a member of a sane society. In order to insure my feeble existence in this chamber of horror, I would have to forget about ethics and morality, etiquette and formality.

Jamesburg thrived on, and gobbled up, every ounce of strength, animal cunning, and physical dexterity a person could possibly muster. At the end of every day I found myself physically and mentally exhausted, but thankful that another day had passed, that I still remained alive, and that I hadn't had to kill someone for the privilege.

Though it should have served to cultivate strong minds and healthy bodies, Jamesburg did just the opposite. The administration looked upon and used the inmates as simple automated labor tools who were placed at the beck and call of the state legislature to enhance New Jersey's child slavery system. We were sent, conveyor-like, through the prison system—from Jamesburg to Annandale to Bordentown to State Prison—and made to work like dogs, with the death house coming as our ultimate reward.

Most of the Jamesburg kids had only committed the same violations of rules as had endeared Huckleberry Finn to millions of people, but in us society found these deeds intolerable. Not many of us had committed what could be called serious crimes, but, serious or not, once caught we were thrust into the same degrading criminal categories as an adult offender. Even down to having the same strait-laced kind of parole.

Thus, general opinion of Jamesburg's population was that we were criminals before we got there, would remain criminals throughout our stay, and would be hardened criminals when we left. The public's attitude was, work us as hard as possible, feed us as little as they could get away with, and beat the hell out of us whenever we got out of hand. That was the institutional policy, and it worked, too. Sometimes.

The ensuing years decisively changed my thinking. I witnessed many deaths and attempted suicides by frustrated inmates seeking refuge from atrocities committed against them—young boys who had first gone to the higher authorities begging for their help, only to be met by sadistic technicians who literally burned their brains out by experimenting with electric shocks, and then sent them right back to Jamesburg smoking. (They claimed that these shocks removed a troublesome inmate's hostilities.)

As I grew older, and more and more embittered with life, I became more and more committed to a philosophy of hardcore determinism. I began to believe that every human being born on this earth, and every atom residing within the universe, had to follow its destiny, and only survived to minister to its purpose; that a greater ruling power, call it what you will, shaped and formed all of life.

I believed that everything I had done in my life had been the natural and logical thing for me to do, under the circumstances. If by chance I performed a gracious deed, I laid claim to no credit. If I committed a crime in the eyes of society, I took no blame. I felt no more responsible for my actions than for the winds.

I believed that the omnipotent entity, the capricious ruling power, that had fiendishly set cyclone and hurricane forces free on this earth was the same fickle energy that had created me. If I overturned a basket of social concepts, or violated a few rigid conventions in pursuit of my destiny, it was not my fault, but Fate's. I felt no compunction for the act that I had been forced to commit, which, according to society's standards, was a crime. At the time it happened, my behavior seemed to me to be natural, just as natural as a cyclone wind will demolish a building standing in its way. I came to believe that no man could actually be the master of his own frail destiny and that everything under the sun was as it should be, or it wouldn't be.

So, I accepted the inevitable, and with this acceptance came the belief that I had been betrayed by the white distributors of equal justice. I bitterly resented being confined to this pus-filled New Jersey pit. I despised the sadistic men and latent homosexuals who worked there in the guise of correctional officers, and it was no well-kept secret how I felt.

To me, the people who worked at Jamesburg were lower than a

skunk with fallen arches, and everytime I had the chance, I attempted to break my foot off in one of their butts. Each such incident would invariably require hospitalization for the scumbag officer, and segregation—locked up in an iron cage with no clothes or bedding—for me.

A small, isolated building situated deep in the woods, Segregation was an honest-to-God shithouse containing sixteen cells and no place to relieve oneself but the cold cement floor. The entire paint-hungry building reeked of maggot-infested wolf pussy, and its inhabitants looked like death standing on the street corner eating lifesavers.

I came to spend a great deal of my time in this place—so much time, in fact, that one cell was always held in reserve for me. Just as sure as water is wet or small brush grows into big timber, I would sooner or later be sent down there to stay.

The last time it happened, I was almost seventeen years old and still a runt—one of the shortest guys in an all-black cottage called the Big Six. It was, without question, the roughest on the grounds.

Each cottage had its own dukes, fellows who could outfight anybody else in their respective houses, but the duke of our house was generally accepted as the Duke Upstate, the Kingpin, and I was it. Oh, don't get me wrong, there were plenty who could have made their presence felt in a good old rough'n'tumble, some who even came on like a thunderstorm. But there was only one Hurricane: the Rube—Number One—me.

The fool cop responsible for my going into Segregation that last time was a fairly new one. He had come on duty while I was out practicing with the drum and bugle corps, so we didn't bump heads with each other until after the evening meal. He was a young hack, big, white, tough, and known to favor tender black kids.

The floors had to be scrubbed every night, under my supervision, and had to meet my approval before any recreation could take place. By the time I reached the cottage that night, everyone was down in the basement, stripped to the waist and waiting. I guess the officer wondered what everybody was waiting for. When I came in, he was leaning impatiently against the wall, near the stairs, smoking a cigarette. Without saying a word, I went over to my locker and stood up on it, my arms folded across my chest. When the water boys saw that I was ready, they began flooding the floor with hot soapy water, and the scrubbers went to work with their deck brushes. Everybody else stood by for the mop-up detail.

Since this cop was so new, he didn't know me from Adam's house cat, and that was his first mistake. Had he known how I felt about bullying correctional officers, he would not have made his next move.

"Hey, boy!" he called.

I looked around, wondering to whom he was talking. But there wasn't anyone called "boy" near me, so I just ignored him.

"Hey! I'm talking to you, nigger," he growled, pointing to me. "Get your self down here and grab one of these mops, and let me see you with your ass in the air, cleaning this floor!"

I didn't move. I couldn't have budged if I'd wanted to.

The officer came away from the stairs and squished through the water towards me. His face was red. A sudden rage seemed to have swept through him.

"Didn't you hear what I said, nigger?" he demanded. "Get your narrow ass off that bench and get down here like I told you to, goddammit—now!"

Tarzan, the other line sergeant, six-feet and about two hundred pounds, jumped down off his locker on the other side of the room and intercepted the advancing cop before he could reach me. The scrubbers had stopped scrubbing by now.

"You better take it easy, Jim!" he told the man. "It's not his job to scrub the floors. That's the head line sergeant."

"I wouldn't give a shit if he was Jesus fuckin' Christ!" the cop yelled. "I'm running this goddamn cottage tonight, not you nor him!"

"I'm telling you, fool,' Tarzan warned the man. "You had better cool it while you got a chance, because you're just about ready to let your mouth write a check that your ass can't cash!"

The cop's lips curled up at the corners while he disdainfully looked me up and down. "Shit!" he snarled in scorn. "I'll kick this little punk's ass into the middle of next week!" Then he barked at me again: "Are you gonna do what I told you to do, boy? Or do I have to drag your black ass off that bench?"

I tried to warn the man, but all I could do was sputter and stomp my foot. Not knowing that I couldn't talk, and probably thinking that I was trying to make fun of him, his face turned livid with rage—a blinding, searing, tearing rage—and he reached up for me. That was his second mistake. Because I pounced on his ass and proceeded to whup him all around the basement, raining a hailstorm of fists and knuckles against his head that quickly rendered his face a bleeding pulp.

It was when he let me bulldoze him into the broom closet that he made his third and final mistake. It must have really been a frightful shock for him when he woke up in the hospital with both arms in casts and four broken ribs. But if he felt any pain at all, he had Tarzan and a few others to blame, because if they hadn't taken that baseball bat away from me when they did, he would have awakened in the Valley of Hinnom, with Lucifer's pitchfork stuck in his nasty ass.

That was why I was put down in Segregation again, with a bunch of guards crowded around my cell door.

"Well, Carter," the superintendent said to me, shaking his head in disbelief. "I see you've done it again," he murmured sadly. "Goddammit, you've done it again!"

I sat up and looked at the man, knowing that he had already been to the hospital and heard the officer's side of the story. Well, the superintendent was a fair man, if nothing else.

"Ha-have you t-ta-talked to him yet?" I stammered.

"Jesus Christ, boy!" he exploded, cursing for only the second time I could remember. "When is it going to sink into that fuckin' thick skull of yours that it doesn't help matters just because an officer is wrong? That isn't the point. The fact remains that you hurt that man! Can't you understand that?"

I understood exactly what Mr. Moore was saying, but evidently he didn't understand where I was coming from. "He had no business putting his hands on me!" I told him heatedly. "So it was his mistake—not mine!"

"Yes, but he didn't know who you were," he explained patiently, as if that were the solution to the whole problem.

"Well, he'll know the next time, won't he!" I threw back at him sarcastically, getting carried away, still thinking about what the man had done.

Mr. Moore backed away from the bars in surprise. His eyes were slits of blue silver, looking right through me, reading my mind—reading the hatred like it was two-inch-high print.

"No, I don't think so, Rube," he said after a while, spacing his words carefully. "I don't think there will be a next time," he said. "You're getting too big for your britches. You've hurt your last

man at this institution. I think I'm going to send you away from
here."

Dirty sonofabitch, I thought. Annandale Reformatory, here I
come. Then I got mad because I was locked up and making it
easier for them to come and get me. "Well—well, if yo-yo-you—"
I began to stutter, trying to tell him that they would have to fight to
get me.

"Just shut up!" he broke in. "Just be quiet, before you say something you might be sorry for."

I was so mad I couldn't say anything anyhow. So I sat back
down on the floor, and looked forward to the day when they would
have to come down here and get me. I relished the thought.

"Carter?" Mr. Moore said, his soft voice interrupting my meal.
"I'll tell you what I am prepared to do, and it's beyond me why I
even bother. But because you've been here for such a long time,
son, and also because I'm afraid of what's happening to you, I'm
going to make you a proposition."

My ears perked up. I started to ask him what it was—anything
was better than going to Annandale—but he motioned for me to
be still.

"If you can bring me three months, three full months without
any trouble," he went on, "I will personally guarantee that you go
home on the last of that ninety days. Will you accept that?" he
asked. "Will you give it a try?" He looked intense.

Had I been knocked in the head with the moon, the shock
couldn't have been any greater. I mean, I was flabbergasted. I'd
have been at a loss for words even if I could talk.

"Well?" asked Mr. Moore again, expectantly. "Will you give it a
try?"

I leaped to my feet, clinging to the bars so that I wouldn't fall.
My knees were nearly buckling beneath me. I gasped for breath,
sputtering for words, and tried to tell him, "Hell, yeah, I'll do it!
You goddamn right I will!" But I couldn't speak. This was a
helluva time to be speechless. But he seemed to get my message
anyway, and he smiled wearily.

"I understand," he said, "but now I want you to understand
something, too. I want you to understand without any reservation
that the very first time you violate any of the institution's rules—be
they big, small, or whatever—I will immediately pack your black

ass up and ship you out—and on a stretcher, if need be. Do you understand that?" he asked. "Have I made myself clear?"

"Yes, sir!" I blurted, the words rushing out of me all of a sudden. I was happy for the first time in years.

Thus, when Mr. Moore unlocked my cell and set me free, he released a determined young man. I was resolved to capitalize on his mercy. For the first time, I could see a little daylight at the end of the long, dark tunnel. At long last I had a reason—and the desire—to live again, to feel, to be a part of a world which in the past had been of no great concern to me. Now I would walk through hell with a pair of gasoline drawers on before I would mess up my chances to go home.

But oh, how hard and how slowly the days came, and the long nights never seemed to pass. My mind was constantly in a state of turmoil and confusion. Seven days passed into a week, and then another, and soon one agonizing month was gone.

And still I had no trouble.

Jamesburg's entire population was happily in my corner, standing firm behind my cause—a few because they were really glad to see me going home, and others, I imagine, because they were tickled pink just to get rid of me. I didn't have too many friends. But I had a lover.

Somewhere, someplace, I had once read that loneliness at times is as important as a lover . . . and that a true individualist has got to be lonely. Well, I didn't know if I was an individualist or not, but I must have had that lover, because I was lonely as hell.

By the twenty-ninth of June, the jailhouse grapevine was popping with the news that I had received a further reduction in time, and that now I would be going home on the first of July, rather than the fifth as previously arranged, because of the Fourth of July holiday.

My boredom had gone, the bitterness was dissolved, the hatred forgotten. Throughout the long day I waited expectantly, impatient to find out if the rumors were true. I didn't dare leave the laundry, where I was then working, not even for lunch. I hung right in there, working straight through the meal, me and the man. And just before the quitting whistle sounded, a messenger came from Main Building and gave the laundry supervisor my traveling pass to the superintendent's office. A pass was the only way that we could move around the institution without being stopped.

"Here it is, Rube!" he shouted gleefully, holding the pass up for everybody to see. "You're going home, kid. You're finally going home! Congratulations, and God bless your ornery hide!" He smiled affectionately and shook my hand.

Then all the workers crowded around me, and their expressions of assorted pleasure came from every direction. "This is what I wanted to see!" a happy voice blared in delight. "And, goddammit, I knew you could do it!" it said fervently. "Now where's that mother-fucker who's got my money?" the voice's owner cried, moving through the crowd in search of a boy with whom he had made a bet.

"Oh, shut up, nigger, I got your damn money!" an inmate answered irritably. "You don't have to look for me—I was coming to find you," he went on. "And I'd bet you again, too! Because if anybody ever told me that Rubin Carter went three whole months without fuckin' up at least one cop, I would have called him a lying sonofabitch and went straight to war!" He turned to me. It was Salty Dog. "Good luck, Rube," he said, "and take care of yourself."

Then Little A, who had already been home once and sent back, and who was the only person I considered a real friend, tearfully clutched my hand in a burst of emotion that was foreign to the both of us. I had never known him to express anything but anger very strongly before. Now he looked almost naked, because the bitterness was missing from his face. It had been replaced by several other emotions, predominantly sorrow.

"Yeah, take care of yourself," he whispered passionately, all wet-eyed and serious, angrily brushing away the tears that spilled down his dark cheeks. "And man, stay out of these goddamn places!" he added more forcefully. "Because this ain't your stick, ole buddy-buddy." He flashed a tearful smile.

I frowned at him fiercely. He was clinging to my hand as if I would disappear suddenly if he turned me loose, and his pathetic look almost melted the shield that I had thrown up to protect myself with. I looked at the boy for whom I would gladly have given my life, and dammit, I couldn't help it, tears began trickling down my face, too.

Mine were eyes that hadn't been moist with tears in a long time, and it embarrassed me. Some of these people were closer to me than I could dare admit. Now that I was going home, going to America,

I couldn't say a goddamn thing—not a solitary word. But I could feel. And I felt more empathy and understanding at that time than I could remember feeling in my entire life. I couldn't do anything but stand there and look, shivers streaking up and down my spine. So, with my eyes brimming over and my heart bursting with gratitude, I shamefacedly turned away from the crowd and walked out the door.

Two minutes later I crashed into Mr. Moore's office like a wild bat out of hell, breathless with excitement. I gave my pass to the secretary behind the desk, and sputtered out why I was there.

"Please have a seat, Mr. Carter." She smiled radiantly. "Someone will be with you in just a moment," she sang.

At any other time I would gladly have sat down in hope of getting a peek at the woman's legs. (In the past I had gotten some pretty good shots.) But today I was too impatient. Today I wanted to go home. I strolled over to the window and looked out, watching the work details slowly trickling in and thinking that all this was in the past for me now; nothing else mattered except tomorrow.

"Okay, Rubin," the secretary called to me pleasantly. "You may go in now."

With a rapturous, shit-eating grin plastered across my face, I knocked on the door and entered at the sound of a voice. Then my smile faded and was replaced by what I'm sure was a grimace of pure, unadulterated hatred. The man sitting behind the desk was not Mr. Moore. It was a man I'll call Mr. Wallace, an officer I hated more than anyone else in the world.

His gaunt face was the color of jaundice. His short, undernourished body, emphasized by funny shoulder-padded suits, reminded me of a broken-down, wasted skeleton. He had two thick, purplish lips that seemed to drool continuously, and to make matters worse, he never looked a man straight in the face but always at his crotch.

He was the reason I once had to suffer six agonizing months of solitary confinement in a six-foot-tall, three-foot-wide box that almost drove me insane. The only thing that had kept me from going completely mad during that time was the fact that he was in the intensive care unit of a hospital, hovering between life and death from the ass-whupping I had draped on his back. That had been a pleasure that by far outweighed my penalty.

I had caught him a year before in Cottage Seven, the little boys' quarters, where I was going to check the laundry count, just as he was attempting to force a little light-skinned fellow into a homosexual act. I became so enraged at the sight that I whupped on him until my arms were weary, and I'd be whupping on him today if it hadn't been for that little boy grabbing my legs and pleading with me to stop.

Since that time, this man had let it be known that he was going to "pay me back" sooner or later. I thought it would probably be later, if ever, because he always made it his business to be wherever I wasn't. And happy as I was on that June day in 1954, when I found him in the superintendent's office instead of Mr. Moore, I still hated him with an unfulfilled passion.

"Where's Mr. Moore at, man?" I demanded, moving closer to the desk.

Mr. Wallace was sweating cinder seeds, but he must have been looking forward to this moment all day long. Because his eyes were puffy and bloodshot, and his lips drooled excessively as he glanced down at my swipe.

"Ah—ah—ah, Mr. Moore is away on vacation, Carter." He cleared his throat nervously, wiping the sweat from his mottled face. "However," he purred, "he left me with explicit orders to deal with you whenever the occasion arose."

Whewwwwww! My breath gushed out in relief, my heart almost jumping out of my chest. Then I grew angry with myself for having shown a sign of weakness in front of this sissy. Luckily he didn't see it. He wasn't aware of my discomfort. All his attention was directed to a yellow document that he held clutched in his hands.

"Carter," he said, looking up at me finally, "do you know what this is?"

I just stood there and looked at the creep. I didn't even try to answer his stupid question. I don't think he really expected me to. He knew damn well I recognized the paper he sat there pretending to read. How could I mistake the institution's disciplinary report for anything else, after having had hundreds of them? I started to tell him about his crippled, bald-headed mammy, but then I thought better of it and just kept quiet.

The silence became deep, and then eerie forewarnings of doom seeped into my system. Something had gone wrong. I could taste it. My frazzled nerves slowly bunched up in my stomach. What in hell is this fool waiting for? I asked myself impatiently. Then, taking the initiative, I stalked up to the desk stiff-legged, and snatched the paper out of his hands.

I could hardly believe it as my own name reared back and kicked me in the face. I sank into the nearest chair, shaking my head in bewilderment. The words on the paper became blurred.

"Dear Sir," the report began, "The above-mentioned inmate, Rubin Carter, today, June 29, on his way to work at 12:45, maliciously referred to the cottage supervisor as 'a bald-headed son of a bitch.' As pre-instructed, concerning this inmate's behavior, I am accordingly submitting this report."

I just couldn't believe it. This was pure bullshit, and whoever wrote it was a goddamn liar, his feet stunk, his stupid heart pumped shit, and he didn't love his Jesus. I searched frantically for the officer's name, praying that it was there—so I could stomp the lying bastard back into the ground for the worm that he was. But the signature was missing. After reading it for the sixth or seventh time, it finally dawned on me, like a left jab and a straight right cross to my jaw, what was wrong with the report.

"Don't play with me, man!" I shouted indignantly, throwing the charge on the desk. " 'Cause I'll fuck you up in here right now!" And I started around after him.

His eyes got big as silver dollars. Then he screamed and leaped for the door. His coattails flew straight out from his smoke, but when he saw that he wasn't being followed, he stopped on the threshold and got brave again. "Now take it easy, Carter," he whimpered. "Just take it easy."

"Moth-mo-motherfucker," I stammered, "You-yo-you know this is a god-god-god-goddamn lie!" I stomped my foot, trying to force the words out. I failed to hold back a flood of frustrated tears. Mr. Wallace smiled, a victorious twinkle flashing in his eyes.

"Sorry, Carter," he gloated, "but that's for me to decide." Then he made it out the door, smoking.

I should have run him down right there, but all I could manage to do was scream and smash my fist through a plate glass window, which cut my hand to ribbons. I felt so—so helpless and humiliated at being tricked and double-crossed. I was disgusted. I wished I could swell up and explode, demolishing the building and anything else that got in my way with me.

I stood there and brooded about the three long, hard months I had passed without any trouble. Then my mind returned to the disciplinary report. "Lies!" I hollered in despair to the empty room. My voice bounced off the woodwork like it was an echo chamber. I was crying. "All goddamn lies!" How could I have called any officer any kind of names at noontime? I had been working in the laundry since eight o'clock that morning. I could prove it. But I knew it was too late.

My memory is foggy now over how and when I finally stumbled away from the building, but my next recollection is of waking up in surprise, listening to the sounds of marching feet, and of being alone in the darkened basement of a quiet cottage. Just how long I had been sitting there, I haven't any idea. But the return of the inmates from evening mess reactivated my senses.

Bright-eyed, flint-faced and quiet, the boys sluggishly shuffled in with their lips set in grim determination. They threw off an electric current that made the air in the room snap, crackle, and pop. I could see their compassion for me and my troubles, and their respectful silence was their way of telling me just how they felt. They looked like advance scouts for the Grim Reaper, with his sharp scythe drawn and ready to harvest a bloody crop. All it would take was a word from me.

One word, and I had a million of them running through my mind, a million fires of reciprocation for desecrating the chapel which had been my temple of resolution for the past ninety days. I didn't care then if Jamesburg were torn down and burnt to the ground.

Then a sudden wild surge of rebellion against Fate, and not the institution, erupted within my mind. What right had Fate to treat me in this way? Where was the justice? And why was destiny toying with my life so? I felt I had been the brunt of all its nasty jokes. Well, I'm not taking that shit anymore, I wanted to shout. I was ready to do my thing. I'm going home anyway, I decided. And I'm going home tonight.

Tonight? I sat there momentarily stunned at the thought. A green light illuminated my mind. The word "escape" registered with a pleasing clarity. I asked myself why I hadn't thought of it before. But I had to be careful. I had to go easy. One false move could detonate a bloodbath that would be hard to equal for a long time to come. But first I had to re-establish my authority as line sergeant and maintain the status quo.

"Awright, you guys," I barked, and stood up before the silent population. Their eyes swung my way and became riveted to mine. "Let's hit this floor," I said forcefully. "I want to watch some television tonight!" It was the same thing I said every night.

Immediately, the basement came alive with relieved, babbling voices and nervous laughter. "Hitting the floor," in our language, was scrubbing it—something that none of us particularly relished. It was an essential part of our everyday lives though, and it had to be done. Like it or not, it was a cheerful group that scrubbed the floors that night, and by the time the work was finished and the showers begun, I had found my escape route.

In the basement, directly above our heads, was a small fifteen-by-thirty-inch window that was locked in with a heavily wired screen. Twenty minutes after the basement had been cleared, I was working like a dog, pushing and pulling, jerking and yanking, trying to break that cage. I cussed Fate and her double-crossing mammy with every sound I made, while each tiny noise seemed to laugh back at me and grow louder, echoing throughout the building and trying to give me away, stop me from going home.

I kept wiggling and jiggling, fussing and cussing, straining my back to break that wire, and straining my mind to find somebody to take with me—somebody I could use for a scapegoat, if necessary. Even as I pondered this little bit of treachery, the screen nearly came unshackled in my hands. I stopped then to inspect the window and its fractured cage, making sure that nothing unusual could be detected.

The 10:00 p.m. changing of the guards would tell me finally if I was really going home, or off to another institution, to another hellhole of degradation. The new officer, freshly awakened from his nice warm bed, would be searching the building for breaks of this kind. If he were to find my disconnected window cage, the cottage would become flooded with a human sea of cops and black-jacks in a matter of minutes. You could bet your bottom dollar on that.

When I was satisfied that nothing unusual was apparent, I laid out the clothing I wanted to wear. The answer to my next problem unexpectedly jumped right on my back. Two inmates, the Werewolf and Simpson—one of whom I thought I might be able to use for a sacrificial lamb—were sneaking down the stairs to steal a smoke. Five minutes earlier, and they would have caught me.

"Whatcha cats doing down here?" I growled, hoping they hadn't seen what I was doing.

The Werewolf, a tall, wiry, deceptive kind of guy, was always where you wouldn't expect him to be. A real nosy sonofabitch. He claimed to be a car thief, or at least that's what he was busted for, and he swore to God there wasn't a machine made that he couldn't steal. I believed him. He smiled at me now, his heavy mustache and beard making him look more mature than his years.

"We came down to grab a quick smoke, Rube," he said, pointing to his partner. "We didn't know you was still down here, man."

I looked at the Wolf, and then at Simpson, a quiet, good-looking boy from south Jersey. I knew nothing about him, except that he had been in jail a long time. The Wolf was from Newark, just a few miles from Paterson, and I thought he could prove helpful in many ways. When it came down to fist fighting, the cat could really deal, and he had a heart as big as all outdoors.

"That's all right," I told him. "Go ahead and smoke."

I stayed there until they had finished their cigarettes. I wasn't about to leave and let them mess up my thing. Anyway, I wanted to talk to the Werewolf alone, if I could, and persuade him to run with me. I remembered that the parole board had just hit him with more time the previous week.

"Hey, Wolf!" I called as he and his partner started up the stairs. "Wait a minute," I said. "I wanna rap with you for a minute." His partner kept on going, but Wolf turned around and came back.

"Whatcha want, man?"

"When are you going home?" I asked, knowing the answer already. I just wanted to see if he was mad or not.

"Going home?" he snorted in disgust, wrinkling up his face. "Shit, man," he said bitterly. "The bastards just hit me with more time last week!"

That was all I wanted to hear. I knew then that he was ready. He was angry. "Do you want to go?" I asked him quietly.

"Home, you mean?" He was puzzled.

"That's exactly what I mean," I said, nodding my head in agreement, and whispering that beautiful, "home, man, home!"

I could almost hear the excitement race through his body while the full significance of "home" penetrated his mind. For a moment, he was speechless. Then he almost shouted, "When, man, when?" His eyes were sparkling.

"Shshshshsh," I warned, looking around to make certain that we were still alone. "Just be ready when I want you," I told him quietly. "And don't tell anybody else, either!"

"Solid, Jim, solid!" he whispered back excitedly. "You can count on me and my partner, anytime!"

Partner?

Partner! I clenched my fist. I don't want your goddamn partner, I started to say. All I want is you, you dumb-ass motherfucker, you! But I didn't tell him that. Time had joined forces against me, as the call for bedtime and prayers floated down from upstairs to interrupt my reply.

"Awright, Wolf," I gave in reluctantly. "It's you and your partner, then. But you better go upstairs now; it's time to go to bed."

He joyfully bounced away.

As soon as he was gone, I laid out their clothing and then went upstairs myself. As I passed the first-floor landing, the third-shift officer was reporting in for duty. I almost died—with relief. This old man was the inmates' favorite. He didn't give a fuck about nothing, and went to sleep as soon as the lights went out. He was old, senile, and disgustingly friendly. Fate was finally looking out for me again, damn her miserable heart.

When the count was cleared and the second-shift officer was gone, the old man leaned back in his chair and the cottage settled down for the night. I couldn't have slept if I'd wanted to. My mind was busy planning and scheming, rehashing the many things I had to do to make it home. I thought about my treachery, almost hated myself for it, but I knew if push came to shove, I was going to do it anyhow, and damn my thoughts. I wanted to go home.

The minutes ticked by with a sluggishness that was slowly killing me, and the hot, stuffy room only added to my irritation as my dwindling patience began to fade completely. I looked at the old man through the murky dimness, hoping that he would stick to his normal routine, and prayed that bad luck (or Fate) would not hinder me now. I couldn't help but remember that Fate and I were no longer friends. If it hadn't been for all the bad luck I'd had in my life, I probably wouldn't have had any luck at all.

Finally the old man's head began to nod. His chin had almost touched his chest when he jerked it up again. Two seconds later it dipped once more, and giving in to the power of sleep, his chin once again sank down upon his chest. This time he didn't lift it up. Ten minutes later and I knew that he was fast asleep.

I had to fight down the impulse to get up and go immediately, and it was the hardest thing I'd ever had to do in my life. I did my best trying to give the old man some extra time, but all I could manage was five more excruciating minutes. Then I slipped noiselessly out of bed and sank to the floor, slithering along on my belly until I came to the Werewolf's bunk. Reaching up, I shook him gently, warning him to be quiet when his eyes snapped open. I did the same thing with his partner. When I was sure that both of them were awake and that they understood what was happening, we slipped past the snoring guardian of the damned and crept silently down the stairs.

When we reached the dark basement, I went straight to the damaged cage and broke it off completely, raised up the window and let in the coolness of damp, sweet-smelling grass. Not a word had passed between us. I turned away from the window and started putting on my clothes, and my partners quickly followed my lead. When we were dressed and ready to go, I called the Wolf to my side and softly stuttered in his ear, "You go out first. Then wait in the shadows up against the building, and if anybody comes before we're finished putting this window back, it's up to you to take him out. You understand?"

"I'll beat the motherfucker to death!" he whispered back anxiously. Then we boosted him up and out. Simpson and I quickly followed.

The cool summer night was peaceful and complacent, full of fragrant odors and twinkling stars. Small animal life was busily in abundance all around us: the industrious crickets chirped their heads off, the little frogs croaked their croaks, and I sweated like a champ trying to fix that window. After we had done all that was possible, I motioned to the Wolf and we took off across the fields, flying like three bats out of hell.

On our way to America.

Going to find Ray Charles.

THE EIGHTH ROUND

Free, Free at Last!

"Free! I'm free! I'm free at last! Great googamoogoa, I am free at last!"

Those were the joyful words my heart cried out as my feet carried me swiftly across ditches and over fences, through streams and thorn-spiked thickets. I ran, floating on a cloud, unaware of how high I was stepping, or of much of anything else around me. There was room in my head for only one word, one thought—freedom. Nothing else was worth thinking about.

Then a gasping, wheezing moan penetrated the sounds of the woods and reached my ears. Slowing down to a trot, I looked back over my shoulder, and saw the Wolf and Simpson pounding hard on my trail, but faltering badly.

"Wait for us, Rube!" the Wolf huffed and puffed as he caught up with me. "Slow down, man, and wait for us!"

"Don't—don't slow me down now, Wolf," I sputtered angrily. "It took me six years to get this far," I said, picking up the pace once more, "and we've got to get out of these goddamned woods before the sun comes up. So if you're coming, man, you better come *on*—because I'm making it!"

Tired and winded as they were, they didn't stop to argue. They knew I was right. The downfall of all inmates who had ever chosen to flee that madhouse at Jamesburg had been the woods, the daytime, and the farmers—not to mention the state police, the dogs, and the shotguns.

As we were scrambling out of that window in our bid to escape, I had figured it to be close to eleven o'clock. I had also figured that we had roughly three or four more hours before we were missed. We had now been running about an hour.

"Goddammit," I muttered to myself, and put on a new burst of speed. Four hours wasn't enough time for people traveling on foot. But what the hell, it was the best we could hope for.

As my pounding feet propelled me through strands of grasping, tugging brier patches, my thoughts flew to conversations I'd had with other inmates who had tried escaping in the past, only to be caught wandering around hopelessly in the woods, rambling in circles, lost in the chaparral as it were, not knowing what to do; glad, even, when they were finally apprehended—rescued, actually. They'd been scared to death by the farmers and their dogs. I was determined not to become another celebrated statistic.

We ran on and on and on, and eventually we came to a dusty dirt road, pitted with holes and rough stones. I trotted along its shoulder, keeping a sharp lookout for houses, cars, and small hamlets. These were the stumbling blocks which had to be avoided at all costs: it was almost impossible to pass a farmhouse without some canine setting off enough racket to wake up the dead, let alone the farmer and his household.

As we ran, I wondered how we could manage to stay clear of the thousand-and-one pitfalls that could send us back to Jamesburg in chains. Suddenly I felt a hand grab my shoulder. I spun around and fired, my fist snaking out and catching the Werewolf flush on his chin. He went down like a dead man. When I saw who it was I had hit, I bent down and helped him up.

"God-god-god-goddammit, Wolf!" I sputtered heatedly. "*Say* something when you come up behind me. Don't grab me like that, man!"

The Wolf shook the cobwebs out of his head and looked at me with a sickly grin. "You won't have to worry about that happening anymore," he said. "Goddamn, but you hit hard!"

"Now, what did you want?" I demanded impatiently, nervously glancing around. I didn't like this standing still, and I guess it showed in the tone of my voice, because the Wolf looked over at his partner and hesitated.

"Why don't we steal a car from one of these farms?" he said, looking off across the field. "Then we could get out of these woods in no time, you know what I mean?" It sounded good to me. I would have liked nothing better than to be able to ride all the way to Paterson. But the only way we could steal a car would be to get close to one of those farmhouses, and that meant tangling with the dogs and with some farmer's ever-loving shotgun. Once these backwoods farmers got wind of our trail in the woods, they would hunt us down just like we were chicken thieves, and they wouldn't mind busting a cap or two in our black asses, either. So I decided against Wolf's idea, shook my head, and trotted off down the road again.

But Wolf was not to be so easily discouraged. He put on a burst of speed, leaving his partner behind, and puffed up alongside me.

"Why not, man?" he demanded.

"Because I want to get home, motherfucker," I snapped at him, impatient with this bullshit. "But don't let me stop *you* from doing it," I said. "Just give me time enough to get out of sight. If you want to risk fucking with these farmers, that's your business. But I'm walking!"

"Walking!" The Wolf was incredulous. "All the way to Paterson? Man, you gotta be out of your mind!"

"All the way to Paterson," I said, more to myself than to him, liking the way it sounded. "All the way to Paterson," I whispered again, and increased my speed. "All the way to Paterson," my feet echoed in return, skimming over the dusty road.

All the way to Paterson.

We ran for miles, and time became a thief, stealing away rapidly. The night was warm, brightly lit by a brilliant moon and erratically twinkling stars. The darkness was filled with strange sounds, alive with moving shadows that overlapped the road and made bizarre patterns whenever the slight breeze riffled the leaves on the forest's trees.

The steady pounding of our feet was muffled by the spongy sand that hugged the shores of the road. So far, I thought I knew where we were going, but now I saw that about a mile or two up ahead was a crossroads that would either take us out of these woods, or lead us right back to Jamesburg.

When we reached the intersection, we had to choose which direction to take. It was a hard decision to make. In the darkness I could feel my partners' eyes watching me curiously as I walked up one road and down the other, trying to single out the right one. We all knew from common knowledge that only one of these roads would lead us to freedom, while the other three deceptively wound their way back in the direction from which we had just come.

I was stumped. I had never been this far away from the institution before, and I was just about to surrender the choice to Fate and let come what may when I spied, thirty or forty yards down the road, a white guideline painted in the center.

"This is it!" I shouted to my partners, pointing to my discovery and motioning for them to come on. I took off at a fast trot, my logic being that the white stripe would lead us to a main highway—and freedom, I hoped.

Hours upon endless hours we ran. We slowed down occasionally to catch our breath, but we never stopped to rest. Time was still against us. Already the dawn was breaking, sweeping away our cover of darkness, and the daylight would bring the state police, the farmers, and their shotguns. This knowledge, coupled with my willingness to die before allowing myself to be caught, only made me run harder. But soon the pace began to take its toll.

My heavy legs began trembling painfully. Spasms ripped through my chest, causing my breath to come in gulps, but I pushed on anyway, running the white line and searching the road ahead for cars and farmers. I knew that the police had to be out looking for us by this time, and the only hope we had was to gain more distance. Even so, we had to leap off the road at times to keep from being spotted.

Finally, after what seemed like a million years, we reached the main highway and, dead-tired, gathered around a directional sign. I wanted to die on the spot. The arrow was pointing in the direction of Newark, which was our destination, but which it said was twenty miles to the north—back the way we had just come. I stomped my foot, sputtered and fumed.

"Halt!" called out a sharp, authoritative voice. "Halt in the name of the Law!"

I spun around. A highway patrol car had crept up behind us, and a state trooper was barreling toward us with his pistol drawn. Throwing all caution to the wind, I dashed across the congested highway. Car and truck brakes screeched and screamed in protest, the vehicles swerving wildly out of control. I darted around a car that had skidded violently, narrowly missing me, and cut across the road toward an overpass on my right.

The Wolf and Simpson stayed hot on my heels. Reaching the overpass, with the state troopers right behind us, we struck out across it. Midway over the bridge, another police car came racing toward us from the opposite direction. Their sirens shrieking, the cops leaned out their windows, drew their pistols, and pointed them directly at us.

"Look out!" I shouted. Wheeling around, I saw state troopers

heading for us from that direction too. We were trapped. I ran over
to the guard rail and looked down. The turnpike twenty-five feet
below looked up. Heavy traffic zoomed by. I hesitated one second,
then leaped the railing, and found myself falling through empty air.
Down, down, and down I fell, falling forever, it seemed.

The concrete of the highway rushed up and greeted me with
tooth-shattering impact. Luckily I was unhurt, and was quickly up
and running again. My ears filled with the squealing confusion we
had created by jumping into the early morning traffic. As I sped
across the highway toward an open field, trying to make it to the
other side, I heard the whip-like, crackling snarl of a bullet just
miss my head, and the pop-pop-popping reports of more pistol
shots. They were all close, the snapping sounds drilling me as if the
slugs were burrowing into my skull. Bullets ricocheted from the
ground all around me, searching, but we galloped onwards—on
our way to America.

At three o'clock on that cloudy afternoon we arrived in Newark,
tired, nasty, smelling like wild apeshit—but we arrived. I was so
hungry my poor stomach must have thought that my throat had
been cut. Waving goodbye to my partners (it was the last time I
would ever see the Wolf; Simpson was caught that same afternoon
and sent back to Jamesburg in chains), I ambled off in the direction of Paterson, thirteen miles to the northwest, and I pursued that
course at a brisk trot, going home, ever mindful of the police traps
that could be lurking around every bend in the road.

Whenever an inmate had escaped successfully from New Jersey's
child-labor camp in the past, the first thing the institution did—
after calling the state police—was to notify the fugitive's parents
and rush to his hometown themselves. In this way, the institution
thoughtfully contrived to relinquish any legal responsibility for injuries which might befall the inmate during his escape. This noti-
fication of divorce also served as an officer's protection against
prosecution when the inmate was finally caught, or maybe killed.
That had been known to happen.

Anyway, what seemed like two centuries and thirteen million
miles later, trudging very wearily, I finally reached Paterson. The
skies were overcast, darkened by ominous storm clouds, and the
street lamps spilled across the sidewalks into my shadow. One
minute the rain seemed to be threatening; the next, the heavens

opened up and poured buckets-full down upon the earth. Catching sight of a police car slowly approaching, I darted into an alley past rows of stinking, uncovered garbage cans, climbed over high picket fences, burrowed through thick binding hedges, and was chased (and almost bitten) by a dog as I swept across hundreds of back-yards. Finally I reached an alleyway across the street from my house.

I carefully searched the streets for any unmarked police cars that might be prowling the gloomy shadows until I felt sure I was safe. Then I drifted back to my house, crept up on the porch, and looked in the window. The venetian blinds partially obscured my vision, but vaguely I could see my mother moving about in the kitchen, placing something on the table, and then leaving my view.

I entered the house and walked into the hallway. "Hi, Mom," I said with forced casualness, not sure how she would react to my coming home.

"Hi there yourself, stranger," she smiled, with the same forced casualness, trying to show me that she was unconcerned. She should have taken acting lessons, because I could see unmitigated relief flooding her face. "How are you? Are you all right?" she asked anxiously. "You're not hurt or anything, are you?"

"No, ma'am," I answered. "I'm all right."

"Thank God!" she sighed, nearly giving up the ghost. "Now come sit down and eat before your food gets cold."

I stood there for a long moment and looked at my mother, noticing how small and fragile she appeared since I had grown up. I examined her sweet face quizzically, and wondered how could she have known I would be coming home, when there was a fifty-fifty chance my father would turn me in if I did.

"Was this plate put here especially for me?" I asked suspiciously.

"Uh-huh," she answered, humming, taking down some bath towels from the pantry.

"But—but—but—" I stammered. "How did you know I'd be home?" She looked at me with the smile of an angel. It tugged at my heart. It was a smile of gay and infinite tenderness.

"Oh, sit down and eat, Rubin," she flipped at me affectionately, still smiling her angelic smile. "A mother knows and understands her children, and I know and understand you, child—even if you don't understand yourself at times." Then she went into the bath-room and closed the door.

I sat down and greased, devouring what food was on my plate and ready to destroy what was left on the stove, when my brother and sisters came into the kitchen. I understood then why the house had been empty when I arrived—they had all been out looking for me. Everybody was here except my father and Lloyd Junior, who was still in Korea.

But things just didn't seem right to me. I could almost smell the aroma of suspicion and fear as it settled over the room, turning what should have been a jubilant moment into a cold-blooded wake. And that was a goddamn shame. My brother and sisters seemed to be afraid of me. When I looked at them, they dropped their eyes. When I dropped my eyes, they looked at me.

Damn!

It was a good thing my mother chose that moment to come out of the bathroom, because I was looking for my brother and sisters to bolt the room at any second.

"Rubin, the tub is full now," my mother said. "Go in and take a bath. Scrub yourself good and throw those filthy clothes away."

After bathing and dressing in some of my brother's clothing, I went back into the kitchen. Mom was the only one there, and she was waiting for me with a suitcase in her hands.

"What're you planning to do with yourself, Rubin?" she asked, looking me straight in the eye. "You're not a little boy anymore, you know."

I could tell by her tone and the expression on her face that she was deeply concerned. Not that I had ever thought any different, but this time her anxieties were a bit more pronounced. My heart went out to her like it never had before. There is no assurance like the reassurance of a mother's love. And I knew that she was not in the habit of defying the law.

"I'm going to try and get into the paratroopers," I explained to her. "I'm through getting into trouble, Momma."

Her expression of relief made me more determined than ever to make something out of my worthless life. When she smiled, I felt good. When she was happy, I felt marvelous. It was just that way with us. She handed me the suitcase and thrust some money into my hand.

"Lillian's waiting outside," she said. "Go with her . . . and take care of yourself . . . please!"

There were tears in her eyes and there were a million things I wanted to say—a million things we should have said. But we knew each other, and when she looked at me for a long moment and smiled sadly, that said it all. It was all contained in that one smile: bigger than all of Texas, taller than the Empire State Building, more beautiful than a symphony by Beethoven. That said it all and that was saying a lot.

Lillian was waiting for me outside in a taxicab. I climbed in with my suitcase and we rode to the bus station. From there we took a bus to New York. I had no idea what my final destination was going to be, and I didn't ask. This was my sister, my blood, my family; if I couldn't trust her, then whom? So I went to sleep. I was tired.

It seemed as if I had just closed my eyes when Lillian shook me awake. We were at Pennsylvania Station, New York City. This was my first trip to the Big Apple—despite the fact that I'd lived only twelve miles away—but I wasn't very impressed. The hustle and bustle of swarming humans, all going their own impersonal little ways, reminded me of a giant anthill alive with activity.

Lillian left me for a moment by a newsstand, and when she disappeared into the crowd of people, I became very uneasy and distrustful. But a short time later she was back with a train ticket in her hand. I was so ashamed I couldn't look her in the face.

"This will get you to Philadelphia, Rubin. You're going to stay with our Cousin Hazel," she said, glancing quickly at her watch and grabbing me by the arm. "Come on, your train's leaving in a few minutes."

The words were scarcely out of her mouth before a loudspeaker blared from somewhere, "Silver Coach Express for Newark, Trenton, Philadelphia, and all points South, now leaving on Track Four!"

Lillian moved ahead of me, pulling me by the arm. "Come on," she said. "That's your train. Now hurry up!"

"Wait a minute, Lilly," I said, holding back. "How do I get to this Hazel's house? I don't even know her."

"Oh, yeah," she said smiling sheepishly, but still pulling me up the flight of stairs to the platform. "I almost forgot. Mother called her while you were taking a bath, and Hazel will be at the Thirtieth Street Station when you get there. Now remember," she added, "you're to get off at the Thirtieth Street Station in Philly. You got that?" I nodded.

The train was ready to pull out when we reached the platform, so Lillian hustled me onto the steps of a slowly moving car and walked alongside it. She held on to my hand, as if she couldn't let go, and stared into my face with an odd curiosity.

My sister was a fair-complexioned, very attractive young woman with smooth, unblemished skin, and a smile that could have melted all the snow in Alaska. Meeting her eyes with a look of my own, I gazed deep into their hazel depths. The longer I looked at her, the more bewildered I became. Then a sharp, nagging suspicion began eating away at my mind, going away, then coming back again more strongly, festering until it became an awareness, a reality. It was a phenomenon that would haunt me for the rest of my life.

People were actually afraid of me—even my own family, even Lillian. Her eyes, her whole face was filled with puzzled questions, and just the fact that she didn't know any of the answers pained me. She seemed to be asking, "Would you hurt me, Rubin?" Her sweet eyes begged me pitifully, "Would you hurt Momma? Would you hurt any of us?" I wanted to give her a loud, emphatic *"Never!"* but something held me back. I didn't know what it was, and even now I can't explain it. But that intangible something that had entered the hallowed archway of Jamesburg with me never left me again.

I had never gone out looking for friends or buddies, nor would I accept any who made friendly overtures. I trusted no one, nor any material thing. I never could talk, and when incarcerated at Jamesburg, I had stopped trying. But I knew that all it would have taken to bring a sweet smile to Lillian's lips, erasing that half-tortured expression from her beautiful face, would be a word, a touch, a tender look. I wanted to give her all three of them and a kiss to boot, but I couldn't.

And so, in the instant before Lillian came to the end of the platform and had to let go of my hand, I ached. I ached because I couldn't even open my mouth to ease the pain of someone that I loved dearly. The treacherous years of living in Jamesburg had done their job of emotional homicide to perfection: they had killed my poor heart dead.

Near a window at the back of the train, I found an empty seat and sat down. I put the suitcase on the floor in front of me and propped my feet up on it.

"Clat-clat . . . clat-clat," the wheels of the train on the tracks said as they moved away from the tall buildings into the open country. "Clat-clat . . . clat-clat," said the wheels of the train.

Philadelphia-Philadelphia, I thought in time to the sound. A new town, new people, and perhaps a new life.

"Clat-clat . . . clat-clat."

"Jamesburg-Jamesburg," I whispered aloud.

I started thinking about that stinking rat hole.

People feared me only for the way I looked. Until I had been sent to Jamesburg, I hadn't acquired much hatred for white authority, nor had I distinguished people by the color of their skin. While it could be said that I had displayed my fair share of naked aggression, it could not be said that I had ever fought with racial prejudice dominating my emotions. I fought simply because I loved to fight, and in jail, that jungle of violence that bred either punks or young savages, I had found a fighting heaven.

I had never actually gone looking for a fight, but if one happened to come my way, you wouldn't find me with my ass in the wind. At Jamesburg I had learned to fight better than most, and I learned with a dedication toward perfection. I made it a point to be the best at whatever I tried to do.

There were no fence-straddlers at Jamesburg. A man sitting on a fence at high noon casts a shadow on both sides, and an inmate was either a "touch-off" or somebody's "wife," a duke or a dip. And there were always those who were eager to find out which.

If I had wanted, or tried, to be a faggot and somebody's wife, I would no doubt have been the hottest flame in the State of New Jersey. It's not what a man says that makes him what he is, it's what he does, and my conduct was in complete harmony with the opinions I couldn't express verbally: whenever anyone saw me in action, fighting and kicking and biting and scratching, there was no need for me to open my mouth—they all knew exactly what I was trying to say. It was the only way I had of releasing my pent-up frustrations; it was my way of crying without tears.

But what really burned me during my stay at the State Home for Boys were the atrocities committed by the officers. It was bad enough that we inmates were beating, starving, and fucking each other in the ass, without the sadistic officers doing likewise. There's no justification for an inmate to pick on someone weaker than himself, but at least we were all in the same boat and things were a bit more balanced between us. But for a correction officer, a representative of the state, to use his position and his badge to force young kids into degrading sexual acts, well—as far as I was concerned, there wasn't a tree high enough to hang the dirty sonofabitch! I didn't like it then, and I don't like it now. I hate that kind of animal. I would ruin such a man now—and I ruined quite a few then.

The conductor's singsong voice jarred me away from my reverie. "Thirtieth Street Station," he called as he walked through the car. "Coming up. Next stop, Thirtieth Street Station—"

I waited for the train to grind to its squeaking halt, then picked up my suitcase and made my way off. I didn't know who to look for, or who might be coming to meet me, so the only thing I could do was stand on the platform and hope that someone would recognize me. All I saw was a thinning swarm of ant-like people disappearing through a maze of exits.

"Rubin—"

I spun around, and found myself facing a coffee-skinned young woman, not much older than myself, who would have enhanced any cover of *Ebony* magazine. Her black hair hung down over her shoulders, framing a face of pure mahogany beauty, and her clothes accentuated her lovely sophistication. Her long, blood-red brocade dress made her black hair seem startling.

I stood there, speechless, and she took my silence—correctly—for openmouthed astonishment. She smiled, showing a row of pearly white teeth, and it was like the sun coming over a mountain.

"You are Rubin Carter, aren't you?" she asked.

I could only manage a stupefied nod.

She laughed softly, a delightful tinkle that sent a sharp thrill streaking through me. Then she stepped in closer and sweetly kissed my cheek.

"Hi, I'm Hazel," she purred, and my face must have been stained with disbelief, because she laughed again and said, "Believe it or not, baby, we're first cousins—and I'm the married one. So you can just get that leering gleam out of your eyes." She laughed again. "Did you enjoy your trip?"

"It was all right," I answered slyly, knowing that she had read my mind. She just put her arm around my waist and steered me toward the nearest exit.

When we reached the street, Hazel was carrying my suitcase,

laughing and talking as if we were sweethearts instead of cousins. Her casual attitude had the effect of erasing everything that had happened to me during that hectic day, and as we strolled through a parking lot, she stopped and pointed to a sleek, canary-yellow Pontiac.

"How do you dig my new chariot?" she asked with a smile.

How did I dig it? Now that was the world's most understated question, if I had ever heard one. Why, this car was my fantasy, this woman the embodiment of all my romanticizing. I had been dreaming about such fine things for six long miserable years. I walked slowly around the shiny car and caressed it lovingly. "It's real pretty," I said with a passion. "Almost as pretty as you are!" I blurted, and probably would have blushed, if I wasn't so dark.

"Aha," she chuckled impishly, her white teeth gleaming in the darkness. "Flattery will get you everywhere, cousin! But right now, I'd better get you home."

When we reached the house in West Philadelphia, David, her husband, greeted us at the door. He was a tall, dark-skinned man with unusually big eyes, and by no stretch of the imagination could he be called handsome, or even good-looking. But there was an air about him, a kind of niceness that I had found lacking in most people, and when he smiled that great big smile of his, I couldn't help but like him. The minute he opened his mouth I knew we were friends forever: he stuttered as badly as I did.

"Hi, there cou-cou-cousin," he grinned broadly. "Co-co-come on in and si-si-sit down!"

We stepped into the living room, and then I was afraid to move any farther. The room was breathtaking. Soft blue lights glowed dully off the ceiling and accentuated the texture of a thick-piled golden carpet that ran from one wall to the other. A smattering of sofas, easy chairs, and mahogany inlaid tables and stands complemented the room. I found myself staring at the biggest console television set I had ever seen. I imagined it must have been there to project cinemascope movies. But in a few short moments, David and Hazel had me feeling as if I had always belonged there.

Hazel made some coffee (which I didn't drink), and then we all sat down to talk. David and I stuttered and sputtered so much that we must have sounded like two angry machine guns firing across the room at each other, but I had never felt so relaxed, and I'm sure I talked more in those few hours than I had at any time in my life.

Eventually, my cousins got around to the subject of my going into the Army. Both of them were against the idea, especially Hazel. "Rubin," she said anxiously, "this isn't a personal Carter war. We didn't start the damn thing, and it's not up to us to finish it off single-handedly either! There's too goddamned many Carters still in Korea now, as far as I'm concerned.

"Aunt Maude's two sons are there," she went on; "Uncle Prince has his two boys there; your sister's husband is in the fighting; David was wounded in Korea; and God knows how many more Carters are there. Aunt Bert has enough to worry about with your brother Lloyd over there, and now you want to go. Ohhhhh," she cried, "how I wish there was some way to make you men understand how we women feel—"

I was surprised at the agitation in her voice, the frustration, the hurt, but most of all I was surprised at her tears—how the mere thought shook her up. She didn't change my mind, but I went to bed thinking about it, and woke up resolved to leave Philly as soon as I could. A few more nights of Hazel's type of persuasion, I knew, would make it virtually impossible for me to leave.

Two days later David took me down to the induction center. After showing my birth certificate, I told the recruiting officer that I was born in New Jersey but had lived in Philadelphia all of my life. This knocked out the possibility of them finding out I had a police record. Rubin Carter hadn't been in Philadelphia long enough to take a leak, let alone start shitting around and building up a criminal record at City Hall.

After I had signed endless forms, the induction officer sent us to the Schuylkill Arsenal in North Philly, where I underwent a complete physical examination and took innumerable written tests. When we finally reached home late that night, I collapsed on the sofa from sheer exhaustion, and that was where I woke up the following morning.

THE NINTH ROUND

The Epitome of Ignorance

Two weeks later, on a beautiful, cool summer day in July, I boarded the Army Special that would take me to Fort Jackson, South Carolina, and the famed "Screaming Eagles" of the 101st Airborne. I rode in the last of a long line of coaches—a decrepit old cattle car segregated from the rest of the train—with approximately one hundred fifty black recruits and draftees from the New York and Pennsylvania areas. None of us had ever been to the Deep South before.

When we arrived in a hot and humid Columbia, South Carolina, late that night, we were transferred from the train to trucks. Excuse me: we were not *transferred*, exactly, but prodded in like cattle, and forced to continue on under the same suffocating conditions we had endured all the way down there. The white recruits were loaded into the first twenty-odd vehicles, where they could relax in comparative luxury, while the black guys were herded into the last two trucks, packed in like sardines and more or less stood on top of one another.

As if this wasn't bad enough, in charge of our little Welcome-to-the-Army Committee was a big, brawny, square-jawed sergeant who strutted up and down the line of the caravan with his "cunt cap" cocked at a dangerously rakish angle on the side of his huge head, barking out orders in a Mississippi twang that dripped and drooled with some powerful shit. Roaring over here and cussing over there, he was D Company's top kick, Master Sergeant Claude Hawkins.

Man! I thought to myself, looking at the sergeant. So this is what it's all about. This is what I had been looking forward to. Wow! I must have been a goddamn fool, I reflected. I couldn't help but smile at the irony of the situation.

For basic training, I was assigned to D Company—"Dog" Company—of an airborne infantry regiment quartered in an area of

Fort Jackson known as Tank Hill. My first few days there were swallowed up in the red tape of collecting gear and getting myself together. It was during this period I discovered that the military character of my confinement at Jamesburg had given me several advantages over the rest of the recruits. I already knew how to march and count cadence, spit-shine my jump boots, and handle my weapon properly. I'd been doing all of that in jail for years. By contrast, many of the other fellows (to whom I would later give private marching lessons) seemed like inexperienced children caught up in a world they knew nothing about—an especially physical world that must have been as alien to them as freedom was to me.

Our daily routine, for instance, consisted mostly of running accompanied by hours upon hours of push-ups, pull-ups, sit-ups, and God knows what else that affected the heart, lungs, and muscles of a human being. I found that I could control some of the involuntary responses of my body. If I didn't want to get tired—even when everybody else around me was falling out from sheer exhaustion—I wouldn't. If I didn't want to breathe too hard after a five-mile run in full field gear, I accomplished that easily too. The only part of my anatomy I couldn't seem to master was my idiotically stumbling, bumbling tongue. I still couldn't talk worth a damn.

The food was another problem that sorely affected the majority of soldiers I came in contact with, though it didn't bother me at all. It was a helluva lot better than what Jamesburg had fed me, so naturally I couldn't make any fuss over what I ate at Fort Jackson. I mean, C rations may not be too tasty, but they were definitely better than anything Jamesburg had. By comparison, they tasted like fried steak smothered in onions.

I should mention here that when I first arrived at Fort Jackson, I didn't immediately notice any outward display of racial prejudice of the kind I'd seen on the train going down, but that was probably due to a presidential decree that had recently integrated the armed forces.

But how incredibly naive I found myself to be. How ignorant I was of the deep-seated prejudice that was actually proliferating all around me, the true nature of which I was to discover in—naturally —a violent clash.

It happened early one morning while Dog Company was undergoing a footlocker inspection. These inspections were oft-occurring, middle-of-the-night operations that always caused tempers to flare more quickly than the occasion seemed to warrant. The only reasonable explanation we ever got to justify these impromptu examinations was that the length of a trooper's life span depended upon his being alert every second of the day. Well, I could dig that.

What I couldn't dig was that at two or three o'clock in the morning—when all sensible people would have been fast asleep—a loud, shrill whistle would suddenly blow us out of bed. It demanded, in no uncertain terms, that we get our lazy asses out of those nice, soft sacks, get dressed up in starched uniforms and spit-shined boots (that had taken half the night to polish), pick up our footlockers, jump out the nearest window, and assemble in formation on the company's parade field standing tall, sharp, and ready to be inspected. (A trooper still in training was not permitted to use the doors of any building upon leaving the premises. That was a strict rule. Can you imagine two hundred men skedaddling pell-mell out of every available window in a two-story barracks at three o'clock in the morning, bailing out with footlockers in their arms, and trying to stand tall? Well, that's exactly the way it was.) To top it all off, this had to be done in less than two minutes.

So, on that unforgettable morning, when the sergeant's whistle blasted, I scrambled up and out of my bed, got dressed in less than two shakes of a lamb's tail, grabbed up my footlocker, and "Geronimoed" out the nearest window.

Outside, Sergeant Hawkins nimbly pranced up to where I was standing. Executing a sharp right-face in my direction, he snapped stiffly to attention. His boot heels sounded like a cracked pistol shot. For a long drawn-out second or two, he just stood there before me like petrified wood, his silver-gray eyes sparkling as he slowly inspected my uniform from head to toe.

Suddenly he took a rapid-fire step backwards and lashed out at me, his voice flooding the quiet void. "Gawdammit, soldier!" he said, the words slithering out of his mouth with smug satisfaction. It seemed as if he had been waiting for this a long time. "Boy?" he said with disbelief. "Do you think that you're any gawddamned different than the rest of us standing out heah?"

I didn't know what he was talking about. "No, sir!" I snapped back immediately and then stammered, "I'm a—I'm a—I'm a fiery-eyed paratrooper, sir!"

"You're a *paratrooper!*" he echoed in surprise. "Then where's your gawdamned headgear at, *trooper?*" His gray eyes still sparkled. "I mean the two-dash-fifty-one A that was issued to you by the quartermaster," he sneered. "Your hat, stupid, your gawddamn hat!"

OOOOOh, man! No, I berated myself. *Rubin, you dumb sonof-abitch, you. You done went and left your hat inside, you stupid egg-headed bastard!*

"I'm a—I'm a—I'm a flying shit-bird, sir!" I confessed. "I left my headgear inside." I felt so ashamed I could have cried.

Sergeant Hawkins stood there stern-faced. The muscles in his jaws bunched up and rippled, then rippled and bunched some more. "Then drop down and give me fifty push-ups," he demanded ominously, his face suddenly blood-red with rage. "If you were in a combat zone right now, soldier," he shouted, "you would be dead without your headgear! Dead—dead—dead!!! So drop down and count 'em out smartly, nigger!"

I must have hesitated for a moment when he called me a nigger. I really can't say. But in the next second he yoked me by the head and flipped me over his hips, slamming my stupid ass to the ground.

"*Move, soldier!*" he raged, showering spit down upon me. "When I tell you to move, gawdammit, you *move—move—move!*"

This big Mississippi coming-from-cracker was madder than a Black Muslim at a pork-chop dinner, totally unable to get his thoughts together. He had probably never before had a black man refuse one of his orders.

"I said *move,* gawdammit!" he screamed again, kicking at me but missing. "Move, move, *move!*"

I leaped to my feet, frantic. But common sense made me hesitate. I didn't want to go back to jail. A little shiver passed through me just at the thought of it.

Sergeant Hawkins stood there smiling at my indecision. He probably thought he was seeing fear of *him* in me. His knees were bent slightly as he balanced on the balls of both feet. His attitude reflected a lifetime of giving orders and having them obeyed: from his intimidating fighting stance to the way his big head was tucked in between his two muscle-rippling shoulders, he was a cagey old ostrich laying his eye into the situation.

And I was trembling, now, worried by my doubtfulness, and wondering if my reluctance to fight back was part of a revolt against the violence that had so characterized my life in jail for the past six years, or if it was a whimpering reach for sweetness, mercy, and forgiveness. Or was I just getting weak?

"*Fuck it!*" I grunted, and fired a straight right hand at the grizzly sergeant. I followed it through with a wicked left hook, my fist streaking across the distance between us and crashing against the old man's chin. It stretched him out on the ground, but only for a moment.

Slowly raising himself up from the dirt, blue-black-green rage filled his face. He shook his shaggy head like a wounded bear. Then he spread his huge arms outward, fell into a crouch and started easing his way towards me.

"Woooo-wheeee!" he said from between clenched teeth. "Ah ain't been hit like that nigh onto a month of Sundays, boy," he choked. "But now, you black bastard, you, I'm gonna tear your meathouse down!"

Then he sprang at me, all two hundred and forty pounds of him. I braced my feet against his thunderous attack, and pain began spreading over my face. A crashing right hand had smashed into my mouth, flattening my lip against my teeth. Blood streamed down from my nose. I shook my head and backed away, bobbing and weaving, hunching up my shoulders and forearms to ward off the rainstorm of blows, and when the sergeant's flurry passed, I straightened up with a sizzling left hook, and then another, and a blob of blood flew from the corner of his mouth. I jabbed. I jabbed again, crossing it with a crisp right hand, and the sergeant's knees seemed to buckle. His eyes rolled up into the back of his head. I moved in for the kill.

But the old man had been faking. He hurled himself upon me furiously, hammering away with both fists in a sledge-like manner. One clubbed me fully on the ear, while the other chopped its way into my kidneys and sent me soaring backwards until I shattered against the barracks wall.

I bounced off the building and leapt back in at the sergeant, slamming home a hard right hand in his ribcage and a wicked left hook under his heart. The big man stopped and grunted deeply, blinked, and started to back away, but I shuffled in closer, still slugging, and nailed him on the head, the back of his neck, and in the eye.

He stopped suddenly and side-stepped me, rolled at the hips, and smashed a ham-like fist against my Adam's apple. Another went to the pit of my stomach. At the same time he lashed out viciously with his foot and kicked me in the groin, slamming me into the dirt. "HEEEYAAHH!" he whooped, and smashed his head against the bridge of my nose with a fiendish delight.

A blanket of bright stars covered my vision. I struggled desperately to roll over and get back on my feet, but he came thundering down on me in a battering ram of solid power that crushed me back into the ground.

We rolled over and over in the dust, our legs wrapped tightly around one another as our fists pounded away at each other's faces unmercifully. Our bodies were soaked with grimy grease, sweat, and blood; our snarling faces were only inches apart, straining in a fixed do-or-die battle.

My lips skinned back away from my teeth. Like a hissing panther, I went straight for the sergeant's throat. To rip it open. But before my teeth could even start doing its damage, the man had unleashed a pulverizing right hand which cracked me on top of the head and broke my stranglehold on him.

I don't know how many street fights, brawls, and battle royals I had been in prior to this occasion, but they were usually all five- or six-punch affairs, rarely lasting for more than a couple of minutes, but Sergeant Hawkins and I fought like cats and dogs for an hour or more that morning, almost killing each other within the first ten minutes, while everyone else in the company just stood around and watched us.

After that, it was only a matter of who would drop dead first, of whose hatred was the more intense. The end was near when a mouthful of hairy knuckles smashed into my teeth and ripped open the inside of my gums. A dark cloud began to shroud my mind as one blow struck my jaw, and another, my eye. I tried to rush him and tie up his arms, but Sergeant Hawkins rolled and flipped me over his hips again, smashing me back into the dirt. I jumped up and an iron fist ripped my cheek, my ear. Another one slammed into my belly button. Then he kicked me like a wall-eyed mule, numbing my leg where he struck.

"EEEEEEE-YOW-EEEEEE!" he hollered as he fought.

I retreated backwards, slashing out with long lefts and rights, trying to gain some time to get myself together. Sergeant Hawkins bored in like an enraged animal, kicking me, gouging me, trying to get me to wrestle with him.

But I wasn't going for no more of that shit! I was tired of him throwing me down every time we got in close together, so I kept backpedaling, staying out of his reach, and waiting until I could set myself. Then I slammed home a bone-crunching left hook with all my might, and watched the darkness slip over his eyes.

At the same time, I collapsed from the sheer effort of having thrown the punch. My heart was pounding like some wild, monstrous animal running amuck inside my chest. I looked over at Sergeant Hawkins as he groaned and turned over on his stomach. He tried to push himself up to a sitting position, but his powerful arms strained beneath him.

"OOOOOOh, Lord-Gawd-Almighty!" he gasped, and fell back to the ground. "I'm a dying cock-a-roach, Lord," he moaned. "I'm a dying cock-a-roach!" Then he rolled over with a tortured look and shouted, "You're still a gawddamned *nigger!* You can't change that, boy! You're a gawddamn nigger!"

Indeed, what could this nigger say after that? He had already said it all.

Two or three hours later I was ordered to appear before the company commander to explain away the doings of that eventful inspection and, I imagined, to see what, if anything, the Army was going to do about this little nigger's belligerent assault upon a white man in South Carolina.

The orderly room, where my hearing was to be held, was in a small white building that completed the triangular composition of the company's training unit, the other two sides being lined with the barracks and the mess hall.

Sergeant Hawkins stepped in ahead of me and rapped sharply on the commander's door, snapping stiffly to attention and saluting crisply as we entered the room. "Sir!" he barked. "First Sergeant Hawkins reporting to the Company Commander as ordered, sir!"

The officer sitting behind the desk, a captain, returned the sergeant's salute in a lazy manner. For some reason, I had expected him to be a big burly tobacco-chewing southerner. But he wasn't. He was a dwarfish Mexican, Captain Mendez by name, and, I thought, an unusually small person to be in such a ticklish position as South Carolina put him in: the nigger-lynching Ku Klux Klan down here didn't care any more for his kind than they did for mine. But I realized that many would-be Napoleons were small men such as myself, and I liked the man instantly.

Captain Mendez was very carefully dressed in tailored gabardines that possessively hugged his pint-sized body. His jet-black hair was neatly trimmed, cut real short, and he had a military aura surrounding him that made it seem as though he had an iron rod running from the crack of his ass to the top of his head. Though he seemed to be a young man, his blouse was decorated with what seemed to be every campaign ribbon the Army had issued during World War II and the Korean War. Beneath the smooth gabardine shirt, his chest and shoulders bulged with the animated power of a very strong man, and his face was hard—and almost as dark as mine. His eyes were rock steady, black, and looked straight through you—and yet they were soft at the same time.

"A' ease, Sergeant," he said in halting English, swinging his eyes in my direction. He looked at me closely. "What yo' name, so'dier?" he asked.

"Sir!" I responded instantly, and stammered, "Pri-pri-pri-private E-1 Carter, RA 13-509-6039, sir!"

Then I stood there at attention and listened to Sergeant Hawkins rattle off what he had to say about the incident. He told the captain about the order he had given me to drop down and knock out fifty push-ups for meeting the formation without a hat, and that when he told me to move, I just didn't move fast enough to suit him.

"And then, by Gawd," Hawkins lied, "he told me to go straight to hell, sir." He wore a twisted grin. "And that's when I lost my temper and threw him to the ground."

Captain Mendez's piercing black eyes swung away from Hawkins and settled back on me, closely examining my bruised and battered features. The stillness of his stare was a loud warning bell to me, and I knew that I was in deep water again, sinking rapidly with every passing moment.

"Where's yo' home at, Carter?" the captain asked.

"New York City, sir," I lied. Anywhere but New Jersey.

The man continued looking at me for another long moment, then shook his head up and down. "Uh-huh," he murmured, as if my answer explained everything.

"Do you realize, so'dier, that I could have you court-martialed for striking a noncommissioned officer of the United States Army?"

I confess the idea gave me a moment's pause. But I wondered what the captain would have to say if I were to tell him that I had just recently escaped a very similar fate, and then what he would do if I told him I really didn't give a fuck.

"But the fool hit me, first!" I blurted out instead.

"Well, so'dier"—the captain shrugged philosophically—"while in the Army you will have to accept a lot of things that you normally wouldn't. Because that's—"

I exploded.

"No! Unh-uh, not me!" I interrupted. "Ain't no man gonna *make* me do nothing." I was feeling stubborn now. "The last man who made me do something that I didn't want to do was my father," I said. "And he can't do it no more. So I ain't about to let some *cracker* start doing it down here!" And I meant what I said.

It was the captain's turn to look sharply at me, and I could feel his irritation as he spoke. "You're heading for trouble, so'dier," he said, finally. "But awright, what's done is done. We won't talk about it anymore. You're both dismissed."

So nothing was resolved, but things seemed to go along much more smoothly after that. Sergeant Hawkins and I weren't exactly on what you could call buddy-buddy terms, but we weren't always tearing at each other's throats, either. Sometimes the damn old fool would let his bigotry fade, and act almost human. On rare occasions, I would find myself almost liking that Mississippi hillbilly.

One afternoon, for instance, we were on our way to a parade in which the entire population of Fort Jackson was to be reviewed by the base commander. Every swinging dick had to fall out and make this inspection, from the top-ranking officer to the lowest recruit. Nobody was excluded—no one—not even the dogs and cats, the mascots or the field rats. Every living ass on the post had to be standing tall. Spit and polish was the S.O.P. (Standard Operating Procedure) for the day.

Ten thousand fiery-eyed paratroopers all assembled together, decked out in their finest parade apparel. Twenty thousand spit-shined jump boots gleamed and glittered in the sun, throwing off a multitude of colors like a million tiny rainbows flashing. Red, white, blue, and yellow scarves were looped flamboyantly around their necks, and the hands in which they held their polished mahogany rifle stocks were enclosed in the same color gloves.

These were truly proud men, marching in complete unison, strutting, swaying, singing in fascinating harmonies, prancing with beautifully precisioned rhythms toward the parade ground as if they were all God's gift to the world. Everybody rocked and rolled to the same cadences.

Then here *we* came, *Dog* Company, stumbling and bumbling

like goddamn fools. We couldn't march a lick. But then again, Sergeant Hawkins didn't know as much about calling cadences as a cross-eyed monkey knew about flying an airplane. I had never felt so ashamed.

Goddammit-the-hell! I clenched my teeth as Sergeant Hawkins' methodical southern voice droned on in what he considered to be highfalutin' cadences. *"Jesus fucking Christ!"* I whispered disgustedly, as the soldier in front of me had to skip two or three times just to keep in step. *"Dirty sonofabitch!"* I snorted, outraged. I wished the road would just open up and suck us all away into obscurity.

"Carter!" Sergeant Hawkins' voice boomed through my thoughts. "Fall out and take over, boy!"

"Fall out and take over?" I murmured to myself, bewildered. What could that old reprobate be talking about? Did he actually mean for me to break rank and take the very throne on which he had always reigned supreme? Where every black man in the state of South Carolina feared to tread? Did this mean he had been aware all along that I had been teaching these guys how to march, like I had at Jamesburg? (I had.) Why that sneaky old bastard! I said to myself.

The next thing I knew I had stepped out of line and Sergeant Hawkins had stepped in. Now, maybe I couldn't have rapped out of my face worth a fiddler's fuck, but I knew that I could count cadences just as smoothly as Frank Sinatra could sing a ballad. I looked over my shoulder to see what step everybody else was in, and then laid my head back and cut loose with a boogie-woogie rhythm that would have put James Brown to shame:

"Hup-Ho-o-Ladeeeoooo!"

"Hup-Ho-o-Ladeeo," echoed Dog Company without much spirit.

Awwwww, shit! I said to myself. I knew doggone well we could do better than that.

"Hup-Ho-*An*-a-Ladeeeooooooo-o!" I forced out more briskly.

"Hup-Ho-*An*-a-Ladeeeoooooo-o!" Dog Company shouted back a little more enthusiastically. They began swaying a little bit, starting to roll with the chant.

I smiled inwardly. The rustiness disappeared as the bopping flamboyance started to infect everyone, and every man became an intricate part of a perfectly precisioned unit, strutting and prancing proudly.

I watched several other companies as they passed in review—still singing the same old funny songs—and I detected a subtle hint of envy reflected on their faces. I knew then that we were looking good. Damn good! So I reared back and went for broke.

"Some people say that a preacher don't steal!"

"Hon-eee! Hon-eee!" the marchers chorused.

"Some people say that a preacher don't steal!"

"Ba-abe! Ba-abe!"

We sho 'nuff had the right rhythm now! *Everybody* was walking bowlegged, strutting pigeon-toed, and talking heap plenty of shit, including me.

"Some people say that a preacher don't steal—but I caught *three* in my cornfield!"

"Honey-o-Ba-aa-aby Mine!" the company rang out cheerfully. That did it—Pandora's Box was wide open! It was a brand-new ballgame. Downtrodden heads began to perk up in exultation: Dog Company was on the money and looking good! Stepping out briskly now, prancing, singing, sashaying, and striding with pride and dignity, we swaggered with an authoritative confidence that made it seem as though we had been marching together all of our lives. Even Sergeant Hawkins couldn't hide the smug look in his eye.

Can you imagine how proud I felt? Me, Rubin Carter, a black man in South Carolina giving orders to captains, white lieutenants and cracker sergeants! I'm saying that my pride, my individual dignity, was all that I had ever had in life. Stronger than dirt, mightier than the sword, more satisfying than sex, than life, is pride!

Right then I was saturated with it, doing something I really enjoyed and knew how to do well, and the longer we marched, the better I felt. The better I felt, the more aware I became of the scrutinizing gazes being tossed our way from the top brass. Some seemed to be quite perplexed at Dog Company's bebop style of marching, while others appeared to be smiling their approval. Well, I didn't know if we were being cheered or booed, but whatever it was—it sure felt good to me.

Throwing a quick glance over my left shoulder at the officers sitting on the review board, I snapped my head forward, did a hard foot-stomping dig and straightened out with another ditty: "We're in the jailhouse on our knees!"

"Hon-eee! Hon-eee!"

"Standing in the corner just a-begging please!"

"Ba-abe! Ba-abe!"

We were passing the officers' podium now, making a sharp right turn and approaching the spectators' stand. I did another hard foot-stomping dig and sounded off again.

"We're in the jailhouse on our knees—eatin' stale cornbread and blackeye peas!"

"Honey-o-ba-aby mine!" the soldiers repeated. The spectators laughed and cheered, and we strutted off bowlegged with the marching award for the day.

Dog Company's performance that afternoon was just plain out of sight. There is no other way to describe it. The ditties we sang were new to the Army's never-changing ways, the rhythms different, happier than those out-dated "Jody" songs that had been sung since the beginning of time. From that day on, Dog Company walked away with every marching banner that Fort Jackson had to offer, and if that's not something to be proud about, hominy grits ain't groceries, eggs ain't poultry, and Mona Lisa was a man!

After completing my sixteenth week of basic training at Fort Jackson, I was ready to ship out for Kentucky and three weeks of jump school. Sergeant Hawkins called me into his squad room for a little chat. I knocked on the door and walked in.

"You wanted to see me, Sarge?" I asked, then stopped dead in my tracks.

He had been standing behind the door, and as I entered the room, he quickly threw the latch and locked it shut. I spun around and saw at once a look of cruelty on his face. The room smelled of homemade moonshine and yeast. I felt an icy fear start to trickle into my veins.

Sergeant Hawkins smiled. It was not a pleasant thing to watch. I could see that he was straddling the borderline of racist insanity: this was going to be his last chance to get me, and he was taking advantage of it. The breath came from his nostrils in sharp, hot spurts. He moved towards me like a matador moving in for the kill.

"Carter?" he said, grinning vilely. "I think me and you have got some unfinished business, boy! Something we got to attend to."

I looked back coldly into the sergeant's flushed face, but inwardly I was far from cool. I wondered bitterly if all black men went through these periods of rage and felt this pressing injustice. Why didn't the man just leave me alone? I could see that Hawkins was drunk and almost to the falling-out point. I also realized that the man was dangerous in this condition.

"You're a hard man to convince, Sarge." I spoke very softly.

"Yup, could be," he admitted. "But I just don't believe that a stinking nigger can really whup me!" he said. "I think you just got lucky that first time, and *now* I want to find out for sure!"

Whatever hint of sympathy for Sergeant Hawkins had lain within the inner fibers of my troubled soul I now hid away. I had come to realize that I lived only by caution and chance, and that the next man I fought might be just the one to luck up and kill me dead.

I looked at Sergeant Hawkins, my mind now made up. My former doubt and fear had left me, and in that moment I knew I had but one path open to me, and that was to fight until I died.

"Yo-you-you're pu-pu-pushing me again, man," I stammered heatedly. "And I don't want to fight you! Because the next time that I do, I'm going to kill you!" I promised him, almost out of breath. "I-I-I swear 'fore God I will!" Then I turned and walked out the door.

Had the man pressed the issue any further, though I was glad he didn't, one of us would have died right there on the spot. Of that I am convinced. Not that I was unnecessarily ruthless, but a man has to survive. My life was as important to me as the next man's was to him—only more so, because it was mine, and the only one I had.

THE TENTH ROUND

Getting It All Together

The next day, segregated again—only this time in buses rather than trucks—we left Fort Jackson and rode through South Carolina and Georgia into Alabama, Tennessee, and Kentucky. Stuck in the rear vehicle of the caravan, the black guys in Dog Company were still getting the shitty end of the stick all the way.

We traveled across beautiful mountainsides and through long groves of quaking aspens, their multicolored leaves shimmering in the cool breeze beneath the morning sun. They were dark green above, gray, brown, and yellow below. America, the beautiful!

America, the dirty white racist bitch! I seethed, as the buses stopped for food and drink. The white soldiers were allowed to go into the chophouses while the rest of us were forced to remain where we were, eating cold bologna sandwiches. America, the low-down stinking bastard! I reflected bitterly as I sat there in shame, gnawing on dried-up bread and drinking the lukewarm water that was sold to us as coffee.

I was burning up inside just thinking about the total disregard that the Army was displaying for my people. Every nook and cranny of my body raged at the hypocrisy of it all—at the dirty white lies that I had been indoctrinated with all my life. I was mad at my mother, at my father, at all the niggers who held themselves in contempt of their color. But most of all, I was mad at the world for sending me down South to learn the truth about myself.

"Fuck these crackers!" I announced through clenched teeth. I looked out of the window at a bunch of drunken farmers who were crowding around a radio and disharmoniously yelling their fool-ass heads off to a hillbilly song. Their loud rebel shrieks grated on my nerves. I noticed that they all had the deep cornpone accents of Sergeant Hawkins, and the same cold eyes of that flesh-eating scavenger, the buzzard. I noticed something else, too: all these honkies were wearing guns, every last one of them. I decided I would have to get me one, too. This Army life was not really making me any nastier than what I was, but it wasn't making it any easier for me either. It just made me care a little less than usual, which wasn't really a helluva lot in the first place.

Fort Campbell lies some fifty-odd miles northwest of Nashville, Tennessee, right on the border between Tennessee and Kentucky. By the time we arrived, the leaves on the trees had turned into deep, dark colors and the air held a subtle hint of frost. The climate was fresh and crisp after the long hot drive over the mountains and bottomlands, and the heavy fragrance of the pines, the smell of the long grass shimmering with dew, exotically filled my nose. This was a land for a man to love, a beautiful land of rolling grass and alpine trees, of towering mountains pushing their dark peaks towards majestic skies.

Jump school, however, consisted of three torturous weeks of twenty-four-hour days of corrosive annoyance. During the first weeks, we were kept fully occupied strengthening our bodies and keeping our minds alert: like hanging from the "nut cracker"—a leather harness suspended ten or fifteen feet above the ground— and learning how to fall from the belly of a mock plane; jumping from a forty-foot tower for hours upon hours; and lying on our backs strapped into an opened parachute, while huge windblowers dragged us through piles of sharp gravel until we were able to deflate the chute and gain our footing.

The third week was when we put it all together, and jumped from the bowels of a real airplane. It took five of these jumps to qualify for "blood wings," as they were called, and thus become paratroopers—or goddamned fools; I really didn't know which.

On the morning I embarked on my maiden voyage from the solar plexus of a C-119 Flying Boxcar, I was the fourth man to jump in a "stick" of sixteen. I remember I was trembling as the aircraft left the loading zone and started to roll. It quickly reached its flight speed and went into a ragged lift-off. Things began flashing past outside in a weird kaleidoscope of objects briefly seen and then gone forever.

The airplane shook and shuddered as it left the ground, exploding gusts of fiery flames from the engines as if it would blow up at any moment. When I looked around me, I saw everybody was quiet—scared to death, I knew. Some guys were praying that their parachutes would open on time, and if not, begging forgiveness for any wrongs they might have committed in life; others looked at pictures of their moms, or of their wives and girlfriends. I just kind of wished that I hadn't gotten on the damned thing at all.

The jump master, a full bird colonel, nonchalantly stood in the front part of the aircraft, gazing out of an open door. He stood so close it seemed dangerous, as though the draft from the doors would suck him through them into nothingness at any moment. Suddenly the C-119 tilted sickeningly, then straightened back up and hunched forward into the added acceleration. A green light flashed on a panel behind the colonel.

"Get ready!" the colonel shouted, taking his position in the doorway. "Stand up, hook up, and check your equipment!"

"OOOOOOh, shit" I said to myself. "Here we go!" My head was buzzing loudly, my ears were stopped up, and my blood pounded through my veins like tom-tom drums. What if my chute don't open? I worried. What if I get to the door and freeze up? As these things flashed through my mind, I heard the jump master sound off with equipment check, and the man behind me shouted, "Four, ready!" Then I got myself together and checked out the man's equipment in front of me.

"Three, ready!" I confirmed.

"Two's ready!" signaled the man in front of me.

"All's ready!" the stick leader called.

The thunderously belching airplane banked sharply into its approach pattern and then leveled off again. My stomach leveled out with it. Our altitude was twelve hundred feet, and the wind whipped through the passageways at sixty miles an hour, pushing and pulling, and threatening to drag us off our feet.

"Drop Zone coming up!" the colonel announced. "First man move up and take a 'tee' on me."

The first man, the stick leader, shuffled up to the door and placed his foot against the jump master's instep. The colonel was still standing in the doorway, his arms braced against the sides of the bucking aircraft. His knees were bent slightly, well balanced, and his eyes were riveted to the red light glowing on the wall panel. Suddenly the color changed to green.

"Hit it!" he shouted, and out the door he went. The stick leader followed immediately after him.

There was no time for thought or hesitation. I could only hear the dragging gait of many feet as man after man shuffled up to the door and jumped, was pushed, or just plain fell out of the airplane. The icy winds ripped at my clothing, spinning me as I hit the cold back-blast from the engines, and then I was falling through a soft silky void of emptiness, counting as I fell: "Hup thousand—two thousand—three thousand—four thousand!"

A sharp tug between my legs jerked me to a halt, stopping the count, and I found myself soaring upwards—caught in an air pocket, instead of falling. I looked up above me and saw that big, beautiful silk canopy in full bloom and I knew that everything was all right. The sensation that flooded my body was out of sight! I didn't feel like I was falling at all; rather, the ground seemed to be rushing up to meet me.

I looked down, and a slight breeze whispered through the grass below, turning it from deep green to blue to shifting silver as the wind stirred along the lowlands. It was beautiful. I felt so free up there, just like an eagle soaring over his domain and controlling everything. All the cream in the Milky-White-Way was mine. I was in total command of all that marched across the horizon of my imagination.

All too soon my newly found power was gone. I hit the ground with such force that it shook my body from head to toe, forcing me to go into a five-point landing to absorb the shock and deflate my chute. That's when I really understood what the training had been all about.

My next four jumps went much the same way, and when I finally graduated and received my wings, it was a great day of reckoning in my life. It was a day in which I proved to myself that I could do anything I desired to do, just as long as I had the will and determination to keep on pushing on.

By the time the cold winter winds of 1954 had unleashed their icy fury upon the lands of Tennessee and Kentucky, the 187th R.C.T. (Regimental Combat Team) had been sent home to Fort Campbell from Korea, and shortly thereafter, three hundred of us were involuntarily recruited into the advance party of the 11th Airborne's transfer to Europe. I was one of those fortunate few.

Once in Augsburg, Germany, where we were based, I found it to be more racist than I imagined any southern state in America could ever be. To top that off, *all* of the soldiers stationed there—

black and white—seemed to hate the 11th Airborne. Some said it was because we made twice the money the other G.I.s did—attracting all the fräuleins to us, and running the price of pussy up sky high. They said that in the past they'd only had to pay twenty marks ($5.00) for a quickie on toast. But as soon as *we* got to Deutschland, the price of beef went up to forty and fifty marks for the very same quickie—so you can just imagine how much it costed the soldiers for a hot dinner to take home!

Looking back on the situation now, I think that maybe the guys had a legitimate gripe. But nobody had to worry about me messing with their women. I was having enough troubles of my own. I just couldn't seem to get myself together, and I guess that was my own fault, since I wouldn't talk to anybody. Until one day I met Ali Hasson Muhammad. Then everything started falling in place.

I believe there is an old saying that likens a child to a piece of carbon paper upon which each passerby leaves a mark. It was this way with Hasson and me. He made a giant-size fingerprint on my life that could never be wiped clean from my memory.

The man was just plain too much. He was an *Aswad* Muslim, a Sudanese who had migrated to America during the riots in his own country, and was now trying to earn an early citizenship by pulling time in the Army.

"Serving time," he would correct me. "And not for the racist ideology of this capitalistic country, either!" It was for his own personal freedom as a resident of the United States. He was very adamant about that little distinction.

He imparted to me the astute (I thought) observation that nobody, but *nobody* in the world today could beat a black man when it came down to fighting. Or dancing. Or singing. Nor could anybody outrun him. Or outwork him. In other words, nobody could outdo a black man in *anything*—as long as he put his mind and soul into it.

"So *what* on God's earth," he would exclaim, sometimes wiping tears of frustration from his eyes, "what in Allah's name ever gave the black man in America the stupid, insidious idea that white men could somehow *outthink* him?" And he would shake his head in sorrow.

He once told me a story about a fat countryman of his who fell asleep one night while shelling peas upstairs in the cramped quarters of his hovel—how the hut mysteriously caught on fire, and how the village people had rushed in to save the farmer from burning to death. But they couldn't do it, because the man was too heavy to move, and the attic too small to shift his enormous weight over to the stairs. Hasson told me how the townsmen worked desperately, but without success, to save the man before the house burned to the ground. Then how the village wise man came upon the scene and told the struggling masses trying to save the sleeping man, "Wake him up! Just wake him up and he'll save himself!"

Hasson said that the "Black People" in America would have to wake up in order to save themselves too, that knowledge of Self and Kind is the only true means to a feasible liberation of the common people, but that a good many of the black leaders in America—most especially those jack-legged preachers who were sitting under the tree of wisdom, still hung up on spooks and spirits and a diverse assortment of other irrelevant apparitions—were all pretentious egoists who selfishly hid in the shade of ignorance and had to be kicked in their asses to drive them out into the sunshine.

He said that when a people without any knowledge of themselves blissfully take their individual liberties as indisputable facts —as his countrymen did for such a long period of time, and as the black man in America was still doing—they ultimately built the iron foundations of their own prisons. Ball-and-chain type prisons which, later on in life, would force them to shed precious blood in order to escape the constraints. They were words I would often have occasion to recall.

Ali Hasson Muhammad was about two shades darker than I was—which couldn't be considered light by any means—with long silky hair braided about his head so that it appeared to be cut short. He also wore a shaggy, uncultivated beard over the lower portion of his face. He looked mean, but he was soft-spoken and gentle. Though he always talked in platitudes and euphemisms, he was very steadfast in his religious ideals, and he sported a mean pair of talking eyes that advised a man he'd make a better friend than he would an enemy.

While his brute strength was much less than my own, Hasson's moral self-sufficiency was definitely greater. He had a stamina of the soul that outweighed any of my physical attributes. He was a fiercely proud man under the cool, calm face that he showed the world, and knew exactly what he was all about. Yet, even his frequent efforts at friendship rarely moved me. He just couldn't reach me with his vast knowledge of life and limited command of the English language.

But late one night when we were returning from the service club to our barracks, and I was slightly in my cups from drinking beer, we decided to take a shortcut through the fieldhouse—and that's where we started to communicate. That was where Hasson found the common ground on which he had so diligently sought to reach me, but could never seem to find. That ground was prize fighting.

The regimental boxing team was training in the fieldhouse that night, and we stood there and watched them for a good while. "Shit!" I stammered suddenly, "I-I-I can beat all of these niggers."

Hasson swung around with irritation marking his face, one of the few times I ever saw him disgusted. "I can see why you don't open your mouth much," he snapped. "Because you don't know what to say out of it when you do, do you? Every time you open it up you stick your foot right in it, don't you?" he said. "So why don't you just finish the job and tell that gentleman over there what you've just told me. Maybe he can straighten you out!"

The gentleman Hasson mentioned was standing off to the side by himself—a young blond-headed lieutenant who didn't appear to be much older than I. His hair was sheared in the then fashionable crew cut—so short that you could actually see the pink of his skull. He stood about five feet eight inches and was lean. His blue eyes sparkled and danced with pride as he watched the boxers work out. The smile on his face was friendly, but his eyes were reckless— glowing with a be-damned, go-to-hell little glint—and his smile, inclining somewhat to the left side of his face, seemed to be forever on the alert to challenge whoever doubted his boys' abilities. He was the big honcho around there—the boxing coach.

We walked over to where he was watching the workout, Hasson grinning with joy. "Lieutenant?" he said. "My little buddy here thinks that he can fight. In fact, he honestly feels that he can take most of your boys right now," he smirked. "So he's asked me to ask you if you could somehow give him a chance to try out for the team."

The lieutenant's name was Robert Mullick. He was a straight-leg, a ground-pounder, a Regular Army soldier, as was the rest of his team. Hasson, too. The lieutenant looked back over his shoulder at me as if to say, "You're crazy!" An amused smile flickered in his eyes and came to rest on the parachutist wings fastened to my blouse. I could almost hear the sweet voice of revenge streaking through his mind and saying, Ah-ha! Now's my chance to get even with one of these proud-ass parachute-jumping bastards.

When he turned to me he said, "So you really think you can fight, huh?" He sounded defiant. "Or are you just drunk, and want to get your stupid brains knocked out? Is that what you want to happen, soldier?"

Smoke darker than the outsides of the blackest cat jumped straight from my head. Every fiber in my body told me to knock this clown down, to teach him some respect, to show him that everybody was not to be trifled with, because he just might get burned in the exchange. But the rational side of me was thinking better.

"I-I-I can—I can fight!" I stammered, getting mad because I couldn't say much more. "I'll even betcha on that," I said.

"You will, huh?" he teased, his face breaking into a satisfied grin. "Well, I'm going to give you the chance to do just that, buster," he said then, "but not tonight. You've been drinking, and I don't want any of my boys to hurt you unnecessarily. Just leave your name and I'll call you down tomorrow. Maybe by then you won't think you're so goddamn tough." Then he turned his back and continued to watch the workout as if I was no longer there, signifying that the interview was over.

To be sure, I was kind of glad when he suggested that I come in the next day, because I wasn't too anxious to climb up into that ring at all. I wasn't a complete fool, you know. What the hell did I know about prize fighting? I had never had a pair of gloves on before in my life, and wasn't too particular about starting then. As far as I was concerned, there would be no tomorrow; I had no intention of coming back then, or at any other time. Boxing just wasn't my shot.

But Lieutenant Bob thought otherwise, and he wasn't about to let me off the hook so easily. He had his mind made up not to let me slip out from under the ass-whupping he had in store for me. He wanted to teach me a lesson for low-rating his pride and joy, let the world know that he wasn't going to stand for that kind of bullshit from anybody, especially a paratrooper. So the next day I was ordered to report to Lieutenant Mullick at the fieldhouse.

When I arrived there late in the afternoon—after having given the matter much thought—the arena was jam-packed full of people, alive with unusual activity. Prize fighting was a big thing in Germany, and my inebriated challenge of the night before had not been taken lightly. More than the usual crew of hustlers, curiosity seekers, admirers and fanatical fight fans were on hand—twice the amount than would normally be the case—to witness the jive-ass paratrooper getting his jump boots knocked off. Hasson was there, too, as were the sports reporters from *Stars and Stripes*. It seemed that I was being used as the blunt end of a crude publicity stunt.

As I stood unnoticed in the doorway, watching two fighters in the ring pound away at each other, I knew right then that I was out of my class. They seemed to be trying to kill each other. The short dark one was bleeding like a stuck pig from a gash above his eye, while the other fighter, no longer able to breathe through his smashed-in nose, continually spit out globs of blood from his mutilated mouth. His right eye was closed, too, and was swelling rapidly from the steady mete of right hands it was absorbing.

The crowd leaped up and down in their seats, shouting with ecstatic glee, pleading and begging for the kill—for either one of the fighters. They didn't give a damn who it was that fell, just as long as somebody hit the dust. At that point I realized that people were even sicker than I thought they were, that human beings were addicted to violence and brutality in whatever form would suit their barbaric temperaments—just as long as it didn't personally involve them.

For a fleeting moment, I experienced fear, and the desire to get away quickly. If I could have run and continued living with myself beyond that day, I would have flown. Standing there, I felt a cold chill, a quick shuddering premonition that only comes when, as the saying goes, somebody has just walked on your grave.

When the bloody sparring session in the ring had finally reached its conclusion, Lieutenant Mullick—who had been up in the square jungle officiating as both referee and timekeeper—jumped down from the apron and elbowed his way through the crowd to where I was standing. Silence cradled the gymnasium softly into its arms and rocked it gently to sleep.

"Are you ready for that workout now, mister?" Mullick shot at me, waiting for me to refuse. "Or do you have a hangover from boozing it up too much last night and want to call it off?"

I shook my head.

The lieutenant nodded, wheeled around, and strode back to-wards the ring, where his fighters were grouped in a huddle and talking among themselves. He began explaining something to them and the men became quiet. They were even more quiet by the time I reached them.

I couldn't help but to look in awe at the many sweat-polished, black faces that surrounded me. All of them were scarred, ring-battered and worn. But they had a togetherness about them that went far beyond their blackness. They were men of great courage whom one would have to shoot in order to stop, for their pride and integrity was such that they couldn't be broken. Still, not one of them appeared hostile in the face of my stupid braggadocio.

Then a big black dude separated himself from the rest of the squad, climbed into the ring, and started shadowboxing—shaking out his arms, his legs, and his thick neck muscles to loosen them up. At this sight the mob of spectators came alive, jumped to their feet, and shouted his name. They sensed the kill. The nigger did look good, I had to admit.

He was Nelson Glenn from Atlanta, Georgia, stood six-foot-one in his stocking feet, had thick ropy shoulders like a bull, and one of those short, compact necks that made his head appear to be at-tached directly to his deltoids. His chest was broad, deep, and mas-sive. His stomach was hard and flat, like a washing board, and the muscles flexed and rippled each time he moved. His hands were big, too. He just oozed with the sheer animal power of a gorilla.. (He kinda looked like one, too.) But the powerful shoulders, arms, legs, and hands all spoke of many years of dedicated training.

Lieutenant Mullick climbed through the ropes and began lacing up a pair of gloves on his fighter. At the same time, he motioned for me to get into the ring. It was too late to back down now, so I mounted the apron and climbed in. Hasson was right behind me.

I could feel the adrenaline race through my body, firing up my blood, yet I remained calm in spite of it. I seemed somehow to feel extra light and especially strong at the same time. But I also felt a loneliness, a deep-down vulnerability to be in the ring by my gutter-sniping seventeen-year-old self with a highly trained fighter. There was another twinge of feeling mixed up in there somewhere, too—pride—a sharp, electrifying sense of self-respect.

Over in the opposite corner, Nelson Glenn looked huge and

almost indestructible as he pranced around the ring with a sure-fire cockiness that left very little doubt in my mind as to what would be the outcome of this ill-matched fray. His entire body was glistening, gleaming with sweat. He was a formidable opponent, and I readily accepted him as being the better man with the boxing gloves. Still, I wouldn't yield to him in the least. I couldn't do that! It just wasn't in me. I hadn't challenged him directly, but I was going to attack him as viciously as if he'd just stolen a white-faced mule in Alabama. My best bet was to show him that I wasn't scared, that he wasn't going to just whup on me without getting whupped on himself. I was going to let him know that he would have to *bring* ass to *get* ass; that he couldn't leave his in the corner when he came out to get mine.

My stomach tightened up even more at this thought, tickled by the butterflies, so I turned around and pretended to be listening to the instructions that Hasson was giving me while he tied up my gloves.

". . . so stay down low, and watch out for his right hand," he whispered softly, the depth of his concern very obvious. "And try to protect yourself at all times, you hear?"

I nodded.

Nelson Glenn had been the All-Army Heavyweight Champ for the past two years, and was well on his way to repeating that feat again this season. And here I was getting ready to box him—me!

Then the bell rang.

Glenn danced out of his corner snorting, pecking away at my head with a sharp jab. as we swung around toward the ring's west ropes. I bobbed and weaved, slipping and sliding, fighting him as if it were a street fight and we were out in some alleyway, trying to stay underneath his crisp left hand. I bobbed out, feinted, then darted back in again, and lashed out with my first punch of the fight—a blurring left hook that caught the heavyweight flush on the point of his chin. And down he spilled on the canvas.

It probably startled me more than it did him.

He was up before the count could even start. He was groggy and reeling around in confusion, but able to duck the blows out of pure instinct. Obviously, he was surprised by the power of a mere welterweight. But once again, a relatively short, bone-crunching left hook crashed against his head. With a screech born of nothing I recognized, I leaped in with another left hook, and then another one, and Nelson's mouthpiece flew from between his teeth. His eyes turned glassy, his powerful arms hung down at his side, and he started sinking softly to the canvas.

When the battering explosions of gloves pounding against meat died away, it became so still inside the arena that you could hear the clouds pass by overhead. Then it burst into pandemonium, and the spectators were up and standing in their seats, gaping with disbelief at the quivering champ still stretched out on the floor, knocked cold.

There seemed to be no end to the exhilaration of this mob. They continued to cheer even after Hasson had removed my gloves and Nelson was revived. They were applauding for me, now—the cloudbuster—though I'll bet they would rather have slept in shit than see Nelson Glenn lying there in the dust instead of me.

It was at that moment in my life, after having searched in strife for so many years, that I finally knew exactly what I had been created for: fighting. Street fighting, gutter-sniping, and prize fighting have always been my amazing grace.

The next day—after Lieutenant Mullick had cut through tons of Army red tape and pulled Lord knows how many governmental strings—I was transferred to the Special Service detachment and relieved of any further military obligation, as far as being a weapons-bearing soldier was concerned. I was told that I was fighting for Uncle Sam, now, and as a result I could do no wrong and could have no need too great for the Special Service to satisfy. Now I belonged to the elite!

The boxing team had an entire building allocated to itself, three floors of plush living space to accommodate twenty-five men. On the first was a vast recreational area containing every type of entertainment imaginable—plus its own kitchen and cooking personnel. The second floor was sectioned off into bathtubs and shower stalls, whirlpools and rubbing tables, while the top floor had our sleeping quarters—individually secluded and kept very private. This was the utopia of Army living.

When I sat down to the table at suppertime that first night, I looked at the rugged faces—black, white, and Puerto Rican—around me and suddenly felt at home. At home with people I knew but slightly, but could feel strangely warm and comfortable with. I felt their easy understanding, their awaiting friendship, their obvious sympathy. They were strong, honest people, hard-working and equally hard-fighting, but simple in their ways. There were no complications there whatsoever, no tensions, no fears.

I was accepted immediately by these fellows (even Nelson Glenn) without the slightest hesitation. They all seemed to understand that we were *brother warriors*, each and every one, and as such we should live together in peace and harmony—regardless of individual temperaments. And I liked that.

After that I lived for boxing alone. It was the beginning, middle, and end of everything in my life. Apart from fighting, nothing held much meaning for me. I rapidly built up a strong following and quite a name for myself with a quick knockout style. I had twenty bouts and lost only one, with sixteen kayos to my credit, and I got better and better all the time. I was happy for myself, but something was still missing.

It was Hasson, again, who pulled my coat and showed me the way. He showed me that stuttering was not the root of my speech problem, not the villain I had made it out to be in order to justify my difficulties. He said that stammering was only a small cause of my antisocial behavior, a psychological block that could be very easily removed simply by going back to school. He even promised to enroll himself, if I felt too embarrassed to go it alone.

"Knowledge," he said, "and especially of one's self, has in it the potential power to overcome all barriers. Wisdom is the godfather of it all." And so it was that we enrolled in a Dale Carnegie course at the Institute of Mannheim, where we happened to be based at the time.

As I began learning how to talk with some clarity, all the knowledge that I had picked up in the course of my life simply by remaining quiet and listening, began to pour from my mouth like the unbridled Niagara. I had this beautiful feeling of being able to communicate at last—a big, wide, wonderful world full of my own sounds, where every new word I learned was immediately shoved aside by the force of the one that followed.

I developed a special feeling for verbal expression. Even Hasson couldn't keep me from talking, couldn't stop me from telling him about the million-and-one atrocities in my life that I'd kept bottled up inside me for so long. Silence was no longer a defense mechanism for me; it became, instead, a luxury. If I kept quiet now, it was only because I wanted to, and not because I felt I had to.

My whole life changed. My attitude, even my boxing ability, greatly improved. I had an all-consuming thirst for knowledge. I learned that an education, and especially a European one, could very easily be spread thick over many slices of good times, and that's exactly what I did with it: I boxed and went to school, and tried to combine the pugilistic aspects of myself with the militarism of the Haitian general Dessalines, in the scholarly manner of a Frederick Douglass.

Ali Hasson Muhammad was always there to counsel and assist me, inspiring me to reach for ever greater heights by learning more and more facts about life, about living, about myself. Everything in Hasson's world began and ended with Islam, Islam, Islam. He fasted according to the Holy Koran, ate only by the mathematical maxims of Hadith, and fulfilled Allah's benevolent principles with every ounce of strength in his being.

This fascinated me no end. So I was more than willing to embrace his Allah when he asked me to consider it, and in fact, I was downright honored to be finally unified in soul and spirit with the man who had performed an important miracle in my life. I wanted to know from what Hasson had derived all this incredible strength, who it was that gave it to him, and how I too could become as powerful as he.

The Holy Ghost spookisms of the Protestant religion that my father had shoved down my throat in my childhood, and the asinine Virgin Mary bullshit of Catholicism that was violently thrust upon me in jail (and it was), were all still preserved within the dusty museums of my past. I knew every prayer, and every Apostle from Peter to Judas, but I could never relate to *anything* where ghosts or spirits were concerned. So, I thought to myself, "What the hell, what harm could it possibly do if I checked out this Islam thing?"

So out of the cradle of ignorance came Saladin Abdullah Muhammad—me—the warrior and general!

I was taught that the black man is the Original Man, the maker, the owner, and the Father of Civilization—the cream of the planet earth, and God of the universe; that black man himself placed the sun in the sky over seventy-eight trillion years ago, and the moon sixty-six trillion; that the earth travels at the speed of one thousand thirty-seven and a third miles per hour, and that one cubic foot of common earth weighs sixty pounds. I found out that I had seven and a half ounces of brains lodged in my head, but, in ignorance of self, only functioned on a mere half an ounce; that there were seven inhabitable planets in the outer universe, but that the white man knew of only one.

I looked at my new discovery and it was good! I rejoiced in the knowledge of it. But when I questioned my teachers about ever meeting this extraordinary entity called Allah, I was told that I either would have to die first, or could meet Him in the person of a little black man living in Chicago named Elijah Muhammad, all praises due! This, then, was the same devious God of all the other religions and cults and Daddy Grace practices, I thought, and I could not go for any of that bullshit.

In the school of Islam I attended four nights a week, after my other classes, there were two or three different types of Muslims, who couldn't seem to agree ideologically about who the amazing Allah actually was. But my man knew! My good friend Hasson, who had been born and raised as a Muslim in northeastern Africa, knew, and he vehemently denied that Allah was a separate entity, as was being taught by the American-born Muslims in Germany. He said that Allah was in us all, that man himself was God. And this was an explanation I could readily accept. For if, indeed, I was a god, then everything had been all right all along. Because I had never stopped believing in myself anyway.

Hasson told me that Man's mind was an explanation-seeking organ. Thus a spirit was conceived as an entity roughly shaped from the clay of superstition, which gave Man an excuse for being, and relieved him from the burdens of his own conscience. The mind, Hasson said, was a label-placer to justify the faults inherent in Man's own deeds and weaknesses.

He said that the belief in Holy Spirits merely invoked in Man a response to justify the world's creations and degradations. Because Protestants, Catholics, and skeptics of many other denominations invariably loved mystery better than they did explanation, they could readily believe that God—this spiritual being—actually created heaven and earth. By throwing aside their objectivity, they could conceive of a universe that had not always been here, but could always be here, and that words such as "beginning" and "end" were all man-made symbols to identify a passing phase in life. That's what Hasson believed, and I could believe that part of it, too.

It could have been a day, a week, an eternity—but it was really two years that had slipped past when it came time for me to go home. Two good years, during which I twice racked up the European Light-Welterweight Championship by winning fifty-one bouts— thirty-five by knockouts—and sustained only five losses. I was honored when I was asked to compete in the Olympic Trials that were soon to take place, but was told I would have to re-enlist in order to do so, since my discharge was due before the date they were to begin.

I loved prize fighting, but I wasn't about to prolong my Army career in order to compete in nothing. Shucks! I wanted to go home. I wanted to go back to America and find Ray Charles! Because I had missed him the first time around.

So, in June of 1956, I was shipped back to the States to be discharged.

THE ELEVENTH ROUND

Trying to Make It Real
Compared to What?

Riding the U.S.S. *Grant* back to America from Germany, I latched onto a group of soldiers playing "bid whist" for ten dollars a man. And by the time we docked at the Brooklyn Navy Yard, I was really beat—almost out on my feet from playing cards ten days straight without stopping. But I was fifty-seven beautiful hundred dollars richer, all praises due! I had just won more money than I'd ever seen before at one time. It appeared that with the return of my speech came luck, came peace, and plenty of prosperity. I was mustered out of Fort Dix the next day.

But Paterson, New Jersey, had deteriorated drastically in the years I'd been gone. The "Silk City's" streets were filthy. Garbage was strewn everywhere, as if the people had simply grown tired of trying to dig themselves out from under. Prowling, growling alleycats—fat, vicious, and sassy from fighting and feeding on the equally fat and vicious rats in the streets—patrolled the gutters and trash cans as if they, and not the people, were in control of the community. Many of the most handsome buildings I had known had been gutted and wantonly abandoned. Cars had been stripped of their chrome and then burned, their charred metal hulks a mute testimony to the destruction in the air around them. Homes I remembered as neat and comfortable were now horrifying firetraps, forsaken by their original owners and allowed to fall into decay so that local slumlords could gobble them up cheaply. Then they would pawn them back to ignorant blacks at prices exorbitant enough to assure the city's political fathers that niggers would always be kept in a fixed, concentrated area. Preventing them from spilling over into the affluent white communities.

Even Twelfth Avenue, the street where I was raised and where my mother and father still lived, had felt the greedy fingers of City Hall picking its pockets empty by cutting down all the trees and raping the avenue of its shrubbery. But in spite of the neighborhood's rapid decline into a bona fide black ghetto, it was still the most beautiful place I'd ever known. Because it was home, and I was free—and, as Allah was now my benefactor, I was a changed man.

Al-Hamdilallah!

My entire family was back together again. My oldest brother, Lloyd Junior, was out of the service and married, living a few doors down from my parents. Lillian's husband, Bob, had made it home from Korea too, as did the rest of the Carter men who had trekked off to foreign shores to fight. Brother Jimmy was still going to school, Harvard University now, and sister Beverly was married and living in Passaic. My two youngest sisters, Rosalie and Doris, were both at home and going to high school. So, all in all, the Carter family was in the money and looking good.

After five or six days of acclimating myself back into the stream of civilian life, which meant buying myself a new Lincoln Continental and going on a wild shopping spree to replace my long-lost wardrobe, I got a job driving a tractor-trailer for a paper company in the suburbs of Paterson. Then I settled down to some real easy living.

I met a girl, too! I mean, I met a lot of girls, but this one fox named Regina was my pride and joy—the sweetest bundle of curves to be erected since Allah had placed the sun, moon, and stars in the sky. Lovelier than a full moon on a cloudy night, more graceful than a lustrous, starry-eyed gazelle—she was a *fine* Mizzafizza!

At five-foot-four, weighing a hundred and thirty pounds, she was exquisitely proportioned, a Queen of the Universe, a truly beautiful symphony of lush, firm curvation. Her mouth-watering breasts stood high, hard, and solid, jutting out defiantly like a pair of softly blunted cones. Nowhere on her body was there an excessive wrinkle or an ounce of fat, and her tiny waist voluptuously sloped in around a smooth, flat tummy. Only her legs, and that purely to a true perfectionist, might have seemed a trifle bit shorter than they should have been, but to me they only added to the total vision of her loveliness. They were muscularly lean, smooth and graceful, like the legs of a highly trained athlete.

Regina was pure *blaaack*. A deep unglazed black—not the shiny color of coal, which was so reflective, but the unblemished sheen of virgin soot, with the same dull, soft, ungleaming quality about it.

Her complexion was really flawless, her hair as black as a raven's wing. Only her huge snapping eyes shone through that dusty, unglossed skin. Her voice was deep and melodious, and her beautiful face, with its high cheekbones and deep-pooled, long-lashed eyes, carried an air of dignity.

This girl was the mother of my newly found civilization. Because I had been mentally dead and ignorant as hell for twenty miserable years, this type of woman would have been, in the past, impossible for me even to *think* about dealing with, much less love. I thought I had always known what sort of woman I wanted—a high-yellow, flashy woman; a thin-nosed, straight-haired woman. I didn't want no girl as black as me! And since my nature was that of a fighter, a fighter I wanted her to be. But when I emerged from the graveyard of ignorance by coming into what Hasson had called the wisdom and knowledge of Self and Kind, I no longer aspired to a flashy, gin-guzzling, bleached-skinned woman with burnt-out hair. Shucks! I didn't even want to fight no more. All I wanted now was peace of mind.

On the Fourth of July, me and my little fox were going to spend the morning driving down to Atlantic City for the holiday festivities. The night of the third, I twisted and turned with impatience, lying in my bed wondering if I shouldn't just get up and go pick up Regina, and then get on the highway just a little bit earlier than planned. But then I said to myself, "Nawwwww, fool, it's still too early yet." It was only twelve o'clock. So I lay back down.

But getting back to sleep was hard. I'd been looking forward to going away with Regina for this holiday ever since first meeting her. The mere thought of what the next day might bring sent sparks of joy streaking through my mind.

"Uh-uh-uh!" I closed my eyes and let my mind drown in sweet pleasurable dreams, when suddenly, a loud, crashing noise jerked me back to full consciousness. The door to my room was kicked open, and in rushed two cops, their weapons already drawn.

"Sit still!" one of them hissed as I came up out of my bed. "We're police officers!" He flashed a badge in a leather case up under my nose. "Now, get up slow and easy and put your clothes on. You're under arrest."

"Under arrest!" I exclaimed. "But what—"

"Shut your fuckin' mouth!" the other cop rasped. "Or I'll shut it for you!" The words seemed to have been ripped from his throat.

They silenced me immediately. His face, fraught with tension, burned into a deep red. The fist not holding his gun he rigidly clenched at his side.

I just couldn't believe it. I was frozen by the nastiness that dripped like saliva from the officer's fangs. I couldn't understand why they were doing what they were doing. Hate burned through me like a million torches. I wanted to destroy something, and my strange mental fog drove me towards the two cops. I wanted to get my hands around their necks and squeeze until their eyes popped out of their skins like grapes.

The small hairs on the back of my neck seemed to stand up on end at these reckless thoughts. But then a tiny particle of sanity stirred from within: Rubin! Rubin! What are you doing, fool? I heard it say. Don't give your life away for nothing. Leave these goddamn crackers alone, boy! You haven't done anything.

A look of pure astonishment swept across the two cops' faces. I'm sure they hadn't expected me to give up without a fight—and they were right, because Rubin Carter wouldn't have. But Saladin Abdullah Muhammad did.

Before I met Hasson I would gladly have fought the two cops until I was free again, or had been killed in the process. But since embracing Islam, I tried to look at the practical side of every situation, sorting out the probabilities, cataloging the possibilities, and then mapping out a proper plan to meet the action. Now, I figured I had no reason to fear these people. I had done nothing wrong. So I allowed them to handcuff my wrists behind my back—almost tightly enough to cut off my circulation—and then lead me away from home. I was positive I would be back in a matter of hours. Back in plenty of time for a late breakfast and still be able to get away for the holiday.

But the cops had no intention of taking me downtown to police headquarters, or to court, either. That would have been too much like doing things right. No, the two in my room, along with two others who were waiting for us outside, unlawfully abducted me without any formality, or any opportunity for me to obtain a lawyer. Throwing me to the floor of their car, they drove like madmen straight through the night. They zoomed me up hills and over secondary highways, through dark alleys and down back roads, until we ended up at Annandale Reformatory—the next vicious step up the ladder from Jamesburg in the penal system, going *down!*

Going back to jail was like taking a bath in disaster, and I was hurting. As I sat there in Annandale in the first light of morning, angry and dejected, I sought to look the facts of life straight in the face as best I could. All I could see, however, was sneering cops. I felt that I had struggled, vainly, to become something I wasn't. Sitting in that cell, I realized the lunacy of even having tried.

Maybe it was this vacuum of personal helplessness, of my having taken it for granted that justice would be done, that all wrongs would be righted, and all that other storybook shit. But once thrown back in the penitentiary, without having had a hearing or anything, I felt different.

I berated myself for believing the bullshit about justice in this fucked-up society. My urge for revenge now almost choked me up with its bitterness. Somebody would have to pay for putting me back in jail. Even more than that, somebody would have to pay for destroying my self-respect. For mutilating the "newly found" Rubin, the "at-peace-with-himself" Rubin. Somebody *had* to pay for that!

I wanted to see this insidious juvenile-labor system demolished from stem to stern, and I wanted to see it happen out of pure hatred and vengeance, as atonement for the crimes committed against me, and others just like me who have never had the nerve to voice their legitimate grievances as members of the human race. I wanted to be the Administrator of Justice, the Revealer of Truth, the Inflictor of All Retribution.

I gloried in these thoughts. For all intents and purposes, I meant to wreak havoc upon this lousy cesspool, and I knew there was nothing short of killing me that anyone there could do to stop it, either. I wasn't afraid; my renewed hatred would dull the blows. I experienced a delicious sensation, knowing that these dirty mother-fuckers could do no more to me than I could do to them, quicker. I sucked in my breath and felt the tense knot in my stomach start to expand.

New Jersey's prisons have a grapevine second to none. Despite the fact I had been sneaked into the joint, cloak'n'dagger style, in the wee hours of the morning, my recapture was heralded through-out the institution before the sun was up, and the word kept spread-ing with the vigor of a forest fire gone wild. I heard all about it later.

"The Rube is back," the gossip went. "They brought him in this morning."

"What! But I heard that he'd changed up and went Muslim."

"That's right, he did," the first voice hissed. "But the dirty motherfuckers went and kidnapped him anyhow!"

"Well, in that case," another voice chimed in, "I'm gonna stay the hell out of his way, myself. I mean, I don't know this dude personally, never saw him before in my life. But from what I've heard, that's gonna be a hard nigger to get along with now! So I'm just gonna stay out of his way."

So it seemed that my notoriety had not died in my absence from the system. But this time the Rube that everyone would see would not be the stammering, stumbling, confused man-child they had known at Jamesburg. Annandale had itself a matured Rube, a person who knew what he was all about, and was just that much harder to handle for the knowing. It had a man who understood what it meant to be free, who knew the consequences of selling his soul, were he to allow himself to accept the daily ration of slights and slurs dished out by its faggot, would-be-Gestapo officers. No, sir! They were going to find a Rube who would take shit from no man. They were going to find a young, misused man hell-bent upon his own destruction—a person who just didn't give a fuck anymore.

Annandale Reformatory was just a nastier, bigger, crueler, and more perverted rendition of the slave camp at Jamesburg. Situated in the upper regions of northwestern New Jersey, it had no visible prison walls. They were there, though, in the form of endless rows of hills, mountains, and thick forests. These hang-ups provided by Mother Nature were the chains and shackles that held in those of us who had "rabbit blood" coursing through our veins—those inmates who, like myself, had already proved they would get up and escape.

There were, as at Jamesburg, eight residential cottages, and a power plant, an industrial building, an administrative building, and a tired-looking mess hall that blushed and peaked with embarrassment each time someone commented on its sad appearance. Annandale had a snakepit too—the gymnasium—where differences were settled, fights fought, and semilegal mayhem committed without the threat of getting busted. It was the inmates' meeting place, their warriors' den. Everyone had to enter it sooner or later.

The prison's chain-gang labor system, like Jamesburg's, was more ruthless and more brutal to its inmates than any southern-type road camp could have ever been. Because this one dealt with kids, young people who really should have been getting an education or learning some kind of trade that would be useful to them on their return to society. Instead, they were forced to work on a hot, steaming rock pile for ten hours a day under the menacing eye of a rifle-carrying guard, smashing useless boulders, which were then turned into rocks, crushed into stones, and which finally ended up in a worthless mountain of tiny pebbles that was never used for anything—not a goddamned thing. Not a red penny did they get for this work, but a mighty swift kick in their asses was on its way if they didn't produce their work quota for the day.

The only difference between this institution and Jamesburg was that Annandale didn't waste any time dehumanizing its population. As soon as you were in the door, it started right in trying to break your back, take your will, and kill your spirit. My own first day there was steeped in violence and despair. I sat in my miserable cell that morning wearing nothing more than a pair of state-issued pajamas, waiting for the doors to open and thinking. Finally I heard someone outside fumble with the lock.

When the door opened, a young officer came slinking into my cell carrying the uniform of the institution—a pair of short pants and a shirt. These, like the shave they gave your head when you entered the place, were designed to strip away your manhood and make you feel like a kid again, to wipe out whatever remained of your personal identity.

The man in my cell now was a lean, good-looking fellow with a boy's soft gingerish beard sprinkled over his upper lip, slender cheekbones and stubborn chin. His thin neck rose arrogantly from a collar as stiff as yesterday's oatmeal. The hair on his head was deep red, while his chin whiskers were light brown.

"Okay, Carter," he said, throwing the clothes at my feet. "It's time to get dressed. Chow'll be going out in about five minutes." Then he turned around and left the room, locking the door behind him.

I stood there motionless, looking down at the crumpled garments in distaste. For me, they didn't exist. I didn't know what that clown had in his mind, but I wouldn't even think to infringe upon the image of Little Bo Peep by wearing his sacred uniform. Shit! I hadn't lost no motherfucking sheep, and I goddamn-sure wasn't a little kid anymore, either! So if that boy ever wanted me to leave this building for chow or anything else, he'd have to take this shit back where it came from and bring me some long pants to wear.

I bent down and scooped up the demeaning clothes and tore them to shreds, flinging the humiliating rags into a corner with disgust. I didn't mind it so much when they cut my hair off, but wearing these short pants? That was too goddamned much for me. I'd rather be caught naked in the "Boogaloo," Georgia, living room of the Ku Klux Klan's Grand Dragon—with my feet up on his table and his wife sitting in my lap—than be caught *dead* in those goddamned short pants!

So when the mess bell rang I just stood in my door, watching the other new inmates walking past my cell in their short-shorts on their way to chow. Barely concealing their long black legs, short yellow legs, and fat white legs, their knock-knees, pigeon-toes and bowlegs, those shorts made every one of them look just like they felt—like goddamn fools.

I couldn't help but shake my head in disgust at the whole horrifying scheme. To me, this was worse than being kicked in the ass every day. At least then you had a chance to fight back. But wearing these short pants took your dignity—and men without dignity are like clowns without an audience, pathetic and lost.

How could they allow themselves to be humiliated like that? I wondered. They didn't even shame the inmates like that in Jamesburg, a penitentiary for much younger kids, where short pants would have been more appropriate. But here in Annandale, where the population ranged in age from sixteen to thirty, fully grown men were made to dress like kindergarten children on their way to a coloring class or something. I didn't like it at all, and I wasn't going for none of that funny shit myself. Before I allowed it to happen, the administration would have to run rabbits, sleep in the woods, and bark at the moon singing "Hi-yo Silver!" until the Lone Ranger showed up with Tonto, saying "Hmmmm! Heap 'um good, Kemo Sabe!"

So I stayed in my room while the others went to eat, looking out the window, watching them file past a waiting officer and into the chow hall. It was obvious from where I was standing that the officer didn't know he was one man short until he had counted each inmate going in. Then he swung around in surprise, looked toward the cottage, muttered something, and came storming back in my direction.

I heard him unlock the front door and come stomping down the corridor. His footsteps were hollow-sounding, clopping angrily through the empty building. Then he was standing in the doorway. A hard, reckless gleam of contempt danced in his eyes.

"What in the hell do you think you're doing, mister?" he snapped, furiously marching into the room. "You're supposed to be in the mess hall with everybody else, goddammit!"

"Huh? I'm sorry, what did you say, again?" I asked the man stupidly.

"I said, what the hell do you think you're doing, mister!" he repeated, with emphasis. An ugly light had jumped into his eyes, contorting his face with indignation. "Put those clothes on and get your black ass in the mess hall! Who the fuck do you think you are?"

I didn't say anything. I just stood there.

The man's face turned beet-red, but I wasn't sure if it was from the exertion of having run all the way back to the cottage, or the fact that I was standing there looking at him like he was a goddamned fool. It didn't make too much difference to me one way or the other.

"I ain't going a goddamn place with no short pants on!" I let him know. "So you can just take that funny shit elsewhere, buddy. Because I'm staying right here where I'm at—and ain't nobody gonna move me, either!"

The man was really steaming now. He opened his mouth to say something, but changed his mind about it. He took a quick step forward—and changed his mind again. He started backing out of the room. "I'm not going to stand here and argue with you, goddammit!" he growled, and slammed the door. "I'll see you when mess is over, you stupid bastard. I don't have the time to be bothered with every goddamn idiot in this fucking place!" Still raging, he stomped off down the hall.

I went back to my window and continued watching the inmates plod to and from the mess hall in sullen silence. They were like beaten slaves, no longer possessing the will to resist. Well, not all of the inmates were such submissive types: there were Bennie Burg and Drady Howard, Seaborn Howell and Chuck Carter, Freddie

Johnson and Jump Charleston—all of whom were legitimate bad-motherfuckers—guys who wouldn't take no shit off of nobody, guys like me.

Many of us had fought several times in the past, both with and against one another, but that made no difference. All of it had been in the yesteryear, in another time and another place, and today was the only thing that counted now. They had a healthy respect for what the name of Rubin Carter had once meant, and it was incumbent upon their suspicious natures to convince themselves that what I once had been, I still was.

Standing at my window, I could see Bennie Burg and Brady Howard strutting out of the mess hall. Their pants were slumped down around their butts, their belts open and hanging loose, and their jailhouse caps were cocked ace-deuce-and-a-half on the sides of their heads.

"Hey, Rube!" Bennie called, searching out my window. "Why didn't you come to the mess hall, Jim? All the boys were looking for you. Do you need cigarettes, candy, or cosmetics over there?"

"Yeah," Brady chimed in with his funny way of talking. "If you need, don't plead—just let us know, and it'll show. If things get hard, just send us a card—you might've been gone, but you're still our pard. Just say the word, baby, just say the word."

I didn't say anything.

During the previous four or five hours, I had felt a frigid change take place within me. It was that same old turn-about of body chemistry that sets my heart aflutter whenever I'm in trouble. My whole system gets rearranged, all my nerves and senses become more alert, more careful. Where before I would have vented my rage upon my harmless cell door and kicked it into splinters, would have knocked its windows out and torn the room itself to smithereens—now I was cool. I was able to think more clearly, and every part of my mind was conscious of the dangers that were lurking deep in the bowels of the institution.

Standing there in the harsh, revealing light of early morning, sensing the brutal confrontations awaiting me out there in population, knowing that I had no legal business in this place, certain that I had been kidnapped in the middle of the night for absolutely nothing, made me hotter than a palpitating pussy with the passionate pop!

Somebody is going to tell me something this morning! I promised myself, pacing up and down the floor. "Somebody's going to tell me something or I'm gonna tear this place down!" I cried. "Somebody—the warden, the captain, the sergeant—but somebody is going to show me the papers that are keeping me here."

Hopelessness rolled down upon me like a dark blanket, smothering my pride in everything good that I had worked so hard to accomplish since I had escaped from Jamesburg. My hands started trembling, my whole body was quivering with fury, with the desire to buck the Establishment, to smash it if I could.

But a saner part of my mind kept warning me that nothing would be gained by added stupidity. Another part said that violence begot violence, and that these people wouldn't be satisfied with what they had already done but would try to do even more. They were doing it already with the short pants. So what was to stop them from going even farther, and taking my life? And I couldn't allow that. *I* had to be the one who stopped *them*.

A dozen wildly irrational schemes of revenge swarmed through my mind, flashing with intensity, each as hopeless and futile as the one before it. I felt strangely empty and just a little bit sick. I wondered where I would go from here, but I didn't really care. I was sure of one thing, though: watching the inmates coming back from the mess hall to be locked up again until chow was called at lunchtime, I was sure that I could never withstand the continuous boredom of being in jail again. Although a man's behavior, as well as his emotions, can be controlled to a certain degree, his mind— once it has known freedom—can never again be completely controlled. It was just that simple: either these people were going to turn me loose that day, or they would have to kill me that morning to keep me there.

These thoughts were side-skipping through my misery, glancing off and then grabbing hold, as the door to my cell was flung open to reveal five guards looking as if they meant business. One of them had a bundle of what looked to be clothing in his hand. He threw them on the floor of the room.

"Put that uniform on, boy!" he demanded, kicking the bundle toward me. "And then throw your mattress out here on the floor. Let's see how you like sleeping on the bedsprings for a while. That oughta teach you to do what you're told when somebody tells you to."

"Fuck you, cracker!"

The words slipped out so quickly, they surprised even me. But when I thought about it later, that was exactly what I had wanted to say. My mind unreeled. The quickest route between two points was straight ahead, I knew, and that's where I wanted to go—straight to the warden.

"That's right, that's what I said: 'Fuck you, cracker!' If you want somebody to wear those short pants," I told him bitterly, "then you wear them your goddamn-self! Because I'm not gonna do it for you, or nobody else!"

The man's jaw dropped open with surprise. He was, except for the slight flaring of his nostrils, utterly motionless. Then his brows flew together in a fixed scowl. He hadn't expected any resistance from me with four more dogs at hand.

"What did you say, nigger?" The man spoke with a cold, quiet fervor quite unlike his initial ravings. The acid in his tone ate coldly into my flesh. "Did I hear you right?" he asked, stepping into the room. "Did I hear what I think I thought I heard, you sonofabitch?"

White heat went through my stomach like a boring tapeworm, and I knew that once again I must fight for what I thought to be right, or I would never have any respect for myself again. My fears vanished. I had to get out of the room before the cops smothered me. Nothing else made any sense. So I charged the door.

The man's features showed surprise. His eyes flared with the upswing of his head, and then he lunged at me, whipping across a looping, overhand right that skimmed my chin. With an urge to rip out his backbone, I dug a hard right hand of my own into his stomach, and stopped him dead in his tracks. That left him open for the thundering left hook that followed and crashed into his mouth. He grunted heavily—once—and then slid to the floor.

Without breaking my stride, I continued on out the door into the corridor, right into the flailing mitts of the other four guards. There was a multiple collision, a rainstorm of drenching knuckles and lightning-delivered fists. They were all over me. Swinging wildly in their efforts to get to me, they kept tripping over each other's feet, doing more harm to themselves than they were to me. With a sudden heave, I flipped one of them over my hips, and slammed my fist against another's neck. Then I stood there and methodically poured lefts and rights into their eyes, their mouths, and their flabby, out-of-shape bellies. It was plain to see that these guys weren't equipped to handle me by themselves.

It had been a long time since I was in such a situation, and, quite frankly, I was pleased. I felt right at home, waging war against these vicious, sadistic bastards. When finally I broke away and vaulted up the flight of stairs which led to the second floor, the cops were more than happy to let me go. They did put on an act, however, trying at first to catch me, but when I spun around and made my stand on the landing, they stopped pretending and just stared up at me like I was crazy.

Meanwhile, "Canvas-back Pete," the first officer to come into my room, had spit out a couple of teeth and shaken the crickets from his head. He had gotten on the house telephone and was yelling like a maniac with his ass on fire.

"Goddammit, send us some help!" he screamed to whoever he was talking to. "This nigger's done gone crazy over here! Send us some help, quick!

"What? No, I ain't neither!" he said to an unheard order. "I'll be damned if I'm going up after that fool, and neither are the others! We don't get paid for this stupid shit! I got a family, man! That's right! That's what I said: I got a family. What? Well, then hurry the fuck up! This nigger's gone crazy over here!"

Then, almost before he could hang the phone up good and turn around, there was a small army of guards scrambling through the door and crowding around the bottom of the stairs, all of them carrying clubs. They were led by a tall, lanky, raw-boned guard with a bucket face, who glared up at me maliciously.

"Awright, jerk-off!" he growled with contempt. "Get your black ass down here on the double before we come up there and beat you into the middle of next week." His voice sounded tired, but venomous. "Now come on down from up there, boy."

The rush of passion I had felt just a short while before was rapidly expanding into a full-blown holocaust. Crouching there on the catwalk, I bitterly resented the fact that I couldn't hold out for long against all of these dirty, low-life snakes. But oddly enough, I was also hoping that they *would* rush the stairs. I craved an opportunity to vent my rage against something solid, to eliminate the terrible frustration that was eating away at my breadbasket.

"No, you come up here first, you bucket-faced cracker!" I shouted down at the man who had threatened me. His eyes widened as I spoke. (I had learned, years before, that once I make up my mind to do something, then I do the motherfucker—and I don't back down at the last minute.) "That's right," I said, "you come up here first, because I'm gonna take you with me wherever I go, you bad motherfucker, you!"

Bucket-face hesitated—an intuitive moment of doubt. But then his anger overcame his caution, and he started up the stairs.

"Hold on just a minute, there!" a lean old man named Pop Thompson commanded. He pushed his way through the mob, brandishing a dull, snubnosed pistol. When he reached the stairs, he pointed the gun at my head. His old, gray, dissipated eyes burned holes right through me.

"Come on down from up there, boy," he said slowly, unemotionally. He took time to pronounce each word clearly. "Now come on down before you make me use this thing."

I flinched as an imaginary bullet sent a ball of flaming pain straight to my chest. Looking down into the business end of that gun, I knew he wasn't jiving—and yet, I still couldn't back down. I just couldn't do that. Once a man starts backing away from what he believes is right, he won't easily find a way to go forward again.

"Fuck you, too!" I barked at the old reprobate. "Fuck you! If you wanna shoot, then shoot! 'Cause I don't give a fuck. Shoot!"

The slack folds of flesh in Pop Thompson's jowls clamped tightly around the bulge of tobacco in his teeth. He gently thumbed the hammer on his revolver, slowly easing it back to full cock. But rather than just stand there to be shot down like a sick animal, I tensed up and coiled, and made ready to dive down the stairs right into the mob.

The men standing below all looked at me in concern. They knew Pop would shoot me.

"No—wait!" a frantic voice exploded. A young, dark-haired, bespectacled officer pushed his way through to the stairs and forced the lieutenant's gun aside. "Let me talk to him, Lieutenant," he pleaded. "Maybe he'll listen to somebody now."

The old man didn't say a word. Didn't even look around. Keeping his glare frostily riveted upon his target—my breast pocket—he nodded and stepped aside.

"Didn't you just get out of the Army, Carter?" the newest arrival asked, desperately looking for a common ground on which he could communicate.

I didn't answer him. My mind was filled with contradictory emotions. I was dumfounded as to why this stranger would come to

This is the Hurricane, out-staring Sonny Liston.
(*Sports Illustrated* photo by Walter Iooss, Jr. © Time Inc.)

Private Rubin Carter, paratrooper, in 1955.

The Carter family at my parents' retirement home in south Jersey, July 4, 1966—two and a half weeks after the crime I'm in jail for was committed. Seated: my father, Lloyd, and my mother, Bertha, with Lloyd Jr. Standing (left to right): Beverly, Doris, Jimmy, Rosalie, me, and Lillian.

Oh, Happy Day! My wedding, June 15, 1963.
(Bucky Leggett is second from the right, partially hidden.)

Her name is Theodora, 8 years old here. A very beautiful child, she loves her daddy! Wowie! (Smile.) And daddy loves her, too. She's going to break some poor fool's heart pretty soon. I kinda feel sorry for the sucker already! (Smile.)

I think I knocked more fighters out of the ring than any other prizefighter. Here Florentino Fernandez takes his leave in the first round at Madison Square Garden, October 22, 1962. (Wide World Photos)

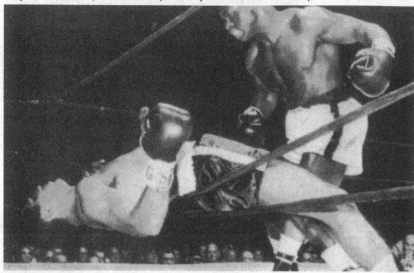

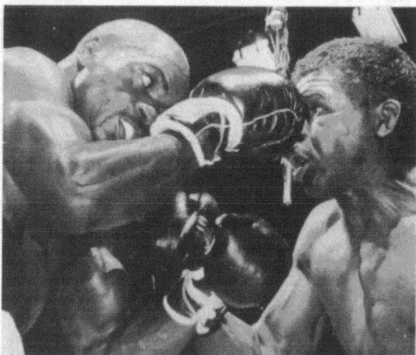

A right to the nose of Holly Mims, December 22, 1962. Holly Mims, Dick Tiger, Sonny Liston, Eddie Machen, Zora Folley: if all these fighters have gone to hell, then that's where I want to go, too. (Wide World Photos)

The hunter trying to lure the rabbit: I did the popping, but Luis Rodriguez won the fight in a split decision, February 12, 1965.
(*Sports Illustrated* photo by Tony Triolo, © Time, Inc.)

Stopping Emile Griffith in Pittsburgh, December 20, 1963. Emile came to fight—but not for long. I knocked him out in the first round.
(United Press International Photo)

May 20, 1965: the night the Tiger tamed the Hurricane. Here I am with
Dick Tiger just after the fight.
(*Sports Illustrated* photo by Herb Scharfman, © Time, Inc.)

"Nigi"—the man with a beautiful beard—as a Zulu chief in Johannesburg,
South Africa, after I KO'd Joe Ngidi in the second round on September
18, 1965.

John Artis and I leaving the Passaic County Courthouse after sentencing, June 29, 1967.
(Wide World Photos)

What would your verdict be? Check out the two people in this picture and the one above against the description of the killers that Bradley first gave to the grand jury: two thin, light-skinned Negroes, both about five feet, eleven inches?

In my "house" at Rahway State Prison, November 1973.   (Mel Williamson)

my rescue, and incensed that he seemed to think I'd give up behind his cheap, bullshit psychology.

"Well, did you go through all of that just to come here and get yourself killed?"

I still wouldn't answer him.

The young officer, Robert T. O'Keefe was his name, had a deep voice that was harsh and gentle at the same time, with just a touch of the Irish in his tone. A little taller than myself, he was about three or four years older, clean-shaven, and ruddy. He looked like he could have come straight out of a Marine recruiting billboard. His uniform was even tailored just so. His slate-blue eyes, magnified by thick-rimmed bifocals, seemed to go from gentleness to fiery fervor and back again, but steadily reflected a calm certainty.

"Why don't you answer me, Carter!" he snapped, losing control for a moment. "All I'm trying to do is help you, man. This is for you, not me; maybe we can get this thing straightened out."

I looked at O'Keefe. I wondered if the guy could be for real, or if he was just bullshitting. I told myself to make one last effort at civilized communication. Then I was going to stop talking forever.

"Awright," I nodded to him. "Let's start with this: what the fuck am I doing in this place? Let's just try that on for size!"

O'Keefe frowned as though he didn't know where I was coming from. "What are you talking about?" he asked, looking genuinely confused. "I thought the problem was about you not wearing the short pants. What do you mean, what are you doing here?"

I watched his forehead contract, and decided that he was honestly interested in what was going down, but didn't understand yet what it was.

"I mean: why am I here?" I wanted to know. "Why are you people holding me here? I didn't commit no crime, and didn't no court send me here, either! So what the fuck am I doing here? That's what I wanta know!"

The man flushed. Different expressions flitted across his face— doubt, a sense of urgency, anger. He scratched his head in bewilderment.

"Well, that's new to me." He paused, looking thoughtfully at nothing in particular. "But I'm sure there's got to be some mistake here someplace," he said, "and that shouldn't be too hard to straighten out. So if you'll just cool down for a second, I'll see what the 'old man' has got to say about this. Will you accept that?"

When I nodded my head, he went to the telephone. Hastily dialing a number, he spoke rapidly and with authority to whoever was listening on the other end. In the hush that followed, I remained at the top of the stairs. I knew my very life was at stake.

When O'Keefe returned from arguing my fate across the telephone wires, he brought back the news that Mr. Goodman, the superintendent, wanted them to bring me to the Control Point immediately. I shuddered, inwardly, relieved to be free of the burden of deciding in which direction I should next proceed, knowing that the wrong decision could finish me.

We all trooped out of the cottage and headed towards the administration building. Ten club-toting cops and one pajama-clad inmate, marching in loose formation.

Run!—the idea dropped into my consciousness like a grenade, but I just shook my head and asked myself, "What's the use?" Outside, the skies had become overcast, mirroring my own thoughts exactly. I felt like a condemned man walking his proverbial last mile to the electric chair.

Upon our arrival at the administration building, I was quickly hustled through the Control Point and ushered into the superintendent's office. A tall, baldheaded man with white bushy brows and a thick white mustache that covered his entire upper lip was sitting behind a large desk. This was Mr. Goodman. His eyes were clear and intelligently alert within a youngish sort of face. But they fixed themselves in a deep scowl of displeasure when the room filled up with all those cops behind me. Then, perhaps taking into consideration all of the protection he had, he nodded his head.

"Sit down, Carter," he said, pursing his lips. He drummed his long fingertips on his desk.

I refused to sit. I wanted to stand.

For a long moment or so, Mr. Goodman continued to beat his fingers against the wood, indicating his desire to hear me out. I proceeded to run down my entire history. I told him why I had been sent to Jamesburg nine years before; why I had escaped and joined the Army; and then how the Paterson police had kidnapped me the night before and brought me to Annandale. By the time I had finished, naked emotion was racing through my voice, my heart was pounding furiously, and I could hear the roar of my own blood.

"You have my sympathy, Carter," Mr. Goodman stated, "but—"

"Sympathy!" I exploded. "I don't want your goddamn sympathy! That's only a word between shit and syphilis in the dictionary, and I ain't got any use for either one of them," I said. "I just wanta go home!"

"So you feel you shouldn't be here. Am I correct in stating that as your position?" he asked patiently.

"You goddamn right!" I snapped back. "Can you show me any kind of papers that says I *should* be here?"

He just sighed and leaned back in his chair, glancing quickly at the lieutenant standing somewhere behind me. He reached for his cigarettes and lit up, took a long, deep drag, and blew the smoke up towards the ceiling. Then he leaned forward across the desk, and squinted at my face as if trying to read my mind.

"Rubin?" he said. "I wasn't here when the Paterson authorities brought you in this morning, but you can bet that I've already chewed some asses for that incident, for accepting you here without the proper commitment papers, for the absence of a direct court order informing us to do so. And I—"

"Then what are you holding me here for?" I quickly wedged in. "If I don't belong in this goddamn place, then turn me aloose!"

Again he only sighed, but there was no compassion for me in his eyes. There was only a grim determination to do his job.

"Well, to be perfectly frank with you, Carter," he said gravely, "I've looked into what little information we have on file concerning your present situation. That is to say, at the escape warrant the police brought here with you this morning. And we—"

"But that ain't—" No good! is what I wanted to say.

"Then," he cut in, "we erroneously accepted that escape warrant as your commitment papers. There was, however, a little notation attached, a memorandum informing us that your records would be forwarded in the very near future. Until then, you are a ward of the state under my jurisdiction."

Goddamn! I stood there looking down at the floor and couldn't say a word, not a mammy-jammy thing. I felt so cold and worn, as if I had just been swallowed by a deep dark pit.

"But what am I going to do now?" I blurted out miserably. "I can't pull no more time in these places," I said, knowing it to be true. "What can I do to straighten this thing out?"

"Unfortunately, Carter, it's not up to you," Mr. Goodman said, shrugging his shoulders. "It is strictly my decision to make. But I don't mind telling you that it could very well be to your benefit if you walked a little softer around this institution. Because I'm the one who has to evaluate your records to see what to do about your situation. That is, whether to let you go back home—or to keep you here with us."

The bald-headed punk had me hooked just like he was a monkey on my back. He knew that. And almost casually, as if just having had the thought, he added, "Pending that time, Carter—and I'm sure you can appreciate my ticklish position—I'm duty-bound to keep you locked up until your records are made available. You do understand that, don't you?"

"What!" I exclaimed, after his words had sunk in. "Naw, hell no! I ain't going for none of that funny shit!" I promised him. "Naw— hell no! The only way you're going to get me to lock-up is to carry me there—dead!"

But the superintendent only smiled faintly, then went right back to drumming his fingers on the desk. His face had lost none of its firmness, but his eyes seemed to soften somewhat. The pause created a small silence.

"No, I've got to keep you locked up, Carter," he said finally, as if the decision had unburdened his soul. "I really have no other choice in the matter. Besides the trouble you've caused today, you still have a history of escape on your record, and there's nothing here to prevent you from doing the same thing again."

"But that was a long time ago," I told the man calmly, hoping to convince him with the soft voice of reason. "And then I only did it because I had a good reason for doing it."

Mr. Goodman looked at me as if to say, Who do you think you're kidding with that funny soft-soap shit? Boy, I've been deal- ing with you people too many years for me to fall for that stuff now. He pursed his lips again briefly before he spoke.

"And you have that very same reason for doing it now," he said, almost to himself. "No, I have no choice but to lock you up—and then maybe that will help keep you out of trouble's way too. Until I have decided this matter, I want you to be out of *everybody's* way. Maybe that will be the best thing for all of us.

"But, Rubin, I'll tell you what I will do," he proceeded thought- fully. "I'll give you my word that once I've had the opportunity to examine your record—and that if what you have told me here today is true—then I'll make it my business to do everything in my power to see that you are released immediately. I can't do any more than that."

"But only if I go to lock-up now, is that it?" I asked him.

"Yes, that's right," he said without hesitation, standing firm. "Only if you'll go to lock-up—and without giving us any more trouble."

How stupid could I have been? Armed with the superintendent's promise to check out my story, I now allowed myself to be led off to another jail for the second time in one short day. It was a jail within a jail, really—"the Graveyard," they called it. I should have known better. My formal education was equivalent to two years of college, but I had also obtained an informal bachelor's degree in the streets of oppression; a master's degree in man's inhumanity to man; and a Ph.D. in prison brutality. But the only thing my education had ever done for me, it seemed, was to inhibit my natural powers to survive, and leave me to fall prey to my most cunning enemies. For one week later Mr. Goodman was gone from Annandale, promoted right out of my life: he had become warden of Trenton State Prison.

The "Graveyard" cell Mr. Goodman had left me to roll around in was just that—a cold, empty hollow in a cement wall. Life inside it was filled with such starvation and a stench of human feces so vile it could have made Dachau seem like a hillbilly heaven.

I was provided with only the barest essentials: a filthy mattress was thrown on the floor for me to sleep on each night, and was snatched away before the sun rose; during the day the unyielding walls were my pillows, the cold floor my bed. The food, or rather the lack of it, invariably consisted of one mushy bowl of cold cereal in the morning for breakfast; a tiny, three-ounce scoop of unseasoned vegetables for lunch; and four slices of stale bread as a nightcap to hold me over till the next morning. But the worst part of living in the Graveyard was not the food. It was the screaming silence, the terrifying hush that pushed against my eardrums till the soundlessness had beaten them into a useless pulp.

One night I was awakened by a strange sound that I wasn't sure I'd actually heard or just dreamt, everything that had gone before seemed so vague and confused. The dim nightlight in the dungeon flicked its shallow glow across the cell's bars and cast eerily patterned shadows on the walls. I picked out the huddled mounds of other inmates sleeping near their doors to gather the heat.

"Psssst, hey Rube?" I definitely heard the whisper that time. It was coming from the cell facing mine. "Psssst, hey man, you awake?"

I rose and peered across the corridor, surprised to find another new inmate had been added to the Graveyard count while I was sleeping. It was "Little Hobo" Murray, a violent-tempered loud-mouth and a dark, good-looking boy who possessed a devilish talent for seeking out a person's weaknesses and then sinking his poisonous fangs deeply into the sores. But as I remembered him from Jamesburg, he was also one of the boys.

"Hey, Rube," he whispered softly (talking wasn't permitted up here), "you remember that helluva fight that you and the Wise brothers had back in Jamesburg, and then ya'll got sho 'nuff tight after that?" he said. "Do you remember that?"

"Yeah, I remember," I answered, and the memory of that encounter burned like fire in my mind. Those two brothers and I had fought like cats and dogs one day for I don't know how long without stopping, after one of them, Harry, had laughed at my stuttering. Because the two brothers were inseparable, I had to fight them both by myself. But after that we became fast friends.

They were the only people I have ever envied. Their close family ties represented everything I had always wanted for myself and my family: the energy to help one another; the spirit to stand by each other; the zeal for enjoying whatever we had together. This was what their mother, a deeply religious woman, had taught all of her children, and she never failed to show them as much love and understanding as she did for her God.

"And you remember Alfred Stokes, too?" Hobo went on more passionately. "Well, all three of them guys went to the electric chair since you been gone. They died this month last year."

"What!" I bellowed, shocked. I felt like my legs had been cut out from under me. I couldn't help moaning. Was this what was in store for all of us?

"Hey, Rube? You awright over there, man?" Hobo hissed loudly. "Say something, Jim—you awright?"

"Shut up down there!" the night watchman blasted. "Where the hell do you think you're at—the Waldorf or someplace?"

"Kiss my ass, you dumb motherfucker!" Hobo shouted right

back. "And if you open your mouth again tonight, you stupid sonofabitch, I'll piss on you in the morning!" He spat vilely. The jack-legged cop shut up.

I got myself back together, but this wretched bit of information had really knocked my socks off. I think I unconsciously made a vow to avenge those beautiful brothers, their mother, and their sisters. I wanted to kill the system that had destroyed them, and if I had to go out sitting in the electric chair like the rest of my friends seemed to be doing—then fuck it! I was going out smoking.

"Do you know how it happened, man?" I asked Hobo.

"Well, yeah," he said. "But if I thought it was going to do *that* to you, man, I would have kept my big mouth shut." He was lying through his teeth, loving every second of my misery.

"Don't hand me none of that funny shit, you black pop-eyed bastard!" I snapped at him. "Just tell me what I want to hear."

This was Hobo's big moment of glory. Finally, after all these years, the little bastard had got to the Rube—and his enjoyment affected him so greatly that he had to walk away from the door to keep from laughing in my face. He knew that if he had, I would have shot him down quicker than sickle cell anemia. But when he returned he was cool, he was sober-faced, and he started telling me the story.

"A few months after you escaped from the 'Burg,' Rube," he said, "maybe a little more than that—I can't remember exactly when—the cops in Elizabeth accused Harry and Albert and Alfred Stokes of stickin' up this fur joint and shooting somebody—a police sergeant," he said.

"Everybody we know claims that there were no witnesses to the crime—but the cop died—and they tricked Harry," Hobo explained. "That's all I know about it—except that when it was time for them to die, Harry wanted to be first. But his brother wouldn't let him. Albert told Harry that he was the oldest, so he'd go first. He'd pave the way for Harry, and then be waiting for him on the other side."

I sat there, enveloped in anger, and cried like a baby. This kind of treachery was the thing that I had fought against all my life: the legal lynching of black people.

"But wait, Rube, that's not all." Hobo had to add his own nasty dig into my misery. "Sconion-Eyed Jones went the same way too! Last September the twentieth. He killed a white fag and they burned him for it," Hobo said, spitting disgustedly on the floor. "Now ain't that a bunch of shit? Man, I'm getting mad just thinking about it! I'm going to sleep."

But I didn't sleep much that night, or many other nights that followed, either. I found out that my brand-new car had been repossessed, that Jody had got my gal (which only showed me that I'd never had her in the first place), and to put the sweet icing of reality on top of my fruitcake of frustration, Uncle Sam sent me a message saying that I had forfeited my rights to his G.I. Bill for entering the Armed Services illegally. What a swift kick in the ass that was.

Finally my day came—that bright, beautiful morning when it was time for me to go home. A brutal, ugly year of wasted energy had gone out of my life. Ten long, worthless months of bitter frustration had blown everything I had achieved, and had tickled my old animosity back to life. On that Tuesday morning when Annandale set me free, they might not have known it (or maybe they did), but they had just unleashed a walking, ticking, short-fused time bomb set to explode on contact with an unsuspecting public. A society which fooled itself into believing that this miniature penitentiary sitting in the hills of its community was really an honest-to-God rehabilitation center.

My mind was in turmoil. I didn't know where I was going, or even where I was at. I didn't even know which way was home, I was so lost, destined to come back to jail even before I had a chance to get started. I had no money in my pocket, and no job waiting for me when I got home. I couldn't help but become just another statistic that gathered dust in the record halls of recidivism.

Back in Paterson, I immediately fell into a deep depression. I was ashamed I had been back to jail again, and humiliated at being a pauper, after having lived like a king for a while. All I did now was go to the job I'd gotten in a plastics factory, come home, eat, sleep, and go back to work again. I was a vegetable, just barely going through the motions of existence.

Nothing seemed to matter to me anymore. I had even stopped talking again. But then, late one night when I was walking home from work, a long, sleek black Cadillac screeched up behind me with a rubber-burning squeal.

"Hey, Blackie!" a jeering voice called out spitefully. "How's your sweet-looking black momma, boy!"

That was it. I spun around and leaped off the curb toward the sarcastic cracker motherfucker. Snatching open the car door, I reached in ready to deliver a bone-crunching knuckle sandwich. I caught myself just in time. There sat my old Jamesburg buddy Little A, still grinning like a Cheshire cat and looking blacker and stronger than ever.

His face was more handsome and mature, the African features more refined, but the ominous scowl was still there, just more serious. His white teeth, so perfectly formed and so even, gleamed against the backdrop of his dark complexion. His black, snapping eyes glinted like bits of obsidian in the bright glare of the interior car light.

"How the hell are you, ugly?" he laughed. "Man, I've been looking for you ever since I heard that you were home from the joint. Get in, nigger; we got a whole lot of rapping to do."

Little A looked ever better from close up. He was dressed to kill in a Hart, Schaffner & Marx's, and in the soft glow of the dashboard his handsome face was dust-colored and smooth as silk. His immaculate appearance, compared to my own, only made me feel that much more ashamed and shabby. But from that night on, he and I became almost inseparable companions.

We started hanging out in Hogan's—the players' lounge, so to speak—where all the half-assed pimps and hustlers, pool sharks, and would-be gangsters thrive in every black community. We would sit there and listen to the "big shots" rap about how much bread they pulled in off the streets every day from their mud-stomping prostitutes, and how many thousands of kickback dollars they had to pay to some graft-taking cop to stay in business. Or how much money they had paid for their fancy homes out in the suburbs and for their custom-made hogs.

I would sit there listening to these lying old bastards and be really smoking sometimes. I knew they were full of shit—talking through their hats—but still I was fascinated by their voices, held in thrall by their diamonds, and captured by the huge bundles of money that nonchalantly kept exchanging hands. Although they were nasty and sometimes even vicious to the community, life was still good to these men. Even the fading sunlight played the game with them, reflecting the sheeny luster off their shoes and onto their expensive clothes. Their silk suits shone like new money.

When Little A and I left Hogan's in the early evening of July 1, 1957, full of the holy spirits and talking heap-plenty o' shit, right then I was in the best mood that I could remember being in since I was kidnapped a year before. Everything was all right again. Not a worry in the world. Life was beautiful to me, and never mind if I had to go to work tonight, I still felt good. Then out of the clear blue sky, without rhyme or reason, I snatched a woman's pocket-book—right there in broad daylight.

Now ain't that a bitch!

I don't know why I did it. With my pockets loaded down, jam-packed full of my own money, it was the most dastardly thing I'd ever done, I simply snatched that poor lady's purse and ran like hell—laughing, no less. I guess it was supposed to be funny. But I have always wished since then that someone who had seen me would have blown my fucking brains out right then and there, because that incident—that woman, and that pocketbook—remains the most humiliating moment of my life. The woman's name was Mrs. E. Deary—a black woman!

Little A ran with me. But since I really didn't know why I had done what I was doing, he couldn't have known what was jumping off. But like I said, he ran with me, and no questions were asked. That was his mistake. Because down the street farther, still giddy with my folly, I hit a man. And still on the run from the first shameful deed, now compounded by this second, I went hog-wild and did it again!

Finally we stopped running and parted company for the night. Little A still hadn't said anything about what I had done, but just before he split he looked at me kinda funny-like, as if to say, Nigger, what in hell is wrong with you? Are you losing your goddamn mind or something? But he didn't say anything—and I couldn't. I was too ashamed. I felt like a stinking hypocrite. With a *friend* like me to help him along, Little A sure didn't need any enemies! I was glad when he dropped me off at work. He was too, I suppose.

Horizontal Plastics—the manufacturer for whom I was working —was a dynamic affair in the Riverside section of Paterson. It was an enormous place, with several hundred men working around the clock, carefully attending the many intricate machines that baked, rolled, and molded raw synthetics into plastic bags and other pliable items. The work wasn't hard, and it was steady.

The towering platforms from which we worked the machines over the smoldering furnaces easily scaled up to thirty or forty feet off the floor; so it wasn't hard for me to see when three or four cops, headed by a black detective named Bobby Ward, tried to slip into the building unnoticed, to arrest me. They didn't surprise me at all. The only thing that really puzzled me was why it had taken them so long to get there. Paterson was full of stool pigeons, and everybody in the neighborhood had witnessed the stupid shit that I did. No, they didn't surprise me when they finally arrived; on the contrary, I was glad.

Two weeks later Little A and I copped out to the charges.

A week after that we were in Trenton State Prison—serving three to nine years.

THE TWELFTH ROUND

Prison Is a Place Called Hell

Trenton State Prison is a nasty, stinking, medieval cubbyhole that was built in 1849 for noncitizens and mules, eight years before the Supreme Kangaroo Court under Chief Racist Taney declared the black man in America should not be considered a citizen of these United States.* It was located right in the heart of the state's Capitol District, in the county of Mercer, and on what is now the property of millionairess Mary G. Roebling. Its ugly gray walls were huge, high, and indestructible, though the black-slated rooftops of the buildings somehow managed to lift their mangy heads up over the towering barricades.

At the entrance gate I could sense the depravity, violence, and racial bigotry within. Everything about it was wrong: from the sissified cops looking up my ass for make-believe contraband to their fingering my swipe for more contraband, the whole place seemed plagued by faggotry and ravaged by deep pockets of corruption.

During the search, Little A's gaze met mine, and I knew that we had finally reached the bottom of the barrel. After this blatant display of disrespect for our bodies and their privates, I felt there could be nothing else worse in the world, except maybe death.

I had heard many grim stories told about Trenton State Prison and its monstrous racism before, and I soon found out that none were wilder or worse than the truth. As soon as Little A and I had been processed through the receiving gate and were inside the prison proper, we were hit by an impalpable wall of unmitigated musk. The air was fouled by the rancid odor of stale feces and

---

* The *Dred Scott* decision. It was handed down by the United States Supreme Court on March 6, 1857, Chief Justice Taney presiding. Dred Scott was a slave who had been taken into free territory, and maintained that he was therefore a free man when brought again into slave territory. But the Court ruled that a Negro was not a citizen of the United States and therefore could not sue in the courts.

mildewed humans, and intensified by the rotten pungency of men sitting idle too long on the shelves, like fetid cans of black caviar. Sitting there doing nothing, killing time, wasting away the years, and growing old, rotten, and stale against life, against people.

We came in at a place called the Center, the focal point of the institution. It was a large and barren, many-times-painted area with five iron gates leading to the seven wings of the jail. All traffic had to pass through this rotunda, and, standing there on an honest-to-God star, flushed with the arrogance of his authority and directing the flow of incarcerated humanity like a traffic cop downtown, was a big, burly, blue-uniformed guard with a blackjack about the size of a small oak tree.

"Hold it up, over there!" he shouted, raising the club for us to stop. "Awright, Two Wing coming out! Move it out, Two Wing!" Then—

"Goddammit! I said hold it up over there, Seven Wing! Can't you fuckin' cons understand English? Youse too, Four Wing! Hold it up over there! Jesus fuckin' Christ!" the man snorted derisively.

And finally—

"Awright, Seven Wing, move it out! Get your hands out of your pockets! Tuck those shirttails in! Stay in line! Move it out!" he ordered. Spinning around then, he shouted, "Hey, Six Wing! Hold it up over there, you fuckin' guys! Jesus fuckin' Christ!" he swore, as if he just couldn't stand it anymore. This would go on day after day, year after year. And he loved every little bit of it.

Like every other jail in New Jersey, Trenton State Prison had its quarantine area, and that's where we were headed—to One Wing. A dimly lit dungeon of about one hundred cells standing side by side on top of each other, it was a huge, run-down warehouse for storing humans away like Christmas parcels. My slot numbered 337 to the fourth power—a dingy little cubbyhole on the fourth floor with a bare iron slat welded to the wall for a bed. Lying in the corner was a small, once-white, cruddy porcelain sink that had died a miserable death of a fractured basin years before.

Goddamn! I thought to myself. There wasn't even a mattress to cover the slat.

After a few minutes we were pulled back out of our cells to have our heads shaved clean and our bodies measured for stripes (though we only had to wear stripes on our pants).

Then we had to march to another part of the jail, where we filled our homemade mattress covers with some moldy straw that we found in a rat-infested bin. We worked up a sweat shooing away the mice and stomping the straw and bugs into tiny bits and pieces until they were flat enough to lie on. These would be our mattresses.

Coming back through the narrow hallways shouldering these ungodly burdens of itchy straw, we cussed and fought tooth 'n' nail with the lice-infested bundles of shit every step of the way. We had to climb sideways up the three flights of stairs of our tier and beat the lumpish bedding through the cramped doorways of our cells. Man, shit! I was tired, and smelling like an angry bull. I needed a shower—bad! Instead, I was given a bucket of scalding hot water, then locked into my cell. Thus began my initiation into the weird ritual of "bird bathing."

"Dip and dunk," they called it. "Dip your towel, and with your soap you dunk, you scrub your tail in your own nasty funk."

There were no showers in the buildings. They were all outside, in an old, dilapidated shack that once had been used as a barn and was now converted into a fifty-stall showering shed. It was a faggot's heaven, a jailhouse punk's haven, a rape artist's happy hunting grounds—and a monument to the living hell the young kids in the joint had to suffer. Everyday, sometimes two or three times a day, some poor unsuspecting fool would get ripped off in the dense clouds of concealing steam. He would be stabbed in his back, then humped in his backside while the shower cop had *his* butt pressed against the wall and his senses shut off from the anguished cries. He was content with just protecting his own nasty ass.

My fifteen days in quarantine passed rather quickly. I was transferred from One Wing to Seven-Right, a predominantly black ghetto of the jail for hard-to-handle prisoners—and faggots—which had been the bloody arena of a riot in 1953. The Ku Klux Klan–minded guards, armed with machine guns, had stormed the tiers and killed everything in sight. The deep, mind-bending scars from the bullet holes were still visible in the repainted walls, the high ceilings, and even in the dented steel of the cages themselves. They still voiced their outrage at the holocaust that had swept through there like a mad broom, swallowing up lives like a greedy vacuum cleaner.

The wing had ten tiers, five floors on each side, and housed three hundred fifty men, thirty-five cells on each shelf, so to speak. It was operated by a noisy locking system that could open one cell at a time, or all of them together. It was *never* quiet in this building during the day. The heavy steel doors created enough racket to keep the living dead on the sharp edge of insanity.

Even so, I felt that I was lucky: I had a window in front of my cell, and that helped a lot. When the old man living next door to me happened to take a shit during the day, or maybe farted in his sleep at night, the window pulled the odor out into the streets and didn't push it down into my lungs. It was good for something else, too. From it I watched children go to school every day, saw them grow up from gangling, knock-kneed youngsters to switching, sophisticated young women and dapper young men. Their growing process fascinated me no end.

But life soon became a dreary ritual. Time inside dragged, though the months flew past my window at an alarming rate. Each morning, at six o'clock sharp, a nerve-shattering bell would blow me out of my bed, demanding I wash, shave, and clean up my cell. Two more bells would dispatch me off to eat. (Garbage! Shit!) Thirty-five minutes later—that's all I had—and another bell would order me to work, to make license plates or sew clothes, mop floors, or just plain lie idle in my cell for twenty-two hours a day.

Eight o'clock at night, after I had worked like a dog all day, the "quiet" bell would ring—no talking was allowed—and an hour or so later three more bells cut the lights off and tucked us into bed. Bells, bells, and more goddamn bells, that's all we heard all day long—bells, bells, them goddamn bells!

I took to constant brooding, which in jail is a dangerous thing. Deep brooding usually leads to loud grumbling, which then becomes plans of mayhem, which then, in anybody's book, becomes a bloody riot.

My hatred for the place and its people grew with each passing day. Discriminate hostility, always directed against the black population, masquerading around in a cloak of discretion, was the means by which racism was injected into prison life. The white inmates had the best of everything.

At the time I entered the penitentiary, the black inmates were locked into the violent throes of racial strife. They were demanding more black guards. The inmate population was eighty percent black, five percent Hispanic, and fifteen percent white, but only three black guards worked in the system. Meanwhile, a multitude of young white boys, who had very little schooling and whose only qualification was being cousin to somebody's uncle who held a high position in the bureaucracy of the administration, came and went through the prison employment system daily. "On-the-job training," they called it. Working piecemeal with their daddies, they dredged up the experience, the expertise for subduing some husky nigger with a stick to strap him into the electric chair.

The penitentiary was geared to making the black inmates rise to the heights of their own incompetencies—even in the protection of themselves. Once I heard somebody—Hasson, I think it was—say that a society that condones the murder of black Americans just because they are men enough to stand up and voice their opinions against a system that does not necessarily benefit them, is not a society at all but a penitentiary with a flag.

A black inmate named Jonesy was locked in the third cell down from my own. A big, bald-headed nigger whose nature was good, but whose expression was habitually wrapped up in the gloom of an embittered man's thoughts, he was set up one morning by the guards and stabbed to death by a bunch of Nazi crackers just because the prison administration was scared to death of him. Forty times the man was stabbed, and nobody was ever prosecuted for the crime. But you let a black man pull a stunt like that, and if they didn't kill him right then, they'd take his dumb ass out to court and add fifty more years to his time. White inmates didn't get an extra day for daily murder.

Such was the nature of Trenton State Prison. It even surrounded its fags with this protective cloak. One day, while up in the movies, when everything was quiet and still, a young black jitterbug called Mother Herb started whupping on his faggot's ass—which was white. That afternoon, Moko Reilly—a good-doing dude who was dedicated to the awesome proposition of peace and was studying law to lift the burden of sixty-five years off his back—went to Mother Herb and told him about the rumor going around that if he (Mother Herb) went out to the yard that afternoon, the white boys would kill him for what he had done to his faggot that morning.

But Mother Herb didn't believe Moko, which only tended to prove his suicidal inclinations, since everybody knew that Moko Reilly didn't play. So Mother Herb went out in the yard anyway. He died on his way back in, lying on a stretcher with his guts hanging out of his ripped-open stomach.

Jail made these men exactly what they were: regimented killing

machines, wicked and deadly and utterly without mercy. They
were hard men who asked for no breaks and gave none in return. I
had to become that way too, to get my air space.

But inside me I felt a need to get something better for myself
than this continual violence. I knew I would never leave this place
of tortured souls alive unless I could change my attitude, reorder
my priorities, and rechannel all aimlessly spent energy. I concluded
that the only thing I really knew how to do was to fight. I was
geared for that. Even born to it, I sometimes felt. So I decided to
give up all of the worthless luxuries that most of the inmates craved
—the cunt books, the fags, the cigarettes, the movies—and I made
up my mind to stop talking again.

In jail, boredom was an inescapable fact of daily life—and an
inmate's worst enemy. It was with boxing that I began to fight this
boredom, this killer adversary, and then everything fell into place
like the picked tumblers of an opened safe. I lived only from day to
day, not even thinking about tomorrow, watching the lonely sun-
sets flame and die outside my window. I watched the dawns come,
saw the morning stir with its first light, while the vicious community inside the walls remained a stifling jungle of hate.

In the yard, in the mess hall, everywhere I went, I demanded to
be left alone. I let my eyes do my talking: I made them glitter like
hot coals. They foreclosed on any communication and made my
message perfectly clear in no uncertain terms: "Leave me alone,
motherfucker, or I'll kill you, dead!"

I even quit my job in the slave quarters of the tailor shop, and
refused to work anywhere else in the penitentiary. At eleven cents
a day they could stick their job up their motherfucking ass! I had
no time for that bullshit. I was trying to get myself together for the
streets. My training program began at four o'clock every morning
when the church bells across the street would chime. While everybody else was sleeping and the scurrying rats were still sneaking in
and out of the roach-infested cells to steal the inmates' bread, I
would get down on the floor and knock out five thousand push-
ups—in sets of a hundred each—before the wake-up bells rang.
And that only started my day.

Once back from the mess hall I would sit down at my desk and
read Sigmund Freud, C. G. Jung, and Machiavelli until the slop in
my stomach had digested enough not to cramp me up with a death-
dealing garbage attack. Then I would put my books away and

furiously shadowbox for a solid hour. I worked in front of my mirror, steaming, sweat popping off my bald head like a wet dog shaking its fur. I followed this with sit-ups, deep knee-bends, and more push-ups. By the time I finished, the working men would be straggling in for lunch, so I'd lay down and wait until the yard was called out after chow, then go outside to finish it up.

The prison's yard was a little fortress in itself, barren-looking, ominous, a death trap if anything untoward should happen in it. The Big Dusty, we called it. An empty space of hard-packed dirt that was washed down in oil each day to keep the soil from blowing away, it was a steel-enforced, four-walled enclosure that measured an even furlong when you walked the edges, and was covered by four disheartening gun towers. Walk eight times around and you had a solid mile of shotguns loaded down with double-ought bucks, cocked and waiting, ready to blow your brains out at the slightest provocation.

In the summertime no air stirred in the quadrangle. It was hot, stifling hot, and tempers flared quickly. On the east wall five hand-ball courts were painted; the dominoes and the checkerboards were on the north side. Weight lifters took the western corner, prize fighters the southern, and right smack-dab in the middle of it all was the intramural softball field, where league games were played daily.

The whole stupid thing was a screaming mass of calculated confusion. Even Barnum and Bailey's three-ring circus was better organized than the activities in the yard, although they certainly didn't have the assortment of talent displayed here. Like the jailhouse pimps, for instance. They leaned against the wall with their silk handkerchiefs out and ready to swoop down on that speck of dust that had the colossal gall to land on their fifty-dollar Stacy Adams, or their thirty-dollar Dino shirts—which were pressed down sharp as a mosquito's peter in starched khaki trousers that had a black stripe down each side.

The pimps got in everybody's way. They stood on the wall surrounded by giggling stables of faggots who clustered all over them and picked their faces and ran their slippery fingers through conk-olene hairdos, ohhhing and ahhhing about how sharp they got their daddies looking today, kissing on them, playing with their swipes, promising them to trick harder the next day so they could buy Daddy another pair of new shoes the next week.

Moving down the wall a little farther you had the "big-time spenders," the penny-ante racketeers. They were the grocery conglomerates of the jail, the cigarette loan-sharkers who talked millions, smoked Bull Durham, and rhapsodized out of the sides of their mouths about the block-long Cadillacs, the five-hundred-dollar suits, and the high-priced call girls that they still had hustling for them out on the streets. With the very next breath, of course, they'd ask you to save them a drag on your cigarette butt. It was a pathetic sight, because everybody out there was for real, serious to the point of death. There was no playing in this penitentiary.

Prison was big business to these guys. On the streets they were nothing. But here, cluttered among the real losers, their glib abilities to phantasmagorize their crimes made them kings. They might have been busted for snatching a pocketbook, the same way I was, but by the time they got finished telling the story, the poor woman had become a bank carrier, her purse the bank's total receipts, and her welfare check was a hundred thousand grand.

Most of these guys lived in a dream world. They simply refused to accept the bitter truth of only being sad and weakly human. Their greed, their ambitions, or their need for some quick money always led them astray. But they were really harmless people—men who had been forced to live too long under a low profile and then suddenly found themselves institutionalized. Physically alert, but mentally dead, they were more comfortable in jail than anywhere else.

But now we come to the big honchos in the joint—the killers, the gamblers, the organizers of the prison sports, the fight managers, the boxing promoters—all the people who really controlled the big money. These were usually quiet types—and they took care of their business on the sly. They bought and sold prison officials, guards, ballplayers, prize fighters, and anything else they wanted like it was going out of style. To them everybody had a price.

They held boxing matches every day for big, big money. Murderous, blood-gushing brawls, they made the TV fights look like kindergarten romps. But the champs of each division had to defend their titles only once a week, on the weekends, when all the inmates could get out into the yard. This was the great extravaganza of the week. A lot of money, cigarettes, and food was won and lost by the mere flick of a gloved hand. So were many lives.

For my first couple of months behind these turbulent walls, I would begin to jog as soon as I was searched and could step out into the yard. Then I would run like a maniac from yard-out until they called yard-back-in, a period of about two and a half hours. I covered more than sixteen miles, running and exercising, jumping rope and shadowboxing, but I didn't want to put the gloves on yet. I didn't think I was ready.

As good as I was, I *knew* I wasn't ready yet. They had some mean mister humdingers out there in those boxing gloves, some real bad motorscooters! I mean, the kind that could make you dance bowlegged, put you to sleep, make you dream, and then wake you back up before you knew you was even hit. Jimmy Isler! Booker Washington! Donald Bird! Fitzgerald! Teddy Roberts! Shannon! Northfleet! Chuck Carter! Bo Jingles! All of them, some bad motherfuckers! And yet, they weren't what I was worried about.

It was the sorry fact that I was born a natural light-middleweight —a hundred and fifty pounds, even if I stuffed myself. Too heavy to be a welterweight, too light to be a middleweight, and too damn short to be anything else. But, proud fool that I am, my aspirations scaled the heights of insanity and rested on the idea of becoming the "heavyweight" champ of this jungle. I wasn't satisfied with just one measly little boxing title. (I never could do anything in moderation.) I was too greedy for that. I wanted them all! And I was working hard to achieve that goal.

When the yard period was over, still running, I would head straight for the shower shed and grab a quick shower, wash my clothes, and go back to my cell. I'd lay down for a few minutes, until the working men dragged in at four, and then go back out in the yard to train some more (in the summer we had two yard periods), beating the heavy bag this time, the speed bag, and heaving the medicine ball. I always watched the other fighters work, familiarizing myself with their styles and mistakes, cataloging their habits and inclinations. It was like being in the Army all over again, only this atmosphere was a thousand times more intense. Stretchers were always on the move out here, scooping up the battered fighters and rushing them, quivering and unconscious, to the infirmary, where they would wake up and come right back out for some more.

At the end of the long hard day, when everything had quieted down and cooled off after chow, I would climb right back into my books. Studying long and hard, I learned new things about myself, and about other people. I was determined to grow rather than become stagnated and conform to the degraded ways that were this penitentiary's wont.

Sometimes I would just talk with Mr. Summers, my next-door neighbor. He was an easygoing, soft-spoken old man who'd been locked up in this hellhole for twenty years or more. For murder, they said. He had caught his wife in bed with a white man—the sheriff—and had killed them both. But he went to trial only for wiping out the cracker. They didn't even try to prosecute him for his wife.

Mr. Summers was a good old man, a God-fearing Christian who really and truly didn't belong in jail, but every time he went up to see the parole board the stinking bastards would hit him with two more years, and he would cry like a baby. He was a kind, experience-smart, humble old man, and I took to him like he was my father.

He used to talk about how the personality of the prison had changed since teenagers started coming into the jail, and how he found it difficult to establish any meaningful relationships with them. They had no respect for their elders, he would say. These were new-fangled people to him. Much different from the children he had left in South Jersey in 1936, and he couldn't understand this new breed of viciousness. His closest friends were all dead, so he didn't try to cultivate any new ones. His married daughter was his only link to the past, and he hadn't seen her in twenty years. But she was still his hope, his salvation, his only real reason for living. He said he prayed to God every night that one day she would come and whisk him away from Trenton before he died. I think we all feared dying in jail.

Most of my conversations with Mr. Summers would be ended rather abruptly by the ringing of the "quiet" bell in the wing. Packing up my books, I would then get into the remaining exercises of my day: more push-ups, sit-ups, and more shadowboxing. Armed with the other fighters' mistakes of the day, the ones I had seen in the afternoon, I would work to cash in on their errors.

Thus, a normal day in prison for me meant working myself down into an exhausted stupor to drive the ever-haunting whammies away from my destiny. I stayed away from the jailhouse politics, and left the flat-backing faggots strictly to their swipeswapping pimps. I dreamed sweet dreams of my future in prize fighting, of big bucks and good times, instead of always thinking about my swipe, which should have been reason enough to send me home right then.

Little A, who shouldn't have ever gone in in the first place, got out on parole two years before I did.

Two of the hardest things about being in jail are, first, that you can never make a decision for yourself—every one, from the time to eat or sleep, walk, talk or even breathe, is already made up for you; the only thing that is yours to decide, which requires no deep concentration, is whether or not to stand up or sit down in your cell.

The other thing is the unreasonable absence of women. We inmates sit in prison and listen to the President of these United States fly all over the world in search of a mate for a jive-ass gorilla in some zoo, but for us, the people in his prisons, he doesn't do a goddamn thing! Our position as humans is relegated to one inferior to that of the wildest beast.

I had never been able to understand what motivated this kind of thinking. But I soon found out. Great Googamoogoa, did I find out! Almost as soon as I walked through the doors of Trenton State Prison. Here were two hard-looking, dewy-eyed sissies straining against each other, kissing passionately in a hidden nook of the jail; a bald-headed, muscular black man withdrawing his oversized swipe from the flushed anus of a skinny, freckled-back white boy in a shower stall; two convicts sitting together in the movies, one of them with his hand in the cut-out pockets of the other one's pants, jerking him off; a black hardcore tough guy titillating the nasty ass of a Confederate flag-tattooed cracker in the Catholic chaplain's office with his nasty tongue; a jailhouse pimp sucking his fag's dick in the officers' locker room during mess. . . . Did I find out?

Jesus fucking Christ!

Faggots and fuck-boys were plentiful in this joint. They proliferated here unchecked. In fact, they owned the goddamn place. This was the prison's little secret of control—the faggot weaponry! These vicious, gutter-sniping, he-shes were ten thousand times more deadly to the men in the jail than sickle cell anemia was to the entire black population on the streets.

They prowled the jail unmolested, searching for a victim. They picked out the weak and the unstable—the ones who were always looking to get their hips out of hock. Gradually, through a series of flip-flopping sex orgies, the fags would strip the masculinity from their victims and turn them into whores. To sisters! Swap-out partners, I mean. Just a few more vicious dick-chewing freaks to help further terrorize the jail.

Swishing their tight, saucy, hip-hugging asses all over the penitentiary, they strutted around looking like Zsa Zsa Gabor in processed hairdos, wearing bright red lipstick and pink panties, dark eye shadow and padded brassieres. The *men* in the jail, meanwhile, knew they had better not be caught dead going too long without shaving, much less wearing a mustache. You had to be just plain crazy to even *think* about a beard. Any prisoner who was caught walking the jail with hair growing on his face, the administration surmised, was either a goddamn fool or trying to assert his manhood. So they would jump on that poor sucker and beat his brains out, while the good-doing "mommas" would lay back and dig it all, laughing, still swishing their nasty asses and glorifying in the fact that they were queens of a big-dick kingdom that had no kings!

If there was a fight going on someplace, all you had to do was just look for the nearest fag to be behind it all; if somebody gambled and won a lot of cigarettes, go down to the faggot's tier and you'd find the winner and his cigarette under the bed buying some head, or getting fucked; if somebody got killed in the jail, either a fag did it, or another inmate "shanked" a fag's husband to have the fag for himself. If the administration couldn't control an inmate in the joint, they'd give him a fuck-boy to calm him down, and use him as a wedge; it was a warning to him to be cool, to slow down before they snatched his fag away, or killed him.

The powers that were didn't care if they promoted more crime by committing crimes themselves, instituting uncivilized behavior with uncivilized actions—the very same traits in us the public was paying them to rehabilitate. The real tragedy of it was that some of these guys could have been saved. With just a little bit of help they could have been restored to society as valuable citizens at little or no expense. But the officials didn't care if they used impatience to curb our impatience, or overbearing force to suppress our wills, or abuse and degradation to eliminate our insubordination, and this browbeating humiliation affected me strongly. I could almost understand why men leaving this penitentiary went out on the streets and at the first sign of danger, went berserk. At the first sign of hostility from the law, they became savage animals—men to be hunted down and ruthlessly destroyed.

They'd been locked away in this torture chamber for too long, living under the constant threat of death, and waking up in the middle of the night to the excruciating cries of some poor devil getting his brains knocked out. They knew that it could very well be themselves next, and they just couldn't take any more of it. All the days, weeks, months, and years of being enslaved under this nigger-hating Nazi mentality and painful passivity would cut loose in their minds, and they just naturally went for broke.

And I could dig it! Never before in my life had I been so sure what my reaction would be to anything violent that jumped off, such as a riot, or a fight, or some kind of altercation with the cops. I thought a lot about it, even dreamed about it sometimes, and I came to the conclusion that I would probably be killed—shot down like a dog mad with rabies. Because I would fight! I would have to.

Quiet rage became my constant companion. It formed, crystal-like, against a solid backdrop of persistent helplessness, terror, and humiliation. It was mind-bending! But one day, out in the yard, it almost got away from me. I suddenly found myself caught up in the tight clutches of this feeling, experiencing a savage exhilaration that knew no bounds.

I was standing by the boxing ring, and saw a young jitterbug whup on my next-door neighbor, Mr. Summers. He was tarpapering the old man playfully and then viciously lashing out with sharp combinations to his head and body, taking pure advantage of his age.

Methodically slamming lefts and rights into Mr. Summers' stomach, the big nigger hurt him deeply, and laughed about it. The old man struggled vainly to fight back, swinging wildly but always missing, tripping over his own graceless feet. He scampered around the ring in an awkward, clumsy shuffle, trying to duck the stinging blows. He threw a frightened glance around at the crowd watching the slaughter, swallowed visibly, and then started backing away. His pain-distorted face was bathed in a slick sheen of cold sweat.

Mr. Summers was built small, a bantam-sized old man in his late fifties or early sixties. He was mostly skin and bone, and his pants hung down off his butt like a huge cape. The only thing that age hadn't caved in yet was his chest. Gray-haired and lean, he was brown-skinned and proud. He looked like a skinny "Uncle Ben" on a box of rice. But his dark eyes were still intelligently alive and flinty, still showing plenty of fire and glitter, though he mostly kept his feelings to himself.

He loved prize fighting dearly, having been a professional once himself, but his twenty years in the joint had stolen his dignity and bankrupted his spirits. It had preserved his health, his strong white teeth, and most of his kinky gray hair, but not his will.

"Whoooa! Hold on there, Mr. Summers!" I called, burrowing my way through the crowd and stepping in between the two men. My vision was blurred with both anger and sorrow. "Why don't you take these gloves off, ole buddy-buddy," I said softly, "before this nigger beats your brains out." Mr. Summers was standing there holding on to me for dear life, his face slack from exhaustion.

"Why don't you mind your own goddamn business!" the big jitterbug barked at me with the belligerence of a conqueror.

"Why don't you *kiss* my motherfucking ass!" I shot right back at him, suddenly gripped in a fit of rage. "If you want to box somebody, nigger, I'll box you! Or fight you! Or do anything else you wanna do, you punk motherfucker!" I said, and snatched the gloves from Mr. Summers.

The whole yard gathered around now.

"Bo Jingles" was the nigger's name. An old archenemy from Jamesburg, now he was the heavyweight champ of this joint. A tough guy, a loud-mouthed touch-off, utterly without scruples, vicious and petty, he was the nasty afterbirth of all the state institutions: a liar, a thief, a jailhouse drug addict; he was the ringleader of all the jitterbugs in the jail. Shorter than me by an inch or more, he had an ugly razor scar stitched all the way around his throat to his ear on the opposite side. Fat, black, and bald-headed, he talked like a little bitch—high and whining-like, with glowering eyes that narrowed down into slits. He gloried in just the thought of a fight. He was big-boned, fast, and full of raw power. But he was also full of shit.

We squared off, and I nailed him with a leaping left hook.

I mean, I thought I did. But he was quicker than a cat on his feet, and I missed. His hands were quicker yet, and he nailed *me* with a left hook of his own. The numbing impact ricocheted off my chin and swept my legs right out from under me. I thought that oomebody had sneaked up from behind me and tried to tear my head clean off. There had been no start to the punch that I could see—it just blurred out and hit me like a sledgehammer, and dropped me to my knees.

I stared down at the ground in a kind of awed wonder: the first punch of the fight, and I'm down on my knees. Goddamn! I pulled myself up out of the dirt and fell into my crouch, hands high and close together, and popped Bo Jingles in the mouth with a jab, then ducked as a whispering left hook zoomed over my head like a guided missile, unerringly controlled and right on target.

But I had his rhythm now, and he could take that left hook and stick it up his ass. I popped him again, and popped him twice more. When he moved that hooking arm I slammed across a straight right hand over the top of it and stopped him in his tracks. He blinked, grunted deeply, then shook his head like a stunned bull in a slaughterhouse when the hammer has only wounded its victim.

Bo Jingles even snorted like a bull. He straightened back up and shuffled flatfootedly forward. He faked a shot with his shiny head, then feinted a right hand, and fired off another sizzling left hook that burned me high on top of the head. But I came right back with a two-fist combination of my own, nailing him solidly in the ribs and his fat gut. It was unexpected; the air whooshed out of him in a loud rush. He bent over double and fell to his knees, then over on his side, clutching his stomach and gasping for breath.

I stood over him as he laid there moaning, and something invisible grabbed me, something from way down deep inside. Quiet fury stung my eyes. Numbly I realized that I wanted to beat this big nigger to death—not only for what he had done to Mr. Summers, but for what this ungodly penitentiary was doing to us all. It lent me the strength to help Bo Jingles up on his feet, and knock him right back down again.

The crowd was stunned by this unsportsmanlike display.

When Bo Jingles got back up once more, he was taking no chances. He let go with a desperate right hand, but I flicked it aside like a fly-swatter swatting a fly, and drove both my hands to his head. Then I rolled at the hips and slammed two more into his kidneys. He screamed, high-pitched, just like a little girl, doubled over and stumbled away, but I was right on top of him again, pounding away. I fought with arrogance now, with a brutal and ferocious desire to maim. At that particular time, the pleasure was not totally in the fighting. The real thrill could come only after I had completely annihilated this overgrown jitterbug.

I stalked him like he was a piece of raw meat and 1 a hungry animal, sending him dazed and reeling from right hands into vicious left hooks, then switching up again and slamming home another shot to his groin. He couldn't take that. He grunted heavily, and stood straight up, splay-footed. Then, in coldly calculated measures, I drove two more thundering right hands solidly home into his unprotected ribs. Next, I hooked one into his stomach, and poleaxed him in the head. He hit the ground as if struck dead by lightning, and sprawled out cold in the dirt.

"Stretcher up!" somebody called. "The Rube done got Bo Jingles!"

And that was only the beginning.

Looking at the faces of the unsavory crew around me, I saw awe, incredulity, and fear, but no hostility. I saw something else, too: tears of shame trickling down Mr. Summers' face. The old man had really been deeply hurt—you could see it in his skin. It was ashen, and beads of sweat glistened on his forehead. I could read the shame in him like it was large-type print written all over his face, and humiliation fit this proud old man about as well as a halo would fit the devil.

As I took my gloves off and walked over to where he was standing, his lips trembled weakly and his dark eyes looked tortured. He seemed close to revealing something terribly important. A shy, hesitant, embarrassed kind of smile crossed his face.

"You—you know what, Rube?" he gulped, his voice cracking. "I've just found out that I'm a tired old man." He snorted in disgust. "Been here in this rotten old penitentiary for so doggone long, doing nothing, that I never even thought about it before. It took what just happened for me to really find out. I—really— found—out—" We walked back to the wing together, and he rambled on like that all the way. I could find nothing at all to say to him.

Later on that night, as I lay in my cell thinking about the day gone by, I promised myself never to underestimate another man again. I had learned something else of importance too—that my aggressive style of fighting would mean coming in off the streets early, working hard, and planning well. It would be my own brute strength, not my boxing ability that would keep me—

"Hey, Rube, you busy over there?" It was Mr. Summers knocking on the steel wall separating our cells. That devilish old "quiet" bell hadn't rung yet, so I rolled off my bunk and stood up by the cell door.

"No, I ain't busy, Mr. Summers. What can I do for you?"

"Put your hand outside the door," he said. "I wanna show you something."

I squeezed my arm out through the bars and stretched it over to his cell. He gave me a paper bag and I pulled it back in. When I opened it up, I saw that it contained his whole month's pay from working in the tag shop making license plates: four packs of cigarettes, two bars of Lifebuoy soap, a packet of Gillette razor blades, and three candy bars—Fifth Avenues. His whole month's pay; his appreciation; the sweat off his brow.

"I can't take these things, Mr. Summers," I told him. I handed them back and tried to think up a good excuse why. I knew the hardships they represented. "Whatcha trying to do—start me to smoking?" I laughed, trying to make a joke out of the whole thing. (But accepting stuff from people in this jail was serious business.)

"I know you don't smoke, nigger!" Mr. Summers shot back briskly, ignoring my attempt to be funny. He was stone serious. "But I want you to have 'em anyway," he said. "Just keep 'em over there until I ask you for 'em. I don't want none of these thieving niggers breaking into my locker and stealing 'em on me."

I was feeling kind of peculiar about the old man now, more embarrassed by this overreaction of his than from what had actually happened out in the yard that afternoon. So I didn't say anything more to him, I just placed his valuables under lock 'n' key and let it go at that. But he wouldn't. After a short pause, he knocked on my wall again.

"You know what I was just thinking about over here, Rube?" he asked. I got up from my bed and stood by the door again.

"No," I answered. "What?"

"I was just thinking about myself over here, and how I used to be able to fight just like you once upon a time. Sho 'nuff," he said. "I did! But now I wake up this morning and find an old man in place of my old self, and I can't even hold my hands up anymore. I'm an old, tired, useless bum just feeding his face and getting in everybody's way."

"Shit!" I snorted. "You ain't old. That's just in your mind because of what happened today." But I knew I was lying, and so did he. He continued to reminisce right over my words.

"I can recollect the time, Rube," he said, "when I could have spanked that young rascal's hindparts and nine or ten more of his jitterbugs all put together. I coulda done that even if I was drunk off moonshine, on crutches and cross-eyed, blind or crippled or crazy! But now I can't even whup one of 'em," he said sadly. "Lord! Lord! Lord!"

There was a long pause, and then he continued as if he hadn't stopped at all. "I remember when I was down home," he said. "I useta beat the sun up out of bed every morning, and be halfway finished with my chores even before that doggone rooster would get his lazy butt up outa bed to crow. I would work all day and I never even *thought* about getting tired!" His voice almost broke into a sob.

"But now I gotta sleep all night and half the next day, just to get ready for tomorrow! Nawwww, Rube," he sighed, really sounding tired now, "there's no further use in me b-s'ing myself any longer. Today showed me up for exactly what I am—a useta-could-do-it, done-done-it, but cain't-do-it-no-more! I'm just a tired old man."

I could have cried. This fierce old man was still independent and proud, respected everybody and hated no one, not even his keepers. But this stifling penitentiary couldn't hold back the hands of time. He was an old, old man, and he had finally realized it.

At some point during that long, dark and lonely night, Mr. Summers' weariness must have given into the lassitude that all inmates are prone to, that deep pit of depression, and he hung it up. They found him the next morning hanging from his cell door, his earphone wires—which every inmate bought to listen to the institutional radio—carefully wrapped around his broken neck. His lips were puffy and swollen and curled up into a grotesque, enigmatic smile. He was a stomp-down trooper, even at the bitter end.

I looked at Mr. Summers lying there on that stretcher in disfigurement and death, and a steady threat of nausea trembled in my stomach. My accomplishments of the day before receded. Even the joy of being alive had ebbed.

As they carried him out, surrounded by a crew of cackling and apathetic guards, right there, I knew, went one hell of an old man, one hell of a human being. But also, I thought very sadly, one hell of a tortured and frustrated soul. He had been betrayed by the vicious ugliness of the times, murdered by the strangling tentacles of this penitentiary's deceptiveness.

Yesterday's final insult had driven the spirit right out of his soul, bowing his proud shoulders with a weight that he could no longer bear. Like one who has diminished from a great reputation in the past and is suddenly cut down to a lesser degree of respect. Mr. Summers had always been undersized in life, and in death he appeared even smaller yet. But looking at him lying on that stretcher that morning, my heart swelled with pride, and moisture stung my eyes. His inner stature was more than enough to make up the difference for his physical size. He was a big, big, little giant of a black man!

Two miserable days later, while I was still smarting from the tragedy of Mr. Summers' death, insult was added to injury when they brought in my childhood buddy and put him in the death house. It was Leroy "Lurkie" White of the old neighborhood Cherokees—the same treacherous little warlord who had helped me terrorize the city of Paterson when we were still hoodlum street kids.

Lurkie had been arrested and placed in the same cell with me and Little A in the Passaic County Jail four days before we had been sent to prison, and that's when I learned his story. In the early 1950s Lurkie had been drafted into the Army, and volunteered for the paratroopers. He was seriously wounded in Korea, and, like so many other thousands of soldiers injured at that time, he was fed a steady diet of alkaloid morphine to numb his pain.

But when Lurkie was brought back to the States, he was discharged straightaway out of his hospital bed, without the Army's even making a pretense of taking him off the drug. Back in civilian life, he soon found that he had come home not only with chunks of shrapnel still lodged in his body but with a hitchhiking habit as well. Uncle Sam had hooked him on dope.

When Lurkie had been a civilian for only a few days, he became sick—deathly sick. He couldn't eat, couldn't sleep, and pain racked his soul. Fever scorched his body and subjected it to ice-cold chills at the same time. Tears streaked down his face continuously, his nose wouldn't stop running, he couldn't control his bowels, and still he was ignorant of the hungry monkey who had thumbed a ride home with him and was now kicking his ass for food.

But the other drug addicts in the community knew. And with his money and their greedy connections, Lurkie was reduced to a pauper in a couple of weeks. Now he was hooked hopelessly on two kinds of drugs: the pain-killing morphine that his injuries craved, and a mind-bending heroin to feed his habit. It demanded more and more "scag," and whupped on his ass if he happened to miss its feeding time. So he started throwing bricks at the penitentiary—stealing!

It happened one day when his "jones" was down, and he was sick and needed a fix. He and another drug addict in the same condition held up a grocery store in the neighborhood. They entered the place with a gun in their hands, subdued the owner, took his money, and then locked him in a closet and left. In trying to free himself, the proprietor suffered a heart attack, and in falling, he struck his head against the edge of the door and died from the concussion.

Lurkie and his partner were arrested and convicted of first-degree murder. His partner, Boobie, got life imprisonment—and at this writing has gone home; Lurkie was sentenced to die in the electric chair.

In my cell the night he arrived, I reflected on the profusion of gross injustice all around me. I was distressed by Lurkie's situation, made all the more critical because the government did not have the patience to detoxify him while he was laid up in the hospital. It had me pacing the floor like a caged animal: three steps forward— that's all I had—then around and three steps back. I experienced the same dreadful anxiety I knew Lurkie must be feeling in the death house.

I resented the treacherous hell that being black had created for all of us—all of us. I stalked that cage all night long, seething in a fit of bitter rage, trying to find some logical answer to it all that I could cling to.

"Why?" I asked myself. "Why is it always that this electric chair seems to be stealing my friends away?" I didn't believe in God, but I *had* to have somebody to talk to.

But who?

Then it hit me like a straight right cross and a thundering left hook smashing into my solar plexus—the solution to all my problems—the electric chair! That was the enemy! That was the dirty bastard who was killing us all off, crackers notwithstanding. Why shouldn't I go and have a talk with that chair, I mused.

Maybe it would tell me something I didn't know. After all, I thought, my future may very well depend upon its wisdom; survival was always at the forefront of my thoughts.

I wondered whom I should approach with this mad idea. Nobody was supposed to be allowed on death row but those condemned to die, but this rule wasn't too strictly enforced at Trenton. Some guys were allowed to go in there all the time. So I decided to see a captain who was one of the few men in the prison system— with two other exceptions—who the inmates could go and talk to and be understood, without kissing somebody's ass. These men had recognized the fact that I was trying to do something to help myself with boxing, and had gone out of their way many times to assist me all they could, and my request—to go visit the electric chair—was granted this time as well.

The death house was a small cement-block building situated within the prison's walls, right outside the hospital—straight across from the iron door that led into the dusty yard, where all the inmates could see it. It was the administration's little reminder to us that chained-lightning death was always present, always at their beck and call. The horrible thought of such a death could be sensed everywhere. Knees had a tendency to quake whenever they passed by that building.

When the captain unlocked the grille-gate door to the death house that morning, my knees were shaking something fierce, and I had to close my eyes when I stepped into the dimly lit corridor of death row. The darkness hurt. The bright sunshine from outside and the sixty-watt light bulbs in there seemed to have no relationship to each other. Strange. It was like stepping out of one weird world that promised you no tomorrow, smack-dab into another that *guaranteed* you none. The change was startling; the noise inside, deafening. I couldn't even hear myself think.

The atmosphere was permeated with doom. It was everywhere —in the ceiling, on the floor. I could sense it, smell it, even almost touch it. Designed to hold only nineteen men, two tiers of the death house covered the whole right-hand side. The narrow passageway the captain and I were in ran straight as an arrow from the front door to the back door, a distance of about fifty feet. I started walking that storied "last mile" to the dark green door that opened onto the dreaded monster. I stopped sometimes, by some of the cells I passed on the way, and looked in at the men condemned to die.

There was Larry Hunt, Joe Grillo, Silvio DeVito, John Kolciek, Edgar Smith, Deathhouse Cleve, Lurkie White, and two others whom I didn't know. Each man looked at me strangely as I passed. It was a sorry sight, I can tell you that, seeing young men caged up like animals to die.

"Whatcha doing down here, Rube?" Lurkie asked, flashing that brilliant smile. "We hear tell that you're really killing 'em out there with the boxing gloves," he said proudly. "You shoulda been doing that years ago. But whatcha doing down here?"

I didn't answer him. I couldn't. I just walked away.

The execution chamber was a windowless little room, painted green, that broadened out to twenty by thirty feet to the left-hand side of the door as you walked in. Three or four wooden benches were placed in the back and to the left for spectators to witness the killings. Straight in front of them stood a waist-high partition that acted as a barrier between them and the murder. Sitting directly behind that, but elevated ten or twelve inches off the floor on a platform, was the electric chair. It glared at me like a wordless indictment.

Dark and impressive, it was still adorned in all of its grisly splendor: from the waistband to the leg straps to the arm braces, and even to the metal headgear, waiting for another poor soul to burn. Deep and dark, it was polished like mahogany, though it was made of black oak. All it needed now was to be hooked up to the telephone pole outside, and it would be ready to go—ready to snuff out another indigent life.

I stood there by the door real quiet-like (the captain had unlocked it and walked away—I imagine because there was nothing in the room that I could damage; everything was bolted down to the floor), in deep reverence for the haunted feeling of the place, and sensed the presence of many lost souls still flitting restlessly about the room: Harry and Albert Wise, Alfred Stokes, Sconion-Eyed Jones, Chink. My heart throbbed with an acute fear of the unknown. That ungodly monster was only twenty-five feet away from me. Oh, how I hated the bastard! But step by trembling step I crept up closer to it, watching, fearful of it, making damn sure that it didn't move. I thought I could hear a peculiar purr of anticipation emanating from it.

"Well, hello there, Rubin Carter," it seemed to say. "So you've finally come to see me, huh?"

I spun around. My heart was pounding like a trip hammer.

"Ooooooh, come off it, man!" the chair said in my mind. "You know you don't believe in ghosts. There's nobody else in this room but us. So turn around and face me, tough guy. Turn around and meet your master, punk!"

I eased back around slowly, on the brink of bolting out of there, and stared at that black monster in defiance. This thing just couldn't be! But then I saw it. A flaw in the chair, I suppose, some kind of defect in the grain of the wood that made a small pattern like a smile. This goddamn thing was laughing at me!

"Nowwww, that's better," I imagined I could hear it say. "I hate talking to people with their backs turned to me, don't you? Why don't you come over here and sit down, boy?" it seemed to be asking me. "You look kinda tired—like you been up all night. Come on. Have a seat—rest."

"I've *got* to be losing my mind!" I exploded.

"Naw-naw, now don't start that shit again!" its voice in my mind taunted. "All you tough guys come to see me sooner or later, and I've been waiting for you to come for a long time now, buddy! So come on. Sit down and take the load off your feet. I won't burn you—yet! Ha-ha-ha-ha-ha-ha—"

This was insane! I thought, that's it! I'm losing my mind! I'm going crazy! But I couldn't seem to stop myself.

"Ooooooh, come on, now—Rube! I was looking for much better things coming from you. Don't let me down now, man, and start getting scared like everybody else. Because we have something in common, you and me. People have been scared of us all our lives. So let's not be afraid of each other. You know that you came here to talk with me about Lurkie's plight. Admit it! Face up to the truth. Don't start being a punk, now! Ha-ha-ha-ha-ha-ha—"

"Shut up, goddammit!" I kicked viciously at the wooden leg of the chair, then hawked a glob of spit on the seat like the foul scab that it was. But I only heard more laughter.

"See! See! That's why I'm gonna get you, nigger!" it seemed to say. "Just like I got all the rest of your friends. Because you've got spirit, boy—hot spirit! Ha-ha-ha-ha. I get all the tough guys like you. Remember Sconion-Eyed Jones? And Chink? I got them, didn't I? Tough guy, I betcha I get you, too!"

I couldn't take it no more. The sweat was pouring off my face and soaking into my shirt, plastering it to my chest like a second skin. I despised that black monster with every beat of my heart, with every breath I drew, with every hateful thought of vengeance that I could possibly work up. I looked wildly around the room in search of a weapon to smash this thing—anything! I was going to crush this crazy maddening mother into harmless splinters, into toothpicks, if I could. Cold fury had swept my mind.

"Ha-ha-ha-ha-ha-ha—just look at yourself, boy!" I could imagine it crackle. "Now you're trying to find something to destroy me with, to kill *me*, if you can! Ha-ha-ha-ha. But the State won't let you hurt me, fool! I'm the salve that soothes their consciences. I get rid of all you bad niggers they're too scared to get rid of themselves. Ha-ha-ha-ha—"

Low venomous growls started out from my throat. "So you're gonna get me too, huh?" I screamed, furious at everything in the room being nailed down to the floor. So I took my Johnson out, and pissed all over that greasy monster.

"Here! You want me?" I said to it. "Take that! Now you got me! Here—take some more of me!" And I stood there pissing on that ungodly thing until my bladder was completely emptied.

"Ahhhhh, that's what I like about you, boy—the fight!" the drenched chair seemed to sigh with glee. "First you spit on me, and then you piss on me, but when I get your tough ass strapped into my hot-seat, I'm gonna make you shit on me! Ha-ha-ha-ha-ha. They all do! All your friends did it! But they weren't you, noooo, they came to me silently. But you will fight! Yeah, you'll jump when I hit you, and squirm to the bitter end."

Fuck that shit! I left the room—smoking!

But Lurkie was lucky. On the fifteenth day of December 1957, just a few short hours before he was scheduled to die, the governor gave him a reprieve which saved his life. And then came a new trial, and life imprisonment.

My time continued just barely moving along, with the days, weeks, months, and years becoming one great big tortured nightmare. The officials in the penitentiary regarded me as a somewhat unstable number who harbored the potential to do great violence if nudged in the wrong direction. They were right too! It was my only means to achieve a democratic solution to my problems. It was very simple: I would never start any trouble, but once it got started, you wouldn't find me backing away from it. It was not a form of hostility by any means, but simply the reality of life and death in Trenton State Prison.

The constant threat of that death-dealing electric monster always grabbing at my life's string, and the penitentiary's ability to make wild animals out of human beings, helped to reinforce my flagging determination to carve something positive out of my life, to stay away from Paterson, and to fight—by boxing, preferably. So I began running through the prison's prize fighters as if they were dry leaves and I was a forest fire burning down everything that got in my way.

Pretty soon the word spread through the grapevine that "Rubin Carter was ready to fight and settle down." Offers started pouring in through the mails from Philadelphia, Chicago, New York, and Los Angeles, and from fight managers all over the world. They sent advance contracts, and some even volunteered money, while others dangled well-paying jobs in front of my nose that I could take when I was finally released. But none of them offered me a way out of jail.

I even got a proposal to be managed by a black guard who worked in the prison named Billy Legget. But if snot was dynamite, and getting me out of jail was the plunger, he couldn't even blow his own nose! But his heart was in the right place—at that time, at least.

I answered each offer I got from elsewhere with the same letter: I told them that I would fight for anybody who could get me out of jail. I didn't care who that person was or where that person was or even how that person was going to do it. If he could get only one day cut from my sentence, a few hours off my back, or even a mere smidgen of a free minute put back into my life, that would be good enough for me. That was all I could ask—just have enough faith in me to take that chance. But my luck was still running bad; nobody would do it.

So I continued my lonely dissection of prize fighting like a mad scientist studies a germ. To reach the pinnacle of prize fighting in the professional field became my ambition. I wanted to show everybody I could rise up from the depths of my humiliation on my own.

But even that wasn't enough.

To really put the cap on top of the whole mammy-jammy thing, out of the grab bag of my future, out of the melting pot of the world, I ended up choosing Billy Legget to fight for after all, and Trenton, New Jersey to live in—as a constant reminder of what was taking place behind these walls. If things got too bad for me outside, I surmised, all I had to do was to walk down here and look at this nasty place. I'd know that as bad as I might be doing on the outside—maybe sleeping in hallways and sucking on raw eggs—I was still better off out there than anybody was in this prison.

On September 21, 1961—four years and two months after first walking in the door—I walked out of Trenton State Prison. I vowed upon everything holy never to come back alive.

THE THIRTEENTH ROUND

Hit 'Em Hard and Hit 'Em Fast

It was a bright Thursday morning when I walked out of Trenton State Prison, and the hot, butter-yellow sun beaming down from directly overhead seemed to be warning me of the hardship yet to befall me—as if the sweetness of life did not necessarily come with being set free, but was based solely upon whether or not somebody was kissing or kicking my ass at any particular moment.

I was free, but I found little pleasure in the fact. I didn't even know where my next meal was coming from. With just ten dollars in my pocket, and only the clothing on my back; with no prospects for a job, and a new home in a city where I had no friends; and with the burden of being an ex-convict to boot, I was a very likely candidate for jailing again before night could fall.

Even as I walked out the front door, I had to stifle a quick surge of resentment against my chances of really making out. The odds were against me, I felt, and it was an emotion that I'd been experiencing too often as of late. Too much dependency in jail subdued a man's ambition and forced him to become a slave to his desires: friends, food, excessive drink, and women—these were things I would have to stay away from.

I knew what I wanted, though, and I knew what to do in order to get it. I didn't fool myself. At twenty-five, it was too late in the game for me to start shucking, tomming, and buck-dancing; I was over the hill in prize fighting almost before I had gotten started. But, luckily, in my mind's eye, I felt like a veteran of a million wars. Billy (or "Bucky") Legget thought so, too.

He was waiting for me outside.

Bucky had been a fair-to-middling prize fighter himself at one time, a lightweight—or so I'd been told. He was still lean and in pretty good shape for a man his age—forty years old on his last birthday—and he still carried himself like a jitterbug, always hip-de-dipping and walking around on his toes with a swagger seen more often in younger men. He was dark-complexioned and neatly dressed, and always carried a toothpick in the corner of his mouth. He called me the Champ—and I liked that!

He had made arrangements for me to live in Trenton with Tommy Brown, a tall, good-natured welterweight. Tommy had been a darn good prospect only a few months earlier, when he had fought Charlie Scott of Philadelphia, the top-ranking welterweight contender. He hurt Tommy enough to put him in the hospital with a brain concussion. It almost killed him, and it did ruin his career. Now he was working in a hospital.

Tommy had inherited his one-family home when his parents had met with an unfortunate accident. Tommy was a beautiful person. He was unmarried, too, so we had the whole house to ourselves.

Trenton was a strange place to me. Though it is the Garden State's capital, the jobs (for blacks) were few, and those were mostly domestic. The main source of employment within the community were in the prison facilities scattered throughout the area: Trenton State Prison, Bordentown Reformatory, the County Jail, and Trenton State Home for Girls. This was a county full of jails. If these places were ever closed down, I thought, it would wipe the city right off the map. Which only proved to me that keeping folks like me locked up inside these iron lungs forever was big, big business.

The day following my release, Bucky Legget came by bright and early to ask me if I wanted to go to Maryland with him. A former welterweight champion, Virgil Akins, and Kenny Lane were scheduled to fight in Annapolis that night. Bucky had been called to work in Virgil's corner. Akins was trying to win back his lost crown.

"When do you want me to be ready?" I asked.

"Right now," Bucky answered. "I'm ready to hit the road."

So off we went to Maryland.

Bucky was driving a green, 1953 Ford with a stick shift, and he scared me to death all the way there. He couldn't drive worth a damn. But then, the car wasn't worth a damn. The wheels wobbled, the brakes wouldn't work, the little monster wouldn't hold the road, and to top it all off, Bucky was trying to go a hundred miles an hour. Goddamn! How I wished for a state trooper to come along and stop us, since then I could ride with him and let Bucky drive on by himself. I was to the point of hysteria when we finally got to where we were going, and thinking very seriously of maybe catching the bus back home. But, I was broke.

The fight was being held outdoors in the Naval Academy's Memorial Stadium. The crowd on that warm September night was as thick as thieves in jail, and twice as horny for blood. I sat up in the bleachers by myself, eating hotdogs, drinking a soda, and waiting for the preliminary fights to begin. It was my first meal of the day; ten dollars didn't go too far.

"Rubin! Rubin!" I heard Bucky calling my name suddenly, and watched him as he came running up the stairs. "Come on, Champ," he exploded. "I've got a fight for you!"

A fight! For me? What kind of foolishness is this man talking about? I thought. Oooooooh, so that's why he wanted me to come down here in the first place—to fight—and here I am eating a hotdog and drinking a mammy-jammy soda. *Jeezus Christ!* But my ego wouldn't let me back down, and I went with him, curious to see what he was going to do next. He brought me straight to the boxing commissioner.

"My fighter says that he'll take the fight," Bucky told the man with a note of pomposity in his voice. "We didn't come all the way down here for nothing!" he said. "And this will pay for our gas." He was talking as if we had planned it.

The commissioner, a big man whose thin lips had twisted up almost into a sneer while Bucky was talking, now turned his frosty eyes speculatively on me. He seemed to be weighing me against my company, then cataloging my looks, and placing me in what he thought to be my proper slot. The opposing fight manager was going through the some changes, walking around me, looking me up and down, appraising me like I was on an auction block and he was going to buy me.

"This guy ain't no fuckin' middleweight!" the fight manager finally snorted. "Who'n hell do you think you're fooling? He's more of a goddamn light heavyweight than anything else," he said. "And my boy ain't fighting out of his class!"

"How many fights have you had?" the commissioner asked me around a dead cigar hanging in his mouth. "Do you have a license to box in this state?"

"I don't have a license to box *anywhere*," I told the man, "because I've never fought professionally before." The hotdogs began barking in my stomach.

"Well, just get up on those scales," the commissioner ordered impassively. He pointed to a little bathroom scale sitting in the middle of the floor. "Let's see how much you weigh."

The scales spun and weighed me in at 156 pounds, fully dressed, since Bucky wouldn't let me take off my clothes. He was afraid the other guy wouldn't fight me. Four and a half years of training behind bars every day had made me into a full-fledged heavyweight, but without the poundage. In the end, the fight was approved.

Bucky ran around the dressing room like a chicken with its head lopped off. He borrowed boxing trunks from this fighter, shoes from that one, other equipment from other fighters. I even had Virgil Akins' cup-protector on. When I finally had all the stuff on together, I looked like a psychedelic mishap on the way to a weird happening: red shoes, purple trunks, green socks, a blue robe, and a wad of toilet paper tucked in between my lips for a mouthpiece. Wow! Not since King Kong came strutting down the pike had anybody even seen anything like it.

But I didn't have much time to ponder my looks. As soon as I was dressed, they hustled me out of the dressing room, through the crowd, and towards the ring. We were late already. The other fighter, Pike Reed, from Washington, D.C., had already been in the ring for five minutes or more, prancing around impatiently and looking pretty for his admirers. These were his stomping grounds.

I climbed up the stairs, under the ropes, and into the bright lights amidst a fury of hoots and jeers, laughter and ridicule—but it didn't bother me a bit. This was the first day of my life, and I was enjoying every second of it.

Then the bell rang.

With all due respect to Pike Reed, it must be said that while he fought me with determination and vigor that laid a steady siege against my abilities—to which a lesser fighter would have easily succumbed—I was more than just a prize fighter. I was a warrior! I was in my element now. Fighting was the pulse beat of my heart, and I loved it.

Unlike Pike Reed, winning or losing had no real significance for me; only the heat of the contest mattered. I wanted only to outfight my opponent and knock him unconscious. If being acclaimed the winner at the end of the fierce struggle added a certain piquancy to the whole affair, then solid—I would take that, too!

When the bell rang, everybody said, we didn't waste any time.

We started fighting like cats and dogs. Standing toe to toe, we slugged it out for the three-minute rounds. For part of the rest periods, too. I can't remember very much of what happened, myself. I was too tired. Every move I made sent new pains streaking through my chest. My vision was blurred, and waves of dizziness swept over me time and time again. I thought I was going to die. But when the fight was over, they had to come and pull us apart. I had won it, my first professional fight, but I couldn't even stand up long enough to acknowledge the victory. The crowd was roaring, the entire stadium was on its feet—and I couldn't get up off my stool.

Ten minutes later, when I finally stumbled back into the dressing room, the place was packed with people: newspaper reporters snapping pictures; the commissioners lined up waiting to question me, and Pike Reed's furious manager, smoking mad, stomping up and down the floor cursing up a blue streak.

"Goddammit, Commissioner!" he raged, clomping back and forth. "I want this sonofabitch barred from *ever* boxing again!" he demanded, pointing a bony finger at me. "This sonofabitch is a ten-round fighter!" he screamed. "Sent down here just to stop my boy! He might be able to fool ya'll, goddammit, but he can't fool me! I want his black ass barred—tonight!"

I didn't even stop to listen to what the man was saying. I left that to Bucky. I was tired. My head was throbbing and reeling, and clouds were forming before my eyes. I was totally exhausted. Now I could understand how fighters got killed in the ring—by not being in shape, and then by listening to some greedy sucker who really didn't give a damn about them. I promised myself I would never let this happen to me again. Then I dragged myself into the showers, fully dressed.

The boxing commissioner, his staff, the newspapermen, and Pike Reed's irate manager were still waiting for me when I returned from the showers. They were standing around mumbling as if they'd been waiting for Sugar Ray or somebody.

"What's your real name, Carter? If that's your name," the commissioner began. "There's no use in your lying about it," he said, thumbing through Nat Fleischer's *Ring Encyclopedia*, "because we've got you cold, mister. And God help you if we find your name in this book!"

"How long have you been fighting?"

"Where did you come from?"

"What's your manager's name?"

"Who sent you down here?"

The questions came at me from every-which-a-way, as though I had just pulled off a royal coup or something. Bucky Legget kept quietly off to the side, not saying a damn word in my defense. For a long moment I couldn't speak. Shame for him and anger for myself seemed to block my throat. Then the anger swallowed the shame.

"What the hell are you people talking about?" I blurted.

"The fight!" the commissioner rapped right back. "That's what we're talking about! You said that you never fought before, but that's a lie. Because that was a professional job you pulled out there tonight, and now we want to know *who* you are, and *where* you come from!"

"I told you before, man, that my name is Rubin Carter." I was getting warm now. "And I've never had a professional fight before in my life. I just got out of the New Jersey State Prison yesterday, and if you don't give me my forty dollars, tonight, I'm coming back tomorrow for whupping on your ass!" I needed that money. It was the only thing between me and starvation. All at once my body came back alive again. If these people thought that I was bullshitting about the money, well, they were going to have another fight here in the dressing room, and it wasn't going to cost them a dime!

Suddenly the place was very quiet. Only the stale odor of dried sweat and stinking feet stirred in the air. Everybody had started backing away from me when I spoke, as if I had suddenly turned into a green-eyed cyclops. They were no doubt thinking, "Wow! Where in hell did this little bald-headed bastard come from?"

"I'm sorry, but we can't pay you tonight, Carter," the commissioner said, stepping forward. "This office will have to investigate you first," he told me. "To find out if this fight was on the up and up. If you're legal. And when we do find out, one way or the other, we have your address on hand, so we'll send the twenty dollars to you. You don't have to worry about that."

"Twenty dollars!" I exclaimed, unable to believe what I'd heard. "Shit, man! You better get your arithmetic together!" I snorted. "I've got *forty* dollars coming to me!"

"Sure you have," the commissioner agreed. "But there's nothing wrong with my arithmetic." He smiled faintly. "You got forty dollars for the fight, right? Now you've got to pay us ten dollars for your license, and ten more for Legget's license, and that leaves you with twenty dollars to splurge with. Check it out," he said, "because your money's as good as in the bank."

Goddamn! I wanted to tell the man. I don't need my money in no doggone bank. I needed it right there in my pockets. I was tired of eating hotdogs. But I didn't say anything. I shut up and got dressed. Then I walked outside, hungrier than ever. Things out here were going to be just a little bit rougher than I expected. But I was going to—

"Hey, kid! Wait a minute!" a shrill voice called from behind me as I entered the parking lot. "Wait a minute, I wanna talk to you!" I turned around and waited until one of the reporters from inside came puffing up to me.

"What do you want, man?" I asked belligerently. I wasn't in the mood for any more talking.

"I want a story," the man replied candidly. "It's obvious that you're broke, and I write for a living. So you talk, and I'll pay!"

But I just stood there looking at him. He must have been in his early fifties or so, but very well preserved, and ruddy-faced. Although his suit was wrinkled up like an accordion, he still appeared distinguished.

"What can I tell you that you don't already know?" I asked him finally, sarcastically, the disgust very obvious in my voice. "I just got out of the penitentiary, yesterday, and I'm broke. I just fought my stupid heart out for forty stinking dollars, and I'm tired, and now they won't even pay me!" I said. "They've got me throwing bricks at the penitentiary, again, because I've got to eat. Is that what you wanted to know?"

The man looked at me patiently while I rapped. His face was like a map of the world, colored and worn, and deeply furrowed by the erosion of many hard years. His eyes were the blue of the sky, specked with gold, and surrounded by tiny crowsfoot wrinkles that deepened into trenches when he smiled.

"Don't let those cynical bastards in there get you down, kid," he said brusquely. "This is a rough business, this boxing game, and the fighter that loses his head is always bound to end up on the bottom of the heap. So hang right in there, and keep punching, because you've got the makings to be somebody! Just keep your head. And let somebody else throw the bricks at the prison. You just throw the punches in the ring," he said with intensity, suddenly shaking my hand. "So take care of yourself, kid—I gotta go now—but I'll be looking for some great things coming from you in the future." Then he rapidly walked away and never even looked back. He left a ten-dollar bill folded up in my fist. My eating money. My no-brick-throwing money. And I didn't even know his name.

In the days that followed the fight in Maryland I worked myself back into fighting shape. Bucky would come by the house at four o'clock every morning to pick me up and take me out on the highway, where, running in the headlights of his car, I would jog, sprint, and run for at least ten miles. I intended never to get tired again. I liked to train—it was my thing—but I loved to fight even more. I was *born* to fight.

In the evening, when everybody else was coming home from work, I would pack up my equipment and walk from East to North Trenton—a distance of about three and a half miles—where Bucky had his little gym. It was a dump, an old, dilapidated red brick building that had once been used as the city's Boys' Club. We trained upstairs in the loft, with a makeshift ring that had to be nailed down to the floor to keep it steady. A heavy punching bag hung from the ceiling, a speed bag was draped in the corner, and an old, wood-burning, pot-bellied stove was situated right in the middle of it all to keep the place warm.

Trenton was also the home town of Mr. Ike Williams, the baddest little lightweight champion ever to lace on a pair of boxing gloves. So, naturally, this was a boxing town, with more than its fair share of young prize fighters on the move, trying to follow in their leader's footsteps. Bucky's little gym was loaded down with them: Gaylord Barnes, Mel Collins, J. D. Ellis, Jimmy McMillan, Georgie Johnson, Tommy Brown, Winnie Winfred, and ten or twenty others. All of us wanted to be champs.

But when I'd been living in Trenton for a solid week, training every day, the gym suddenly began to lose all of its fighters. Everybody became mysteriously ill, or just quit. Finally there was only me, Georgie Johnson, and Winnie Winfred left. All of the others had gone. Bucky had been working me hard, getting me ready for another fight—or so he said—and the guys who had left didn't like the way I boxed. They said I hit too hard! But I wasn't trying to do that, really. I was training the only way that I knew how to train—and that was hard. I wasn't trying to hurt anybody, but I wasn't there to do any bullshitting, either.

And Winnie Winfred, an amateur light welterweight with a heart just as big as all outdoors, was constantly threatening me right into shape, too. This young rascal could really *fight*, and he knew it. He took pleasure in letting you know it, too. Maybe that was his whole trouble. He could fight too doggone good! I really had to whup on him to keep him from whupping on me.

But he would come right back smoking harder, snorting, and firing combinations from who'd-thought-it to who-flung-the-chunk. He was twice as fast as I was. So he forced me to utilize my sheer punching ability to neutralize his speed. I had to slow him down some, if I could, to stop him from cutting me up. His quick hands were like razor blades.

But even my punching power didn't faze him. It only made him work that much harder, raining thunder and lightning at me for every step of the way that I tried to push him around the ring. I liked him for that, and we became very good friends.

Winnie was only seventeen years old, a senior in high school, and graduating that coming June. He had been living right around the corner from me all this time, but I didn't know it. Coming from a fairly large family, he lived with his mother, two younger brothers, and three sisters—one of them older than he was. They were all beautiful, very tan-complexioned with oriental eyes and personalities that would have put the most loving, chicken-eating, jack-legged preacher to shame. They were a very tightly knit family, too: played together, stayed together, and worked together. Winnie supplemented the family's table by doing landscaping work after school every day with his pickup truck.

I was proud to be "adopted" by this family. Hard times were knocking at my door, and if it hadn't been for them, I might have starved to death—or started stealing. There was no food in my house, no oil in my stove, and I was less than able to help better my situation. I was dead broke, and Bucky didn't have any money. He was only making ninety-nine dollars a week working at the prison, and he had a wife and two children at home—and a son away at Lincoln College—so he couldn't very well support me, too. On the other hand, Tommy, my landlord, was in good shape: all of his family lived right there in Trenton; whenever he wanted something to eat, or wanted to go somewhere where it was warm, all he had to do was get in his car and go. All I could do was drink sugar-water, suck my thumb, and suffer.

Finally, one night when it had turned uncommonly cold and I

just couldn't take it anymore, I got myself a job. Or rather, Bucky got it for me, but only after I urged it upon him with the threat of going home. I told him that I didn't have to take this shit. My father owned half of Paterson, and I could go back there if I couldn't go any place else, and eat good, sleep comfortable, and be warm forever.

So the next day I started working in what in 1961 was still called Levittown (now Willingboro), New Jersey, a middle-class community some twenty miles outside of Trenton. I was working for a black man, no less, and I liked that part of it. But when I had to get up at three o'clock in the morning to do my roadwork, then come back home to bathe and run out on the highway to catch the five o'clock bus to work, I didn't appreciate it so much.

And then, when the guy I was working for, whom I'll call Mr. Toms, picked me up at the bus station in his blue-paneled truck and drove me through the streets until we came upon these big, beautiful, colonial-style homes with flowing lawns and swimming pools, green shrubbery and tennis courts out in the backyards, and we had to go in there and scrub the goddamn floors, I liked it even less.

I mean, nasty floors! Wall-to-wall scum! Cock-a-roaches everywhere, ceiling-to-ceiling! All the women, meanwhile, in every house without exception, regardless of what time of day it was when we got there, would be swishing around us in their most revealing negligées, talking out of the sides of their faces, sipping on their morning cocktails, and telling us what to do.

"Dear? Would you move the refrigerator, please, and clean in that corner behind it? Ooooooh, you're such a doll, and so muscular, too!" If I would have looked at her for any longer than a second, she would have hollered rape!

And then there was, "Mr. Toms, would you care for a cup of coffee while your *boy* there is cleaning?"

I was so goddamn mad that I didn't know what to do—shit, spit, or just go blind. "Boy"! I was burning up. Me! Down on my knees like a goddamn nigger, scrubbing a lazy cracker's floor. Jeezzzzzzzzzzzus Christ! If somebody had said something to me right then, there was no doubt about it, I would have beaten them to death—especially this nigger who had me trapped up here in these hills. I would have ruined him, but I didn't know which way Trenton was, and I had no way of getting there if I did.

Well, that bourgeois Uncle Tomming nigger worked me like a

slobbering idiot from seven in the morning till seven that night, stopping only once—to buy me a hamburger when he dropped me off at the bus station. He told me he'd see me in the morning. I looked at that fool like he was crazy. He was *never* going to see me anymore, and if he said too much about it—right then—I was going to bust him in his motherfucking mouth. Oh, man, was I smoking!

Even on the bus, going back to Trenton at eight o'clock, I still hadn't cooled off. The man had worked me like a mad mule skinner, getting the pure marrow from my bones, and all I wanted to do was crawl up the stairs and fall into bed. But guess who was waiting for me out in front of the house when I got home, getting ready to work me some more? That's right! Bucky Legget.

"Hiyah, Champ," he said. "I've been waiting for you." As if I couldn't see that. "Go grab your stuff and let's get on down to the gym. We'll go by Winnie's house and get him, too, so hurry up, it's late already." But I didn't move. I looked at him like he was crazy.

"Man, I ain't going nowhere, tonight!" I told him. "That tomming nigger like to work me to death up there with them rich crackers today. Scrubbing floors and scraping shit off the walls! I was even looking for him to start washing the dishes that was piled up in the sink. Nawwwwww," I told Bucky, "I'm not going anywhere tonight. I'm too tired. I'm going upstairs and get right into bed."

"But, Champ," Bucky tried to explain. "You've got a fight coming up soon, man! You can't be missing any days from the gym. That's not the way to—"

"I know, Bucky, I know!" I interrupted him irritably. "I know that's not the way to train. But *who* am I fighting, and *when* am I fighting! That's all I want to know. Because I'm broke, man. And hungry. Can't you understand that? I *need* the money. So just tell me when am I going to fight this fight that you're always talking about? That's all I wanta know."

Bucky had a funny habit of twisting that toothpick around in his mouth whenever he was trying to get over on somebody, and he was doing it now.

"Er—er, soon, Champ! We're fighting real soon," he said, uncomfortably. "I've got a real sweet one for you this time—plenty of money, plenty of publicity, but you gotta be in shape for this one, Champ. I'm telling you, you just gotta listen to me, man!" Bucky was almost pleading, sounding a little pathetic in his desperation.

"I'm listening to you, Bucky," I said, answering him more civilly this time. "But don't come to me with that sweet shit. There ain't no sweet fights, only hard and bitter ones, and really, I can't do anything tonight. I'm just too tired, man."

"Okay, Champ," Bucky finally relented, grudgingly, but sounding almost relieved. "Try to get some sleep tonight, and I'll see you in the morning for roadwork, Okay? G'night, Champ."

"G'night, Bucky," I said, and went into the house.

Just opening the front door, the cold air hit me like a bucket of ice. It was freezing in there—colder than it was outside. I went upstairs and climbed right into bed, clothes and all, and laid there shivering in the dark with my teeth chattering uncontrollably. I was miserable, hungry and disgusted; what remained of the night was an agony of nearly unendurable cold. But I must have fallen asleep eventually, because the doorbell woke me up with an insistent ring. It was Lloyd Senior and his sidekick, Junior.

"How're you doing there, boy?" my father greeted me in his gruff voice. "Your mother was thinking about you tonight," he said. "So me and Junior just thought that we'd drop down here and see how you're making out. Doggone!" he said suddenly, rubbing his hands together briskly. "It's cold! Put some heat on in here, boy! Before somebody gets pneumonia."

"Ain't no heat," I answered reluctantly. "There's no oil."

"What! No *heat*?" he exclaimed, looking at me kind of wide-eyed. "Then maybe you better pack this in, and come on back home with us," he said. "Who in the world ever heard of staying in a house without heat in the wintertime! What else *ain't* you got down here?" he asked sharply, sounding angry. "I bet you *ain't* got nothing to eat, either! Do you?" And he went stomping off in search of the kitchen, with me and Lloyd Junior bringing up the rear.

My father snatched open the refrigerator door, and instantly recoiled from the empty muskiness he found there. The freezer, too, was barer than Mother Hubbard's cupboard. Not even a cock-eyed cock-a-roach could have survived there.

"Lord, Lord, Lord! Look at here, Junior," my father called to my brother to come there and have a look-see. "This fool is starving to death down here," he said bitterly, "and he's too damn proud to ask for a little help. But that settles it. You're coming back home with us tonight, boy!"

"No, I ain't, either!" I told him. "I can't go back to Paterson. I got to stay here! This is my last chance. And I got to make it! I'll be all right—you'll see."

My father's face was drawn sharp with his pain. It was the same look I've often seen in the eyes of a child before they were flooded with tears, and it surprised me. This was the closest thing to emotion that I'd ever known my father to show—other than when he was whupping on our asses, or in church, which I've always thought was pure bullshit, anyhow. But this was for real. I could see it. His eyes were burning slits, and he was trembling. I could feel for the first time in my life that maybe—just maybe—this cat really did dig me, but just didn't know how to relate to me. But wow, he was doing it now, and his magnificence was powerful. Right then I loved him as at no other time before.

Before he went back to Paterson that night, he took me shopping and we filled up the refrigerator with juicy steaks and chops, prime cuts of ribs, and eggs. And we restocked the closets with vegetables, canned goods, and everything else a man needs to survive. We even got in touch with the oil company that night, and received their promise to come first thing in the morning to fill up the five-hundred-gallon drum out in the backyard. But just to tide me over through the long, cold night ahead, we went out and bought some bottled fuel and started a fire. And then I sat down and greased, and was warm, and for the first time in what seemed a very long time, I was almost happy again. I had finally found my father.

Maybe that was what I had needed all along to push me through. I mean, maybe that night was the turning point in my life, though I really can't say. I only know that after eating a few good, hearty meals, and being warm for a couple of days back-to-back, my entire attitude changed for the better. I became loose and relaxed, both mentally and physically, and even my fighting got better. A little too much better, I'm afraid, because I unwittingly almost destroyed my best friend.

It happened in the early part of October 1961, while I was still in training for the phantom fight that Bucky was always talking about but would never fully explain. The little gym was crowded that afternoon, full of backseat-driving spectators, but no prize fighters. As usual, Winnie Winfred and I were the only ones there, and we were already hooked up in the ring, about to renew our daily war. Bucky called "time," and we moved out to start it.

The sparring session was ferocious from the very beginning. I shuffled out of my corner bobbing and weaving, and Winnie met me in the center of the ring, hooking and jabbing, doubling up on his combinations, determined to drive me back into my corner. I was just as resolved to move forward. So we stood there slugging it out, toe-to-toe, grunting and firing on each other. Both of us were hell-bent upon forcing our respective wills against the other. That's what boxing is all about.

"Don't hit him so hard, Champ!" Bucky called to me.

"Move, Winnie, move!" a spectator advised my little buddy. "Don't stand so flat-footed!" he said.

"Jab the monkey and run, Winnie!" somebody else coached excitedly. "Don't let him keep hitting you with that funny hook, baby!"

But Winnie couldn't hear what they were saying. He was just as hung up in all of this nonsense as I was. The only difference was that I loved the fighting while it was going on, and he enjoyed only what the fighting could bring him when it was over—the grandeur of being somebody.

But this match was pure brutality in its rankest form: coming back from one of Winnie's jolting combinations that had just rocked my socks, I hammered one home to his chin, then nailed two more thundering left hooks to his head. Then, suddenly, I switched around and did something horrible to him: I caught him on the end of a five-punch combination that knocked a crown of sweat from his brow, and stopped him in his tracks. Time and life were suddenly suspended. He fell face forward, out cold.

It had happened the same way on a number of other occasions, but in the past, after he was revived, Winnie would jump right back up and vehemently demand his pound of flesh in revenge. He couldn't stand the thought of being knocked down and not getting back up to fight again. But this time was different. He got up, all right, but not to fight.

Later that night, as we rode home in his little pickup truck, he was the same old good-natured Winnie again, smiling, forever talking about his girlfriend and how it almost blew her mind just *thinking* about their up-and-coming graduation day. And the fact that if he couldn't borrow his mother's car on the night of their prom, with them all dressed up in evening gown and tuxedo, they would have to go to both occasions in Winnie's blankety-blank pickup truck. His girlfriend didn't like that worth a damn! But Winnie and I fell out laughing, just talking about it.

About a half an hour after he dropped me off at my house, though, one of his sisters came bursting in, crying and screaming that her brother had just keeled over suddenly, begun foaming at the mouth and trembling violently, and that they couldn't wake him up. Before she had finished sobbing out her story, I was out the door and halfway around the corner, and by the time she dug that I was gone, I was crashing through the front door of her house. I knew what was wrong. Didn't know exactly how I knew it, but I did.

Winnie's whole family was hysterical. He was laid out on the kitchen floor, twitching, going through shuddering convulsions that violently jerked his body across the floor. Everybody was crowding around him in a frenzy, crying and trying to wake him up. Burrowing my way none too gently through his brothers and sisters, I snatched him up in my arms, ran outside to his truck, and took him straight to the hospital. They rushed him right into the operating room, where he had to fight for his life. Winnie was in big, big trouble.

Moments later, when his friends and family began arriving by the carloads, I left. I couldn't stay there and watch them suffer like that. Five beautiful children and their mother, carrying on something wretched, going through pure hell and agony for something that I had done. I felt guilty about it. The entire family had befriended me, no questions asked, and this was how I repaid them for their kindness. Goddamn! Me and Bucky Legget!

All of this heartache and misery could have been very easily avoided with just a little bit more careful supervision from Bucky. Even so, when everything was said and done, it was still just as much my fault that Winnie got hurt as it was Bucky's. Because I had seen it coming. I'd even warned Bucky about it. I had been telling him to quit putting that boy in the ring with me every day, where, like two goddamn fools losing their minds, we tried to beat each other's brains out, round after round. Somebody had to get hurt. It was bound to happen. But I loved boxing with him too much to stop.

When I got back home, Tommy Brown was there. After I told him about Winnie, he rushed out the door to the hospital himself, telling me I had some mail on the dining room table. The letter was in a long, official-looking envelope, with the seal of the Maryland Boxing Commission on it.

"Ah-ha, my twenty dollars," I thought. But when I opened it up, there was that, and more. It was a contract, signed, sealed, and notarized on the night of my first fight, with Bucky Legget's signature scrawled on the bottom of the page. The thing had come to me by mistake. The contract read, in part:

I, *Billy Legget*, boxing manager for Rubin Carter, of Trenton, New Jersey, have agreed to meet Holly Mims, of Washington, D.C., in a scheduled ten-round bout on Friday, October the Sixth, 1961, in the Memorial Stadium of Annapolis, Maryland.

Each participant is guaranteed the sum of One Thousand Dollars and/or Twenty Percent of the net proceeds, whichever is greatest.

Three Hundred Dollars has thus far been advanced to Billy Legget against Carter's share of the purse.

I sat there and read that contract a million times over if I read it once, and still—I just couldn't believe what I was reading. There had to be some kind of mistake. Holly Mims was the top-ranking middleweight in the country, one of the best fighters in the world. Without even taking off his robe, or working up a sweat, he could undoubtedly splatter my stupid brains all over the arena.

Bucky couldn't be doing this to me. Shit! I'd given that man everything I owned, had even starved for him, laid down to sleep in a cold house for him—he wouldn't be trying to get me killed now, right? But even as I thought it over further, my disbelief started to fade. The urge just to get up and quit swept through me. I wanted to go home and chuck the whole thing. It wasn't the money, or the fact that I was starving, or even fighting Holly Mims. I would have done it, and he would have killed me—but I would have died fighting my heart out, doing the one thing I knew how to do best. At least I would have had that one, final, savage, glorious moment of meeting the best of the best; oblivion would have come as relief.

I snatched up my coat and rushed outside on the run, heading for crosstown and going straight to Bucky's house in North Trenton, a few blocks from where we trained every day. When I finally got there and knocked on the front door—hard—Eleanor, his very beautiful wife, answered.

"Hi, Rubin." She smiled, hesitantly, a worried frown on her lovely face.

I never could hide my feelings. I was the sort of person who always wore his inner thoughts, as well as his heart, right out there for everybody to see, so she knew right away that something was wrong. "It's kind of late for you to be calling, isn't it, young man?" she asked.

"Yes, ma'am," I said. "But it's kind of important that I see your husband tonight, too."

"Well—" Mrs. Legget said, still hesitating. Then, opening the door wider, she decided: "Well, come on in, then. Bucky's in the kitchen."

The Legget home was typical of every other one-family dwelling in Trenton: you entered a large living room as soon as you stepped through the front door; the dining area was really little more than an extension of that. There was no effort to divide the space, except for the placement of furniture and the kitchen wall, which faced the entry side of the house.

I strode through the rooms in a blaze of silent fury. Rage flooded through my every move, and I wouldn't have blamed Mrs. Legget a bit if she hadn't let me into her house at all that night. And, although I felt like knocking her husband dead, I didn't. I just threw the letter in his face and stood there watching him, suppressing a rising urge to wring his scrawny neck.

"Why, man?" I asked him, holding myself in. "What have I done to you that makes you want to do this to me?"

Bucky didn't answer me. He sat at the table with a midnight snack in front of him, pretending to read the contract. His brows were furrowed in deep concentration. The toothpick was moving in his mouth.

"But you can beat this old man, Champ!" he finally blurted out, ignoring my question. "This is what we've been training so hard for. This is your big chance! If you beat Holly Mims, you're on your way—straight to the top! Can't you see that, Champ?"

"Dammit!" I snapped back at him, angrily. "That's not what I'm talking about, nigger, and you know it!" I wanted to call him a motherfucker, but his wife was standing in the doorway. "I would have fought *God*, had you told me to, continued to go hungry, like I've been doing, freezing, like I've been doing," I told him, "because I believed you when you told me that you were *broke!* And all the while you had *my* three hundred dollars, but you wouldn't even give me a nickel to eat with! No! You just let me go hungry." I looked at him with distaste. "And now Winnie's in the hospital, too! Because of you."

"But I had to pay some bills with that money, Champ, and—"

"Bucky?" Mrs. Legget cut in smoothly. "May I speak to you, please? And would you excuse us for a moment, Rubin?"

Bucky seemed glad for his wife's timely intrusion. He jumped right up and followed her out of the kitchen like a disobedient puppy yapping at her heels. Once they were out of sight, I couldn't hear too much of what they were saying, but she seemed to be fussing with him about something or other.

"Bucky, you shouldn't have done that boy like that!" I faintly heard her scold him. "And you ought to be ashamed of yourself, too! Spending up his money, and letting him go hungry, without even trying to feed him. That's what I can't get over!" she said. "You ought to be ashamed!"

I heard Bucky mumble something back to her, but I couldn't understand what it was he said. Then he came back into the kitchen, alone this time, and sat down.

"All right, Champ," he said. "Not telling you about the money was a mistake, I admit it." It wasn't an apology. "But that still leaves the fight, which is only two days away, and you're already in shape, so why not take advantage of it?" he asked. He looked at me as if he had just made the world's great new discovery—that I was in shape (at the expense of another man's life)—and I looked back at him, knowing that I had just uncovered a goddamn fool.

"Bucky?" I said to him, coldly, and felt the indignation wash over me. "I'm doing all that I can just to stand over here and try to talk some sense into you, without putting my hands on you. Because I'll break you in two, if I do." I glared at him murderously. "I oughta put your black ass in the hospital with Winnie," I said. "So if you still want to take that fight with Holly Mims, then *you* fight him! Because I'll be goddamned if I will! I'm not even going down there."

"But they'll take your license away from you, Champ!"

"No they won't, either," I said. "They won't have to, because I'm sending mine back and getting my ten dollars, and if I had your license, I'd send that, too, and get twenty of my dollars back.

"You jive-assed motherfucker!" I finally got it off. "The only thing that you're worried about is giving back those three hundred dollars that you took from those people, and I hope you ain't got it, and I hope they tear your black ass up for it!" And with that, I stomped out of the house before I really blew my cool and ended up doing something really horrible to him.

I started walking aback to East Trenton, really frustrated, with the firm idea of leaving this burg in the morning deeply embedded in my head. But halfway home, I changed my mind about leaving, and when I got there, I changed my direction and went around to Winnie's house. "I'm not going to let that nigger chase me out of town," I said to myself, "because if that boy pulls through with this operation, I'm going to stay right here and fight for him. That's what I'm going to do—and fuck Bucky Legget!"

But when I told the Winfreds about it, they wouldn't even listen to the idea. Being equally as proud as they were gracious, they were satisfied that it hadn't been anybody's fault in particular. Winnie was out of the operating room now, resting quietly under constant supervision. The doctors had diagnosed his condition as stemming from a blood clot in his brain that had placed undue pressure upon a mass of nerves in the cerebrum. Once this pressure was relieved, they felt, and barring any unforeseen complications, he had a fifty-fifty chance of surviving.

When I went to see Winnie with his family a couple of days later, he'd been removed from the intensive care unit and put in a private ward. But it was pitiful. He couldn't talk, could barely even move, and he wasn't aware of anything going on around him. They kept him drugged. He just lay there, floating in a crib-like bed, walled in on all four sides with intravenous whatchamacallits leading into each of his arms, which were tied to the bed. His head was sheathed in white bandages, like a turban made of gauze, and tubes extending from both nostrils were fastened to an oxygen tank at the head of his crib. The whole place smelled of sickness and death.

"Winnie! Winnie!" I whispered to him urgently. The doctors had asked me to do it, to see if he would respond. "Winnie!" I called again. "Can you hear me, little buddy? This is Rubin."

Suddenly his eyes jerked open and started blinking rapidly. He seemed to be trying to focus in on all the people crowded around his bed at once. Only his eyeballs moved. He caught sight of my shiny bald head and ugly bearded face, and I'll be doggoned if he didn't try to smile! It was as if he was saying, "See, nigger! I got back up, didn't I?" And I had to shake my head at that; indeed, he did. His family cried, the doctors sighed. My man was going to be all right—and he was. He completely recovered during the months that followed.

All during this time I hadn't seen Bucky Legget. Didn't know what had happened to him down there in Maryland. But a few days later, on October 11, he stopped by the house and asked me if I wanted to fight up in Reading, Pennsylvania that night. Jimmy McMillan, one of my stablemates from Bucky's gym, was fighting a lightweight named Richie Sue up there in the main event.

As for my opponent, he was as yet unnamed, but would probably be a fighter out of Philly. As soon as Bucky told me that, I felt deep down in my gutworks, that he was trying to put something over on me. Because the prize fighters from across the river, whoever they were, were the worst kind of opponents to run into blindly. They all hit hard, and were left hookers, but I accepted the fight anyhow. Fuck it! I thought. Whoever was coming would have to bring ass to get ass!

I was hit 'em hard and hit 'em fast.

That afternoon, up in Reading, at the boxing commissioner's office, where all of us fighters were weighing in and getting our physicals for the contest that night, everyone showed but my opponent, Joey Cooper. They promised me he would be there that night. He didn't have to weigh in, didn't have to take a physical. They probably thought that he wouldn't have to show up but a minute to bump me off, either. And normally, they would have been right. If he had been fighting somebody else. But he wasn't. He was fighting me, and I planned to ruin him, whoever he was.

Even sitting in the dressing room that night, waiting for the fights to begin, I still hadn't laid eyes on this Joey Cooper. I didn't know what he looked like, or if he would come swinging through the ropes like Tarzan, wearing a loincloth and clutching his spear, mistaking me for Cheeta. I didn't know if he had even showed up. Whatever he was, I was prepared for him. If he looked like Charles Atlas kicking sand in some skinny fool's face out on the beach, I was ready for him. Winnie's mother had made me a brand-new hooded blue robe. She had agreed to make me as many as I wanted, and I agreed to pay for the material and for her time, and from then on I always wore two robes to every fight—one for me, and one for Winnie. I was always fighting for him.

My fight was scheduled as the first bout of the evening that night, and on my way up to the ring, I spied my father sitting out in the audience. I saw Joey Cooper for the first time, too. On the other side of the arena, people had started cheering. The crowd parted as he entered the ring, dancing. He was young, white, not much over twenty years old, and his face was handsomely un-marked—the sure sign of a good prize fighter.

He smiled confidently, and waved to a pretty girl sitting at ring-side while the crowd went crazy, cheering his flamboyant entrance into the square jungle. Then he stripped off his robe and flexed his muscles. I looked at his arms. They were long, very long, and that was bad for me, because I was short. He was also heavily muscled, and they rippled as he moved gracefully and swiftly, but controlled, like a big hunting cat. His eyes were alert, displaying plenty of craft. I felt the breath of disaster on my cheeks. This boy was a puncher. I could see it in the way his shoulders sloped in and thickened up high, rather than broadening out wide like a body builder's.

My black ass was in trouble.

The referee signaled us out into the center of the ring. A kind of surprised sigh went up from the audience when Bucky removed my two robes, revealing my physique: I was black, bald-headed, and shiny with sweat. After we received our instructions, Joey pranced back to his side of the ring, and I to mine, waiting, listening for the sound of the bell.

I was nervous. My mouth was dry, and my pulse beat fast. But I felt a weird mixture of apprehension and a joy at the same time. Once the tension of all the waiting had passed, the apprehension would also vanish, I knew, and leave me with nothing but the pure joy of the thing.

Suddenly it was very quiet in the arena, and I thought I could feel my heart skip a beat. Then—the clang of the bell was startling.

Neither one of us hurried out of our corners, I must admit. We came together in the middle of the ring very cautiously, our knees slightly bent and our bodies tucked well in behind our arms and shoulders. I started circling my young opponent warily, my atten-tion focused upon his feet. Then I popped a stiff jab into his pretty face to get the ball rolling. I could hear the crowd of hillbillies begin their chant for "Joey! Joey! Joey!" and saw a gleam of antic-ipation come into his eyes. When it transferred to his feet, they shifted, and then he fired on me.

"Soooowish!"

Whooooowie! He was fast, faster than I had expected, and I just barely ducked his sizzling left hook as it swept over my head. A shout of pure joy arose from the throats of the bloodthirsty audience. "Git 'im, Joey, git 'im!" they cried. But Joey only smiled. I think it kind of surprised him when he found out I wasn't that easy to hit. I saw it all in his feet. He braced and balanced himself for a new attack, and then darted in at me again, winging his punches now, trying to break through my thick-armed defense.

But in doing that, he let me see through his, and I lashed out with a sharp right hand that caught him flush on his chin. I followed that with a sweeping left hook to the same spot. Joey stopped, blinked, and I whipped another left hook at him, and then another one, and the third one picked him up and flung him through the ropes—right out into the lap of the pretty girl sitting at ringside. Blood splattered everywhere. His nose was broken, and he was unconscious before his head touched her breast.*

For several seconds the crowd remained silent. They were stunned speechless, unable to believe what they had just witnessed. They gaped in astonishment at the fighter lying in their midst, as if to say to themselves, "Is this for real?" Then, accepting it, they suddenly broke out into a loud bedlam of cheers and rebel cries, nearly bringing the house down with their exultation—not particularly for me, and surely not *against* Joey. It was just simply because everybody loves a winner—even my father. He jumped up into the ring and grabbed me, happy and proud that his wayward son had finally settled down to being a man. But I felt no happiness, only a dull throbbing like someone had just poured ice water over my hot skin. This fight was only a small step up that long road to the top, which I fully intended to travel.

My next fight took place two weeks later, in Philadelphia, with Frankie Nelson. At seven o'clock on the night of the fight, I found myself stranded in Trenton, when I should have been seated in my dressing room at six. Bucky was nowhere in sight. Even Mrs. Legget hadn't seen him. So Tommy Brown and his uncle, Andrew Taylor, burned up the highway trying to get me to Philly in time, running red lights, and outrunning the speed limits.

Even so, the first fight of the night was savagely under way when

---

* The record book shows this fight to have been a second-round knockout, and I won't try to dispute that, but this is the only round that I can remember.

we got there, and I had to bogart my way into Charlie Scott's dressing room to have my hands taped up by his trainer. Scott was fighting Jerry Black for the Pennsylvania welterweight title that night. Bucky wasn't there, either. When it was time for me to fight, I had to enter the ring with nobody in my corner but me. People started laughing when I came bouncing down the aisle by myself, carrying my own water bucket, and wearing two robes. They must have thought I was crazy, or something.

My anger was very obvious. It was out there for everybody to see: Stevie Wonder couldn't have missed it! So I put it right to work against Frankie Nelson, and knocked him out in fifty-nine seconds. The people stopped laughing then, and started sitting up and taking notice. When I went to pick up my forty dollars for the fight—yup, you guessed it—Bucky Legget mysteriously appeared, holding his hands out for his share: thirty-three and one-third percent, thirteen dollars and thirty-three cents.

Now ain't that a mizzafizza?

About a month later in Totowa, New Jersey, I fought a young, up-and-coming light heavyweight by the name of Herschell Jacobs, and after knocking him down three or four times during the fight, I beat him in a tough four-round decision.

By late December, when I had been out of the penitentiary for three excruciating months, I'd had four fights, and was still starving and still cold—all of which meant that I was going nowhere pretty damn fast. Shit! I hadn't even cleared a hundred dollars yet. But then, one night, while I was in my heatless house again, my brother Lloyd came to Trenton and told me that my father wanted to see me, and to bring my boxing gear.

The next day my father talked me into going with him down to the Market Street Gym in Paterson. By the time we got there, the place was overrun with more interested people, I am sure, than had ever been inside the joint at any one time before.

Up in the ring, loosening up and getting ready to box, was Attilio Tonda, the newly crowned heavyweight champ of Canada. He was fighting on TV that Friday at Madison Square Garden.

As soon as I walked through the door I felt the tingles of raw nerves wafting through the air, tickling the hairs on my mustache and beard. I knew that somebody had somehow convinced my father to bring me up here from Trenton to fight this man. The fool, I thought! Whoever he was, he was a stupid, egotistical fool.

The Canadian up in the ring must have weighed two hundred and twenty pounds, if he weighed an ounce, even when he was on a strict diet. He was a giant compared to me. The man was a fully grown heavyweight, a professional of long standing, and really, there wasn't the slightest doubt about it, I had no business in the same ring with the guy. But what could I do? I couldn't run—that wouldn't be me. So, being that I was already there, I thought, what the hell—I might as well go along with it.

From the very outset of the sparring session, however, there was little doubt in my mind that this was the real thing and that this guy was trying to hurt me. He didn't pretend *not* to be doing otherwise. He started right out by swinging haymakers from the floor and doubling up on everything, trying to knock my fool head clean off. If it wasn't for the fact that he was so damn slow and cumbersome, like a freight train moving through a prairie town, he probably would have done it, too.

At the end of the first three minutes, I went over to the Canadian's corner and tried to explain to him that although I looked to be heavier, I was only a middleweight and to cool it, to lighten up on his punches. I wasn't getting paid for this shit.

But Attilio Tonda and his manager just ignored me. They pretended not to understand what I was saying, that they spoke only French, and no English. They treated me like I was a babbling idiot.

I decided to use my fists to overcome our language barrier, and let them do my interpreting for me. (It was hard enough for me to speak English, much less French.) When the bell rang for the start of the second round, they went straight to work translating for me, too! I beat that big rascal from his pillar to my post, and when I wouldn't let him fall, his manager got my message right away. When I hung Tonda up on the ropes and in the next minute or so knocked him out, I knew they had understood exactly what I was saying all along, because fifteen minutes later, Attilio Tonda was still laid out cold, just a-farting and a-trembling, kicking puffs of resin dust up off the canvas. Then his manager got scared. He ran out of the gym and brought back a doctor, who gave the unconscious fighter a needle, massaged his head, and finally woke him up again. Before I left the gym that December afternoon, each and every one of those Frenchmen was talking plenty of English, and a little pig Latin, too! But mostly they were the ghetto vernaculars that I'd been used to all my life. Huh, very fascinating! I thought. See how you can learn some relevant facts in such strange places, Rubin? I didn't know they had black ghettos up in Canada, too!

A couple of weeks later, for no apparent reason that I could see—other than just to let me know that some *fool* was still pulling some funny strings behind my back—my stupid trainer signed me up to fight Herschell Jacobs again. I had no choice in the matter, since I was starving again and needed the fight bad.

"But what do I need Herschell Jacobs for?" I asked Bucky. "The man is a light heavyweight. He outweighs me by at least twenty pounds, and I've already fought him once, so what's the point in me fighting him again?" I really wanted to know the answer to that—because Herschell Jacobs was a good, cautious fighter. He was almost purely defensive, and I knew doggone well that it wasn't going to be easy for me to overpower him like I had the first time. And it wasn't.

He beat me in a six-round decision.

I wasn't angry about losing the Jacobs fight, because Herschell was good and on the climb. But I was burning up behind the stupid logic of having to fight him twice. It made my future in boxing look dim. I just couldn't understand the strategy in that.

But that night I finally found out who the Dr. Einstein was—I mean, the brilliant Mister Shadow who had been lurking behind Bucky and my father, pulling all of those shady, undercover deals in the dark, having me brought up from Trenton to box Attilio Tonda, and signing me up to fight a light heavyweight for a second time, when I had already beaten Herschell Jacobs once. All of these moves had been dangerous, unnecessary, and foolish. The genius's name was Carmen Tedeschi, a con man. I mean, a contractor.

He walked into my dressing room with his young son, Johnny, and two other men—Jimmy Colotto, a boxing promoter from Union City, and Duke Stefano, the assistant matchmaker of Madison Square Garden.

"Er—er, Champ," Bucky began lamely, directing my attention to the newcomers. His tone of voice was one of patient conciliation. "This is Carmen Tedeschi—" he told me out of the clear blue sky "—your new manager. He's the man who signed you for this fight here, tonight."

My eyes swung to the three dudes standing by the door. All of them looked alike to me: Italian, swarthy, and short, with nicely styled pepper-gray hair. They were all neatly dressed, in silk suits and paperweight shoes. But one of them looked like he was a trifle too smooth to suit me. Instinctively, I knew him to be Tedeschi.

"Hi, kid," he beamed. And that fucked me up right from the jump—calling me a *kid!* His smile seemed to come too easy, too. It didn't seem real, and I didn't trust people like that. But then I couldn't trust this Bucky-Nigger, either, could I? Goddamn his wretched black ass!

Carmen Tedeschi was a hardnose. A sub-contractor living in Saddlebrook, New Jersey, who raised, bred, and raced pigeons for a hobby—and for money. Married, he was the proud father of three wonderful children, whom he always tried to protect from the harsh realities of this world. His oldest daughter, Carmen Marie, was sixteen years old and a very beautiful girl at that time. Then came his son, Johnny, named after his father's youngest brother, and he was eight. The mother, Nettie—but whom I've always called Mrs. T—had just given birth to their youngest daughter, Niccoletta.

I enjoyed many a good and rewarding moment in their midst, but it took quite some time for me to realize fully that the family really didn't know what it meant to be racist. I didn't know if that was good or bad, but I admired this new sort of freshness, since it came at a time—right after my release from Trenton State—when I could really appreciate it most. Mrs. T. was all hung up on astrology and was a brilliantly intuitive woman. Her husband, on the other hand, was headstrong and rambunctious, quick to accept any challenge that was thrown his way. He was a firm believer in half-truths, with a clever knack of showing one face while hiding the other. He took pride in being called a con man. But he didn't know a damn thing about prize fighting.

From the moment we first met though, helped by a number of important factors—such as Tedeschi's glib tongue, Jimmy Colotto's promotional talents, Madison Square Garden's farm club system, and my natural fighting abilities—my boxing career suddenly spiraled upwards like a giant tornado.

Every couple of weeks or so, somewhere in Union City, or Jersey City, or in the St. Nicholas Arena in New York, you could find me demolishing some poor soul that Jimmy Colotto had placed in my way to block the road to the top. Young fighters, old fighters

—and a few of the referees, too—I ran through my opponents like they were tar-papered shacks standing in the wind on the coast of Florida, and I was that irresistible force Hurricane Beulah. On October 5, 1962, I racked up my tenth knockout in my fourteenth fight.

Rubin "Hurricane" Carter had come into being.

It was during this period that I met Mae Thelma Bosket, the exact female counterpart of myself, who later became my wife. She was slim, pretty, brown-skinned and voluptuous but with an unbending stubborn streak running through her. It was a stubbornness that surpassed even my own at times, because I *would* give in to reason, but once her mind was made up to follow a certain course, not hell, high water, death, or destruction could move her.

This unyielding bullheadedness caused us to have some pretty tense moments. I would say to her, "Thelma"—that's what I called her whenever I was angry—"if you ever get mad at me, baby, I'm going to keep quiet and just walk away. And if I get mad at you? You better walk away. Because if we both get mad together? *You* ain't got no win!"

My wife is an unusual person who doesn't *play* at all: she's a loyal Capricorn—her birth date is December 23—she's a fiery Aries, a natural Taurus, a shrewd Gemini, a moody Cancer, a romantic Leo, a faithful Virgo, a more-than-impartial Libra, a jealous Scorpio, an honest-to-God Sagittarius, a generous Aquarius, and a pleasant Pisces. She doesn't talk too much, either, which I like.

But she did say something, one time, that really got next to me, and reaffirmed my original belief that I hadn't married a fool. It happened in 1964, a year after we were married, when the Sports Writers' Association of New Jersey voted me their Fighter of the Year. We were sitting in the house, Mae Thelma and I, talking it over with a reporter sent there by the *Herald-News* of Passaic. The man had been interviewing me, and then suddenly he switched over and directed a bomb of a question at my wife.

"Mrs. Carter?" he asked. "What kind of person would you say your husband is outside of the ring? I mean, with his police record and all?"

I flinched at the question. That was a double-barreled shotgun, if I'd ever heard one. Thanks to my record, my refusal to kiss anybody's ass, and Tedeschi's publicity-seeking, the newspapers had already made an animal out of me. Now they were bringing this shit into my home, and I didn't appreciate it. But Mae Thelma didn't blink an eye. She took it all in her stride, and whupped it right back on him, jarring me to my heels.

"He's *all* man," she said, right off the top of her head. "When I first met my husband, I realized that he was a lonely and sometimes ruthless man. But I could accept that, coming from him. Because I knew that his ruthlessness would only be applied against his enemies, and not against those of us he loved or against those who didn't bother him. If you didn't—"

"But that's just the point," the reporter edged in. "Isn't it strange that the feeling is there? I mean, with him being the number-one contender and everything, he might soon become addicted to this violence."

"Who would you say was the *most* addicted to this violence?" Mae Thelma snapped back. "The sadistic people who are willing to pay a fortune to watch it, or the man clever enough to make the money? It's not my husband you should worry about. He's only making a living at it. It's the people who are paying him for it who are the ones addicted to violence—not him! Because Rubin would never do you any harm unless you provoked him, and then you really would be in trouble!" She was emphatic.

"And let me tell you something else," she said more coolly. "Never before in my life have I met a person who was so unselfish as my husband is. Only on rare occasions has he even shown any disregard for the feelings of others—including my own. But he's for real! There is no phoniness about him. No airs. So I understand what he's all about, and I love what he is, and together we will conquer it all."

We did, too. We had a beautiful life together.

On October 27, 1962, just a little bit more than a year after I left the penitentiary, I had my first nationally televised fight in Madison Square Garden. It was publicized as "The Battle of the Left-Hookers"—my left-hook against that of Florentino Fernandez. One sportswriter from the *Jersey Journal* predicted I would take Fernandez down within two rounds.

In the dressing room that night, leafing through some old comic books that were left there by the hockey teams, I felt loose and relaxed, almost drowsy, but in shape, both mentally and physically.

I was ready for just about anything. I had knocked out Ernie Burford in August, and since then I had been living up at Eshan's Training Camp in Chatham, New Jersey, coming down only once —to knock out Mel Collins on October 5.

But now, at eight o'clock, sitting in a paint-peeling, gray-walled dungeon under the old Madison Square Garden, with two security guards stationed at my door to keep the spectators out, the time started getting to me. It was still two hours before the fight was scheduled to begin, and I felt myself start to think about it too much.

I had fought this fight a thousand times over in my mind, even during the four years I'd spent in jail. There I had absorbed make-believe punches that always seemed to hurt like hell, but later I learned through trial and error that this pain can become irrelevant when you're fighting for your life, and I knew that was exactly what I would be doing with Fernandez—fighting for my life.

"Okay, Hurricane! It's time to go," the cop outside shouted when he finally opened the door. "Good luck to ya, kid."

Then Tommy Parks, my new black trainer (Tedeschi had gotten rid of Bucky some ten fights earlier), draped my new hooded black velvet robe, which was trimmed with metallic gold thread and had a big black panther crouching on the back of it, around my shoulders over my sky-blue robe—Winnie's robe. I wasn't making it easy for Tommy. I was moving, flexing my arms and shaking my head, trying to get my rhythm together and feeling the flow of power as it oozed through my body. I hated for people to touch me at this moment—it seemed to take something away from me. The corridors outside my door were mobbed with spectators, and I lashed out at a few of them for pulling on me, too. Finally the guards had to surround us and forcibly get us to the ring, uninjured.

The bright lights inside were hot and blinding, and the flashbulbs that kept popping into my eyes from ringside began to irritate me. But I had to be cool. The cameras were rolling. Millions of people were watching me, trying to gauge my reactions, trying to see if I really was the animal that the newspapers had made me out to be.

Such publicity was not too comforting to me, since I was bound to shock them all anyhow. I was fighting this fight with the same philosophy that had controlled my everyday life on the streets. I was never defending myself, as such, but when a person indicated he was about to do me harm, I would attack, viciously. And that's what I planned on doing here tonight with Fernandez—attack.

The hostility adrift in the ring between Fernandez and myself was like a solid sheet of ice. From corner to corner, each of us could see every little detail of the other's state of readiness. With the perception of skilled warriors, each of us was distinctly aware of the other's mental processes. We were both out to knock the other unconscious.

Then the bell rang, and my nervousness fled the ring with my cornerman taking the stool. Without even thinking about it, I stepped right out and popped Fernandez in his nose with one stiff jab, and then another, trying to lure him into my own rhythm. But he flicked out a long left hand of his own, skimming my shiny head, so I stuck him back in the mouth with another jab. Then suddenly I slipped to the side of his returning jab, and whipped across a vicious right hand straight to his chin. He dropped to the canvas on the seat of his britches.

"One! . . . Two! . . . Three! . . ." the referee counted, as I walked to a neutral corner and turned my back on the scene. I faced out into the audience, squinting to penetrate the darkness beyond the lights.

"Rubin! Rubin! Turn around, man!" Tommy Parks yelled at me as he came running around the outside apron of the ring. "Turn around, man! And watch whatcha doing!"

"Turn around, kid! Please turn around!" Tedeschi pleaded right along with Tommy.

"Four! . . . Five! . . . Six! . . ." the count continued behind me.

I looked down from the ring at Tommy Parks and Carmen Tedeschi, thinking, what the hell are you two fools complaining about? I knew what I was doing. I knew that Fernandez had to take the mandatory eight-count, and I didn't want to watch him while he was down. Didn't want to feel sorry for him if he got back up. Because I intended to tear his head clean off his shoulders this time. So what the hell were they yelling about? When the bell rang for each round, they grabbed the stool and ran down the stairs, and sat out there in the audience while I was up paying the dues. I'll just do this thing my way, I told myself.

"Seven! . . . Eight!" The count stopped.

I turned back and faced my opponent, and I could see that he was hurt. He wobbled. His equilibrium was all messed up. But the referee waved me on, and wasting no effort, I moved out to demonstrate why they called me the Hurricane. Shuffling in close to Fernandez, I fired both hands from the hips, and nailed him with a barrage of punches that slammed him through the middle strands of the ropes, and hung him up there in suspension for a long moment.

Only sixty-nine seconds had passed.

Rather than back up, I followed him right into the ropes, still firing from both hands and snarling. For the briefest of moments, the memory of Benny "Kid" Paret's tragic death in this very same ring six months earlier, cruelly battered and pinned in this same corner, flashed to my mind, and then it was gone. The referee was dragging me away, allowing Fernandez to fall from where he was draped over the center strand like an inverted bow. The fight was over.

The Hurricane had done it again.

But three TV fights later, also in Madison Square Garden, I battled José Gonzalez to a virtual standstill, blinded and bathed in my own blood, only to lose the fight. That dirty bitch Success—who had been drinking up my whiskey, sleeping in my bed, and spending up my money—deserted me like I had the bubonic plague.

José was then a noncontender in the middleweight division, unrated and underestimated, while I was ranking number five. Gonzalez was shorter than I by at least two inches, but he was broad and thick-shouldered, powerful from the floor up. But he was scared, too. As soon as the bell rang for the first round to start, I stepped out and busted him in the mouth with a left hook. Fighting from a crouch that was much lower than usual, he leaped up with his head and smashed it into my face, splitting my eyes wide open.

This rascal was a billygoat! He used his head, and the heels of his gloves to keep the blood flowing, while I fought with a single-minded concentration that excluded all else but outraged fury for his cowardice. Every time José Billygoat would so much as touch me (since I couldn't see him clearly after that first hit), I would retaliate with all the savagery in my repertoire, hoping to catch him accidentally-on-purpose. But he had done his job to perfection. The fool had really blinded me.

Each time the bell rang to end a round, my trainer had to come out and lead me back to the corner like a seeing-eye dog. The commissioner's doctor, Alexander Schiff, would examine my eyes and shake his head. Blood was spattered everywhere.

"Please, Doc," I begged him after every round. "Please don't stop the fight! I'll knock him out this time! I can see, now!" But I couldn't.

Between rounds, Tommy Parks fought furiously to stem the flow of blood; sometimes he managed to stop it. But José wasn't going for none of that. He would quickly maul me again, just as soon as we got back out there to fight, rubbing his wiry hair against my eyes until the blood flowed again. Then his cornermen would begin their chant of "Stop the fight. . . . Stop the fight. . . . Stop the fight . . ." while I fired on José in blind desperation, trying to knock him out to save the fight, and knowing all the time that I was fighting a losing cause.

And so it was.

In the sixth round Dr. Schiff couldn't take all that blood anymore. He stepped in and stopped the fight, which gave José Billygoat a TKO over the Hurricane. It was the first and only time that ever happened to me. José hadn't won a single round on any of the score cards all night long. I had whupped the billygoat—blind—but he got that tramp called Success. I got sixteen stitches in one eye, and twenty-seven in the other.

Because I lost that supposedly unimportant fight, along with some of my prestige, a month and a half later—right after my scars had healed—I was pressured into fighting the baddest middleweight nigger in the world—Georgie Benton. He was ranked number three, and all the contenders had been ducking him. Nobody wanted to fight this man—not even me. He was the best boxer in the division, and one of its hardest punchers.

He had fifteen solid head-knocking years of experience behind him, fighting guys like Holly Mims (whom I had beaten myself by this time), Joey Giardello, Bobby Boyd, Henry Hanks, and Charlie Josephs—all warriors from the old school. But I found Georgie Benton's weakness, his Achilles' heel that enabled me to overpower him when we met May 25, 1963.

Georgie was shy up under the left titty. He was a bit more afraid of me than I was of him, and so I relieved him of his long-held third-ranking position in a ten-round decision. Whupped his ass in the process, too!

So, as the year drew to its close, I could total seven lucrative television appearances in twelve months. I was rated the number-one contender in the world, I was married, with a beautiful baby daughter baking in my wife's oven, and I was financially secure. I didn't owe nobody—nothing! My income taxes were always paid. I made damn sure of that, because that was part of my deal with Tedeschi—that the tax money would come right off the top of every purse, even before anything else was sorted out.

So I was sitting pretty right about then, almost without a worry in the world. The only thing that was bothering me was the fact that I didn't have any more black people working in my corner. The closer I came to the championship, it seemed, the quicker my manager would find some reason to get rid of my black trainers. Little Charlie Goldman, the derby-hatted old man who had steered Rocky Marciano to the heavyweight championship of the world, was now my trainer, too, and was trying to do the same thing for me.

Welterweight Champion Emile Griffith and I signed to fight in the Pittsburgh, Pennsylvania, Civic Arena on December 20, 1963. Griffith had become very good friends with my family and me over the past few years, and was always welcome among us. He was a helluva fighter to me, and we got along beautifully. He was riding high on the hog now, dominating his division, and had just been voted Fighter of the Year. So he was feeling his Cheerios and acting foolish. Now he wanted to close out the season with the Fight of the Year, and secure himself a sure shot at the middleweight title.

I couldn't let him do that.

But that left me with a slight problem, because I felt that if he ever got started, the Champ could outbox me. He was definitely more fleet of foot than I was. That meant I had to find some way to make him stand still and fight, instead of getting up on his bicycle and backpedaling all night long. And I had just the thing to do it with, too—his pride. Because Emile Griffith was notoriously proud.

I started right in on my "mad" campaign just as soon as we got to Pittsburgh, at our first press conference, in front of a nation-wide television audience. I picked this time because, living the way I had, I realized that the traps life sometimes laid down for a man were not always those made of steel, and the bait not always what he expected. At first Emile just took the whole thing as a publicity stunt and accepted my digging barbs graciously. But after a while they started getting next to him, as I intended them to. I laid siege to his abilities, and it came to full flower one night while we were appearing on another television program.

"Are you going to run tomorrow night, like all the news reports say you are, Champ?" the television host asked Emile. "Or are you going to stand toe-to-toe with the Hurricane and fight it out?"

I could see Emile was getting annoyed by all this talk about him running. He didn't like that at all.

"I'm the Welterweight Champion of the World," Emile snapped in his precise West Indian accent, surprising the commentator. "I've never run from anyone before, and I'm not about to start with Mr. Hurricane Carter now!"

"Then I'm going to beat your brains in!" I edged in, goading him on. But Emile only laughed, and it was a good laugh, like he was unloading the tension he felt.

"I've never been knocked out, either!" he snapped back at my quip. I sat there glaring at him. "But if you don't stop running off at the mouth, Mister Bad Rubin Hurricane Carter," he said, "I'm going to turn you into a gentle breeze, and then knock you out, besides!" Griffith was fit to be tied by this time, so I slipped the corker in on him.

"Knock me out!" I exclaimed, turning from Emile to face the audience. "If you even *show up* at the Arena tomorrow night, that'll be enough to knock me out!" I said heatedly. "I oughta cloud up and rain all over you right here! You talk like a champ, but you fight like a woman who deep down wants to be raped!" Emile bristled at that and his eyes glinted dangerously.

I knew I had him then.

Just as he had predicted, he came to fight. He brought with him his cheering section, his greatest admirer, and his mother—all of whom happened to be the same person. It was a frigid Friday night, six below zero, and the fight drew a crowd of disappointing size. Rather than brave the sub-zero temperatures outside, it seemed that everybody was staying home to watch the fight on television.

Emile was going into the ring as the 11–5 favorite, not only because he was a champ who hadn't suffered a knockout in forty-two fights, or because of his record-breaking third-time capture of the title (from Luis Rodriguez that June), but because of his speed, his punching ability, and his tried and true stamina.

He started right out like he wanted to win, trying to force the action in the first minutes. That's where he made his mistake. It was exactly what I'd been looking for—his pride to overrule his better judgment. I knew I had him hooked good. He was geared for a swap-out session. Whatever I hit him with, he was determined to hit right back with the same. He wanted to prove to his critics that he could take my best, and return the firepower tenfold; most of all, he wanted to prove that he could outpunch me, fighting my fight.

"Whoooowie!" I thought to myself. "This is going to be a humdinger here tonight."

I popped him in the mouth with a real stiff jab, and before I could get away, he smacked me right back in the mouth. Then I pumped one to his forehead, and he pumped it right back on me. So I backed away a couple of steps and looked at him, then snorted, shuffled back in again and shot another jab in his nose. Then I slipped inside of his countering jab to try and break my left hook off in his gut.

"*Ughhhhhhhhh!*" The air came out of Emile in a rush, and he tried to grab me. I pushed him away.

"Naw-naw, sucker," I mumbled through my mouthpiece, and fired another barrage of lefts and rights that drove him into the ropes. "You made a mistake," I said. "And now you gotta pay the Hurricane!" A left hook dropped him on his back in a neutral corner.

"One! . . . Two! . . . Three! . . ."

The suddenness of it all had stunned the crowd. It took several seconds for them to register what had happened, and then they came to their feet, cheering, as Griffith staggered to his feet just in time to beat the count. But I wasn't going to let him off the hook now. I moved right back in to bombard the bewildered champion, smashing devastating left hooks into his body, right hands to his head. One of these dropped him back to the canvas again.

Emile was hurt, bad, but he was game, too. He tried to get back up, and stumbled. The referee, Buck McTiernan, stepped in and stopped the fight to save the Champ from further punishment. The time was 2:13 of the first round.

The Hurricane had done it again!

On February 3, 1964, on a chilly winter morning up at Eshan's

Training Camp, where I was preparing for my fight with Jimmy Ellis on the twenty-eighth in Madison Square Garden, I was suddenly called back home. Mae Thelma had just given birth to our beautiful baby daughter. Her name is Theodora, and I was then and still am the proudest father in the world.

Jimmy Ellis, who later became the W.B.A.'s Heavyweight Champion of the World, was the chief sparring partner of the Louisville Lip—Cassius Clay—who had three days earlier defeated my main kazam, Sonny Liston, for the world heavyweight crown. Now Clay was working in Ellis's corner against me, trying to make it a dual victory for the Kentuckians over the Bears. He called Sonny the Big Bear, and me the Little Bear, because I'd never missed the opportunity to tell him about his loud-mouthed self.

Clay was always trying to get me whupped, sending his sparring partners to do something that he wasn't certain he could do himself. But that night he would have been better off if he had tried it himself, because Jimmy Ellis just wasn't man enough to do the job. He didn't come to fight, he only came to stay on his feet for ten rounds, and the one time he did take a chance—after Clay kept hollering at him—I knocked him on his ass! From that point on—if I had stayed in my corner—Ellis would have stayed in his, and the spectators would have gone to sleep.

So I chased him all night for a ten-round decision.

A couple of days later, while sitting at home and playing with my daughter, I received a telephone call from the Internal Revenue Service explaining that they wanted to see me and that it was important. So I went. When I got there, I almost had a heart attack. They told me that I owed Uncle Sam $90,000 in back taxes! That I hadn't filed in three years.

"You got to be kidding, man!" I told the people, after I got over the shock. "My income taxes are paid after every fight! Even before I get a dime myself. There must be some mistake here somewhere."

But there was no mistake, and they weren't kidding. I saw that Tedeschi had been beating me for my money all along.

When I confronted him with this bit of clever thievery, hoping upon hope that he would somehow be able to explain away the missing money, he just shrugged it off and told me not to worry about it. That he'd take care of it. But I was tired of him taking care of my money, and me getting beat in the process. He had proved to be a man to whom nothing was sacred; everything to him was open to insult and ridicule. I told him just to forget about it, that I would no longer fight for a man that I couldn't respect, and that we were through. I added that if he had been any longer than what he was, I would whup his motherfucking ass for him, too.

But even that didn't bother him.

Fighting was my bread and butter, the only livelihood I had. It paid the bills, and kept the "haints" away from my wife and daughter. But with Tedeschi, fighting was just a hobby. He thought that he could freeze me back into line by forcing me to remain idle until I really needed the money. Then he would be able to call the shots again. But he overlooked one important factor in his lopsided way of thinking: he blew the most binding ingredient of our entire relationship—the contract.

It had run out on him a few months before.

But Tedeschi wasn't finished with me yet. One day, about two weeks later, I picked up the evening newspaper and read in bold two-inch high print that Rubin Hurricane Carter had been suspended from boxing! The New York commissioner had just revoked my license for failing to appear at my hearing after their third notice to me.

The next day I went to New York to see about these charges, to explain to the commissioner that I hadn't received *one* notice, much less three. But the Commission chairman, Edwin B. Dooley, informed me that he himself had sent me three written notices requiring my presence.

"Where did you send your notices to?" I asked him, but I knew the answer before he gave it.

"We sent them to Carmen Tedeschi, your manager," he said. "The same place we always send your mail. After all, it was *he* who really came to us asking for this appointment, so that you two guys could renew your expired contract."

I just shook my head. That Tedeschi had a lot of try, boy! A lot of try.

A little over a week later, after a new hearing at which both Tedeschi and myself were present and at which he still tried to pull his con game off on the commissioners—as if this whole thing had just been one big mistake—my suspension was lifted and my license reinstated. I was declared a free agent to boot.

I watched in disgust as many legal thieveries like those I experienced at my manager's hands were lived and relived every day of my life, and how the news media suddenly became indignant and grabbed the bone of my career and tried to bury it because I was leaving my Masta. He had *made* me what I am, they claimed, and now I was deserting him like a black rat on a floundering ship.

They refused to see fight managers like Tedeschi in their true light, as they dispassionately signed away a fighter's life with little more than the flick of a fountain pen. Always polite and confident, they regarded a fighter's life as though it were only a footnote to a *Ring* magazine article that might have been written by Joe Louis and prefaced by Sugar Ray Robinson. Their feeling was never one of love—though they were very fond of saying it was—or of crushed skulls and bloody faces, or even doubt that maybe their fighter just wouldn't be up to the struggle that night.

No, No. Money was always the motive.

THE FOURTEENTH ROUND

The Awful Scream of Silence

By the spring of 1964 I had become the number one middleweight challenger. My success aside, I now accepted as a foregone conclusion that nobody really cared about us prize fighters, and that we were looked upon with favor only as somebody else's fighting machines—or, rather, as his meal tickets. When we finally grew old and tired, or maybe got hurt while fighting and the machine just didn't work as well as it had in the past, we were simply scrapped and sent to the junkyard to rot, to lay in waste upon the heaps of other discarded prize fighters who were already decomposing in the bin—just like any other machine rusts without the proper care.

While earlier in my career my concern was for the welfare of all prize fighters, it later narrowed down only to black fighters, and then came to be for black people in general. I had no religious convictions to define my position, no moral feelings to explain away my attitude. I only knew that white people always stuck together, no matter what the cause, in order to break the independent black man. This discovery had worked itself into a deeply grooved furrow of my mind, and I began to resent what was happening to me in public. The newspapers were out to destroy me because Tedeschi had said that I was hooked up with the Mafia, managed by a member of the family of "Bayonne Joe" Zicarelli, and while I could forgive very easily, it was impossible for me to forget.

I considered myself a fairly quiet person. Others may have thought me flamboyant and not overly bright (I sometimes questioned the matter myself), but I had my own ideas about the people around me. I believed that, basically, they were all full of shit. So I began to refuse all interviews. I declined to attend any more banquets. Even after a fight sometimes, when the dressing room was crowded with newspapermen, sportswriters, and commentators all spouting their praise of—or disappointment in—what they had just seen, I would be appreciative and sort of humble, but never open and aboveboard with my thoughts.

I discovered how viciously the press could affect my life in April 1964, when an incident now known as the Harlem Fruit Riot jumped off.

No one (especially not me) seems to know what actually touched off the terrible violence that swept through the streets of Harlem the afternoon of April 17, indiscriminately striking down little kids who were not yet even of high-school age. Some said it was because several of the children had overturned a fruit stand while coming home from school; the police have since lodged other accusations to justify their brutality—mainly that six teen-agers had robbed and killed a Harlem shopkeeper. The man who owned the fruit stand, however, claimed that the kids who had overturned his stand were not from the neighborhood.

I won't go into any aspects of innocence or guilt in the situation, because I really don't know. But there seems to be general agreement with the point to which I eventually addressed myself: that hundreds of sadistic policemen arrived on the scene with their pistols drawn, and started kicking and cuffing and beating those little children over the head with their billy clubs until they were lying out in the streets, torn and bleeding like the abused lumps of helpless humanity they were.

This fiendish display of brutality compelled me to disregard my prior cool and voice my outrage against the trouncing those little children—and grownups as well—received. In anger, I told a supposedly friendly reporter that the black public ought to protect its own against this type of tyrannical invasion by white cops into black neighborhoods. Anyone else in the world would have fought back: a little cockroach, an ant, or even a bedbug; everything, from the smallest creature to the very largest, would have fought back in self-defense, everything but a goddamn nigger!

But I went further with this reporter and said that during the riot, when scores of children were being trampled, stomped, and mutilated by a legion of club-wielding police—while other cops held their guns to the children's heads—the black community should have arisen right then and fought to their death in the streets, if it was necessary. Because self-protection is the absolute right of every living being on the face of the earth. No matter who he is, what color he is, a person has a right to live, and to do so without always being dangled over the political edge of genocide every day of his life.

I told the man that *dreams* do not make reality, and reality for black people may not be all that ideal, but that it's the only real thing we've got. A black preacher who because of his beliefs remains passive while a nigger-hating cop holds a gun barrel to his head may close his eyes, if he chooses to, and imagine himself being a million miles away praying humbly to his God, but when that cop pulls that trigger and the hammer falls, it's going to blow his goddamn brains out just the same! That's reality.

Some trigger-happy cops would kill a black man with icy calm as long as they had the law backing them up, I said. But let that same man face death unarmed, like the people he was killing had to do, and that icy calm would evaporate like dewdrops hitting the first rays of the morning sun. Without that gun, without the official backing of that little tin shield, every man in the world was equal in one very important way: we all had to pull our pants down and shit between two legs. All of us.

This reporter promised to keep most of the things that I told him off the record and confidential—and he did, too—everything I've noted above. Nonetheless, he did print, in an article published in *The Saturday Evening Post*, one statement that spelled my doom: "During last summer's Harlem riots [that followed the Fruit Riot] for instance," he wrote, "[Carter] suggested, in jest, to Elwood Tuck, his closest friend, 'Let's get our guns and go up there and get us some of those cops. I know I can get four or five before they get me. How many can you get?' "

Although the article more or less indicated that I'd meant it as a joke—and I really did, then—the police didn't see it that way. Thus, its appearance in print accomplished something that all my years of being in and out of jail could never do: it brought the entire country's law enforcement agencies crashing down on my head with blood in their eyes. I'll explain about that in a minute.

At first it surprised me that what I'd said had such an impact upon the police. Because—Good Lord!—three short years before, the cops couldn't have cared less what Rubin Carter had to say. But now they were all in an uproar. The Harlem Fruit Riot, as we'll soon see, only foreshadowed the first political repercussions of trying to keep the niggers in their places, President Johnson's civil rights bills notwithstanding.

The first I became aware that this article had been published at all was when I received a call from Sugar Ray Robinson, who told me about it. There were then two men in the world whom I respected more than anybody else: Miles Davis was one, Sugar Ray was the other.

"Hurricane? This is Ray," he said, as soon as I picked up the telephone. "Man, what are you trying to do, get yourself killed or something? Have you got any idea what this article is saying?" he asked. But I had no idea what he was even talking about.

"What article?" I asked. "What the hell are you talking about, Ray?"

"The magazine article!" he said, exasperated. "The *Post*! What the hell did you think I was talking about!" Then: "Do you mean to tell me that you haven't even read this thing, yet?" He was incredulous.

"No," I answered. "Why? Should I have read it?"

"You damn right you should have read it!" Sugar Ray snapped right back. He'd been this route himself, before. "But even more, you shouldn't have even said it," he went on, "because your ass is in the fire now! So you better read it. No! Wait!" he said, changing his mind. "I'll read it to you!" And as he read it word by word, line by line, I realized to what depths an eager reporter would stoop to sell his story.

"That's a goddamn lie!" I told Ray heatedly after he had finished. "I didn't mean—"

"You mean to tell me that you didn't say that?" he interrupted me, swiftly, knowing that some of it was my philosophy. "It sounds like you, Rubin!"

"Sure," I admitted. "I said some of it. And meant it, too! But it's not in its proper context. A lot of what I said was left out—all the qualifying parts. I was talking about defense! Not attacking those goddamn people," I told him bitterly. "That man just used what he wanted, and disregarded the rest! But thanks, Sugar, I'll get back to you later, man. I've got to try to stop this thing before it goes too far."

But the pendulum had swung too far already.

Even at that moment I was hog-tied and branded as a mad-dog, cop-killing nigger who was hell-bent on wiping out the law—singlehandedly, no less. I'd never claimed to be a pulpit angel, and I don't intend to claim it now, but I didn't deserve that. Quite a few people who I could call my friends were lawmen—black and white.

In fact, all of my brothers-in-law in Washington are cops. There was also Peter Rush, a Secret Service man, who always did his roadwork with me whenever he wasn't out guarding some president, and who told me what the law people around the country were saying about me after that article was published. (He later came to testify for me at my trial.) There was Billy Kilroy, a U.S. marshal and an old friend, whose wife and mine always exchanged dinner engagements; Ray Sadowski, a state trooper, who actually got me started in boxing while I was still in prison; Bobby Ward, the detective who had sent me to Trenton State Prison, but who turned out to be a helluva friend later on; Fred Hogan, an Atlantic Highlands cop who always stayed up in training camp with me; Ronald Lipton, a Jersey City detective who was one of my sparring partners; Howard Kline, a Paterson detective, and probably one of my friendliest of friends; Ernie Hutcherson, Melvin Jenkins, Moody—all Paterson cops—men I had grown up with. All of them were telling me the same story: "The *Law* was out to pin the Hurricane's black ass to the wall!"

I began to feel the heat almost immediately. Early one morning, shortly after the Fruit Riot, my car broke down on the highway near Hackensack, New Jersey. The voltage regulator had suddenly gone dead. The road was deserted. It was almost three o'clock the morning, and cold, and what few cars did pass me wouldn't stop. So I pushed my monster off to the side and started hoofing it down the highway to find some help.

It was dark, and lonely, and the wind whipped right through my clothes. My feet were cold. Then I saw a black and white patrol car heading down the highway in the opposite direction. I ran across the divider and flagged it down, and asked the officer to help me find an open service station, or take me to a telephone booth, whichever was easiest.

"Why, certainly," the young white cop smiled. "Get in, man! It's cold out there, isn't it? I've got some jumper cables in my trunk. Maybe they'll start your car without you having to pay some tow truck to do it." It was nice and warm inside his car, and on the way back to mine, we got into a hip conversation about nothing in particular.

But the moment the man laid eyes on my black custom Eldorado, with "Rubin Hurricane Carter" engraved in small silver letters on each side of the headlights, his entire attitude changed.

He didn't say anything about it though. When we couldn't get the car started, he pretended to take me to a telephone downtown, but he was really bringing me to headquarters, to get me in there with the rest of his boys. And that's exactly what he did—locked my dumb ass up! Now he claimed that a meat-packing factory, right across the highway from where my car had broken down, had been burglarized during the night. I was now the prime suspect. Sonofabitch!

Had the man just reached over in the car and smacked me dead in the mouth, I would have been less surprised—and much less angry too. But when I found out how he had tricked me into this den of iniquity just to set me up, I felt something ugly rise up inside of me. Headquarters was manned by a totally white crew of cops, and they reveled in the pleasure of having me in their jail, of being able to lock up this loudmouthed nigger who talked too goddamned much!

When I asked if I could use the telephone to call my wife or my lawyer, they sneeringly refused, and then drew their pistols on me when I became insistent about it. Just standing there facing all of that saintly hatred oozing from the pores of all those big brave "servants of the people" with their weapons already drawn, I experienced a feeling that I hadn't felt to the same degree since that fat cop in Paterson had smacked me when I was nine years old, and this incident reminded me of it for the first time in years. I was furious, and humiliated too, because I felt helpless. They locked me up in a stinking cage as if I were a mad gorilla, while a steady flow of their giggling brethren trickled passed the cell door to taunt me, laughing like the scared fools they were.

Four hours later I was still locked up, pacing the cell in a cold fury and wondering how could I get a message out to somebody. I knew that if I didn't, I was going back to prison—and for nothing —because this was the way the police operated when they wanted to get rid of somebody; putting that person in jail was the easiest thing they could do. Finally, a big black patrolman coming in for his tour of duty passed by cell and recognized me.

"Hurricane?" He stopped suddenly and peered into the cell, looking at my bald head and beard. Not too many people had the nerve to wear such a style at that time. "Is that you in there, Carter? What the hell did you get busted for, man?" he asked, and for the first time since being locked up in that nasty cage, I dared let my hopes fly. I told him exactly what I had been busted for—for nothing—and I didn't mince my words, either.

The other cops in the squad room quietly started to disappear, one by one, because when I got through rapping, that brother was smoking, cussing out everybody in sight and talking about their knock-kneed mammys, their flat-footed daddys, and their snuff-dipping daughters, too. Everyone now asserted his ignorance. No one had any idea what I was locked up for. In fact, now they even pretended not to know who I was, or who it was that locked me up.

But if that righteous brother hadn't shown up on the scene when he did, those cops would probably have gone right back down to that meat-packing factory—if there ever was one—and really torn the door off the hinges, loading my Eldorado up with hamhocks, pigs' feet, hog maws, and chitterlings, and then charged me with breaking into the place, while their families ate the T-bone steaks, prime ribs, and the other choice cuts of meat that they would have kept for themselves. As it was though, because of that brother, they had to let me go.

Not to be outdone by the Hackensack police, however, my home town of Paterson started right in on their own campaign to "get Carter." Only their first attempt was made simpler one night when one of my sparring partners, whom I had *thought* to be my friend, asked me to drive him to a bar where he thought he could find his girlfriend. He went inside while I stayed out in the car. It was the first time that I had ever been near this particular place.

Five minutes passed, then ten, so I went inside to see what was holding him up. I found him hemmed into a corner by three white men crowding around him threateningly, and a black bartender climbing over the bar with a blackjack in his hand. I intervened and got him out of there before anything else could happen. But ten minutes later, Frank X. Graves, the mayor of Paterson, and ninety of his goon-squad policemen were out looking for me.

The cracker who owned the nigger ginmill had called the police and charged me with assault and battery to himself and one of his flunky Negroes—the bartender who had the billy club in his hand. But neither one had to be rushed to the hospital in dire straits, so that proved it couldn't have been me put my hands on them. Because if I had, they would have been ruint! Forever!

But the thing that really stroked my anger was the stridency with which the black community of Paterson assumed its position: they resented me for statements which I had made in private but which had come out in the press about protecting those little children in Harlem. Or *any* children. Anywhere. And I just couldn't grasp that type of logic. But I did understand black people's phobia concerning the law. They didn't resent me, actually; they were only disliking themselves. Desperate and afraid, they hated me because I was *not* afraid, and their fear had driven them to surrender.

Like Malcolm X, whom they hated for his tolerance and feared for his wisdom, my willingness to fight their battles to protect their own children only threw their shame right back into their faces. When they looked at themselves through the mirror of somebody else's eyes, they just didn't like what they saw. So instead of hating themselves for their own human frailties, they started hating me for my strength. And in their inability to fight back, they hated me all the more.

Meanwhile, the police escalated their guerrilla warfare.

The month of July that year was a very important month in the lives of every black person living in America. That was the month the Civil Rights Act was signed into law. For me it brought the signing for the championship fight, and the coming-to-life of my predictions concerning the political fate of my people. For the many black people who felt no pressing need to protect themselves from becoming mutilated under the Jim Crow-foot of their ungodly albino God, there would be death in abundance. Innocent blood would flow in the streets of nearly every major black community in the United States.

Almost from the moment President Johnson stepped in front of the television cameras and signed the 1964 Civil Rights Act, the disorders began. Policemen throughout the country began using lethal persuasion to contain the now supposedly emancipated niggers. Check it out! Look into your history books. See how many black men, women, and children died, and countless numbers of others lost all their worldly possessions—reducing their hard years of labor into nothing more than a fast-burning fire—just because they wouldn't fight to protect themselves.

And civil rights? Bullshit!

That was just another straw on the camel's back. Isn't it strange that if a black man kills a white man, no matter what the circumstances, that ultimately, if he isn't killed on the spot, he's charged with first-degree murder and sentenced to life imprisonment or death? Meanwhile, the same white man could massacre ten black men, five women, and three little children, but he would only be charged with violating the dead nigger's civil rights. A penalty which would net him only three years in prison, if anything. Where's the equality of that? In the White House?

That place in Washington, D.C., ought to be revealed to all black and poor people as the little swamp that it is. Though geographically small, to my mind that White House controls the entire world and every living thing within it, bending everybody to suit its own capricious needs. Each hallowed hall, each green, pink, blue, or whatever color room, only survives at the inhuman expense of many tortured souls forced to live under its demagogic domain.

The black plague of death began just two weeks after President Johnson signed the Proclamation. In New York City—the very same place of the Harlem Fruit Riot in April. This time an off-duty police lieutenant killed a kid. To my mind, he shot the kid down for absolutely nothing. And that started five years of open hunting season on blacks. Nineteen people were shot that time, a hundred and sixteen injured.

During the second day of the rioting, after the funeral services for little Jimmy Powell (the fifteen-year-old who was killed by the cop), James Farmer, then national director of CORE, went to Harlem and checked out the destruction for himself—and was shocked. As he looked about, he saw only havoc, the results of an orgy of death and destruction. Later that day, at a news conference, he said:

"I saw a bloodbath. I saw with my own eyes violence, a bloody orgy of police . . . a woman climbing into a taxi and indiscriminately shot in the groin . . . police charging into a grocery store and indiscriminately swinging clubs . . . police shooting into tenement windows and into the Theresa Hotel. I entered the hotel and saw bullet holes in the walls. . . .

"I saw bloodshed as never before. . . . people threw bottles and bricks. I'm not saying they were not partly to blame. But it is the duty of the police to arrest, not indiscriminately shoot and beat."

Other similarly barbaric shootings and killings were taking place up and down Lenox Avenue between 125th and 130th streets, as wave after wave of riot-gear-armed cops were rushed to the scene, accompanied by carloads of cartridges to replenish the fast-dwindling supply at the riot site. Before daybreak on that bullet-ridden morning, after cruising the area in an unmarked car, Police Commissioner Michael J. Murphy countered James Farmer's charges with the asinine observation, "Some persons have used this unfortunate incident [the Powell shooting] as an excuse for looting and vicious, unprovoked attacks against police. In our estimation this is a crime problem and not a social problem."

What has always escaped me is why couldn't it have been a civil problem rather than a criminal one? After all, Civil Rights did start it! Commissioner Murphy had definitely missed his calling in life: he should have been a chemist instead of a cop, because this man was a genius at changing hard facts into soft shit. What he was really saying was that any civil rights movement that lacked the clear power and purpose to affect the controlling majority was nothing more than a deep bowel movement that should be confined to the bathroom and not be littering up the streets.

John Brown clearly had the right idea a hundred and fifteen years earlier after the Harper's Ferry Raid. He declared to the court in his last written statement, given to one of the guards on the morning of his execution, December 2, 1859:

> That this Court acknowledges, as I suppose, the validity of the law of God. I see a book kissed here which I suppose to be the Bible, or at least the New Testament. That teaches me that all things whatsoever I would that man should do to me, I should do even so to them. It teaches me, further, to remember them that are in bonds, as bound with them. . . .
>
> So I, John Brown, am now quite certain that the crimes of this *guilty land will* never be purged away but with *blood*. I had, as I now think vainly, flattered myself that without very much bloodshed it might be done.

This had been the astute ideology, I thought, that had influenced the black leaders of the sixties, and especially Martin Luther King. But after the riots, they began to change their views. The deep shock of that first flash of indiscriminate brutality hit them like a thunderbolt, and the quick succession of similar outbursts in Rochester, Jersey City, Paterson, Elizabeth, and Chicago likewise dealt them a savage blow where they lived.

Shortly after these major disturbances were fascistically quelled by the police, whose actions officially announced the beginning of their long hot summer's hunting season, many of the more prominent black leaders came to see me in Las Vegas, where I was training for an October championship fight with Joey Giardello. They admitted that maybe I had been right all along—even though I didn't know it myself—and now they wanted to know how I thought this sudden brush fire of violence could be extinguished— to give them a chance to validate the ballot, rather than the bullet. I couldn't even begin to answer their questions. My life had been predicated more or less upon a Machiavellian concept: that once you harmed a man, you must either reconcile that person completely or destroy him utterly. I didn't know a damn thing about politics.

But ignorance is no excuse. Our history has proved, down through the years of legalized slavery, that the real danger lies not in the possession of power, but in the abuse of it. On August 4, 1964, the mutilated bodies of James Chaney, Andrew Goodman, and Michael Schwerner—three young civil rights workers missing since June of that year—were unearthed by the F.B.I. from under a farm pond dam near Philadelphia, Mississippi, where they had been buried. The sheriff of Neshoba County, Lawrence Rainey, and his deputy, Cecil Price, were among nineteen of those indicted for violating the civil rights of the three murdered victims. Price and six others were convicted in October 1967 and sentenced to three years in prison. Rainey and seven others were acquitted. The Federal Government dropped the charges on the remaining eight.

So where was the justice? In a ballot, or a bullet?

It was December when I finally got the chance to fight Giardello for the middleweight title. The bout had been postponed in Vegas and moved to Philly, the champ's home town—he wouldn't fight me anywhere else. I lost a controversial fifteen-round decision.

By then I had acquired another manager, a new trainer, and a black personal advisor who functioned as a buffer between the police and myself, because I was catching pure hell from cops all over the country. Every state that I visited—for pleasure or for business—the local authorities would come and get me immediately upon reaching a town, take me down to headquarters, mug me, fingerprint me, and then make me carry an I.D. card attesting to the fact that I was a registered exconvict. Later even England got in on the deal. On one occasion they refused to let me into the country for three solid hours until I had received a special work permit from their Minister of Commerce.

It was my advisor's job to be with me at all times and to eliminate this constant harassment as quickly as possible. Quite frankly, I was worried that the police would soon get tired of this game they were playing and find some reason to kill me anyhow. So company was my only protection. My advisor's name was Elwood Tuck. Patty Amato, the assistant warden of Hudson County Jail, was my manager. And Jimmy Wilde, a former trainer of five world champions, was my cornerman, the best I ever had.

The following year, 1965, really kept me busy. But it was necessary. It was my way of trying to avoid the inevitable, but it also caused me to criminally neglect the two most important people in my life—Mae Thelma and little Theodora. On the twelfth of February, I fought Luis Rodriguez in New York City; then it was Paris on the twenty-second, and London on the ninth of March. Only one time during this period did my wife ever interfere with anything that I was doing.

It happened a month after Malcolm X was assassinated. I had just returned home from a successful tour of Europe, the highlight of which had been my nine-round knockout of the British middleweight champ in London. The telephone rang early one morning. Mae Thelma answered it. It was from Dr. Martin Luther King. He wanted to know if I would consider coming down to Selma, Alabama, to march in his demonstration to dramatize the voting discrimination. I had made the March on Washington with him in 1963.

"Alabama!" I exclaimed aloud, and saw the fright in my wife's face. She emphatically shook her head from side to side, telling me, "No! Hell, no!" Her grandparents lived in the South, and she went to see them quite often, but would never let me go with her. She was scared that them honkies would get me down there and kill me because of my arrogant attitude toward tobacco-chewing crackers. But she really had no cause to worry, because I was thinking about the same damn thing myself.

"No, I can't go down there," I told the good Reverend. "That would be foolishness at the risk of suicide. Those people would kill me dead! I wouldn't stand a snowball's chance in hell." And it's a good thing I didn't go, too, because the march was brought to a swift and violent conclusion by Alabama dogs and law enforcement officers—which I would say are synonymous.

After I'd been home with my family for just a few days, I had to fly to Kansas City, and then back to London for a fight on April 20. Ten days later I returned to Paterson to fight Johnny Torres, knocked him out, and got locked up again right after the fight. But let me explain that to you.

I was, by nature, a devoted night owl whenever I wasn't in training—would much rather sleep all day and stay up all night. (I'm still the same way now.) So early one morning I went to see a friend named Edgar "Slam" Shewmaker, who was a member of a small group of interior decorators just going into business—called the Hurricane Painters—of which I was the sponsor.

As I pulled up in front of his house that morning, I noticed a white guy standing back in the shadows against the building. His name was Thomas Cappucio—although I didn't know it at the time—so I just dismissed him from my mind.

Upstairs, inside the house, there were five other people sitting around with Slam listening to tapes and talking. I must have been sitting down for less than two minutes when there was a loud knock on the front door.

"Who is it?" Slam called, getting up to answer it.

"The police!" came the barked reply as the door was flung open and a white patrolman walked in with the fellow who had been standing downstairs, Cappucio.

"Awright, give it up!" the cop started right in without saying another word. "Who's got this man's money? He claims that you guys cheated him at craps. So just give him back the bread that he's lost, and everything'll be cool," the cop said, trying to talk hip.

I was sitting way back in a corner of the room, where the lights were dim, and was hoping that the man wouldn't recognize me. I didn't gamble, and I didn't know what he was talking about. There had been no crap game in progress when I arrived, so I just sat back and listened to what was being said.

"Ain't nobody beat that man out of his money," Slam told the cop. "In fact, there hasn't even been a game here tonight." But the cop didn't want to hear that. He was a nasty bastard.

"Don't hand me that fuckin' shit!" he spat. "Or why would this poor sucker flag us down outside and tell us that, if you fuckin' people didn't beat him out of his bread? So cough the man's dough up! That's all, so I can get the hell outta here! Or do you want me to lock all of your black asses up?"

"But we ain't got his money," Slam said. "The man's just bull-shitting you!"

"Awwww, fuck it!" the cop snorted, disgustedly. "I tried to give you fuckin' jokers a break. But now I'm locking all of your dumb asses up!" And he started for the door.

Oooooh, shit! I said to myself. Let me get out of here. Getting locked up right then would have been all I needed to have my forthcoming May 20 bout with Dick Tiger in Madison Square Garden canceled out permanently. That was my only chance of getting another shot at the title. Whoever won that bout was guaranteed the championship fight a few months later. So, as the cop walked over to the door and called down for his buddy to send for the paddy wagon, I stood up to identify myself.

I didn't know the cop, had never seen him before in my life, to my knowledge, and I was sure that the man who had gotten beat for the money would tell him that I wasn't there when it had happened—if it had happened.

"Er—officer?" I addressed the man, in a carefully modulated tone of voice. I wanted to let him know, in case he did recognize me, that I wanted to be conciliatory. "I just got here a few minutes before you did," I tried to explain. "So I would like to be able to leave now before the wagon gets here, if it's all right with you, because this man will tell you that I had nothing to do with whatever happened here."

"That's right, officer," the victim spoke right up without my asking him to. "He wasn't here when—" But the cop had already recognized me.

"Shut up!" he ordered Cappucio, and then turned to me. "And you, Mister Bigshot, sit your fuckin' ass down! I'm especially locking *you* up!"

I don't know why I was surprised, but I was. I couldn't help but grit my teeth and growl at this nasty bastard. The law! That pop-eyed sonofabitch. He stood there with his fist wrapped around his pistol, laughing mirthlessly—priming himself up for the kill, allowing his hatred of me to reach full flood. His face ran the gamut of expressions from ice-cold dispassion to boiling virulence. If there had been no one else there but me, he would have snaked his gun out and shot me down. In self-defense, he would have claimed! The nasty scum-sucking sonofabitch.

So I went to jail again, and the next day the local papers read, in tall print:

RUBIN "HURRICANE" CARTER'S IN AGAIN—FOR CRAP-SHOOTING, ABUSE

Middleweight boxer Rubin (Hurricane) Carter found himself in another brush with the law early Saturday morning. He faces two charges of disorderly conduct as well. . . .

Carter and eight others, also charged with disorderly conduct, were found in what in what police described as a "disorderly house" at 5:15 a.m. Saturday. . . .

Patrolmen Joseph Guidice and Joseph LaBark were responding to a noise complaint. At the apartment of . . . Edgar L. Shewmaker, they found what appeared to be an illegal night club. . . .

Carter was released in $100 bail. Four others were committed to the county jail in default of bail $100 each. Released on $50 bail were Gene Tierno, a technician, and Thomas Cappucio, a truck driver. The second charge against Carter was made by Patrolman Guidice for allegedly becoming abusive when arrested. . . .

Magistrate Charles J. Alfano Saturday set May 4 for a hearing on the charge. . . .

Carter faces court hearings on two assault charges. Last year he was charged by George Shaw, owner of the Kit Kat Club, with assaulting him during a fracas in the saloon. . . .

Also on last July 2, Carter is alleged to have assaulted another man in a tavern fight. He's been out on $5,000 bail on those charges.

The Paterson press, especially the *Evening News*, had consistently shown itself to be a racist arm of the law. The only time that a black resident of the community would get sufficient news coverage in Paterson was when the police had killed or arrested him, and then finally when they framed his ass and sent him away to prison for the rest of his life—with the help of the paper's vicious lies.

But the real cleverness of the whole scheme came out later when Elwood Tuck was approached by some cop who offered to accept a bribe to have the charges withdrawn. We had to pay out five hundred dollars of my hard-earned money, which would be split between the two arresting officers.

Elwood had to accept the deal. The court hearing had been set for sixteen days before my scheduled bout with Dick Tiger, and I couldn't fight in New York with these charges pending against me. If I happened to be convicted on any one of them, the boxing commissioner would snatch my license away immediately. That was a sure-pop! Risking twenty thousand dollars for the five hundred it would cost me to have the charges withdrawn just wasn't worth it to my way of thinking. No way! Besides, I had no choice in the matter.

Thus, with the help of the bribe, I beat all of those trumped-up charges in court and was able to go on with my career. But Dick Tiger beat the shit out of me in the ring! Knocked me down three times for the worst whupping I ever had in my life, but in my heart it hurt me even more—because I felt that he couldn't really beat me. The constant police and press harassment was slowly taking its toll on me. The cops were killing me without even pulling the triggers on their guns, destroying the one thing I loved to do best— fight—and therefore destroying me. Killing me softly. Just because I had happened to stumble upon their plan of black mass murder.

Not long after the Tiger fight I flew up to Akron, Ohio, and knocked out Fate Davis in the first round. Then I went out to California to fight Luis Rodriguez again, and got hung up in the Watts Riot. And that's when I found out that the F.B.I. had been following me all the while.

As soon as I'd checked into a motel on Olympia Boulevard in L.A., I received a phone call from Chief William T. Parker of the Los Angeles Police, telling me that I'd better get my ass down to headquarters to register my exconvict title before he sent some of his boys over to get me.

"So you thought you were sneaking into town on me, huh, Carter?" Chief Parker asked smugly, when I finally got down to his office. He sounded very satisfied with himself. "But we knew you were coming, boy; the F.B.I. had you pegged every foot of the way," he said. "You couldn't have gotten into this city—no way!" He was actually gloating.

But he hadn't fooled me at all. I had a feeling for this sort of thing. From the moment I stepped off the plane, walked through the air terminal, caught a cab, checked into the motel, and grabbed a quick bite to eat in the dining room, and even down at the police headquarters, I had noticed the same person tailing behind me, trying to look inconspicuous—which was a laugh in itself.

"No, I wasn't trying to sneak into your town," I told him quite candidly. "I just came a little earlier than expected, that's all. But you should get somebody else to follow me around the next time." I nodded toward the woman who was trying—and failing miser- ably—to hide in his office. "My, God!" I marveled, just to make him mad, "she's got a beautiful ass on her, ain't she?"

And Chief Parker burned.

Unfortunately, he wasn't the only thing that burned in Los Angeles that week. Just as I had predicted to the *Saturday Evening*

Post reporter eighteen months earlier—but what he didn't print—every time that President Johnson signed some kind of legislation that would benefit the black masses, black people died in the streets. It was Harlem after the Civil Rights Act of 1964, and now it was the Voting Rights Bill of '65, signed only five days before the Watts Riot jumped off. Goddamn! It's a good thing that black folks weren't asking to get *civil wrongs* passed in Congress, or the cops would have massacred all of us like the United States Army did the Indians, I'm sure.

For the next five days in Watts, the rioting raged and destroyed forty million dollars' worth of the community's property; thirty-four people died, and there were 1032 reported injuries.* The entire black community was destroyed. There were fifteen thousand National Guardsmen and a thousand policemen occupying the neighborhood, killing off black folks in a turkey-shoot, and they still didn't dig it. Goddamn! Black people just refused to defend themselves, unless it was against another black.

After that, I needed a rest, so I went to Africa. *South* Africa, no less. The black people got together and invited me. And there I found the most beautiful brothers and sisters I have ever known—oppressed, but together! In a little Bantu village right outside of Johannesburg, after my fight with their welterweight and middleweight champ, Joe "Ax-killer" Ngidi, who I knocked out in the second round, I was named a Chief of the Zulu Tribe. "Nigi" they christened me—the man with the beautiful beard.

The first part of 1966 started off for me at the same furious pace as the previous year had: on January 8 I was in Chicago to fight Skeeter McClure; then Johnny Morris in Pittsburgh on the eighteenth, and Stan Harrington on the twenty-fifth in Honolulu. In February I went back to South Africa to fight Ernie Burford. Then, back home, I fought a return bout with Skeeter McClure in March. By then I was sick of airplanes and traveling, tired of living out of suitcases, and stone cold weary to the bone of readjusting to the different time zones around the world. I wanted to spend more time at home with my family before I started collecting social security, so I decided to take a much needed vacation.

I was still lazying around on the night of June 16, 1966, just

* According to the Report by the Governor's Commission on the Los Angeles Riot, *Violence in the City—An End or a Beginning?*, December 2, 1965, pp. 22–25.

sitting at home watching James Brown on TV with my wife and daughter, when I got a phone call from my new personal advisor, Nathan Sermond. (Elwood Tuck and I had had a slight falling-out over the police pressure and the fact that we stayed away from home so much.) He had received an offer for me to fight Rocky Rivero in South America and Sermond wanted me to meet him at his Club La Petite to discuss money matters. I had been out of action long enough to be jubilant at just the thought of a canvas beneath my feet. So I called my chief sparring partner, Wild Bill Hardney, and told him to get his shaggy butt ready for camp. He told me that he was coming into Paterson that night anyway, so we agreed to meet at the Nite Spot, one of the few places I frequented whenever I was in town—mostly because Elwood Tuck was the manager there.

I didn't get out of the house until late that night, and before I turned into downtown Bridge Street near midnight, I had picked up a passenger, John "Bucks" Royster, the friendly neighborhood alcoholic—though damn good people. When I slowed down to make the left-hand turn to the Club La Petite, somebody else called to me and I pulled over to the curb and waited. A minute later, a young fellow named John Artis sprinted up to the car.

John was a tall and rangy light-skinned boy whom I had met twice since I'd been home. He was a whiz at most sports, but had turned down several athletic scholarships to college, deciding instead to enlist in the Army. He leaned in the window past Bucks. They didn't know each other. John was too young (only twenty).

"You going up to the Nite Spot, Hurricane?" he asked me. "And if so, would you drop me off?"

"Okay," I told him. "But I have some business to take care of down here first. But if you want to wait, I'll take you up there when I go."

So John climbed in.

Nathan Sermond was all business at the Club La Petite. He was quiet, smooth, and self-controlled—there was no play in him. He came right to the point and told me that the promoter in South America was willing to pay for only two air fares, which meant that I would have to travel without a sparring partner, and I didn't like that at all. Too many times in the past I had been made to fight with that same disadvantage, and I knew the severe handicap it placed on a fighter. I simply couldn't get any boxing if I didn't bring my own. Other managers wouldn't let their fighters spar with me—even though I used special twenty-four-ounce gloves—and this promoter wanted me to arrive in Buenos Aires a month before the fight for publicity's sake.

I was rusty already from laying off for so long, and without any boxing—other than what I would be getting up in camp—I would have to go into the ring stale, and I wasn't going for that. That's how people get hurt. So I told Nate to call the promoter back and get him to guarantee me some sparring in South America, or I wasn't going to accept the fight. Nate promised to call and told me to drop back by the club later on that night to find out what was happening. Then I drove John Artis up to the Nite Spot, dropped him off, and Bucks and I went to another club called Richie's Hideaway. That was where the best band in town was playing that night.

It wasn't 'til around 2:00 a.m. that we wound up back at the Nite Spot to meet up with Wild Bill Hardney, who was already there. He had brought two other people with him. Big John and Norris were their names. While I was standing there talking to them, a woman that I knew named Cathy McGuire came over with her mother and asked if I would drive them home. Both mother and daughter, Mrs. Mapes and Mrs. McGuire, lived in the same building. It was only a few blocks away, but it was on a long dark street without many lights—Governor Street—and violent death was not taken very seriously in that area by the Paterson police. This was only June, and already there were eleven unsolved murders on the books.

At about 2:15 I drove the two women home, gladly, though I was beginning to feel like the ever-ready neighborhood taxicab company. But a long time before, I had decided that no matter how high I flew in my career, or to what heights I scaled, I would never get too big to remember my people—or forget that I was still one of them. Too many times in the past, and even right then with some of my friends, I had seen black men and women make their mark in theaters and nightclubs, and then sit back on their rusty-dusty little pedestals, squinting down their long noses at the ghetto folks who were no longer their cup of tea. I promised myself that I would never let that happen to me. Besides, it was only a five-minute ride to Cathy McGuire's, and ten minutes later I was back inside the Nite Spot.

But that's when my money got funny. With my pocketbook lying on "E," I asked Wild Bill to come home with me while I picked up some more bread. It wasn't that I thought my wife would actually try to stop me from going back out, but knowing that woman, she might have just worked it. So I figured it would be best to bring along some support. Mae Thelma knew Wild Bill, and liked him, which was why I asked him to come with me. But Wild Bill was wrapped up with his girlfriend, so he told me that he'd wait there for me to return.

On the way out of the club to my car, I saw John Artis again. He was standing by the door with Bucks, and I invited them along for the ride. What the hell, I thought. If my wife tried to put the slammers on me for the night, I could always tell her that I had to take them home.

They both agreed to come, and John wanted to drive. Since this wasn't my Eldorado but my expense car—a 1966 white Dodge—I tossed him the keys, gave him the directions, and settled down in the back seat. I lived about three miles away. The shit started four blocks from my home, when a police car rolled up alongside of us and motioned us over to the side. When we had pulled over, a uniformed officer approached John and asked for his license and registration. John gave the cop his license but didn't know where I kept the registration.

"It's on the steering post, John," I spoke up from the rear. The cop flashed his light in my face and I saw that it was Sergeant Theodore Capter. This area was his regular patrol.

"How you doing, Hurricane?" Sergeant Capter asked. He had always been a friendly type, and I had never had any trouble with him.

"I'm okay," I replied. "But what's wrong? Why did you stop us?" There was another cop out there looking at the license plates. This car had New York tags on it.

"Oh, nothing really," Capter said, offhandedly. "We're just looking for a white car with two Negroes in it." He handed John back his license. "But you're okay," he said. "Take care of yourself." Then he walked away.

But little did I know what was really jumping off. While I had been in the Nite Spot talking to Wild Bill about making this trip home, the shooting at the Lafayette Bar and Grill that I mentioned at the beginning of this book had occurred, and an alarm was out for two Negroes in a white car. Sergeant Capter and his sidekick,

Officer DeChellis, armed with this description, had spotted a white car with out-of-state plates speeding toward the highway and New York. They picked up the chase, but lost the car miles away on the highway. Then, while coming back into the city, up over a hill of the dividing line, they looked down and saw my white Dodge crossing the main drag at a normal rate of speed and flagged us down. This was at 2:40 a.m., by the cop's report, and being familiar with the constant harassment tactics employed by the Paterson Police Department in stopping my car whenever they had nothing else better to do, I just forgot about it.

I encountered no problems at home and arrived back at the Nite Spot just as Wild Bill and his friends were leaving to go back to Newark. It was late now, and the bars were closing. Too late even to go back to see Nate at the Club La Petite. So I figured I might as well call it a night myself, and drove Bucks home. Then, as we were waiting at a stoplight for the signals to change, on the way to John Artis's house, which was only a couple of blocks away from Bucks's house, Sergeant Capter rolled up behind us again. All he saw this time were two Negroes in a white car. It was obvious that he didn't know it was us again until after he had climbed out of his patrol car.

"Awwww, shit! Hurricane," he said, shaking his head. "I didn't realize it was—" But before he could say anything else, patrol cars had come from everywhere but out of the sky. I never saw so many shotguns and pistols in my life. For a long moment I just stared at Sergeant Capter. I was disgusted. I didn't think *he* would do this to me. Although he did seem to be embarrassed about it, all it would have taken was for him to admit that he had made a mistake, that he had stopped us earlier with three people in the car, and miles away from where we were then. But, for some reason, he didn't. Instead, he told us to fall in behind his car, and to follow it, while the other cop cars fell in behind us.

There isn't much in the world that can scare me, but if you can imagine five police cars loaded down with shotgun-bearing cops leaning out their windows with their guns pointed in my direction, leading two *Negroes* off into the night to God knows where (and we dared not balk), then you can understand that this was one of those times in my life that justifiably made me scared.

We sped down the street at eighty or ninety miles an hour, past the Nite Spot to twelve blocks beyond, where we screeched to a halt in front of the Lafayette Bar and Grill. The crowd of white people in the street split out of the way of our cars like raindrops hitting on a rooftop. Some flew to the side of the squad cars, some to the front; others gathered around my Dodge.

This situation stunk! I could smell it. The people moved too quickly and wore very tense expressions. They whispered altogether too loudly, cussed too profusely, and appeared in my mind's eye to be all on the verge of nervous hysteria. There were tears everywhere. Few people seemed to be actually aware of what they were doing.

Holding my breath, I looked around at the shotguns pointed at me and the angry faces pressing around my car. Suddenly I knew exactly how a black man in the South must feel when a white mob is about to lynch him and the law is going to turn its head. I sat there very quietly, trying to look noncommittal. I wanted to create no opportunity for anyone to interpret any of my expressions as aggressive or hateful. My self-preservation instinct did not allow for any foolishness.

What happened immediately after that, I've already written about at the beginning of this book—the confusion in the street, the trip to the hospital, the direct confrontation with a wounded man laying on a table, and the bull-faced cop almost begging him to identify us. But still, the one-eyed man just shook his head. No, we were not the people. There was disappointment in the cops' eyes when they took us down to headquarters—where they should have brought us in the first place. Taking us instead to the scene of the crime had been—or could have been—a very costly, if not to say illegal, maneuver on the part of the overzealous police.

Back in the familiar little Detective Bureau interrogation room, everything seemed the same as it had when I'd been brought there at the age of nine for stealing clothes. It was still sparsely furnished, with the same battered table and one chair. The ceiling was still cracked and dirty, the walls still bore the pockmarks of the busted heads that had been slammed against it over the years. And just as had happened years before, I was not permitted to contact a lawyer at any time during my stay.

Sitting in that room alone for I don't know how long, I began to worry about John Artis. The only reason he was in jail was because the police wanted me, and they didn't care who they swept up in their quest to get me. So I felt sorry for him. I didn't know if he could protect himself, or if he had ever been involved with the cops before. (I found out later he hadn't.) But I knew how they operated. So there was no telling what that boy might be going through. These guys had a big bag of tricks. I didn't know if they were whupping on him right now, trying to get him to sign a confession to something he didn't know a damn thing about, or what was happening to him. Shit! He was still considered a minor, wasn't twenty-one years old yet, and it had been done plenty of times before. The New Jersey prison system was full of people who could very easily attest to that fact.

But for the most part, after a Captain Gourly had brought me into his office and let me listen in on the telephone calls that he was getting from his nigger stool pigeons out on the street (it shocked me to hear so many voices that I recognized), the cops left me alone again. They did, that is, after they had paraded me in front of all the witnesses brought down there from the Lafayette Bar and Grill to make their statements about the crime. Not one of them could finger either Artis or myself.

It was close to 11:00 a.m. before I saw anyone else that day. The door opened and in walked a lieutenant. His face wore an expression at once stupid and cunning. An old-timer, he was pudgy, going to fat. He had a batch of yellow legal pads in his fist.

"I'm Lieutenant DeSimone, Rubin. You know me," he said. "I'm from the Prosecutor's Office." He wanted to know how I could account for my whereabouts the previous night. "You can answer these questions or not," he said. "That's strictly up to you. But I'm going to record whatever you say, and it might be used against you in court, if it ever comes to that. But there's a dark cloud hanging over your head, and I think that it would be wise for you to try to clear it up."

Vincent DeSimone was his full name, a hard man. As far as I was concerned, he knew no half-rights or half-wrongs where black people were involved, for the deepest groove worn into that granite brain of his was saved for his own self-righteousness. Oh, yeahhhh, I knew him all right! I remembered him from waaaay back.

I sat there and told him everything that he wanted to know (not out of any rising fear of him, but because I had done nothing to make me fear), from the time I had eaten supper at home to the moment I left after the James Brown special had gone off the idiot-box. Then my meeting up first with John "Bucks" Royster and later John Artis. And talking to Nate Sermond about the fight in South America; then driving the two women home. I told him about the cops stopping me four blocks away from my home, first, and then finally when they locked me up.

All during the time I was talking to him, DeSimone was steadily writing, filling page after page of his legal pad, recording every little word that I said. Nothing was given in question and answer form, but he would interrupt me whenever he wanted certain definite times of places I'd been during the night, and how long it took to get from one place to another. The interview must have taken up a full hour and a half.

"Okay, Rubin," he said finally, and stood up to gather in all of the loose papers. "That's good enough for the time being. But there is one thing more that I must ask of you," he said. "Would you be willing to submit to a lie detector test?"

"A paraffin test, too," I told him without hesitation. "But not if any of these cops down here are going to give it to me. You get somebody else who knows what he's doing, and you won't have any problem with me. I'll take it, because I ain't got nothing to hide." DeSimone raised his eyebrows.

"Oh, I wouldn't *think* of letting these clowns down here give it to you," he said, as if it was out of the question. "What I had in mind to do was to send down to the State Trooper's Barracks for an expert, and let him give it to you. Would that be all right with you?"

I told him that it would.

At three o'clock that afternoon the state trooper arrived—a Sergeant McGuire, who didn't pull any punches when we were in a room by ourselves and he was setting up his little machine. I could see the burning indignation in his face after he was briefed about the crime by Captain Gourly, the head man in charge of the investigation.

"Carter?" McGuire said in a tight voice, "let me tell you something before you sit down and take this test. If you have anything to hide that you don't want me to know, then don't take it, because this machine is going to tell me about it. And if I find anything indicating that you had *anything* to do with the killing of all those people, I'm going to try to put your ass *underneath* the electric chair!"

"Why don't you quit running off at the mouth, and just give me the goddamn thing!" I told him. "You ain't scaring me with all that funny shit." I was bone-weary from sitting in that hard chair all night and day, and I didn't feel like hearing any more of this gung-ho shit.

The test covered the better part of two hours, I would say, and when it was over I was again locked up in my little room until the good sergeant could sit down and study the results at his leisure. He said he had to gauge the graphs against some kind of technical slide rule. But he still hadn't said a damn thing to me. I was anxious to find out what the machine had to say, not him, but it didn't take as long as I had expected. The door suddenly flew open, and the room filled with cops—black and white, this time. Ooooh, shit! I thought. Here they come.

"Carter?" It was McGuire talking. "Come over here, I want to show you something," he said, laying out several charts on the battered table. The other cops crowded around us.

"See this long line running straight through there?" the sergeant asked, talking to everybody in the room as much as he was to me. "It measures your respiratory reaction to questions given." He was pointing to what looked to me like a whole bunch of scribbling. I still didn't understand a damn thing about it.

"Well," he said, "that indicates your answer to my question, 'Have you ever been inside of the Lafayette Bar and Grill?' Your answer was, 'No.' The line on the chart continued on uninterrupted, so that was the truth. All the answers for the questions on the lines are the same," Sergeant McGuire announced to Captain Gourly standing at his side. "So you can turn him loose, Captain," he said. "And Artis, too. Both of them are clean. They had nothing to do with the crime."*

Seventeen hours after being locked up, John Artis and I were released. They returned the keys to my car, which was in the police garage downstairs. They had driven it there from the scene of the crime. Somebody had torn it up while searching it. All the paneling in the doors was ripped out. The dashboard, the seats were torn up. The radio was hanging loose. Goddamn! If I wasn't so glad to be out of there, I would have gone back upstairs, and they would really have had a reason to lock me up then. Because I'd have

---

* Unfortunately, at that time a lie detector test was not admissible as evidence in a court of law.

whupped on somebody's nasty ass! Goddamn his treacherous soul.

The next day the Paterson *Evening News* read:

POLICE DRAW BLANK IN DOUBLE MURDER
BOXER QUERIED, FREED

The intensive investigation of two cold-blooded murders at the Lafayette Grill at 2:30 A.M. yesterday apparently was at a dead end last night as more than 130 law enforcement officers were assigned to the bizarre killings.

The murders reportedly were committed suddenly and without warning. Two gunmen barged into the Lafayette Grill and fired at those at the bar. They killed the bartender and a patron and seriously wounded two other customers.

. . . An object of great speculation yesterday, Rubin "Hurricane" Carter, the flamboyant middleweight boxer, left police headquarters at 6 P.M. last night after being questioned throughout the day.

However, Vincent E. Hull, Assistant County Proecutor, emphasized that the 29-year-old fighter . . . was never a suspect, nor at any time charged with the shooting. . . .

Hull refused to answer any questions as to why the men were at the police station. He said there were no suspects, but that many people in the neighborhood were questioned as witnesses.

. . . Despite an intensive search for weapons, none was uncovered yesterday in the vicinity of the tavern. Police were looking for a shotgun and a revolver in the sewers on 18th Street and Lafayette and along the Susquehanna Railroad tracks near Graham Avenue and Lafayette Street.

. . . Many persons in the neighborhood told newsmen they heard gunshots. One woman said she saw two well-dressed Negro men leave the tavern. . . .

Another man said he was en route to buy a pack of cigarettes in the tavern when he heard the shots. As he approached the door, he was confronted by two men. He turned and ran west on Lafayette Street, chased by the men. Evading them by ducking into a sideyard, he said, he returned to the tavern to call police.

It is important to remember that last statement.

Meanwhile, I was "an object of great speculation." From the very first moment that the newspapers splashed the story and my picture across the country that Rubin "Hurricane" Carter—the cop-hating, cracker-hating, nigger-hating prize fighter, who hated everybody, including himself—had been somehow linked to the shooting of four white persons, the amateur criminologists and sociologists of the world started fitting the pegs of haphazard insight into the open holes of speculation. There were but a few good fits, in their immodest estimation: racism gone amuck; robbery; or that Carter was a "hit" man for the Mafia! Nobody ever thought to place the square block into the square hole that Carter didn't have a damn thing to do with it! No! No! That would have been too easy. Too much like doing things *right*!

The public couldn't see the forest for all the trees. They were simply too blinded by these periodical flashes to understand the Hurricane's constant fight against a society that didn't necessarily benefit poor people. They were brainwashed into thinking that he was just a crazy punch-drunk nigger. The cops didn't want the public to listen to me, didn't want the people to become aware of the genocide that was heading their way in the name of the law. Because—shit!—if the poor, black masses could be educated against the acceptance of violent death, that would mean self-protection—destroying their enemy. But destroying the poor people's enemy would mean destroying the government—the cops! And they couldn't go for that.

So the Hurricane had to go.

Unlike the time two years earlier in Hackensack when my car had broken down on the highway and those police officers were about to send me to prison for breaking into a meat-packing factory that I'd never seen, this time I had nobody to help me frustrate the elaborate plans that were slowly being hand-woven for me. This crime had been a godsend to the cops. And the circumstances surrounding it were like heaven. With just a little touch-touch of imagination, they were able to kill two birds with one stone: rid the books of the city's most heinous crime, and send that troublesome nigger to the electric chair, too! A reward of $12,500 for information leading to the killers' arrest was offered immediately.

I flew to Argentina and fought Rocky Rivero on the sixth of August, and when I got back, I signed for the championship fight with Dick Tiger. On October 14, 1966, four months after the crime had been committed, John Artis and I were arrested and charged with triple murder.

THE FIFTEENTH ROUND

American Justice—Jersey Style

The Passaic County Jail is located in the downtown district of Paterson, on Marshall Street. As jails go, it was no different from the other million-and-one sewertraps like it that are breeding criminals in this country like big mother alligators in a swamp. And since the state was going to ask for the death penalty in our case, John and I were being held there without bail. I sat alone in my little tin cubicle twenty-four hours a day, waiting for my moment in court —which wasn't to come for another seven months. The fare was a jelly sandwich in the morning, a bowl of vegetables in the afternoon, and two bologna sandwiches at night.

During the first few days of my confinement, I felt totally lost. My acclimation came hard and slow, as I was still laboring under the delusion that what was happening to me was merely an example of law-and-order at its usual creepy norm. I still believed that the paragons of justice around me would never actually bring me to trial on their trumped-up charges. How could they serve as anything more than political fodder for the elections coming up that November, good platform rhetoric for the candidates to lure back to sleep a gullible community that had been only temporarily aroused by the recent rash of bloody murders in its midst? But I had little idea of the traps that were then being laid for me, or of all the underlying political elements involved. I did know that locking up black people in the morning was like bacon and eggs on toast to some of these cops, and icing one at night was equivalent to their drinking sherry in front of a warm fireplace. Still, I just could not believe that anyone would go to such extremes to frame me.

But the jailhouse grapevine believed it. In fact, everybody else in the motherfucking joint *knew* it, except me. One morning about three days after my arrest, as I lay in my cell watching a squad of bedbugs stomp mudholes in a team of roaches and worrying about the welfare of my family, a trusty in charge of the sandwiches for that day slipped a sealed envelope into my cell and hurried away before I could stop him. The note related the how, what, and why of my being in jail, and also reported the method that the state intended to use to make sure I never got out again. The more I read, the more incredulous I became, because the letter unfolded a tale straight from a horror movie.

The message had been sent to me by Arthur Dexter Bradley, who was one of the supporting actors in the scheme and was being held in protective custody on the third floor of the jail. He had already testified before two grand juries, but he had not told the truth and everyone in the jail knew it, and knew he was partly responsible for my being there. Now fearing for his life, he wrote me that the conspiracy to charge me with murder had materialized in August, while I was in South America. He claimed not to be implicated in any way, although he was being held as a material witness to the crime. He also explained that all indications clearly pointed to the fact that nobody living in Paterson, as far as the cops were concerned, could possibly have committed this crime and still have remained in the city. There were too many paid informers, free-lance stool pigeons, dope fiends, and numbers runners out on the streets for the police not to have heard something concrete long before—especially since there was that enticing $12,500 reward being offered.

Then I remembered that in the four months that had passed since the murders, the only thing the police had managed to come up with was a false alarm turned in by a greedy Negro woman who was stranded in Florida, and who prompted the arrest of two brothers in the Paterson area. However, the cops fooled her dumb treacherous ass and locked her up too, as a material witness, they claimed. Thus they made her suffer the same fate as the two people she had caused to be arrested. Two months later, after living behind bars like the outcast scrag that she was, she couldn't take it anymore and finally admitted that the reward money had been her motive all along and that the brothers were innocent. So the police ran her black ass out of town on a rail. The two brothers were released. But that meant the police still needed somebody to hang the real shit on.

Bradley's letter said that suddenly, out of the clear blue sky, like a beam of golden fortune blazing down on Paterson's finest, a woman who lived above the Lafayette Bar and Grill remembered a few events that she had failed to mention to the police on the night of the crime. Her name was Mrs. Patricia Graham Valentine. She had already revealed seeing two well-dressed Negro men fleeing the Lafayette right after the shooting. Now she remembered seeing still another person, who, she said, had been hurrying behind the bar toward the cash register while the first two men sped away in the white car.

The man she saw was Alfred Bello, an ex-convict and a known thief. When Mrs. Valentine informed the police of this refreshed recollection, Bello was arrested. Then being the half-assed punk that he was, he immediately ratted on his partner, Arthur Dexter Bradley, who then turned in *his* two partners, Kenny Kellogg and Hector Martinez, the latter having been in with Bradley on some unrelated crimes. It's a good thing for the state there were no more partners around, or the already overcrowded Passaic County Jail would have been bursting at the seams.

Anyway, Bello, Bradley, and Martinez were wanted in various parts of New Jersey for armed robbery, and had acquired quite a reputation as the "motel bandits" who ran up and down the Jersey Shore terrorizing hotels and motels. Bello and Bradley admitted to being at the scene of the Lafayette crime to break into a factory around the corner, and to driving a car that seemed to fit the description of the one that the police had been looking for. By the time the caravan of patrol cars escorting John Artis and me arrived at the scene of the crime on June 17, Bello and Bradley had mixed in with the crowd. However, knowing that the woman who lived upstairs had seen them (they'd seen her), they stayed within earshot of her at all times, listening closely to what she told the police. When she didn't mention them, Bello stepped forward and, in an effort to account for his presence at the bar (see news article on page 249), said the two killers had chased him down the street. He later gave the same description of the two killers that Mrs. Valentine had given, and again as she had, at first told the police that John Artis and I were not the men who had chased him. (Mrs. Valentine later admitted at my trial that she had seen no one chasing Bello at all.) Everyone else in the crowd with any knowledge of the crime had twice on that night also made statements to the same effect—that John and I were not the men.

But after having probed the Lafayette Bar and Grill massacre for four long fruitless months, the police had ended up with nothing more than the "motel bandits," and an endless list of *their* stick-ups. Now Bradley didn't say this in his letter, but he and Bello changed their original statements from the night of the crime, and in October, just before we were arrested, they positively identified John and me as the killers. In my opinion, the only thing that had saved them from being charged with the crime themselves was the fact that they were white, while William Marins, the lone survivor, still claimed the killers were black.

I *know* these two slobs agreed to perjure themselves in open court in return for immunity from further prosecution, and I believe I can prove it, because the prosecutor not only went along with the deal but also apparently promised to dismiss all outstanding charges against them, and to pay them the reward money as well, if a conviction resulted. Bello and Bradley evidently grabbed at the deal, but Hector Martinez, who, I have reason to believe, was offered the same arrangement, was having no part of it; later he came to testify in my behalf. Or tried to, anyway.

So the state's case against me looked good, but the circle of duplicity was yet to be completed, as a grand jury in June and another entirely new grand jury in October refused to indict us, even after Bello and Bradley had been dragged before them to give their rehearsed testimonies. But the grand juries dismissed their stories as being ridiculous lies having no foundation.

That left the prosecutor with his nuts in the sand, so to speak, and with only one other alternative: if he didn't want to risk getting sued for false arrest and imprisonment, he would have to take his case to the Kavanaugh Grand Jury, which had been previously empaneled for the sole purpose of investigating the death of a young housewife named Judy Kavanaugh.

When I finished reading of all this treachery in Bradley's letter, I started thinking about finding myself a lawyer. The first name that popped into my mind was F. Lee Bailey's. No question about it, F. Lee was a legal wizard, but he was white, and so were the county prosecutors, the victims, the state's witnesses, and probably so would be the judge and jury. With John and I being the only two flies in the buttermilk, I figured I had best try and find me a black attorney, someone who would at least have some idea of the raw deal that was going down.

There was only one black man who I thought would be capable of bailing me out of this frame-up. He was Raymond A. Brown, one of the finest lawyers in the United States, black or white—if he really wants to go to work for you.

The same night that I received the letter from Bradley, which was my third day in jail, Mae Thelma came to see me and I told her to get in touch with Ray Brown. Two days later she returned with the message that he would take the case for $20,000—$10,000 for me, and $10,000 for John Artis, whose lawyer would be an associate of Raymond Brown's law firm. (He couldn't handle us both at once due to the conflict of interest.)

The first thing Brown did was to tell the prosecutor either to indict us or turn us aloose. Then, on November 30, a month and a half later, as I listened to the news on the radio being piped in over the jail loudspeakers, I knew sho 'nuff I was going to need that lawyer. The newscaster reported the results of the Kavanaugh Grand Jury investigation: they had just indicted six people for murder, he said, and then added that they had also handed down indictments against John and me, charging us with the triple slaying at the Lafayette Bar and Grill.

I didn't actually see Raymond Brown until four months after my wife had retained him. It was February 1967. He didn't appear very spectacular as he ambled into the consultation room wearing a dumpy brown suit. He was tall, and high yellow in complexion—what most black people refer to as a redbone. His hair was short and kinky, dust colored, and he walked with a slouch, like he was ready to sit down after every step. I learned later that his appearance was deceptive and that there was nothing slouchy about his mind. He was sharp, and I felt that I was in good hands.

One thing did bother me though: I had been writing him regularly (as well as everybody else in the world, it seemed), explaining in full detail everything that Arthur Dexter Bradley had been telling me, but this was the first time I had seen or heard from him—only one month before my trial was due to begin. Somehow, this just didn't grab me right. It didn't feel good at all.

Jury selection began on April 7, 1967, at the Passaic County Courthouse in Paterson. An ambitious lawyer named Samuel A. Larner, who had been appointed to the Superior Court less than a month before John and I were arrested and had been shipped over from Essex County to fill in for a vacationing judge, assigned himself to our case. He appeared very irritable and in a hurry to get the mess over with.

The prosecuting attorney was Vincent E. Hull, Jr., the son of a New Jersey state senator, who was trying to earn his spurs, so to speak, at my expense. At his side sat Lieutenant DeSimone, the bulldog, whose face was one that only a mother could love (provided she wore blinders).

The only thing I knew about the law at that time was that it was a violation to feed razor blades to hogs in Arkansas, to dance with less than an inch of daylight showing between couples in Missouri, and attend church services on Sunday in South Carolina without toting a pistol. These silly outmoded laws aside, I soon learned of yet another outdated judicial practice: that in New Jersey it's against the law to give a black man a fair trial—and especially one who's been in trouble before.

Every day for three weeks we tried to select an impartial jury, but most of the prospective jurors were from the immediate area. Because of the way the local news media were reporting the case, it was extremely difficult to find people who had no knowledge of the crime.

The papers had said at first that John Artis was my sparring partner. When that turned out to be false, he suddenly became my cousin. Then I was a Black Muslim who was religiously bent on killing all blue-eyed devils. The papers said that a white man had shotgunned to death my uncle in a tavern earlier on the night of the seventeenth and that I had gone to the Lafayette Bar and Grill and killed everyone in it for revenge. (A motive was never even established at the trial.)

Everyone seemed to know more about the crime than I did. Moreover, of the four hundred potential jurors that came to the bar, only eight were black, and if the prosecutor didn't get rid of them with his peremptory challenges, the judge dismissed them, I suppose because they didn't soft-shoe into the courtroom looking like Uncle Remus and acting like Amos 'n' Andy.

It was during the third week that Judge Larner showed clearly what frame of mind he was in. Thirteen jurors had been accepted by both sides—reluctantly, on our part—and only one more was needed to start the trial. (In New Jersey, fourteen people sit on the jury during the trial, and when both sides have rested, two alternates are chosen by lot and the other twelve go off to reach a verdict.) We had used up all of our peremptory challenges in an effort to prevent the prosecutor from empaneling an all-white, death-penalty-prone jury, and the judge had just dismissed a black woman because her formal education went only to grade six. Next under cross-examination on the witness stand sat a white man who, we felt, was definitely prejudiced against us. He had recently been mugged by a black and openly admitted that he didn't particularly dig black people, period. So Ray Brown challenged him, and said something like, "I respectfully submit that this juror be excused from duty inasmuch as he has been the victim of a past crime committed on his person by a Negro. [We weren't Black then, you see, we were Negroes, or niggers.] This fact has obviously influenced his judgment against the defense."

But Judge Larner decided the man was competent. He leaned back in the traditional style of those pious representatives of the blind lady of justice, who seems to have dollar signs for eyeballs, and looked out a nearby window. "We need one more juror and we've haggled enough, Mr. Brown," I remember him saying. "Of course, you may continue to interrogate him, if you so choose. That's up to you."

Ray Brown then took a shot in the dark and asked the man to tell the court the extent of *his* formal education.

"I completed the fifth grade in school," he answered. But his voice really said, "The nerve of you, nigger, to question me!"

"Your Honor," Brown said, turning to the bench, "I respectfully request that this juror be excused at this time for cause, inasmuch as Your Honor has seen fit to disqualify a black juror for having a sixth-grade education. This man has had only fifth-grade schooling."

Judge Larner would have none of it. The man was empaneled. The jury selection was completed, and the panel duly sworn.

Somewhere in the United States Constitution it says that a defendant must be tried by a jury of his peers; that an accused man shall not suffer death or imprisonment when convicted by those who are not his equals. Well, I had fourteen jurors here who were definitely not my equals: four white women, nine white men and one black man—a West Indian. My peers? Shit! Aside from being a different color than all but one of them, I probably had more education than any person sitting on the jury, and even *I* didn't understand a damn thing that was going on. So how could they? My God! All I could do was sit there and glare at what was happening around me, unblinking and disgusted.

My trial began Tuesday, May 9, 1967. The courtroom quickly filled up with plainclothes detectives and court attendants wearing guns. The cops knew they were fucking me with a dry dick, and knew that I knew it, too. So not many spectators were allowed in. The cops were waiting for me to explode, knowing that the Hurricane wasn't going for this shit passively, and they were right. I sat there while the surge and countersurge of emotions played across my mind, watching my white "peers" file into the jury box and sit down. I knew that trying to convince them of my innocence would be about as effective as a handful of snow on a forest fire. And I could hear the electric chair laughing at me again.*

"Ladies and gentlemen," the judge addressed the jury from the bench. "I want to welcome you back to the courtroom. I am sure you had a tough time waiting, but everything comes to an end and we are finally going to start this trial. There are a few words I wish to convey to you before the trial starts." The judge then advised the jurors of the legal trial procedures involved in the case, and cautioned them against drawing any conclusions or holding any discussions about the evidence until the trial was over. He told them that they would be sequestered and would occasionally be excused from the courtroom while he heard legal arguments on questions of law, which, he told them, were not for them to decide, and were not to influence their ultimate deliberations. Finally, he wanted Vincent Hull, the prosecutor, to open.

Hull rose from his table to his full six-foot height. He was young and slim and conservatively dressed, and his prematurely gray hair gave him the appearance of a man much older than he was. He approached the jury box with dignity, and gravely read into the record the indictment charging John Artis and me with the three murders.

"Ladies and gentlemen of the jury," he said. "In this case the state will prove to you beyond a reasonable doubt that on Friday, June 17, 1966, there was located at the intersection of Lafayette and East 18th Street in Paterson, a tavern by the name of the Lafayette Grill.

"The state will further prove to you beyond a reasonable doubt that at about two thirty on that morning, Friday, June 17, 1966, there were four individuals in that tavern, James Oliver, the bartender; Fred Nauyaks, a patron; and Hazel Tanis, a patron; and William Marins, another patron.

"The state will prove to you beyond a reasonable doubt that

---

* All of the dialogue that follows is taken straight from the official court record.

about 2:30 a.m. . . . while the four people were in that bar, the defendants, Rubin Carter and John Artis, after circling this intersection in Mr. Carter's car, a 1966 Dodge with New York license plates, circled the block and parked the car on the Lafayette Street side of the tavern several feet away from the curb. The state will prove to you that the defendants, Rubin Carter and John Artis, got out of that vehicle. Mr. Carter was armed with a shotgun and Mr. Artis with a revolver. They entered the tavern. Without uttering one word they came towards the patrons and the bartender, and that Mr. Carter premeditatedly, deliberately, and willfully fired a shotgun blast into the left side of the back of the bartender, James Oliver. . . . Mr. Oliver fell to the floor behind the bar near the cash register, dead.

"The state will further prove to you beyond a reasonable doubt that Mr. Artis, armed with a revolver, fired a bullet into the head and brain of Mr. Nauyaks, who was seated at the bar. And Mr. Artis, when he did this, did this premeditatedly, deliberately, and willfully. Mr. Nauyaks died seated on his bar stool. His head was slumped over the bar.

"The state will prove to you beyond a reasonable doubt that the defendant John Artis fired a bullet through the head of William Marins, who was seated at the bar. . . . This bullet entered into the left side of Mr. Marins' head. Mr. Marins lived, but he lost his sight of his left eye because of the shooting.

"The state will prove to you beyond a reasonable doubt that Mrs. Hazel Tanis, seated in the corner of the bottom of [the L-shaped bar] was fired upon . . . by both defendants. Mr. Carter fired a shotgun blast at Mrs. Hazel Tanis, part of which struck her in the left arm, the bulk of which wound up in the wall to the rear of where Mrs. Tanis was seated.

"The state will prove to you beyond a reasonable doubt that the defendant John Artis fired five shots at Mrs. Tanis, one of which missed the mark and went through the window to the rear of where Mrs. Tanis was seated. Four of these shots met their mark. . . . Mrs. Tanis fell to the floor in front of the air conditioner of the tavern. She was removed to the Paterson General Hospital.

"She lived until July 14, 1966. At that time she expired. . . .

"The state will further prove to you that after these defendants, premeditatedly, and deliberately, and willfully fired these shots into these four people, they left the tavern and appeared on Lafayette

Street laughing. And they got into Mr. Carter's car and . . . fled from the scene in the car down Lafayette Street away from East 18th Street. . . . The police were summoned, and the state will prove to you beyond a reasonable doubt that at 2:40 a.m. on this same morning, June 17, 1966, two Paterson police officers with certain information stopped Mr. Carter's car at the intersection of 14th Avenue and East 28th Street in Paterson. At this time there was in that vehicle Mr. Artis driving the car. Mr. Carter was in the back seat. There was an individual by the name of John Royster in the front passenger seat. Sergeant Capter and Officer DeChellis, two members of the Paterson Police Department, checked the license and registration and let the car go. They went to the scene and there they had a discussion [with Alfred Bello], and got more information, and left the Lafayette Grill and went out, and at 2:55 a.m. on June 17, 1966, this Friday morning, some fifteen minutes after they stopped Mr. Carter's car, they again stopped the car at Broadway and East 18th Street. In the car at that time were the defendants, John Artis and Rubin Carter.

"Sergeant Capter and Officer DeChellis got assistance from other police officers, and the car was escorted to the scene of the Lafayette Grill. At that point Mr. Carter and Mr. Artis were taken into custody, placed in a police van and taken to the Paterson Police Headquarters." (At this point the prosecutor conveniently forgot to tell the jury that we were taken *not* to police headquarters immediately, but to the hospital, where William Marins told the cops that we weren't the ones who had shot him.)

"Mr. Carter's car," the prosecutor continued, "the 1966 Dodge with the New York license plates, was impounded by the Paterson police and taken into the police garage, and at 3:45 a.m. on Friday morning, June 17, 1966, Detective Emil DeRobbio of the Paterson Police Department searched Mr. Carter's car."

Both defense lawyers jumped to their feet. Because the cops had never been able to find the murder weapons, a 12-gauge shotgun and a .32-caliber pistol, the state was going to claim to have found two live shells in my car on the morning of the crime, one shell belonging to each weapon.

"Your Honor, at this time I must object," Brown called. "It is quite obvious from pretrial motions that this may or may not be admissible. There is only one issue that has been settled with reference to it, and I urge Your Honor to restrict mention of it. It cannot be stricken once it is advanced in this fashion, and either admitted or denied as Your Honor rules."

Judge Larner was sitting in a swivel chair behind a tall impressive desk. Upon it rested a black Bible with its red-edged pages facing out toward the audience. The American flag stood right beside it, its white robe hanging down as a strangling tribute to all black people. He had kept his back to the courtroom when the prosecutor began his opening remarks, but now he swung back around to face us.

"As you know, I assume you wish to join in the application?" the judge jauntily asked John's lawyer, Arnold Stein. A white man of medium height, with sandy hair and glasses, he reminded me vaguely of television's "Mr. Peepers," and appeared as if he would be much more comfortable inside a classroom than a court of law.

"Yes, sir," Mr. Stein said. "That is why I got on my feet immediately."

A thick-coated silence had now settled over the gloomy, high-ceilinged courtroom. Everybody was waiting to hear how the judge would rule on this important legal question—to see how the remainder of the trial would be conducted. Samuel Larner squinted his eyes up into a faraway, thoughtful expression. Then he pinched his lips together with forefinger and thumb.

"This issue was determined on pretrial application as far as I know," the judge finally said, "and counsel can refer to that which he intends to prove. If he doesn't prove it, it is up to the jury to disregard it. I will not limit him [the prosecutor] in that connection." So the tenor was set. The defense was in for big, big trouble.

"Thank you, Your Honor," Hull said with an air of relief. He knew now that the door of impropriety was left open to him, and he took up his story from where he had left off.

"The state will further prove to you beyond a reasonable doubt that at 3:45 a.m., Friday morning, June 17, 1966, Detective Emil DeRobbio . . . searched Mr. Carter's car. . . . In the trunk . . . amid certain boxing equipment, Detective DeRobbio found a Western live 12-gauge shotgun shell. A further search of the car by Detective DeRobbio revealed . . . on the floor of the front seat underneath the right passenger seat a live .32 S&W long bullet.

"The state will prove to you beyond a reasonable doubt that the shotgun shells used by Mr. Carter when he blasted Mr. Oliver [came from] a 12-gauge shotgun shell. The state will prove to you beyond a reasonable doubt that the bullet removed from the brain of Mr. Nauyaks was a .32 S&W long bullet. The state will prove . . . that the two bullets removed from Mrs. Tanis on July 14, 1966, after she died, during the autopsy . . . were .32 S&W long bullets. . . ."

Hull was really sweating now.

"The state will prove to you," he said, wiping his face with his handkerchief, "that all of these bullets recovered by the police in the tavern, from the bodies of the victims, and the one found in the house across the street were all fired from the same gun. . . .

"The state will further prove to you in this case that on this morning, June 17, 1966, there were money, bills, taken from the cash register of the Lafayette Grill. This money was not taken from this cash register by either defendant, Rubin Carter or John Artis.

"The state will prove to you beyond a reasonable doubt that this money was taken from the cash register by one Alfred Bello, who entered the tavern after the shooting.

"The state will further prove to you beyond a reasonable doubt that in this area before and at the time of the shooting were Alfred Bello and Arthur Dexter Bradley. The two of them were up to no good on this morning. They were down on East 16th Street attempting to break into a factory by the name of Ace Sheet Metal Company, on East 16th Street. The state will prove to you that they were up to no good. These two individuals are the individuals that I spoke to you about on the voir dire. They are individuals who have criminal records. . . ."

The prosecutor then finished and thanked the jury. In the silence that followed, the judge turned to the defense table.

"Mr. Brown," he said simply.

Raymond Brown was dressed in a charcoal-gray suit that morning, and it was just as badly wrinkled as his brown one had been when I first saw him back in February. He had Ben Franklin–type spectacles precariously perched on the tip of his nose. He rose from the table and slouched over to the jury box, a legal document held disdainfully in his hand.

". . . I am certain that as you sat and listened to Mr. Hull, your mind must have analyzed the position that the state has taken, and realized that there are certain grave errors of reason . . . in this entire indictment," he said. "It is always interesting to hear the state as it comes in its full majesty, after a long period of preparation, investigation, and culmination . . . get up and in a very few minutes tell you briefly what they will prove beyond a reasonable doubt, and precisely what the results should be, and precisely what is going to happen, without, of course, having the time or perhaps the will to tell you of the many areas where you will have the very real questions which they will be unable to answer.

"In this case as it develops, you are going to find so many areas of human doubt. By that I mean areas which will not require proof, either side, because Mr. Hull won't be able to fill them, and I shall not be able to present proof to fill them. At the end of this case there will be so many unanswered questions in your mind that I know that reasonable doubt on top of reasonable doubt will exist."

Then he gave them our side of the story, the details of which I have already related: that we didn't know what happened in the bar; that I had been riding in a rented car with John Artis and Bucks Royster; how the police had stopped us just after chasing another car out of town and then let us go; how they stopped us again, when there were only two of us in the car, and brought us to the scene of the crime in front of but not into the bar; and then how they took us to the hospital. Brown reminded them that we had not been arrested or charged with anything until four months later, and told them that since I had not been permitted to observe the search of my car on the day of the crime, the state could claim to have found a *cannon* in my trunk and there was absolutely nothing that I could do about it. He said that I had consistently denied knowing anything about the shooting or the people who were shot, and further pointed out that no guns had ever been found. Also, he asked, why wasn't John "Bucks" Royster sitting in the courtroom today as a defendant, too, inasmuch as he was identified by the prosecutor as being in the car when the police first stopped us, shortly after the crime occurred? To wind it up, Brown called into question the credibility of Bello and Bradley as witnesses, and informed the jury of our own complete cooperation with the police. He concluded:

"The proof in this case will be the answer to the complete vindication of this man. I don't think it can be forgotten in this case that as an outstanding athlete and in a sense a person [in] whom the public would have a greater interest than ordinarily, because that is our culture, sports figures are sometimes—well, they are just sometimes people in whom the general public is so interested that they have a strange position when something begins to embroil them, in a sense.

"This is a disadvantage to any person. He suffers when he is a little out of the ordinary, whether he is an athlete or a workman of outstanding skill. It is all the same. You just become kind of a center of attention that you wouldn't normally have directed at you. . . .

"I think you will find that without question the state will not be able to prove a case against Rubin Carter, not because he is clever and not because he had a grand design, and not because he committed a perfect crime, but because Rubin Carter was singled out on that morning of June 17 for two reasons. One reason was because he was a Negro. Why do I say that? I say that because you will find that some of the broad identification, and when I say broad identification, 'All I could see was the back of his neck. I knew he was colored.' So, any Negro on the street that night would be a suspect. That the second reason [was] he drove a white 1966 Dodge. The only reason in the world why he was brought to the scene at Lafayette and 18th Street, the only reason known to the police or to the defense, and you will find no deviation from this, was the car and the color. Had he been white, every white man would have been a suspect. But, someone said the back of the neck, colored. Every Negro became a suspect. Someone said a white Dodge of a certain kind with certain kinds of lights in the back. Every Dodge to that kind became a suspect. . . .

"Maybe there is an answer. I don't know. Why? Why, when this car was searched with Rubin Carter in the police station, feet away on the other side of the wall, was he not taken back and that trunk lifted and asked, 'Bud, is this your stuff? Here. Look what I found?' No. That isn't what happened.

"Well, why, when the shotgun shell that Mr. Hull talks about is found and the .32-caliber he makes much of, why weren't they arrested? Because oddly enough you will find in this case that had they been charged instead of played with like human beings on a string, they would have certain rights, certain protections, and certain privileges which immediately rests when an American citizen is put into custody.* But no. This did not happen in this case. . . .

"Some of you talked about what you read in the newspapers. That I tell you is part of the calculated development of an atmo-

* The *Miranda* warnings.

sphere as dangerous as poison to gas. The very fact that some of you had to wait three weeks before a jury could be selected in this community was because of the publicity, and some of you described it very aptly at the time. Every man has a right to demand to be accused rather than played with by the state, rather than to have his nerves shredded and his guts torn out without a direct charge."

"Mr. Brown!" the judge exploded, "I don't want to interrupt you, but I think it is time that you limited yourself to the facts to be shown, and let's get beyond the speeches on philosophy."

"That is not philosophy, Your Honor," Brown responded. His face was drawn, and quietly angry. "This is a fact."

"I am sorry," the judge snapped again. "I think you are going beyond it."

"If you consider it to be," Brown said agreeably, cooling down somewhat, "I will desist immediately. I will only say this. These are facts as real as any others and that is all I will say about it." And he slouched back to the table and changed his glasses.

". . . This has been a long opening," he said, leveling his words directly at the West Indian on the jury, "because it is not a simple case. I think you are going to find it one of the most engrossing that you have ever read about. . . . But, the one thing I beg of you . . . please view as facts the effect on people of time and attitude, because none of us lives as a mechanical thing.

"Some of you have had that special training, analytic discipline, but please view Rubin Carter as a person. Please view the witnesses as persons, and please deal with this in the name of American justice as that which effects persons.

"Thank you," he said, and dropped like a tired old man.

The judge then invited Arnold Stein to take the floor. He reviewed the events already outlined in Brown's opening statement and also questioned the credibility of the state's two star witnesses, Bello and Bradley.

"I can only reiterate, restate, and emphasize to you, ladies and gentlemen, one fact," he said. "John Artis was not in that tavern. He didn't do this act. He does not belong in this courtroom today as a criminal defendant. You people are going to determine that when this whole case is over, and you have an opportunity to listen and carefully weigh all of the evidence in this case. You have to consider another factor in this particular case. Mr. Hull says Artis didn't rob the place. He wasn't there for a robbery. *His* witness was in there for a robbery. John Artis didn't know any of the people in this tavern who are the unfortunate victims of what we all have to admit was a senseless and tragic slaying.

"So, you should explore this whole case when you listen to it in the context of what conceivable reason this young man . . . would have to be in that tavern shooting down four innocent people with whom he had had no contact at all." And that ended the first morning session of our trial.

In the afternoon the action proceeded with amazing swiftness. The first four witnesses called were police officers and engineers, bringing in charts and designs, laying out the groundwork with maps which designated the inside proper of the Lafayette Bar, and photographs of the victims as they were situated inside. No finger-prints had ever been taken. (I wonder why?) No paraffin tests had been given to anybody to determine whether or not they had fired a weapon that day. Our names were never mentioned in the development of this evidence.

The next day of the trial, the first witness to be called to the stand was William Marins himself, the lone survivor of the tragedy. He was a man in his middle forties, stocky, round-faced, completely bald, and definitely hostile to our case. He told the court that on the morning of the crime he was sitting inside the tavern with Jim Oliver, the bartender, Fred Nauyaks, and Hazel Tanis, talking, when two colored men came in between two-thirty and three o'clock and shot everybody. One of them, he said, had a shotgun, and a pencil-thin mustache. The other, standing directly behind him, had a pistol. He said that they were both the same height. Then, he said, he felt a sharp pain in the left side of his head, noticed smoke curling out of the barrel of the shotgun, and passed out on the bar. He regained consciousness before the police arrived, and remembered them taking him to St. Joseph's Hospital. He didn't say that John Artis and I were the guilty parties, but he wouldn't say in court that we weren't, either.

Throughout his examination, Marins kept stressing that he was in a complete state of shock on the morning following the shooting and couldn't possibly have known what he was saying when he was being questioned at the hospital by the police. He was very adamant on that point. When Raymond Brown began his cross-examination, it was clear that he had his work cut out for him.

"Do you feel up to testifying some more, Mr. Marins?" he asked, "or would you like a glass of water?"

"No," Marins snapped. He was completely unfriendly.

"You gave a statement to the police about what happened in this place, did you not?"

"Yes," Marins said, again very sharply. "But I was in a state—" Of shock, he started to say, before Brown broke in on him.

"I didn't ask you, sir—" Ray Brown began to snap back at him.

At this point Judge Larner interrupted the proceedings. The courtroom was quiet as a rat pissing on cotton. "Just answer the particular question, Mr. Marins," the judge advised him. But the man had gotten Ray Brown's dander up, and Brown was now preparing to have at him full tilt. He slouched back to the table and changed glasses again, putting on his Ben Franklins, and then he stood up erect.

"You also testified before the grand jury, is that correct?"

"True," Marins said.

"If Your Honor please," Brown said in a clear crisp voice that rang throughout the courtroom. "On the basis [of this testimony], I ask the Court for the statements, all of them, and for the grand jury testimony of this witness."

"Yes," the judge answered, very sadly it seemed.

As with the other state witnesses to come, there were six written statements taken from Marins all told, all testifying to the same facts, and all of which proved to be of a different nature than what he was trying to testify to in court. It appeared that all the witnesses who testified were now changing the substance of their original statements of June 17, 1966, to conform with the prosecutor's theories.

"Now, Mr. Marins," Ray Brown said, "you talked with the police on several occasions, didn't you, about this case? As a matter of fact, while you were in the hospital the police talked to you, is that right?"

"True."

"When you were in the hospital the police came and asked you about the people who you say came in the tavern; that is correct, isn't it?"

"True," Marins said again.

"And at that time," Brown went on, "you were able to talk to them? The doctor okayed it and allowed the police to talk to you, isn't that right?"

"True."

"And several of the officers came in, not just on the morning of the seventeenth or eighteenth, but later on. In fact, you gave one statement to Lieutenant DeSimone as late as October 20, 1966. Do you remember that?"

"True."

"Now, you repeatedly told these officers, did you not, that they were thin, tall, light-skinned Negroes, didn't you?"

"I said they were colored!" Marins snapped.

Brown just shook his head, shuffled back to the defense table to pick up a batch of statements, and shuffled back up to the witness stand again.

"Now," he said, facing the jury, especially the West Indian, "I show you, Mr. Marins, D-2, which purports to be a copy of statements given to Detective Callahan in the emergency room at St. Joseph's Hospital. . . . This was not signed by you at all."

"No, sir."

"But Detective Callahan had set down what purports to be a conversation with you in the emergency room at St. Joseph's Hospital and he states: 'He told me the same story as Hazel Tanis, stating both men were Negroes and the one with the shotgun about six feet, slim build, light complexion, and pencil-line mustache.' Is that correct?"

"No!" Marins shouted. "I told him the man had a dark mustache, or, well, it was a mustache. I didn't look at him that long," he said. But Ray Brown didn't let that outburst disturb him.

"I show you what purports to be a typewritten report of detectives, said report indicating that on the morning of the seventeenth, you told the police officers at the hospital: 'He describes the two male Negroes as follows: one, five feet ten inches, thin build, light-skinned, wearing a hat. The man armed with rifle.' Does that represent correctly what you told the police officers?"

Marins, now glaring at my black attorney, wouldn't even answer the question. He turned away from Brown and haughtily asked the judge, "Do I have to say this or do I have to—because at that present time I was in a state of shock."

"Mr. Marins, that will all be brought out," Judge Larner told him. "The question is, is that what you said to the police officers or not, if you know," he said, giving him his clue to fake amnesia.

"I don't remember," replied the witness, now speaking to Brown.

"You don't remember that," Brown said. "Do you remember

that Dr. Dwyer, the attending surgeon, was present and allowed the officer to question you? Do you remember that?"

"A lot of people were there."

"Do you recall telling the police officer as follows: 'He turned around and saw two colored men in the tavern. One of the men held a rifle. The second was behind the first man and he was unable to see what this man held, if anything. Without saying anything he heard at least four shots. He doesn't remember anything else except there was a woman on the floor. That she was screaming and he describes the two fellows as—.' I just read that. That is what you told that officer?"

"I don't remember."

"Because you were in shock, is that right?"

"True," the witness replied, very smugly.

He was really hostile now, sullen, short-tempered and vicious. It was a frightening thing to watch. He knew the killers were supposed to have been black, and he seemed willing to send us to the electric chair just because John and I happened to be black, not because he thought we were guilty of the crime. He knew that the jury would be more sympathetic to him and his lost eye, and to those three dead people, than to anything that we had to say. And Brown knew it, too. He didn't want to push this man around, but he had to. Otherwise the witness just might change up completely, and claim that John and I were definitely the ones who shot those people. So Brown turned to the judge.

"Your Honor, please," he said gravely, "at this time I ask that Your Honor unseal depositions given by this man in a civil suit brought by him in January of 1967."

The prosecuting attorney, Lieutenant DeSimone, and the entire courtroom leaned forward in their seats at this new development. A deposition? I thought. What kind of deposition? What is he talking about?

"Mr. Marins, do you know that you are the plaintiff in an action against Elizabeth Paraglia [owner of the Lafayette] trading at the Lafayette Bar and Grill?" Brown asked, opening up a sealed envelope, and taking out its contents.

"True."

"Do you recall having testified in depositions taken before a notary public . . . on December 16, 1966?"

"True."

"Do you recall signing these depositions and stating under oath they were true?"

"True."

Raymond Brown then took off his glasses and wiped his eyes. Then he began to shatter the state's grand scheme with indisputable facts. "Now, Mr. Marins," he began. "I call your attention to page 13 of the depositions, which you gave on December 16, 1966; is that correct?"

"Yes," Marins answered cautiously, looking very uncomfortable now.

"You were out of the hospital?"

"True."

"You had been discharged?"

"True."

"Your health then permitted you to go to a lawyer's office and give depositions, is that correct?"

"True."

"Your lawyer was present?"

"True."

Brown then reared back and socked it to him. ". . . Is it not a fact, *sir*, that you told Officer Callahan on June 17, 'He told the same story as Hazel Tanis stating both men were Negroes. The one with the shotgun being about six feet, slim build, light complexion, and pencil-line mustache.' Did you not here state in December, 1966, they were light colored and one in particular, the first one . . . 'with a shotgun had a mustache that I just happened to see and the man in back of him was about the same height.' Is that correct? That is true, isn't it, Mr. Marins?"

"Yes," he replied dejectedly, giving up the ghost. There was nothing else he could do.

I sat there in amazement and watched the courtroom strategy bear fruit, and in my mind, I sort of chalked that round up as one for our side. Because if there was anyone in the world who should have known what the people who committed this crime looked like, it would have to be William Marins—and Hazel Tanis before she died—and I knew damn well that the cops had shown her our pictures a thousand times before then. But, still, as the record clearly showed, she and Marins clung to their original identifications given on the night of the crime. Which definitely excluded John Artis and me.

The next witness for the state was Mrs. Patricia Graham Valentine, the woman who lived over the tavern. She was a thin, mousy brunette, nervous, and wanting to be helpful—to the state. On direct examination she testified that at about two thirty on the night of the crime, she was asleep on her living room couch in front of the television. She was awakened suddenly by a loud noise. She got up from the couch and went over to the front window, where she heard two more noises, which she said sounded like the tavern doors slamming. She said she thought it was Jim Oliver closing up. But she noticed the neon bar sign was still lit. Then she heard an excited woman's voice from downstairs saying, "Oh, no!" So Mrs. Valentine ran over to her bedroom window. From there she saw two colored men running to a white car parked in the street. (She said later that she knew they were colored because she saw the back of one of their necks.) Both of them were wearing sport jackets. The one who got into the passenger side of the car wore a hat. The taillights were shaped "like triangles" or butterflies, wider at the outside. The license plate, she said, was dark blue with yellow and gold lettering. When the car pulled away, she threw her raincoat over her pajamas and went downstairs. When she walked into the side door of the bar there was a fellow standing by the front door and he told her to stay by the door. This fellow was Alfred Bello.

All the people who were shot were friends of Mrs. Valentine's. She said she saw Marins holding onto a pole, though he had testified he had not been. Then she saw Hazel Tanis lying out on the floor, and Fred Nauyaks sitting on a bar stool. She screamed and ran back upstairs and called the police. As she was going out the side door, she saw Bello run back behind the bar. After she had gone upstairs and phoned, she came back downstairs and saw Bello running back up Lafayette Street toward the tavern. Then the police arrived.

"Was this on the morning of June 17," the prosecutor asked, "that you gave this statement to the police?"

"Yes," she answered, nervously fidgeting around in her chair.

"I have no further questions of this witness," Hull said, and sat down, relinquishing the floor to the defense.

From the outset of Ray Brown's cross-examination, there were several flare-ups and interruptions from the judge. Larner seemed unmindful of the fact that the state was seeking the death penalty, and the only thing this witness was really used for was to introduce Alfred Bello into the scheme of things, and to pin down the time of the crime.

"The fact is that before you heard the doors slam you were sound asleep?" Brown asked, looking steadily at Mrs. Valentine.

"Yes."

"You had been watching TV?"

"Yes."

"And fell asleep?"

"Yes," she said again.

"Do you know what time it was when you heard the slamming of the doors?" Brown asked. "Or what you took to be the slamming of doors?"

"About two thirty," Mrs. Valentine stated positively.

"How do you gauge that time?"

"Because when I woke up there was no more picture on my television," the woman answered, and then realized that wasn't any gauge at all.

"And that is the only reason you say that it was two thirty? Seriously," Brown asked, "do you say that the reason you say it is two thirty was because there was no picture?"

"The picture that I had been watching was off and there was nothing left on."

"So the fact is that all you know is that you had a blank television screen? You didn't check the time at all?"

"No." Irritably.

"Could it have been two, two forty-five as far as you know?"

"Yes." Very irritably.

Then Brown wheeled away from the witness stand and heavily strode back to the defense table, his eyes narrowed in thought. He started shuffling through a bunch of pictures of my car on the table. When he found what he was looking for, he returned to Mrs. Valentine, slouching again, like a cunning old rooster about to pounce on a hen. In his hands were two photographs showing the outside of the building in which she lived, and the street directly in front where she allegedly had seen the two killers escape in their getaway car. He wanted to know how far she could see down the street from her window. She had testified that she couldn't see as far as the next building because of a tree that obscured her vision. But the photographs contradicted that testimony.

"Your Honor"—Brown turned to the bench with obvious annoyance—"may I show these pictures to the jury and let them judge?" he asked.

"What!" the judge exploded, glaring down at the attorney, leaning forward over his desk. His eyes were snapping.

"And let them judge?" Brown repeated, simply. It was clear to everybody that you could see almost halfway down the block.

"Please leave the remarks off, Mr. Brown," the judge snapped. "Just act as an attorney without the remarks!"

"Are you suggesting that I am not acting as an attorney?" Brown snapped right back at him. I didn't know if I was really on trial, or if this was just a private war between the two of them. But it seemed like every time the defense would attempt to send an important point home to the jury, the judge would interfere and effectively neutralize the evidence with unwarranted aggression designed to divert the jury's attention, and to let them know exactly where he stood—for the state.

"I am suggesting that your remarks, 'let them judge,' be stricken," Judge Larner told Brown.

"I object to Your Honor's remarks and ask for a mistrial."

"Your application is denied," the judge stated flatly. "You are not to comment in handing out photographs to the jury."

"Do they not judge, Your Honor?" asked Mr. Brown.

"Don't argue with me!" Judge Larner shouted down. "I have ruled on it."

"I have heard you, *sir!*" Brown responded. "And I shall not argue with you."

Both defending attorneys had been forced to work around this kind of autocratic behavior all during the pretrial motions and the discovery of evidence, and again when they submitted legal documents to the court. There was a definite hands-off attitude surrounding the entire case. Had it not been for the reliable grapevine in the county jail, I knew, we would have come into this courtroom totally blind—and the state would have led us right into the electric chair—still blinded and dumbfounded, looking for justice. The whole family of the trusty who had been the letter-carrier between Arthur Dexter Bradley and myself were on friendly terms with this Patricia Graham Valentine, and he had given me another good tip. So Brown eventually went to work in that vein.

"Do you know a family named Van Blocken," he asked the witness, "one of whom is Joseph Van Blocken?"

"Yes," Mrs. Valentine answered.

"Did you have a conversation with them after this case had occurred?" he asked.

Mrs. Valentine began to get the drift of it. "That is my husband's ex-wife's family," she said, evading the question—but not for long.

"My question is," Brown repeated, "did you have a conversation with them about this case?"

"We talked," Mrs. Valentine snapped. Clearly, she didn't like where this interrogation was heading.

". . . Did you tell the Van Blocken family, and Joseph Van Blocken, that you saw these defendants and could not identify them as the men at the scene?"

"I told them I couldn't identify them," she said.

"You told them that," Mr. Brown said, slouching past the jury box and over to the defense table. "And that's exactly what you said, is that right?"

"Yes," the witness admitted, defeated.

"Then I have no further questions, Your Honor," Brown said. As he sat down, I chalked up that round for us, too. To my mind, though, the question should have been: "Did you tell the Van Blocken family that you were *positive* that Carter and Artis were *not* the two men whom you saw running to the white car at the scene of the crime?" Because that's what Joseph Van Blocken had told me she had said to his family after returning home from making her statement to the police. So I couldn't understand why Brown didn't ask her exactly that.

Then Ronald Francis Ruggierio, a white prize fighter, came to the stand, and proved to be just another stage-setter for Alfred Bello's grand entrance. The state needed to prove Bello had been at the scene of the crime robbing the dead bodies and breaking into the factory around the corner in order to validate his testimony. I was anxious to hear his story myself, because if he was capable of sitting up there on that witness stand and, looking straight at me, still be able to lie, then I was going to be capable of tearing that courtroom down with his motherfucking ass! But Ruggiero's testimony did bring to light one very important fact that had not been touched on before: he said that, in his estimation, it was a Chevy that had sped away from the scene of the crime and not my Dodge. He knew my car when he saw it, because he had been a passenger in it before.

When the state finally called Alfred Bello to the stand, a hush came over the courtroom, and everybody leaned forward—the spectators, and the fourteen members of the jury. Ray Brown leaned against me, warning me to take it easy and not give the jury any reason to convict me because of my actions. He said *he* would take care of Bello up on the witness stand. The cops crept up closer to me, leaning, crouching. Then the doors swung open and in sauntered Mr. Alfred Bello, elaborately nonchalant, wearing high-heeled shoes (though they weren't in style at that time). He was twenty-three, Italian, short and fat—too much *pasta vazula*—with black hair pasted down on his head with greasy kid stuff. He strutted past the jurors with an air of extreme arrogance, knowing that he was the star of this well-rehearsed show.

"Mr. Bello," the prosecutor began, parading up and down in front of the jury, "would you tell this court where you live, sir?"

"138 Redwood Avenue," was his instant reply. "Paterson, New Jersey."

"How long have you lived there?" the prosecutor asked.

"For two years, sir," answered Bello.

The preliminaries over now, the prosecutor continued with the following: "On or about June 15, 1962, were you convicted of robbery in the Passaic County Court and sentenced to an indeterminate term at Annandale?"

"Yes, sir," answered Bello very loudly.

"On or about June 15, 1962, were you convicted of assault with intent to rob in Passaic County Court and given an indeterminate sentence at Annandale, to run concurrent with the first conviction that I mentioned?"

"Yes, sir."

"On or about June 15, 1962, were you convicted of breaking and entering with intent to steal, and larceny, and sentenced to Annandale for an indeterminate term to run concurrent with the first charge I mentioned?"

"Yes, sir."

"On or about January 22, 1963, were you convicted of larceny in the Bergen County Court and sentenced to Annandale . . . ?"

"Yes, sir."

"On or about October 9, 1964, were you convicted of larceny . . . in the Passaic County Court and sentenced to an indeterminate term at Bordentown?"

"Yes, sir," Bello answered again. He seemed to be enjoying himself!

"With reference to that last charge," Hull asked, "were you paroled in February of 1966?"

"Yes," was the same old tired answer.

Then Bello went on to testify that he was in the area of the Lafayette Bar and Grill with Arthur Dexter Bradley and Kenny Kellogg to pull a breaking and entering job on the Ace Sheet Metal Company. They were driving a Chevy Malibu convertible, blue, with a white top. He was playing "chickie" while Bradley was breaking into the factory. Kellogg went down the street in the direction of the Lafayette Bar and Grill, where Bello had told him to wait. (It came out later that Bello had actually told Kellogg to wait in the car.) While Bello was waiting for Bradley, he said he saw a white car driving around the block. It had two colored people in it. He thought he saw something sticking up between one of their legs that looked like a rifle barrel. The car was a white Dodge. He was certain of that. He said he thought at first they were black detectives cruising the area.

Then Bello had decided he wanted a cigarette. But he had only one left in his pack. So he walked down to the Lafayette Bar and Grill to buy another pack. As he started down the street, he said, he heard two shots coming from the tavern. He kept walking. Then he heard two more shots. But he still kept on walking towards the bar. Then, he said, he saw two colored fellows walking around the corner, talking loud and laughing. One had a shotgun, and the other had a pistol in his hand. He was fourteen feet away from them at this time—very close. The two men were Carter and Artis, he said. They saw him at the same time as he saw them. So he turned around and ran. They chased him for a block, he said. But he was too fast and got away. They drove off in a white car.

Bello then returned to the bar, ostensibly to call the police. That was when Mrs. Valentine came in. She screamed, he said, and ran back out.

Bello walked around behind the bar and found a dead man back there. Money was lying around on the floor. He went to the open cash register for a dime to call the police (he said he had no change), and instead took all the money in the register. He left the bar and met up with Bradley, gave him the money, and told him that he had to go back because a woman had seen him inside.

When he returned to the bar, the police were there. Not very long after that, the cops brought Artis and me up in my Dodge. (Bello identified us in court, but he didn't at the scene of the crime.) Then the cops took him down to the police station to make a statement. And he still didn't identify us. In October he gave another statement to Lieutenant DeSimone, which contradicted his first statement. The prosecutor asked him if he had ever been indicted or charged for the breaking and entering, or for the robbery of the bar.

"I object to that, Your Honor!" Brown leaped to his feet. "This is a deliberate attempt to preclude the defense from asking questions which relate to this man's credibility and not within the province of the state, if Your Honor please," he said.

"The basis for your objection is inappropriate," Judge Larner announced. "It doesn't preclude you at all from anything. However, I sustain the objection on other grounds."

"Of course," Brown added, "it goes to the impeachment of the witness."

"I have ruled already," Larner told him. "You can use whatever you see fit for purposes of impeachment if it is proper at that time." Irritation seemed to be this man's trademark.

The prosecutor then had Bello confirm that he was wearing high-heeled shoes on the night of the crime, and ended his examination. He returned to his seat with a jaunty bounce.

When Ray Brown began his cross-examination of that dirty stinking lying sonofabitch, he had to do it from behind my chair to keep me there, because I was a mad motherfucker. My God! How could anyone who knew me believe this stupid shit? Had I been the killer and walked outside that bar to find Alfred Bello, Jesus Christ, or anyone else there, I would have run him down like the foul scab that he was and beaten him to a pulp. He not only had the audacity to say that we were there, which was the biggest lie he could have ever told, but that we had also chased him down the street and couldn't catch him because he was too fast. Goddamn the greasy fat bastard! Running was my long suit, and John Artis had several scholarships for speed. No, I thought, these people can't believe that. Why would I let the police bring me over to that place if I knew somebody had seen me? Shit! I wouldn't have lost anything by killing them, too. *If* I'd been the killer.

With the first question that Brown put to Bello, he caught the punk in a lie. It turned out that Bello had not lived where he had told the prosecutor he did for the length of time he had stated.

"Where did you live in August of 1966? This being May of 1967," Brown asked him.

"Well"—the witness hesitated—"in a reformatory, an institution."

"In August of 1966?" Brown asked, peering over his Ben Franklins. "You were in Bordentown at that time?"

"No," the witness answered, flippantly, changing his mind.

"Didn't you just say you were?" asked Mr. Brown.

"No. You said I was!" snapped the witness.

"All right," Judge Larner cut in, annoyed. "Let us stop arguing and let us find out."

Raymond Brown just stood there for a moment with his hands on his hips, shaking his head. Little muscles began bunching up in his jawbone and then they relaxed. "Where were you living in August of 1966?" he asked again.

"August?" Bello was playing stupid now.

"Pardon?"

"1966?"

"Yes!" the judge cut in, sharply. "Two months after these events."

"I was out on the streets," the witness mumbled sullenly now. "The same Redwood Avenue [address]," he said.

"Where were you living in June of 1966?" asked Brown, now that the fool was talking again.

"138 Redwood Avenue," he answered.

Brown turned away from that lying sonofabitch and spoke to the judge. "This has already been marked as state's exhibit 40 for identification, Your Honor," he said, holding up Bello's statement for him to see. Then he turned back to the witness.

"Did you tell the police on June 17, 1966, where you lived?" asked Brown.

"Yes," Bello answered, real surly.

"Where did you tell them you lived?"

"It had to be on Redwood Avenue," he said.

"Would you look at this, please," Brown showed him the statement now. "I show you S-40 for identification. Is there a date in the upper left-hand corner?" he asked.

"June 17, 1966," Bello replied.

"Nineteen sixty-six, is that correct?"

"Yes."

"Is that your signature?"

"Yes."

"What does it say with respect to your full name, age, and address?" Brown asked him again.

"Maple Avenue," the witness answered, meekly.

"Where did you live in June of 1966?" Brown started all over again.

"On Maple Avenue," the witness replied.

"You lived in Clifton?"

"Yes."

"You have difficulty recalling where you lived less than a year ago?"

"I'm not very good on dates," the witness smirked.

"You are not very good on memory either, are you?" Brown snapped right back at him, and slouched over to the table to pick up some more papers. He had shown the jury that they were dealing with a pathological liar. He then read Bello's indictments for his previous crimes to the jury. Bello affirmed he had pleaded guilty to all of them, but his memory was a little hazy as to his convictions and time served. He did state, however, that he had not been charged with larceny from the night of the crime. He claimed that the job at the Ace Sheet Metal Company was the first he had pulled since his release from Bordentown Reformatory the February before. He said he had known Patricia Graham Valentine for a long time, though she had testified to the contrary. He said he had refused to testify about these murders before the grand jury, invoking his rights against self-incrimination.

"You said that when the two men came down the street laughing, they just kept walking towards you, is that right?" Brown asked. "They didn't say anything to you, did they?"

"I didn't stop to ask," the witness smirked again, as if he had just made a funny. He had just turned and run. No one chased him, though he had told Ruggierio, a newspaper reporter, and the police that the two men had. He admitted this was untrue.

I could feel his vicious lies burning holes straight through my guts. This fat jitterbug was really a nasty bastard. He wouldn't give the people the courtesy of even *acting* like he was telling the truth. He knew that all they wanted was me. But if my freedom had depended on the jury's coming to a verdict that day, I'll bet I would have been sitting at home with my wife and daughter that night. The four women jurors were cutting him eyes of pure disgust; the men, too. Bello even told them, "Basically, I am a thief."

Brown continued with the charade: "Did you tell Sergeant Capter of the Paterson Police that whomever you had seen had chased you up the street?"

"Yes," Bello stated, now back on solid ground.

"Now that is not true, is it?" Brown gave him a pitying look.

"Well," Bello then decided, "not actually." Brown had shifted gears on him and come up with some more information. The point was the two killers hadn't paid him any attention at all—and he hadn't gotten a good look at them at all. They simply got in the car and drove past him. (I wonder if even *that* was the truth.)

"You told the police on the very morning that this happened that you didn't see the faces of the men walking down the street from the bar, is that correct or not?"

"Well," the witness hedged, "it is possible."

"Well, it is a fact, isn't it?" Ray Brown was getting warm now, I could see.

"I had a reason why I didn't," the witness rapped back defiantly.

"I didn't ask you, *mister*, anything about your reasons," Brown returned. "I asked you one question and that alone. Is it not a fact that you told the police on the morning of June 17, 1966, that, 'I didn't see their faces.' Is that correct?"

"Yes, sir." The room was quiet.

"It is a fact, is it not, that the statement which I have just shown you given on June 17, 1966, to a lieutenant of the police, was given after you saw a car occupied by Mr. Rubin Carter returned to the vicinity of the tavern, under escort of the police?"

"Yes." The quiet courtroom seemed even quieter now.

"Speak up!" my cagey old lawyer roared. "Did you tell [the Lieutenant] that Mr. Carter and Mr. Artis were the men whom you had seen coming around that corner?"

"I don't recall," Bello said. But Ray Brown was pushing him now for the truth.

". . . Sir, I show you a statement . . . in which you deny knowing these people; isn't that clear?"

"If it is on the statement," Bello answered nastily.

"Don't you know what you told them?"

"Sure I know what I told them."

"Did you tell them that you didn't know them?"

"At that point," Bello said, "yes."

"Yes?" Brown repeated.

"Yes, *sir*," Bello said with disdain, the "sir" dripping off his tongue with pure venom.

"We are not in the Army right now," the judge broke in, as if he too were disgusted with a white witness "yes-sirring" a black man who was defending two other black men against the charges of killing three white people. "So, the question is, you said yes to what? That you did know them or did not know them at that time?"

"I didn't identify those men at that time," Bello told him.

"You did not?" Larner said. "All right."

Bello, as a state's witness, was a hard customer to tear down completely, because he really didn't know the shades of difference between the truth and his fiction. That $12,500 reward made a cash register out of his mind. He knew that if he got me convicted at this trial, not only would he get the reward and be relieved of prosecution for his own crimes, but what the state would be doing was tantamount to issuing him a license to steal, because he would never be sent to prison in New Jersey again. (And he hasn't been. Even though his criminal activities have not ceased a bit, the farthest he's gotten so far is the county jail.)

Bello was on the witness stand for two days, relentlessly pummeled by the defending attorneys. He denied he had been promised any favors for giving these statements, *even though he had never been charged with any crime*. He also denied ever hearing about any reward. Then Brown turned Perry Mason on the punk.

"Mr. Bello," he said, with all the outraged indignation he could muster. "When you stole that money from the cash register sitting behind the bar, did you not have to pass by Mrs. Hazel Tanis lying there on the floor begging for help?"

"Yes," the witness answered.

"And Mr. William Marins slumped on a bar stool shot in the head?"

"Yes."

"And Fred Nauyaks lying dead at the bar?"

"Yes, Mr. Brown." Bello was getting the drift of it now.

"Then you stepped over Jim Oliver lying dead behind the bar to get to the cash register. When did you do all of this, mister?"

"Do what?" the judge exploded, almost busting his gullet.

Brown's eyes whipped around and fastened on Judge Larner's. "Slay the bartender," he said.

"What?" The judge couldn't believe what he was hearing.

"When did he slay the bartender?" Brown repeated. "That is addressed to him," he said, pointing to Bello.

"Objection!" the prosecutor shouted, frantically.

"Answer that," the judge ordered the witness, ignoring the state's opposition. His face showed fury.

"It is not to my knowledge," the witness smirked.

"No further questions, *Your Honor*," Brown snarled in disgust, and stalked away stiff-legged. "Not to his *knowledge*," he said derisively as he passed the jury.

Judge Larner was fit to be tied. "The jury will disregard the question, 'When did you slay the bartender?' There is nothing to support it thus far in my opinion."

"If Your Honor please"—Ray Brown was immediately back on his feet—"there is a great deal to support it. The question was not objected to and I ask Your Honor to respectfully review your rules and let it stand for whatever weight it may have."

"I have instructed the jury as I see it," Larner replied, angrily. "I think it should be stricken in due justice to all parties." But he really meant in the state's interest.

"Perhaps Your Honor may reconsider it at a later time," Brown suggested, and hurried on. "Your Honor, here is this man who was in there—"

"Please don't argue that question now!" the judge quickly interrupted him. He definitely didn't want the jury even to *think* about it again. So Bello was excused.

Arthur Dexter Bradley was the next witness on the stand. He was a skinny, red-haired, acne-faced twenty-three-year-old boy who whispered when he talked and picked his fingernails the whole time he was up testifying. The first thing the prosecutor did, of course, was to bring out his criminal record. It included convictions for larceny, breaking and entering with intent to steal, and time served.

"Mr. Bradley," asked the prosecutor. "Where are you at the present time?"

"Morris County Jail."

Bradley then testified that between 2:00 and 2:30 a.m. on June

17, 1966, he and Bello were in the vicinity of the Lafayette Bar and Grill to burglarize the Ace Sheet Metal Company. After he had removed a tire iron from under the seat of Kenny Kellogg's car, he and Bello went out to pull the job (while Kenny went to the Lafayette to wait for them). Bradley tried to force open the front door of the factory with a tire iron, while Bello played "chickie" for him. Suddenly he heard a car coming by and threw the tire iron into some weeds and walked up to the corner. He returned and began to look for the tire iron, then became worried about being seen. He walked back to Lafayette Street. There he saw a white car with four Negroes in it. He said he thought it was a 1964 Ford. The passenger on the far side had something sticking up between his legs, which he could only identify as being long and thin. He didn't know me personally, but he said he knew my face and recognized me in the driver's seat. He didn't know the others.

He went back to work on the factory door, and while he was struggling with it, he heard something that sounded like backfiring or gunshots. He went back out to Lafayette Street toward the bar. There was somebody walking in front of him. From an earlier conversation, he knew Bello was going to the bar and thought that he could reach Bello before he got there. So he started running after the guy in front of him. He said he wasn't yet sure it was Bello. Then he heard some more backfiring noises. He looked down the street past Bello and saw two Negroes. One had a shotgun in his hand. The other had something in his hand too, but he wasn't sure what it was. One was short and the other was tall. He described their clothing as being dark.

"Is the man who was wearing [*sic*] the shotgun or rifle in this courtroom?" Hull asked him.

"Yes," Bradley replied.

"Where is he?" asked the prosecutor. "Point him out, please."

"He is right there," Bradley said, pointing at me.

"Pointing where?" asked the judge, getting his two cents' worth of credibility in. "Tell us again," he said.

"That *Negro*, right there!" Bradley bellowed. He wanted to say "nigger" so bad that his lips were trembling.

"He said, 'That *Negro* right there'?" Brown asked the judge indignantly. "Is that what he said?"

"Yes," Judge Larner said, beaming down from the bench, a satisfied note in his authoritarian voice. "That is what he said, pointing to Rubin Carter. The record will indicate that he has pointed to the defendant Carter."

Bradley continued testifying to the fact that he couldn't recognize the other Negro. He had turned and run back to the Ace Sheet Metal Company. A minute later Bello joined him and gave him some money he had stolen. Then Bradley went back to their car, but it was no longer there. He kept going and came out on another street, saw nothing, and turned around again. Then he saw Kellogg's car going down the street. He went to another street, waited fifteen minutes, and eventually wound up across from the bar. The police had already arrived. He walked to the bar, met Bello, and then went downtown with Detective Lawless and Ronnie Ruggiero. But they dropped Bradley off before they reached headquarters, and he took a taxicab to a girl's apartment and met Kennie Kellogg there. All three of them drove back to Ace Sheet Metal, and broke in. He looked for money, found a safe he couldn't open, and gave up. The area was crawling with cops conducting a house-to-house investigation. So he went home.

"I have no further questions of this witness," the prosecutor said. He sat down, satisfied that his case was won. It wasn't a question of law and truth, of course, it was simply black against white. And in that, he definitely had the upper hand.

This was the third day of the trial, and though the courtroom had been noticeably barren of civilian spectators during the earlier stages of the proceedings—with the exception of my wife and daughter and John Artis's family—black folks started trickling in. The word had been passed by somebody who knew, that we were downtown getting shafted by two cracker convicts, while they were sitting home on their black asses doing absolutely nothing. So the people started coming to court, and the police were up on the rooftops brandishing their shotguns and trying to scare them away. The cops didn't want too much exposure of this thing that they were doing. They had already threatened some of my witnesses, and driven some others away. Because there should have been a truckload of people coming down here to testify for me, but there wasn't. They were all scared.

However, when Ray Brown rose to cross-examine Arthur Dexter Bradley, he was no longer working in a totally hostile atmosphere. There were plenty of black people behind him now, though silent in their support. Even my father and some of his preacher friends had shown up.

Brown started off his interrogation by obtaining from the prosecutor all relevant information that proved, without exception, that Bradley, just like all the other state witnesses, had given the police three or four previous statements, all of which were taken in October and November—after my arrest—and which differed from his court testimony. The defense attorneys also brought to light that unlike Bello, who had simply refused to testify before the grand jury about this crime, Bradley did testify, and had committed perjury, but he had never been charged with that offense. (Before the trial was quite over, Brown did establish that in October, when Bradley had first given his statement to the police, he was up on charges of having committed four armed robberies, two breaking and entering and larceny jobs, and one car theft, of escape from police, and of possession of stolen property. All of these charges were still pending against him at the time of my trial.)

Now Raymond Brown, oak-tree-tall with brown snapping eyes, stood there and looked at Bradley for a long while, as if he was sizing him up. Then he went to work on him. "Mr. Bello—I beg your pardon," he apologized. "Your partner is Mr. Bello and you are Mr. Bradley. . . .

"Mr. Bradley, the first time that you told the police anything about this was in October 1966; is that right?"

"Yes," the witness whispered.

"And they came down to Bordentown and talked to you about it?"

"Yes."

". . . Now," Brown said, "one [of these two Negroes] you said you recognized?"

"Yes," Bradley answered.

". . . How long prior to this night on the seventeenth of June had you seen Mr. Carter?"

Bradley started fidgeting around in his seat, wrinkling up his forehead in what was supposed to pass for deep concentration. He thought about it for a minute or two. "About in February," he said. "I saw him in a magazine."

"You saw him in a magazine in February?"

"Yes."

"As far as in person, when did you see him?"

"I saw him that same night," Bradley said. But he was talking about when the police brought me to the Lafayette Bar.

"My question is," Brown repeated, "prior means before. How long before June 17 had you seen Mr. Carter in the flesh?"

"In '64," the witness answered.

". . . In 1964!" Brown exclaimed. "That would be two years prior to this event?"

"Yes."

"And that was the occasion when you passed him in a car with a friend who said, 'That's Rubin Carter,' and the other time was in February when you read about him in a magazine?"

"Yes."

"Incredible!" Brown seemed to snort, and slouched back to our table, shaking his head. A low rumble of disgust quickly built up behind us into a loud crescendo of dissent from the audience. The judge banged his gavel for silence. He warned the spectators that he would clear the courtroom immediately upon any further demonstrations of this nature. His frosty-looking features dispelled any further commotion.

Meanwhile, Raymond Brown, as if he had heard none of this at all, was leafing through a pile of papers strewn carelessly over the table, and when he seemed to find what he was looking for, he straightened back up. ". . . Now, as I understand it, sir," he asked Bradley, "there was a man about twenty feet in front of you, is that correct?"

"Yes."

"And you couldn't identify that man as Bello, right?" he asked.

"No," the witness told him. "I wasn't really sure."

"Although you had been with him since early evening," Brown stated, and then inquired, "You had known him for how long?"

"A few hours," Bradley decided.

"You only knew Bello for a few hours?" Brown turned in surprise.

"No," the witness quickly changed his mind. "I have known him a long time." That's what Brown thought.

"You have known him a long time," Brown repeated, "but although you couldn't recognize the man twenty feet in front of you, a man coming around the corner whom you had seen in a magazine and once in 1964 you recognized in a flash, is that right?"

". . . Yes," Bradley said.

"Incredible!" Brown whispered to me when he came dragging back to our table.

The remainder of Bradley's testimony was so warped with more such incredible utterances as to displace all human logic in a person who was thought to be sane, unless that person was prejudiced beyond belief. Ray Brown did bring out, however, that it wasn't until October 14, the day that John and I were arrested, that Lieutenant DeSimone went down to Bordentown to ask Bradley, in effect, to change his statements into one that would incriminate John Artis and me. DeSimone had even brought our pictures down there to show Bradley who we were and what my car had looked like.

To offset this testimony we intended to bring from Bordentown Hector Martinez, Bradley's partner on all of his armed robberies, to testify that he too had been offered the same deal by DeSimone. But Bradley denied that he was offered any deal at all. So Ray Brown let him go. We were going to sock it to him with the testimony of his partner, Martinez. The only trouble was, Brown hadn't asked Bradley the proper questions necessary to permit Martinez's rebuttal in court—which we didn't realize until it was too late.

When Officer Alexander Greenough—the first cop to arrive at the scene of the crime—came to the stand, he testified that at 2:34 a.m. he had received a call to go to the Lafayette Bar, and that he had reached the place at 2:35. His partner, Officer George Unger, went into the tavern while he spoke to Bello outside. Bello told him that people had been shot. Greenough escorted a very excited Patricia Valentine upstairs to her apartment. She described the getaway car as white with a dark license plate. Two Negroes. She even drew a sketch of the taillight on his scratch pad. Greenough took a statement from Bello shortly after coming back downstairs with Mrs. Valentine. Bello was standing with them when the police brought John and me to the scene. But nobody then could identify us as the guilty parties.

"Officer Greenough," Brown began his cross-examination. "[When you arrived at the scene] Bello told you what the people whom he said he had seen looked like, didn't he?"

"Yes."

"Each five eleven."

"Yes, sir."

"Thin build, fedora, and sports jackets, right?"

"Yes, sir. That's what I have on my—"

"And that's what he told you, right?" Brown interrupted.

"Yes, sir," the cop admitted.

"He also told you that those people chased him up into the alley, didn't he?" Brown asked.

"Yes, sir."

Greenough hadn't asked Bello what he had done after he ran up the alley, nor did he bother to search for any weapons. He had simply gone upstairs with Mrs. Valentine to try to get a description of the getaway car from her. When he brought her back down to the street, my car was there, and the sight of it made her hysterical, he said. Had the cops taken us straight down to headquarters instead, we probably would never have been involved at all. It could have happened to any two black men riding the streets that night.

Brown wanted Greenough to tell him how Mrs. Valentine had described the car, the taillights of which she had sketched for him in his notebook.

"Now, did you preserve this piece of paper for any length of time, Officer? You say it was in your notebook."

"No," Greenough answered. "It was a page torn from my notebook to use for this purpose."

"And you discarded it, do you know, or did you lose it or did you just—"

"I can't really say what happened to it," Greenough said. Then Brown took a shot in the dark, because all the evidence was falling that way.

"There was nothing about this drawing," Brown said, "just two tapered lights, and that's it; is that all; just two triangles?" he asked.

"They weren't triangles at all actually," the witness stated. "She was trying to describe the taillights with these drawings to me."

". . . It didn't help [you] at all," Brown said. "There are many lights like that you've seen in your experience, haven't you?"

"That was the problem," Greenough decided. "They looked like nothing I had seen. That was it. I couldn't think—I was thinking in the line of Chevy and this type of car that has the lights across the back. . . ." Bello and Bradley and Kellogg had come there in a Chevy.

"The Chevy has them?" Brown asked, hammering home his shot.

"But they're square," the officer said, so he figured it to be a sports model Chevy. Brown had proven his point: Kellogg's car was a Malibu, a sports model.

"All right, that's all, Your Honor," he said, and sat down.

Sergeant Theodore Capter soon came up to the witness stand to testify. He was a nineteen-year veteran. He and his partner, De-Chellis, had received a call at 2:34 that there was trouble over at the Lafayette Bar and Grill.

"We were going to the scene of the trouble," the sergeant said, "when we saw a white car shoot across in front of us going in an easterly direction on 12th Avenue. The first car that arrived at the scene [of the crime] threw out a description over the air to be on the lookout for a white car with two colored male occupants. So when we saw this car go by, we shot across 10th Avenue . . . because . . . I noticed that it had a foreign plate on it," Capter said, "an out-of-state plate." So he called over the radio to block off the highway. He and DeChellis took off into East Paterson to go after it. But they lost the car, and they never found out what really happened to it.

On the way back into town they saw a white car—my car—come across Broadway and go south. They stopped the car a few blocks away, he said. John Artis was behind the wheel. Another man was sitting next to him. Rubin Carter was seated in the back, Capter said. After checking the registration, he let us go. Then he and DeChellis went to the Lafayette Bar and Grill, talked to Bello, and went back out on the streets, where they saw my Dodge—this time with "two colored males"—in front of them waiting for a traffic light to change. He called over the radio for some help. Then he pulled up alongside, and told us to make a right turn and stop. Which we did, most agreeably. Then they had us follow them back to the scene of the crime, where there was an "enormous" crowd gathered.

On cross-examination, Brown had Sergeant Capter retrace the route he had taken on the morning of the seventeenth while chasing the first white car out of the city and onto the highway, where he and his partner had lost it. The retracing was done on a large chart in the courtroom that was scaled down to represent the entire area. It proved conclusively that it couldn't have been the same car he had stopped on his way back to the city—which was my car. Brown was nothing if not thorough in his cross-examination.

". . . Now, Officer, on the occasion when you stopped the car in which Artis, Carter, and Bucks were riding at about 2:40 a.m. or thereabouts, you allowed them to proceed. Is that correct?"

"Yes, sir."

". . . The second time you stopped the car at Broadway and East 18th," Brown asked, "did you have to stop them? Were they being run down?"

"They were stopped [while] waiting for a traffic light," Capter answered.

"Nothing unusual?"

"No," the sergeant answered. "The only thing [with two colored males in it now], it fit the description that I received at the scene of the crime."

". . . Sergeant," Brown asked, seriously, "why did you bring these men to the scene where this big crowd was milling about as opposed to taking them to headquarters or a precinct?"

"I had no reason actually to take them to headquarters," answered the veteran sergeant. "I figured I'd bring them to the scene of the crime because they're only suspects," he said.

And that's what put us in jail—bringing us to the scene.

Following Capter's testimony, there was a long line of cop witnesses coming and going, all testifying to some small detail of what they had performed in their lines of duty. But none ever mentioned John Artis or me, except, indirectly, the detective who had interrogated Hazel Tanis before she died and William Marins while he was still on the critical list.

"And Mr. Marins told you that he couldn't identify these men, is that correct?" Brown asked him.

"That's correct."

"And he had a full chance to look at them there?"

"Yes, sir," the detective answered.

"And he told you it was the tall man with the shotgun, is that right . . . about six feet, slim built, light complexion, pencil-line mustache?"

"He said he may have had a small mustache."

"I'm reading your report," Brown said. "I'm not making this up."

"I know," the witness said quietly.

"I'm reading," 'Six feet, slim built, light complexion, pencil-line mustache,' " Brown said. "And you put that down."

"Yes."

"And he looked at these two defendants and he could not identify them?"

"That's right," the detective said, and added that his report of
Hazel Tanis's description was nearly identical to Marins'.

At this point the prosecution seemed to get really desperate.
They began throwing all kinds of legal obstacles in front of us: Lt.
DeSimone got up on the witness stand and claimed to have recorded the dying declaration of Hazel Tanis's just a few days before she died. But all the hospital records showed just the contrary
—that she had died suddenly and, up until that time, had been on
the road to a complete recovery. Then the state tried to introduce a
composite drawing into evidence that only showed the face of a
clean-shaven Negro who could have resembled anybody, so both
defense attorneys fought vigorously against its being offered into
evidence. That was one of the few legal rounds that we won—or
did we?

Ray Brown was steady on the move trying to outthink their next
moves, but then they threw a real dickhead at us: the police had
never found the weapons that had been used to kill all those
people, so they did the next best thing—they brought in a cop to
testify that he found in my car one shell belonging to each gun the
police claimed had been the murder weapons. This detective, Di-
Robbio, said that at 3:45 a.m. he had gone downstairs at headquarters into the police garage and searched my car (without a
warrant). He opened the front door and found a .32-caliber lead
bullet on the floor under the right front seat. Then he opened up
the trunk of the car and found a Super X Wesson 12-gauge shotgun shell under some boxing equipment. He put these items in his
pocket and turned them in to the police property clerk the next
morning. That was his testimony.

That afternoon, the prosecutor brought two ballistics experts
into court. They testified that the bullets in all of the people who
were shot and the shells found on the Lafayette Bar's floor were all
.32 S&W long copper-coated bullets and Remington Express plastic
shells, as opposed to the lead bullets and riot-type Super X Wesson
shell the police allegedly found in my car. The two trooper firearms
experts testified that there were absolutely no similarities to the
ones used in the killings and the ones allegedly found in my car
other than the gauges and calibers. So Judge Larner excluded the
shotgun shell from evidence as simply being too remote from those

found at the scene of the crime, but he allowed the *lead* bullet into evidence because, as he said, it could have been fired from a .32-caliber pistol. Well, hell! The 12-gauge shell could have been fired from a 12-gauge shotgun, too! I couldn't understand the logic being used here.

After three more weeks and fifty witnesses, of whom only Bello and Bradley ever specifically mentioned John Artis and myself in connection with the crime, the prosecution rested. Lieutenant De-Simone had been to the witness stand four or five times to help boost the state's case with his lies—vicious, legal lies, which would soon become the legal block to regaining my freedom. For example, he told the court that on the morning of the crime, he had properly given John and me our *Miranda* warnings.

The *Miranda* decision had been handed down by the United States Supreme Court on June 13, just *four days* before the murders had been committed. Not even the state and federal judges, let alone the lawyers, had yet deciphered exactly what the decision meant. But DeSimone claimed to have already had, on the morning that he questioned us, a card made up giving the exact *Miranda* warnings. And it was from this card that he said he had read us our rights.

This part of DeSimone's testimony was not supported by any written notes, but came entirely from his memory—a full year later—which he acknowledged was hazy at best. He claimed to have destroyed his original records on the same morning he conducted our interrogations, but that was a lie. He still had those original records when we appeared before the grand jury on June 29, 1966, so he couldn't have destroyed them when he said he had. As it was, I remembered him saying at the time he questioned me only that my statement could be used against me in court later, but nothing about my being entitled to a lawyer, as per *Miranda*. Another thing, I had told him then that I had driven Mrs. Mapes and Mrs. McGuire home from the Nite Spot on the morning of June 17th, not the 18th—a fact he was able to conceal in court by saying he no longer had the records. It became a crucial point of contention later on in the trial, as we'll soon see.

Though both the statements John and I had given DeSimone on that fateful morning could in no way be construed as incriminating evidence, they were inconsistent in terms of certain times, because we hadn't always been together throughout that previous night. But since DeSimone was now claiming to have destroyed his original written records—and we could not effectively cross-examine his recollections—his unimpeachable testimony was of the most insidious nature. After having listened to the damaging discrepancies recited by this man—one statement following the other in rapid-fire succession—the jury could draw only one of three conclusions: that John Artis was lying, that I was lying, or that both of us were liars. It also meant that I was forced to take the witness stand and reveal my criminal past.

The defense case began with Ray Brown asking Judge Larner for a direct verdict of acquittal, but Brown knew the judge really wouldn't go for it, of course not. It was just a matter of form. So he went ahead and began calling up our defense witnesses.

This was where Larner emerged in all his horrifying majesty. From the very outset of our portion of the trial, he judiciously helped snatch away, with snip remarks and slurs against their characters, the credibility of my most important witnesses. It was for that reason—what I sensed to be Larner's attitude toward my defense—that I refused to let my wife testify in my behalf. It was an effort to maintain what little bit of cool I had throughout this farce; if the judge had shown Mae Thelma the disrespect that he inflicted upon the others, I don't know what I would have done.

So I was the first witness Brown called to the stand, where I repeated the story I had given to Lieutenant DeSimone and to the grand jury investigating the case in June 1966. Cathy McGuire, a young and beautiful black woman and the proud mother of three children, followed me.

She had gone to the Nite Spot on the evening in question, accompanied by her mother, Mrs. Anna Mapes. She testified that at about 2:15 a.m. the three of us had gotten into the front seat of my car, and that I had driven them home from the bar. She said she knew what time it was because her mother had to go to work the next day and kept checking her watch to see how late it was.

The trouble was that her court testimony conflicted with her statement to Lieutenant DeSimone, who had tried to get her to say that she had not been with me on Thursday night the sixteenth going into the seventeenth, but Friday night going into the eighteenth. She said in court that DeSimone had succeeded in confusing her to the point where she signed a statement saying that it was June 18 when I had given her and her mother the ride home. But she said she was sure it was the seventeenth. She pointed out that when she went to the Nite Spot it was usually on Thursdays, because that was Ladies Night.

"What day of the week did you tell Lieutenant DeSimone it was?" Brown asked Cathy, trying to clear up the discrepancy.

"I told him it was the seventeenth," she said, and seemed like she wanted to add something more.

"Go ahead," Brown told her. But the judge interrupted her.

"The *question* is," Larner snarled down at the woman, "what *day* of the week did you tell him?"

"He didn't ask me the day," Cathy replied, frightened. "He asked me the date."

"Oh, he didn't ask you the day at all, is that your testimony?" the judge ridiculed in disbelief.

"I don't think so," Cathy murmured.

"You don't *think* so?" Larner slammed home his advantage.

"I don't remember," Cathy replied, falling right into his trap.

"Before you said, '*I don't think so.*' All right," he said. Then he swung around to face the jury. ". . . Incidentally," he started right back in on Cathy again, "do you go to the Nite Spot quite often?"

"Yes, I do," she replied.

"Regularly?"

"Yes."

"What night of the week usually?" Larner wanted to know.

"Well, Thursday night is Ladies Night."

"Thursday night is Ladies Night?"

"Yes."

"Did you go there on Friday night?" the judge asked.

"Well, I didn't go there every night in a row," Cathy replied. "On weekends I went maybe other nights."

"Weekends include Friday?" questioned the prosecutor—I mean, the judge.

"Friday and Saturday."

"All right," the judge swung back around, dismissing the witness. He had done his duty by creating doubt. Goddamn!

Nine other defense witnesses followed: Mrs. Mapes, Peter Rush, Hector Martinez, Nathan Sermond, and Elwood Tuck, among others. Tuck exemplified the naked fear with which the prosecutor's office had dissuaded all prospective witnesses in the black community away from testifying for our case. Wild Bill Hardney, my chief sparring partner, was another example. As soon as his name appeared on my list as a witness, the cops started hunting him down so hot and heavy that he got scared and left town before he ever got near the stand. Which was what the cops wanted in the first place.

Lieutenant DeSimone's methods of interrogating black people were more than obvious throughout the defense case. Every witness who did take the stand had in some way been pressured and coerced into signing statements they insisted in court could not be true. For instance, Cathy McGuire testified that DeSimone (who of course denied it) had called her a liar and warned her that if she was not telling the truth, he would tear her limb to limb when she got up on the witness stand. But she was telling the truth, and she stuck to it, insisting she had been with me on the night of the crime and not the following night, as the prosecutor was pressing her to say.

John "Bucks" Royster was another case. He was so scared that he hid out in his attic during most of the trial to stay out of the hands of the police, who, he was sure, would arrest him. He had been identified throughout the state's case as being the third person in my car, so the jury would have to be more than anxious to learn what he would have to say about his presence in my car at just about the time the shootings had occurred. It seemed very obvious that anybody with just a little bit of sense would expect that if John Artis and Rubin Carter were sitting there as defendants against these murder charges, then John "Bucks" Royster should have been sitting there as a defendant, too. He said as much in court himself.

Toward the end of his testimony, the judge suddenly wheeled around and lashed out at him, "How many drinks did you have this morning?"

"Who, me?" Bucks said, stunned.

"Yes, yes!" Larner growled down at him, glaring, red-faced.

"I don't know," he answered meekly.

"*You don't know,*" Judge Larner snorted with contempt, then shook his head and looked over at the jury. "All right," he said, satisfied. He had just snatched the credibility away from another of my witnesses. Under this type of tyrannical questioning, even Jesus Christ couldn't have walked away from that courtroom as a free man.

The pattern of judicial interference was soon to make its presence felt by the brevity of the jury's deliberations. Our entire case had been specifically directed at the West Indian sitting in the box, because this had clearly been a case of white law being meted out to black defendants, and nobody had attempted to show it off as anything else.

At the end of the trial, Ray Brown was still wearing his Ben Franklins and his wrinkled-up suits, and after Arnold Stein had spoken for John, he slouched up in front of the jury box to deliver his summation. Would the verdict be life imprisonment, or death? Acquittal now seemed out of the question, and conviction for murder in the first degree meant the electric chair at that time. But the state had a built-in conscience-soother to pacify the jury of my "peers." If the panel could believe us guilty beyond a reasonable doubt, but considered other, extenuating circumstances—such as the judge's obvious disbelief in our innocence—they could recommend mercy, and life imprisonment, instead of letting us go free as the evidence, or the lack of it, demanded. This luxury would allow them to sleep at night, and still get along with their neighbors during the day.

"In all the instructions to the jury, and in all the attitudes that are determined to be properly that of the jury, reason is always the issue," Brown told them in his summation, "not passion, not prejudice, not bias. Reason—reason—reason—reason.

"There wasn't a person who appeared for the defense who did not come in voluntarily, including the defendant. There wasn't a person who appeared for the defense who didn't tell you flatly— even though there were contradictions from prior statements, very expertly and capably handled by Mr. Hull—who said, 'Between two and two thirty I was around Rubin Carter.' Two ladies said he took them home, Mrs. McGuire, Mrs. Mapes. Consider that with reason, because you must determine the life or death of two persons here. . . .

"I would not try to apply reason to a Bello. I would not try to apply reason to a Bradley, because that alone will not answer it. How can one . . . believe them? Who can determine why a Bradley at this tender age already has six, *six* convictions? Who can determine why a Bello, who is on parole and knows that his maximum is 1969, will deliberately go to break in when he says he is working . . . why he will go down and admittedly commit two acts of thievery? . . . A very patronizing young man, quite confident, suave in dress and very self-assured. How does one account for that? I don't know.

"Well, tell me, can you believe him? Can you believe him when police officers who had no interest in this . . . come in and testify that on the morning of the event he described the persons, and . . . the car. One officer says he told them it was a white car with a blue plate. He also told them that it was one, not Negro, one colored male. I suppose that is police department shorthand. One C.M., one colored male, was wearing a fedora, was wearing a jacket, thin build, five eleven. The second C.M., colored male, five eleven. Well, that is what he told them, and then of course he has reason for changing this, because he realized that this description does not fit either one of these men, and most assuredly not Carter, but he had a reason, and let me read for the record what his reason was, if you will. . . .

"He was asked by Mr. Hull and permitted by the Court to an- swer . . . the following: 'Why did you not identify Mr. Carter and Mr. Artis at that time?' And His Honor permitted the answer. . . . 'Because I recognized the fact that I was down in the area and I was on a conspiracy to break and enter and helping to break and enter, and later on as I walked up the street I got involved in a murder, and I also realized that I had recognized the two men that had come around the corner, and I realized if I had recognized them, they had recognized myself' . . . and he went on: 'Knowing that I am a parolee and this was a violation and I didn't want the repercussion to fall on my family, and I . . . realized that if I ever would take a fall for my crime and go back to a reformatory, and be incarcerated—' and then there was another objection, and then he continued: 'Yes, I realized that I committed a crime. There is a seriouser one committed and I should just tell my crime,' and then the Court said, 'Proceed,' and the witness said, 'I don't have any- thing else to say.' . . .

"Now, it appears to me that if the rules of law, the rule of reason, which the Court will instruct you is to be applied, that there are two attitudes permissible where his testimony was concerned. One is, of course, the past offenses to go to his credibility, but, secondly, to consider whether or not with the parole and other things hanging over him, and the crime which he knew he com- mitted, he is not testifying for favor, for hope. This is a very real issue, and I submit to you that you must consider that in deciding whether you believe him or not, in trying to decide why he changed his testimony. . . .

"What about the white car that went streaking out of town? What about the car that was first seen by Sergeant Capter and his driver after getting the signal at two thirty? What about the people that he chased around this place and made all these loops out at Route 20, whatever that is, and all the rest of it, and then came rushing back? What about that car? It couldn't have been the same Carter car, but you wouldn't think that that would be important if you were a police officer who was determined to solve what he had already solved. . . .

"But I know that when Mr. Hull sums up and when you consider this case you are going to say that there is evidence here, there is evidence of a white car, there is evidence of a bullet. That is what you are going to say. That is true, it is in evidence, but speaking of the white car, the manager of the Citgo station [from whom I had rented my car] said very clearly that this was not the only one of its kind in the area. But, let's go beyond that. Ronnie Ruggiero, who . . . saw some of this, had ridden in Rubin Carter's car and knew it, and said he could not identify it as Rubin Carter's car. . . .

"Suppose you had learned that three people had been mown down by some fiend who walked in that door and one of you police officers had to go back and stop the car with these people in it— would you search them? Capter didn't bother, nor did anyone else; but they did something which I tell you helped to set the stage. They brought them to where there were seventy-five to a hundred people milling around, and most significant, most significant, it would appear to me, would be Bello standing next to Sergeant Capter while these two defendants were taken out of their car and held against the building, and at this time, why did he not say, 'These are the men'? . . .

"He says, to return to his answer . . . he knew that he was in a conspiracy, and that he had committed a crime. Well, wouldn't it have been safer if he said, 'Those are the two birds that did all of this,' if he knew them? What better way to get rid of them if you are afraid of them, to get them off the streets. But to have a man he was afraid of to walk the streets for months, literally months— Rubin Carter walked these streets where you walked, ladies and gentlemen, from June 17th he walked out of the station house; they gave him his automobile in which they had already found this 'damning' bullet; they gave him his automobile and said, 'Drive away.' . . .

"On cross-examination it was developed that Bello was either a pathological liar or otherwise couldn't even give his own correct address. And then I asked him this scintillating question, ladies and gentlemen—it sounds so ridiculous as I read it back: 'You have difficulty recalling where you lived less than a year ago?' And he said, 'I am not very good on dates.'

"Well, I then said, 'You are not very good on memory, are you?' And he said, 'Well, I wouldn't say that.' And then I asked him about his service record in the Armed Forces and his undesirable discharge, and so forth. But these are small things, you say. Well, let's go on to things a little bigger. Let's see how good his memory is. . . .

"I said . . . 'Let me ask you if you did in fact tell Officer Greenough that one colored, C.M., was wearing a fedora and sport jacket, thin built, five eleven; number-two colored man, thin build, five eleven—did you tell Officer Greenough that?' And his answer: 'Yes, I might have. I don't recall exactly. I can't recall the exact words.' . . .

"Now, that is the kind of memory on which you are asked to rely and condemn somebody. That is the kind of man who made other statements, such as this. . . . Question: Is it not a fact that you told the police on the morning of the seventeenth of June 1966, 'I didn't see their faces,' isn't that correct? And his answer: 'Yes, sir.' . . .

"The Bench has stopped me once or twice in this case from implying, perhaps, these witnesses, Bello and Bradley, had something to do with this . . . but I will imply with all my might that there is something more to the story of Bello, Bradley, and Kellogg than has been brought forth in this courtroom, and that somebody knows it. . . .

"Remember what [Bradley] said. It will remain with me forever for a special reason. I remember . . . he said, 'That *Negro* over there.' What is that, an animal? Well, I will tell you, in his voice, it was there, and everything around this case revolves around that simple fact. They were Negro. Does it matter if the eyewitness, the man alive, said they were light-skinned and five feet eleven? No. They were Negroes. What difference does it make? Somebody is going to go, and the only description we have is Negro. . . . I tell you, ladies and gentlemen, that if in this case you don't recognize this thread of the fact that these men would not be here if they weren't black, and if it weren't a white car, and those two things alone—talk about your butterfly stoplights. Butterfly stoplights, my foot. Three of the witnesses talked about Chevrolets. Who paid any attention to that? Does anybody care? We have another animal in tow.

"Well, let me tell you something, ladies and gentlemen, the issue here is more than life and death. The issue here is dignity. The issue here is evaluating another person. The issue here is who counts, a man because he is white and wears a uniform, or because he is black and is forthright? And I challenge you, in all this testimony, in all this case, to find one instance where this man didn't come forward. He came forward and faced you. He came forward and faced you wearing the same jacket, the same beard, the same attitude he has had all his life. . . .

"Mrs. Valentine testified, not only did she tell the police that she couldn't identify the men, but she told the local family related to her in some way by marriage, 'I couldn't identify these people.'

"Well, just look at Rubin Carter, ladies and gentlemen. Here is a man who carries himself differently, a man who looks differently, whose appearance is not . . . perhaps as easily forgotten or over-looked as yours or mine. You have seen it. There he sits. That is the way he was that night. [I was wearing the same clothes—a light beige, candy-striped jacket, a black vest, and black pants; bald head and a beard.] . . . If you had just seen somebody who had slain somebody . . . you had seen this terror, you had seen this defendant, you mean you wouldn't remember he had a derby and a white coat or a black coat on, and the other had a sweater on . . . ?

"Inconceivable. Inconceivable. These had to be people who were not as striking as they. These had to be people who were somewhat different, and let me tell you if it were not for the steady insistence of Negroes, it would be improper.

"That's all you have here—Negro, Negro, Negro. I have heard it until I am—I have heard it from Bradley and from Bello and heard it from every living soul here. Apparently that means you are either suspect or more guilty. I don't know what it means, but in this case, ladies and gentlemen, if we are to reach the high plateau this court demands, it can't mean anything. It can't! . . .

"When the story was being told by Mr. Hull [in his opening remarks], I was shattered because I thought surely there was either a movie camera or a witness, because he told how the persons walked in from this door. He told specifically how Artis had a pistol, specifically how Carter had a gun, a pump shotgun—he didn't say, but it was later said—and how they walked in and one shot the other and the other shot the other and then turned and walked out. This seemed to me so remarkable and so bizarre, I said, 'Nobody appearing for the state would make that kind of statement unless he could prove it.' Tell me, ladies and gentlemen, if you can recall anybody demonstrating that. I will tell you what was demonstrated conclusively and beyond peradventure, that the people who were seen by the jackals Bello and Bradley were supposedly coming around the corner, and not out of either door as was stated by each of these ghouls when they were interrogated on June 17. That is for sure. Nobody saw any one of these men anywhere. That is for sure. Nobody thereafter found any weapons. That is for sure, although catch basins were searched, everything around the area was searched. Nobody found a single weapon. Did they stop the right persons? Is this the issue? You must decide. I say, no. Not a question of whether they stopped the right persons or not, the question is, Have they proved beyond a reasonable doubt that these are the right persons and that they committed the acts?

"I don't know how you can discount [the testimony of all the defense witnesses]. All of these people just exuded truth, and under pressure. You can bet they were under pressure. This is not a proper case to be a witness. No murder trial is, because somehow you become allied with the defendant. . . . But there was one little witness nobody wants to talk about. I think they just wish he would go away, a little man who came in here early this week . . . named Hector Martinez. Hector came from Bordentown, and he went back to Bordentown, not in protective custody, not expecting any hope. . . .

"I asked Mr. Bradley one question about this: 'Did you ever tell, were you in the same jail with Hector Martinez in August?' 'Yes, I was.' 'Did you tell Hector Martinez that you were going to play off this Carter case against the other things pending against you?' He said, 'No.' Hector Martinez from Bordentown. One question: 'Were you in jail with him?' 'Yes, I was.' Uncontroverted. . . . 'Did this man tell you he was going to play off the Carter case against the other matters pending against him?' 'Yes, sir.' And then the last question which is in the record: 'And did he tell you that on that night he did not see these defendants?' Answer: 'Yes, sir.'

"That was the end of that. Mr. Martinez departed. No extensive cross. No rebuttal. Would you say then, in terms of human behavior, that a young man like Martinez, who is still in custody, he went back to Bordentown, who told the story unfavorable to the state, with all the pressures, would be more likely to do what Peter Rush did and say, 'I will tell the truth regardless of the consequences,' or a Bradley with five armed robberies, breaking and entries, escape from the police, no charges pending against him. The price may be high, ladies and gentlemen, but the state is willing to pay.

"I can't leave you without this last note," Ray Brown said, pointing to me. "This man is a human being who has lived since 1957 without blemish. This man's record is available to you for only one purpose. That is to assess it against his credibility. In other words, to determine whether you would believe him, believe what he says, all or part of it, because he has had a charge, pleaded to it and served time. The distinction between Bradley and Bello is that they have pending charges, and, therefore, you may not only consider what they have said in terms of their believability, but consider what is hanging over them, in terms of whether they are doing what they did and testified as they have wanting favor and reward and expecting it.

"This is a human being standing in fear of his life. These two young men, Bello and Bradley, have only to gain. . . . This man's life is not bound up in automobiles, but this is one of the reasons he is here. He is bound up in his skin though, and that is the other reason he is here. Can you believe that this man who did not run, who did not hide, did this, did these things? How can one believe this? These are terrible photographs. This is a stark tragedy. Could this man have done this?

"But, that is not the question, is it? The question is, did the state prove it beyond a reasonable doubt, and, of course, you have to answer, 'No.' And what do you say about the Patricia Graham Valentine? [sic] She couldn't identify them within feet. What do you say of the William Marins' five feet eleven, light-skinned? What do you say of the Bello's five feet eleven, light-skinned? Do you write all that off? Do you discount that, although it is testimony in this case, and do you say that this is so terrible that a sacrifice must be made? . . .

"This is probably the last place in the entire world where a trial like this could go on. Where else would they tolerate three weeks of picking a jury? Where else would they tolerate lawyers sometimes bumbling, sometimes stumbling, but each time trying to prove or disprove? Where else do they tolerate this in the world, where else but here? Why then must this man suffer because he rode the streets of Paterson, minding his own business, a black man driving a white car? I know you won't stand for it."

Tears were now trickling from Brown's eyes. "Thank you," he said, and staggered back to the defense table. The six long weeks of strain had taken its toll, and the longest wait was yet to begin. The courtroom was suddenly astir—a confused mixture of muffled sniffling and angry voices. Everybody seemed to be affected by Brown's passionate plea, with the exception of the ones who counted the most: thirteen members of the jury, and me. Only the West Indian displayed a little emotion, though he tried to appear casual when he brushed a hand across his red-rimmed eyes. But the others' faces were pure granite. The judge was affected, too, but in a different manner. When Brown started saying that he was tired of hearing the word "Negro, Negro, Negro" so much, Judge Larner's jaws seemed to swell up and actually turn purple. For a minute there I thought His Honor was going to jump down off his bench and kick Ray Brown dead in his ass, screaming, "The nerve of you, nigger, to put our prejudices right out in the open!" But he must have figured that that would have been too raw, so he just rolled his eyes up at the ceiling and let his breath out in a silent "Whooose."

At the direction of the judge, the prosecutor began his summation right after the lunch recess. "Thank you, Your Honor," he said as he rose to face the jury. The courtroom was deathly quiet again. Heavy tension, like thousand-pound weights, pressed downward from the rafters.

Vincent E. Hull, Jr., was not nearly as voluble as Ray Brown. In fact, he was very blunt, almost to the point of being brutal, and got right to the issues at hand. He explained to the jury why Bello and Bradley could not have been lying for gain or favor—because, he said, the state had not promised them anything, and their statements were not tailor-made to identify the both of us.

"Ladies and gentlemen," Hull said, "when you retire to the jury room, all of the exhibits in this case that have been admitted in evidence will be in there with you, including this bullet, this .32 S&W long Remington Peters. That will be one of the items that goes into the jury room with you, and after you deliberate upon the facts in this case, and weigh all of them carefully, that bullet, small in size, will get larger and larger and larger, and that bullet will call out to you and say to you, Bello and Bradley told the truth. That bullet will call out to you and say to you Carter and Artis lied, and that bullet will get louder and larger and it will cry out to you like three voices from the dead, and it will say to you Rubin Carter and John Artis are guilty of murder in the first degree, and then it will come your function to determine the question of penalty. You know from all the questions posed to you on the voir dire that under the law of the State of New Jersey that the penalty for first-degree murder in this state is either the death penalty or life imprisonment, and each and every one of you, before you were selected as jurors here, stated under oath that you could bring in one of the alternatives, either the death penalty or life imprisonment, based upon whatever the facts of this case might be, and the facts of this case speak for themselves."

The prosecutor then emptied out three bags of bloody clothes on a table situated directly in front of the jury, each bag in a separate pile. Beside each heap he placed the picture of the deceased person whose clothes they were, and in the pictures the deceased were laid out on slabs in the morgue.

"There once was a man," Hull continued gravely, "a human being by the name of James Oliver, a bartender at the Lafayette Grill, and he wore this shirt, and he looked like this when he was placed into eternity by a 12-gauge shotgun shell.

"There once was a man, a fellow human being by the name of Fred Nauyaks who lived in Cedar Grove, and he had the misfortune of going to the Lafayette Grill on June 16–17, 1966, and this is how his life ended when he was murdered in cold blood with a .32-caliber bullet through his brain.

"And there once was a human being, a woman by the name of Hazel Tanis, and she wore these clothes, these bullet-riddled clothes, when she was shot, not once, not twice, not three times—four times; two of the bullets which passed through her and two remained in her body, and she clung to life for nearly one month, and on July 14 of 1966 she passed away, and this is what became of this fellow human being.

"Ladies and gentlemen, on the question of punishment, the facts of this case clearly indicate that on the morning of June the seventeenth of 1966, the defendants, Rubin Carter and John Artis, forfeited their right to live, and the state asks that you extend to them the same measure of mercy that they extended to James Oliver, Fred Nauyaks, and Hazel Tanis, and that you return verdicts of Murder in the First Degree on all the charges *without a recommendation.*

"Thank you," Hull said, and sat down.

The court recessed then, and Judge Larner made his charge to the jury on the following day, May 26, 1967. "Ladies and gentlemen of the jury," he began, "You have sat through a long and arduous trial. You have heard a lot of testimony. You have heard the arguments of counsel for the respective parties, and now the trial in chief is completed, except for the instructions of the Court, which I am about to give you."

Larner went on then to define "reasonable doubt" as "simply an honest and reasonable uncertainty as to the guilt of the defendant or defendants which may exist in your minds after you have given full and impartial consideration to all of the evidence."

He pointed out that the evidence on which the state had relied was primarily circumstantial, and not direct.

He told the jurors that one of their prime functions was to judge the credibility of the witnesses, as well as whether anyone's testimony had been affected by any hope of reward or favor.

He called their attention to Bello's and Bradley's criminal records, as well as to my own, saying that it was up to them (the jury) to determine whether or not these records affected our respective credibility. He added that my previous convictions were not to be thought of as evidence.

He spoke of the conflict over the state's claim that John and I had been properly and fully warned of our rights before we were interrogated by the police, and defined what was meant by first and second degree murder. "It is apparent," he continued, "that among other factual issues, the most important one for your consideration which is involved in this case is whether the defendants were present in the Lafayette Grill at the time and place of the shooting. The state contends that the defendants were the individuals in the bar who committed the murder on the night in question, and has sought to prove that fact through a chain of circumstantial evidence. The defendants, on the other hand, deny the commission of the crime and say that they were not in the bar or on the street outside the bar at the time involved, and that the identification by the state's witness is false and erroneous. These respective contentions have created conflicts in the testimony which must be resolved by you in order to determine whether the state has proved guilt beyond a reasonable doubt."

Before he finished speaking, Judge Larner added one other small note which I thought was the real dickhead of all: he tried to clear the court of all the vicious racism that was shown to us throughout this trial, and which Ray Brown had finally brought out into the open.

"It goes without saying," Larner said, his voice trembling, and his eyes burning directly into Raymond Brown's at the defense table, "that the race of the defendants is of no significance in this case except as it may be pertinent to the problem of identification. The defendants are entitled to full justice under the law whatever their color. The state has not and does not bring this proceeding against them simply because they are Negroes. Such an issue is not in this case, and any suggestion to the contrary is wholly improper. This issue should not enter your minds in any respect in determining the guilt or innocence of these defendants. Your decision must be based upon the evidence, and you should perform your sworn duty with favor and without fear and without consideration of any extraneous matters or influences, in toto, with justice and fairness to the state and to the defendants."

Then, after advising the jurors that they had to return a unanimous verdict, he allowed time for some legal arguments out of their presence. When they returned to the courtroom, Larner turned to a woman who had been seated at a desk beside him throughout the trial. "All right. You may proceed, Miss Clerk," he said.

When this woman got up and started to spin the lottery box that was supposedly holding the names of the fourteen jurors still sitting on the panel, I pulled Ray Brown's coat sleeve. I suspected that the state was getting ready to play another one of its wild jokers, and I wanted Brown to stop it before it happened.

"Hey! What the hell is she doing?" I hissed into his ear. "Get her away from that damn box!"

"Shhh, Rubin," he hissed right back. "She's only going to pick the twelve jurors who will have to decide the verdict. Two of the fourteen will have to go," he said.

And with the first stroke of the woman's hand, the West Indian was snatched off the jury panel. That left us with a totally white jury to decide if two black men had killed three white people— with the accusation coming from two white convicts, a white prosecutor, and a white judge who did just about everything but to tell the jury straightout not to believe the black witnesses. What a kick in the ass that was. Our whole case had been directed at the only black man on the panel; pointing up to him the fallacy of the identification, the lies, the inducements, the coercion, the conspiracy of the state. But now he was gone. Removed by a slip of paper in a spinning box. The electric chair was staring me dead in the face, and the futility of it all made me so angry that all I could do was just sit there and shake my head.

At about noon, the jury went out to begin its deliberations. They had an hour off for lunch, another hour to smoke and get comfortable in the jury room. It took them about an hour and a half more to reach a verdict. Six whole weeks of legal arguments, crying, pleading, tearing, picking, digging, demanding some motherfucking justice, and these crackers had their shit together within two hours. Goddamn! The four women on the jury returned to the courtroom crying; the men were stonefaced. Their verdict was guilty as charged on all three counts, but with a recommendation of mercy, or life imprisonment.

Life? That only proved to me that they still had doubts. If they had truly thought us guilty of triple murder, how in the world could they have twisted their mouths up to give us life? What life? Being abused in jail forever? It would have been more merciful to shoot me down on the spot. Mercy, my black ass! I would rather they had swung me from the courtroom rafters than for them to come in with that mercy shit. That was only a sham, and everybody had to know it. But the worst part of it was my wife: she fell out in the courtroom when the verdict was announced, and that hurt. Goddammit, that hurt. In a sense, they killed me right then. It tore my heart apart to see my beautiful woman like that. Inside, I wept for death.

THE SIXTEENTH ROUND

What Will Your Verdict Be?

Short speeches linger a long time in some memories, and Judge Larner's final speech will remain with me forever. He banged his gavel on the desk for order, then turned to me with the cold dignity of a Caesar.

"Rubin Carter," he announced with lordly grandeur, "although you still contend that you are not guilty of the crimes charged in the indictment against you, you were afforded a full and fair trial before a jury which was carefully selected by counsel in a long and tedious process. That jury found you guilty and the Court is duty bound to impose sentence on the basis of that finding by the jury, and not on the basis of your continued contention of non-guilt.

"I might say from my analysis of the evidence and the witnesses that I have no hesitation in stating that the jury's verdict was fully warranted by the proofs submitted during the trial. The killings for which you were indicted and tried can only be described as the result of a cold-blooded massacre of innocent victims who were wholly unknown to you. There is not a single factor in these killings which can serve as mitigation of the heinousness of the offense. In fact, there is totally absent any understandable reason for motive which can be said to have compelled you for the moment to commit this horrible crime. . . .

"There is no point in my going into it in detail. I am sure you are fully aware of your prior criminal record. . . . In addition, I am sure you are also aware of your antisocial behavior in the past years. Of course, as your counsel has said, not in recent years, but in past years. . . .

"The evidence here reflects a clear-cut intent to kill every person in the tavern at the time. Under the law as I see it, where you have separate victims of a killing with an incident applicable to each individual victim, the killing of each presents a separate murder.

"It is therefore the Court's sentence as to the first count involving the murder of James Oliver that you be imprisoned in the New Jersey State's Prison for the remainder of your natural life. . . .

"As to the second count involving the murder of Fred Nauyaks, it is the sentence of this Court that you be imprisoned in the New Jersey State's Prison for the remainder of your natural life, and this sentence shall be consecutive to the sentence on the first count.

"As to the third count involving the murder of Hazel Tanis, it is the sentence of this Court that you be imprisoned in the New Jersey State's Prison for the remainder of your natural life, and this sentence shall be concurrent with the sentence imposed on the second count."

John's clear record got him three concurrent life sentences, and the fraud was completed, adjudicated, and closed. Judge Larner was transferred back to Essex County and shifted into civil law.

Back at Trenton State Prison that afternoon, I found it to be the same old obsolete hole of depravity and death that it was when I'd left it five years before. The little racist guards that I'd left behind were all big-shot guards now, working in the upper echelons of the administration. They controlled the jail with an iron fist of brutality, a minimum of compassion, and a maximum of security. The deliberate execution of each inmate's personality seemed to be their favorite pastime. First they wiped out his mind, his name, and his manhood, and then they drew him into their subtle web of institutionalization. Everything about the place seemed geared to break the man and praise the homosexual, to kill the spirit and save the punk.

A generation of young kids now made up the prison's population. All the old-timers were gone, free, dead, or shipped out to the farms, while this new breed of whatchamacallits staggered around the jailhouse with nothing on their minds but finger-popping, watching TV, shooting dope, and sucking dicks. They cradled huge radios in their arms like they were babies, and told the "man" on each other for spite and favor. There were no clear lines of demarcation anymore between the men and the homosexuals in the joint, or between the stool pigeons and the jailhouse punks; Trenton State Prison now was just one great big happy family of fools.

My self-respect would not allow me to stoop to this prison's ungodly level of nonexistence. I realized deep down in my gut-works that the twisted-tongued police who had sent me back here, the two convicts who testified against me, and even the prison authorities themselves expected—and hoped—I would go on a rampage and kill somebody in the jail, or be killed myself. I refused to let this happen, although just thinking about the treachery involved almost wiped my mind right out. Triple life? Goddamn! It was as if the cops were telling me, "Yeah, nigger, we fucked you! Now whatcha gonna do about it?"

For the entire month of July I stayed locked away in my cell in deep meditation, going into myself with silence, gathering up all three of my souls—Rubin, Hurricane, and Carter—and wondering what we should do. But as usual, we couldn't seem to come to terms—although we all agreed, for the moment, to continue on with our fight to be free. Rubin, being the quick learner of the three, decided to study the law and get us back into court that way, if he could, while the Hurricane just said "Fuck it!" and was ready to demolish everything in the prison; but Carter, usually the most quiet and reserved of all, thought he ought to write a book and bring our case before the public. Because one thing was accepted by us all, and that was we would definitely not submit to this prison's nastiness. We would study the law and write this book, and if that didn't work, then let the Hurricane take over and do what must be done.

From that day to this, I have kept myself removed from the institution and its people. I have studied the law, beginning under the wizardly guidance of Bobby "Irish" Cullen, a little Irishman who was serving ninety-nine years at Trenton for armed robbery. (He ended up serving only seven of those years, due to his knowledge of the law, and he's home at this time.)

Little Irish was one of the most fascinating people I have ever had the pleasure to meet, and the most jolly, by far. Each day at Trenton State, we met in the library and researched the dusty law books from cover to cover, backwards and forwards, reading, deciphering thousands of Supreme Court opinions to look for that legal loophole. We found many, but always reached the same conclusion: that I'd been given a royal judicial fucking—first class! —and was still getting fucked!

We had to do all the research for my case from memory, because my lawyer wouldn't even answer my letters, much less send me a copy of the trial transcripts. I found many clear instances of legal impropriety and reversible errors, such as the illegal search and seizure of my car; the *Miranda* issue; the judge overstepping his bounds; the cops' sloppy investigation. And then there was my contention that the police had offered those two convicts a deal to elicit their perjured testimony on the witness stand.

And then there was Ray Brown. On the surface of it, he did indeed fulfill his legal obligations to me. That is, whenever an eloquent argument was called for, or when his type of courtroom strategy managed to pry the truth from the sealed lips of the prosecution witnesses. But that's not what I'm talking about at all. I have no quarrels with his oral presentations, because I was as intoxicated by his elegant language as was everyone else in the courtroom—with the exception of the jury, of course.

But John Artis and I should never have been brought to trial in Passaic County. The local press certainly saw to that. Their highly publicized accounts of a racially motivated triple murder of white citizens by two Negroes made it impossible for us to receive a fair trial in Paterson, and Brown should have asked for an immediate change of venue. At least, I'm convinced of that.

Then there was this Martinez business: When Hector came to testify for the defense to refute Arthur Dexter Bradley's vicious lies, Judge Larner wouldn't permit his testimony because, as he said, Raymond Brown simply had not laid the proper foundation for it when Bradley was up on the witness stand. So that left Bradley's testimony standing virtually unimpeached.

And last, but perhaps grossest of all, was when my lawyer had not properly instructed my two alibi witnesses what to do in the event that the cops tried to intimidate them: Mrs. Mapes, and her daughter, Cathy McGuire, had been verbally abused, frightened, and confused by Lieutenant DeSimone some four or five months before my trial, and Brown knew it. I feel certain all of that could have been prevented. But it wasn't, so the prosecutor was able to create a shred of doubt in the minds of the jury as to when it really was that I drove the two women home—Friday morning of the seventeenth, or Saturday morning of the eighteenth—a shred of doubt where none should have existed.

But I couldn't find any way to bring out all the underlying pressures in my case in the law library. I did find out through my research, however, that the question of my innocence or guilt was no longer of any real significance in a court of law, and that was the hardest thing for me to accept. The only issues that I could deal with concretely were those pertaining to whether nor not I had received a fair trial, free from constitutional error or racial prejudice, or whether the conviction was obtained through underhanded methods. That was the big question: did the state know of the witnesses' perjured testimony, and induce it, and had they knowingly suppressed exculpatory evidence?

Yeah! Hell, yeah! *I* knew it was so. But how could I prove it?

During the two and a half years before my appeal was heard by the New Jersey State Supreme Court, which time I spent conscientiously studying the law, I noted the changes taking place on the outside: the Newark riots of 1967 that had killed 26 people; the Detroit uprising that gobbled up 43 lives; the people in the streets who believed that all brothers were valiant and all sisters fair, and were hollering, "Black is beautiful," and "Right on, brother!" The walls of this medieval prison were high, but not high enough to keep out the sounds of violence and racism. The cries of unity and of getting it together fairly thundered in over the walls. Huh! That's funny, I thought to myself one day; that's what I had been trying to tell the people all along.

Via the newspapers and various other media, I learned of some other starting events taking place in my absence. I learned that Alfred Bello—that pillar of society, the state's star witness, who had denied that his mangled testimony was prefabricated to keep his nasty ass out of jail or for personal gain—had appeared before the Paterson City Council to lay claim to the $12,500 reward—except that by this time it had been reduced to only $10,500. (I wonder what happened to the other $2,000?) He even brought some lawyer along, threatening the city fathers with a lawsuit if they didn't come up with the bounty bread. But the city told him he would have to wait until my final appeal was decided before he could get paid for his lies.

At about the same time, Arthur Dexter Bradley, our other paragon of virtue, was being sentenced in Union County for armed robbery. The Passaic County prosecutor appeared in his behalf, however, asking the court for leniency in recognition for his aid in getting me convicted for triple murder, and explaining further that sending him to prison would be putting his life in danger. The judge didn't agree. He felt that Bradley was a criminal of the worst sort and said that if ever a man belonged in prison, Bradley surely did. The judge sentenced him to from three to five years to be served at Trenton State Prison, and, in all honesty, the Hurricane's lips started drooling in joyful anticipation. The prison authorities refused to accept him, however, and so he was shipped off to Bordentown instead.

All of these things I brought to the attention of the State Supreme Court in the form of writs, briefs, and *coram nobises*, offering up the above allegations as new evidence. Any one of them, I felt, should have been adequate grounds to order me a new trial free from perjured testimony, but on July 15, 1969, an opinion written by Chief Justice Joseph Weintraub stated in part:

> At about 2:30 a.m. on June 17, 1966, two men entered the Lafayette Bar and Grill in the City of Paterson. One man held a .32-caliber revolver, the other a 12-gauge shotgun. Their motive was obscure, no doubt because events moved so rapidly. We gather from the testimony of the sole surviving victim that the bartender saw the armed men as they entered and threw a bottle at them, precipitating the shooting before a word was said. The bartender was killed instantly, as was also one of the patrons. Another patron, Mrs. Tanis, who suffered multiple wounds, died four weeks later. The lone survivor, also a patron, was shot in the head. His ability to tell what happened was obviously impaired; he could contribute little more than that the armed men were Negroes. *The State failed in its effort to prove a dying declaration by Mrs. Tanis. We know only that she and also the surviving patron were unable to identify either defendant, but the testimony does not suggest that either patron was able to say affirmatively that the defendants were not the offenders* [my italics].
>
> Both Carter and Artis testified. They produced a number of witnesses in an effort to place themselves at a bar at the time of the murders. It, however, was virtually impossible to establish an alibi, for at all times defendants were concededly within minutes of the murder scene and the moment of the killings could not be established precisely. It is fair to say that the case had to turn upon the State's proof and the defendants' denial of guilt, unaided by the testimony which sought to establish an incompatible presence elsewhere. . . .
>
> The judgements are therefore affirmed.

I could have cried.

The State of New Jersey was pulling its old set of double standards on me again, and the Chief Justice had put the cap on it. He claimed that Marins, the sole survivor, was coherent enough to be believable when he said that it was two Negroes who walked into the tavern and was hit with a bottle. But as soon as the lone survivor described the killers as someone different than John Artis and myself, the man's testimony suddenly became "obviously impaired."

Not once did Weintraub even mention anything concerning Bello and Bradley's credibility as key witnesses on the stand, except for when he said later on in his deceitful opinion, "The sight of money was too much for Bello who, explaining he was a thief, admitted he scooped some bills from the register." With that one insipid statement Chief Justice Weintraub legally sanctioned not only a lie but the easiest robbery in the State of New Jersey as well. The two "bounty hunters" had only to testimony-capture *any* two Negroes in the state to go for the $10,500 reward. But Weintraub didn't say a goddamn thing about that!

For all the shit that a black man goes through in his life, perhaps the most significant thing he learns is that his life is capricious at best. He's always subjected to someone else's whim. Anybody who claims that a man is the master of his own fate should jump ass-first off the tallest building, and then try to master getting his black ass back up on that bad motherfucker. It was this way for me with the courts and with this prison, both of which were designed to defeat the human spirit. The judges, lawyers, and educators of the world all spoke reverently of honor, justice, and truth, but these were merely glib words spewed out of plastic pigs, and the people didn't really believe that shit themselves.

But I knew what the truth was—it was death! Because I would rather be dead than alive in this prison. Now that's the truth.

The Saturday following the denial of my appeal, my wife and daughter came down to visit me at the prison. As I looked through the thick bulletproof, bubble-stained glass at the two people I loved the most in the world, I knew right then that my string of patience had played out. I couldn't take this anymore. The news of my denial had been blasting over the radio for a solid week, and the emotions that swam in their eyes were overpowering, to say the least. Too goddamn much for me to take: love, pity, loss, anguish, pain, heartache. I wanted to break down and cry. Mae Thelma was still young and beautiful, only two years my junior, and the world should have been her oyster. She ought not to have had to go husbandless because her man was locked up in jail on a trumped-up charge. Just by being alive, I was limiting her life.

For a brief moment I sat there seriously contemplating suicide.

Then I thought of Mr. Summers, the old man who had gotten tired twelve years earlier and not only thought about it but went ahead and committed suicide in this hellhole because of this same deadly feeling of hopelessness. Just remembering the sight of his grotesque face as the crew of apathic guards carried what remained of him from the tier made me shiver where I sat. My God! No way. I wouldn't let that happen to me. Still, I couldn't stomach the thought of my wife and daughter traveling 140 miles once a month, year in and year out, just to watch me turn into a useless old man, withering away on a rotten vine that promised me no life, until finally I would just up and die dead of loneliness in this scum-infested puspit, either.

I thought of hurling curses at Mae Thelma and screaming at Theodora, of shouting harsh invectives at them to drive them away from me in hatred. Then they could have just walked out of my life and been glad to have seen the last of me. I really cried then— because I was much too weak to do it. My heart wept for them, for everything they meant to me, for loving the grouchy old Rube and sticking in my corner when everybody else had already packed in their tents and bailed out on me. But mostly I cried because I had reduced their state of living into a financial mess by trying to defend myself against the treachery that had put me in jail. Now I had become an anchor around their beautiful necks, choking them, trying to pull them down even further. No, motherfuckers, no! I wasn't going for that.

The state gave me the name of murderer, I thought then, so now I'm going to play the game of one. I decided that as soon as my family left this prison, and I left this visiting hall, I had me some fools who needed killing bad. There were too many gutless wonders working in that prison just standing in the way and stifling everything progressive like meaningful change. So, I thought, I'm just going to take some of these greasy motherfuckers with me. With that settled in my mind, I immediately felt better, and the Hurricane inside me started dancing around in his corner, putting on his ugly face and getting ready to sho 'nuff smoke.

Well, Mae Thelma, Theodora, and I sat there crying all through the visit. Loving one another something fierce. But we were hurting. The more they cried, I cried, and the more I cried, they cried. I cried because I wasn't going see them anymore. I had made my decision and there wasn't much else I could do: I was determined to free my two beautiful ladies, to give them back the chance in life they needed to live the rich and rewarding lives they so rightfully deserved.

When the visiting hour was over, I just sat there and sadly watched them walk out the door, out of my life, and even after they were out of my sight I remained rooted to the stool, unable to move. I must have sat there for an hour or more, before the shuffling sound of feet behind me brought my mind back into the prison.

"All right, Carter," a guard's harsh voice ordered from behind me. "Your visit's over. Get back to your cell."

"Ah-ha," I thought. "Number one!" But I continued looking through the glass, not even caring who it was behind me. I must have trembled involuntarily in anticipation of his putting his slimy hands on my shoulder, because my brain coiled. I still couldn't do anything to anybody unless they did something to me first. And perhaps there is something to this extrasensory perception theory, because I somehow got the feeling that he knew that if he touched me, he would have to gamble for his life. He must have relayed this same message to the center too, because I was still sitting there hours later when mess had started. The count was taken and cleared, but I still hadn't seen a goddamn soul. I was desperate. And the administration must have known it, too, because they shipped me out to Rahway State Prison the very next morning.

Rahway State Prison is easily identifiable by its big green center dome sitting out in the middle of nowhere, and the cursed stench of pigeon shit polluting the air. If it weren't for the high brick walls and the armed guards constantly patrolling the grounds around it, it might look almost innocent, like the rest of the industrial plants in that particular area. Only it wasn't innocent, because this factory manufactured hardened criminals, and Rahway was the refinery where they gold-plated their product.

This subhuman outlet was rather new among New Jersey penitentiaries. It had been in use only since 1896, when it was a reformatory for juvenile delinquents. But in 1948 it was pressed into service as a full-fledged prison. It was more spacious and less confining than Trenton State Prison, and housed only half the population that Trenton did. It was also the only adult institution in the state which allowed contact visits.

There are five wings in the jail: One Wing was lock-up, Two

Wing was a dormitory, Three Wing a unit of rooms without bars; Five Wing was the sex offenders' quarters, and Four Wing was a vicious black ghetto that would have put the "Big Apple" to shame.

There was no brutality or racism when I got to Rahway in 1969—only apathy, in the form of overindulgence. Everything that the other institutions lacked, Rahway had: contact visits every Sunday, which was equal to mouth-to-mouth resuscitation for us inmates; the Theater of the Forgotten came in on a weekly basis to perform their plays, and community volunteers came in each week to participate in various programs; the inmates put together a variety show each year, and their families were invited into the prison for a night of relaxation; Achievement Night was much the same, when the inmates "graduating" from school were allowed to invite their loved ones inside to watch the ceremonies.

Rahway, then, was a beehive of activity. There were so many places to go at once, and so many things to occupy one's mind, that few people really knew if they were coming or going. The only time a man was locked in his cell was when he got tired and locked his own self up, and that might not be until two or three o'clock in the morning. This was the administration's way of minimizing trouble just as surely as faggots were for Trenton. Only here they kept everyone so busy looking at movies, watching live shows, shooting pool, and drinking hooch that nobody seemed to remember that he was still in jail. This is what I called living in a "cinematic concept"—going to the movies each week to assume a new role: *Superfly* today, and *Shaft* tomorrow—but always shunning the reality of being in jail.

If ever a more subtle form of compliance has been employed to dehumanize a man than those techniques used at Rahway, I would surely like to see it. The inmates were allowed to run wild, and they thought they were hip and getting over. Meanwhile, the only person really getting over was Warren Pinto, the superintendent, who let the fools run themselves ragged and never had a day of trouble.

The inmates' politics, though, were treacherous. The institution had given up so much over the years that some misguided individuals thought themselves to be cops, and not prisoners. Most of the old-timers I'd known from the past, those who would have snatched somebody's head clean off their shoulders if anyone showed them disrespect, were now in control of all the graft-taking programs, and they maintained their precarious positions by turning stool pigeon for the administration. Most of these inmates were serving life sentences, but were so happy in this place that the mere thought of going home would have been a cruel shock to their senses. They'd found it much easier to get along in jail as punks than to survive it as men.

Pinto's administration was certainly aware of why Trenton had suddenly elected to get rid of me at that particular time, and they didn't want me, either. They were afraid that I would upset their delicate balance of control over these wild niggers. But they had naught to fear. The inmates had so whittled up their allegiances into such a multitude of polarized black groups and religious sects that they had completely deserted the strong body of blackness and rendered it weak and futile in its struggle for unity. There was simply too much division among us to give the prison authorities any cause for alarm, and as long as the inmates remained divided, they continued to fall, fall, fall right into the debilitating ways of this insane asylum's custom.

So nobody wanted the Hurricane in his place of business, and, of course, I didn't want to stay, either. But somebody had to keep me, since they wouldn't let me go home, so Rahway thought it best to keep me in lock-up, rather than out in the population stirring up trouble. However, the administration had underestimated their own proficiency in dehumanizing their wards, because I had more contempt than comradeship for what I saw. Never in my life had I witnessed such a worthless breed of nothings. It was a goddamn shame! Most of the young people in Rahway thought that being a man was a simple matter of standing up to take a piss, hollering "Right on!"—and then dropping their pants to let somebody hump 'em in the ass for a bag of dope. "Doing their own thing," they called it.

By 1970 I had reached my wits' end. Black people had gotten so goddamn proud of themselves outside on the streets that they had completely forgotten about the poor brothers still in jail. So it was a white man again—and a cop at that—who came to my rescue. He was Frederick W. Hogan, the same police officer who had stayed with me up in my training camp. He had been overseas while I was on trial for my life. When he came back home, he quit the police force and joined the Public Defender's Office as an investigator.

Fred was a squat, husky, good-looking kind of guy, with brownish-red hair and gray-green eyes flecked with a faint tinge of brown. He sported a thick handlebar mustache above his upper lip, and the firm, jutting chin below indicated a very purposeful nature. He was a "My Country 'Tis of Thee" Irish-American—what you could call a cop's cop. To him, you were either right or wrong, it was as simple as that. He had a young man's stubborn philosophy about where the world was heading, but not too much taste for the likelihood. His reason for leaving the police department, he told me, was to get into a field that somehow prevented crime rather than just solved it after it had been committed.

Fred was full of vim 'n' vigor for life. Though hard and service-worn beyond belief, he was still capable of showing compassion for a man in trouble. But it took him nearly six months just to get me to talk about my case. Every Saturday morning like clockwork, he would travel more than seventy miles to visit me at Rahway. Sometimes he stayed more than ten hours at a clip, interrogating me, continuously questioning certain aspects of my case, trying to break through the barrier of resistance that I had built up around me—that citadel of distrust which had kept me silent for the past three years. I dared not let my hopes fly in the face of the seething corruption, deceit, and fraud that Passaic County had draped on my back.

But the pigheaded Irish in Hogan's makeup made him a hard man to dissuade. No matter how unresponsive I was to his relentless probing into matters I dared not even think about too long—for fear of losing what little control I had—the next week he would be back again, prying up my buried past. Never once did he ask me if I was guilty or not. Each night in my cell I asked myself why was he doing all of this for me, or who might have sent him, and where he was really coming from. I mean, I didn't have one thin dime, and no way of getting a fat quarter, either. So what was he trying to prove? That was my main concern. Who was he working for?—especially since he had me drawing up legal briefs of my case.

During one of our many rap sessions he brought a tape recorder with him, and, although I was skeptical about talking into a microphone at first, we finally went over the entire case piece by piece. Beginning with the initial arrest and the trial itself, and going finally to the awful verdict, we ripped it apart and put it back together again. The verdict was the dickhead that really seemed to blow Hogan's mind the most. It was then that anger, candid and unmistakable, always flared up in his voice.

"That's bullshit!" he would snort every time. "If any *one* of those twelve lily-white middle-class American citizens sitting on that jury even *thought* that you two niggers had killed those white people," he would say, "they would have burnt your black asses to bacon-rinds! And rightly so." This cat has a helluva sense of humor.

But little did I know that Frederick W. Hogan, a real true-to-life Dick Tracy, had also been doing some pretty thorough investigative work on my case on his own. He did this to dispel any doubts of my innocence from his own mind, but he did it in his own way, without leaning on our personal relationship.

He showed me a package of photographs that he had taken of the Lafayette Bar and Grill in Paterson, New Jersey, to prove to me that he had indeed been out on the case. Then, beaming confidently, he began telling me about all the midnight hours he had spent tracking down, through some uncanny method of his own, several people who had been incarcerated with Arthur Dexter Bradley while he was waiting to get his charges dropped in four different counties. Bello never had gone to jail again, it turned out.

Hogan also uncovered a police captain in Bergen County and a correctional officer in Morris County who both claimed to know for a fact that Bradley had been continuously telling inmates in their jails that he had indeed lied in court. But the captain and the correctional officer wouldn't give Fred a deposition because they were afraid of being fired from their jobs.

Nonetheless, this was the best news that I had heard in a month of Sundays. Great googamoogoa! I shouted to myself, things just might be looking up for me.

But then a sober thought crossed my mind. "What good is this information going to do me, Fred?" I said. "I have no more money to retain a lawyer."

"I'll tell you what we're going to do with it," Hogan said, grinning like a mischievous imp. "With those legal briefs that I've had you draw up, along with this other information, I'm going to submit it all to the Appellate Section of my office and request that we take your case into the Federal District Court.

"I realize that this is an unusual procedure for us to undertake," he said, "because our office just doesn't have the budget to handle cases in the Federal Court. But with this new evidence that I've uncovered, which only substantiates your original claim of deceit all along, I have a feeling they might just surprise us this one time.

"But even if they don't," Fred said, "we still haven't lost anything, because I'm going to find us some lawyers somewhere, somehow."

Then he showed me a letter he was about to send to a Mr. Gerald Foley, the man in charge of the Appellate Section in the Public Defender's Office. Fred was enclosing with it the briefs I'd drawn up dealing with the search and seizure of my car and the *Miranda* warnings that Lieutenant DeSimone allegedly gave me, along with a list of the "startling facts" he'd uncovered during his investigation. He hoped that the package would move the Appellate Section to accept my case for appeal.

The letter was out of sight! In fact, it kind of touched me that someone still believed in me, when it was so easy to doubt. But what really threw me for a loop was the list of "new evidence" that Fred had enclosed with the letter. It proved that he had sho 'nuff been digging in somebody else's ass besides my own these past few months, like he said. It was a refreshing change, I kid you not—yeah, yeah, yeah—somebody still dug the Rube! And Fred Hogan wasn't bullshitting, either. The new evidence spoke for itself. (I've changed the names on the affidavits here to protect the people out there, so that the prosecutor can't get to them before I do. The following is only a brief summary of what was recorded.)

1. Thomas Janssen: While incarcerated at Bordentown Reformatory, he spoke with Arthur Dexter Bradley, and now states that Bradley was angry because Bello was trying to cut him out of his share of the reward money, and the prosecutor hadn't kept Bradley out of jail as he had promised. Bradley threatened to blow the Carter case wide open and tell everything, if he didn't receive his share of the money. He said that he would reveal that he had lied, that the prosecutor told him what to say, and promised to pay him if he testified in court against Carter and Artis. Bradley had all but one of the criminal charges pending against him dropped.

2. Chuck Norman: Norman was incarcerated at the Bergen County Jail with Arthur Dexter Bradley in September of 1967. Chuck was from New York City and didn't know anyone in New Jersey. He was locked in the same cell with Bradley. Bradley told Norman how the prosecutor took him and Bello before the grand jury to testify against Carter and Artis, and that the grand jury didn't believe them, returning a no bill. Bradley stated that Lieutenant DeSimone then had him change his story and say that he did see Carter and Artis in the area of the shooting. Bradley went on to

say that Lieutenant DeSimone took him back before another grand jury, alone, this time, with only a statement from Bello, and he got Carter and Artis indicted with this new story. He was promised half of the reward money if he would testify to this in court.

3. Bartram Nathan: Nathan was incarcerated with Arthur Dexter Bradley in the Union County Jail, and Bradley told him that he saw a white Cadillac at the scene of the crime and had assumed it to be Carter's. He knew that Carter had a white Cadillac. But he did not see anyone at the scene of the shooting. Bradley stated that the prosecutor of Passaic County paid him to testify in court that he saw Carter commit the crime of murder, and in return Bradley received monies well over $10,000.

4. Jim Driscoll; James Peters; and William Charles: These three individuals were together with Arthur Dexter Bradley in the Morris County Jail, when Bradley was bragging to them about all the armed robbery charges that he had pending against him, and how he wasn't worried about going to jail because he had made a deal with the Passaic County Prosecutor to testify in court against Rubin Hurricane Carter. Bradley said that he didn't know a damn thing about Carter, but if Carter was convicted he would have nothing to worry about. Bradley said that he also qualified for the $10,500 reward being offered. Bradley spoke many times of killing Carter and Artis if they were not convicted. Bradley did not care what anybody else thought about him, he was still going to turn state's evidence, even though he did not know anything about what happened.

That was the new evidence that Fred had uncovered.

While I anxiously awaited a reply from the Appellate Section, a rumor started floating around the jail that Rahway State Prison was getting a new superintendent. Warren Pinto had decided to retire. In prison an isolated guess rapidly becomes cause for immediate speculation among the inmates, but a rumor twice repeated becomes a fact. We did indeed get a new superintendent, and everything started going downhill from there.

The new man's name was Ulysses Samuel Vukcevich, or, Smilin' Sam Buck Savage, as the inmates soon renamed him. He was muscular, slim, dark, and inordinately good-looking, with a slight lisp in his speech. He smiled continuously, but that was only a front. Because he used his smile as a smoke screen to cover up his true feelings. If you talked with this man for many hours, you still wouldn't learn anything more about him that you didn't know at first glance. Whatever lay inside this man's heart was effectively concealed. He was thirty-nine years old and a past master in the art of psychological manipulation, for deep down inside of him lurked a sleeping monster, which he kept immaculately dressed at all times. He appeared to be much more a Hollywood personality than a serious-minded penologist.

As I understand it, Vukcevich had moved up the ladder of success from a schoolteacher in the reformatory to the administrator of this penitentiary, and at Rahway he found the same old jitterbugs doing the same old stupid shit that they had done in the other joints with him. So he had nothing but contempt for them, and this attitude caused him to make his first mistake in the performance of his duties: he lumped every inmate into this sorry bag and considered himself the big tough in a jail full of punks. He may have had, as I've heard, a Ph.D. in every imaginable science in the books, but one thing became obvious as soon as he took over the reins of the prison: he didn't know a damn thing about handling men— juveniles and jitterbugs, maybe—but men? Forget it!

This colony of lepers called Rahway had been standing here, as is, for seventy-five excruciating years, surviving only at the cost of human adaptability, and even the former leader of its wild bunch had been smart enough to let the inmates defeat their own purposes by running amuck and keeping their minds off where they really were. (In Hell!) But the new superintendent wasn't geared for it, and that was his second mistake. He chose instead to put up iron gates inside the jail's halls, which slowed the inmates down. This gave them time to think. At the same time, he began arbitrarily to disband many of the programs that the inmates had fought so hard with the previous administration to get. He tried to take away their hooch, too, and sober inmates are always unpredictable, without their means to mentally escape.

Before Smilin' Sam Buck Savage had been in office even for six months, Rahway State Prison had definitely undergone a terrible change. Two murders were committed, and there were ten escapes; three inmates died for lack of proper medical attention; an officer was stabbed; another was hospitalized by a poolstick, and a costly strike was called by the prison guards. The previous administration had had none of these problems, so something had to be wrong here. The prison became an armed camp, and it got worse and worse. The formerly carefree and happy-go-lucky inmates were cold sober and disgruntled now, and everybody was walking around the joint all shanked down with knives, clubs, and sharpened steel. They were just waiting for somebody to say something wrong, and on the day before Thanksgiving of 1971, somebody did say something, and the inmates rose—or maybe I should say, staggered—to the occasion.

Somebody had said that the little old winemaker in Four-Wing had done this thing again and now had some *baaaaad* hooch to sell, and soon everybody in the jail was on the move to cop some of his dynamite wine. I even went over there myself and bought a couple of quarts. And while I was standing there still drinking my wine, another inmate, whom I'll call Slick Joe, came over from One Wing, paid his money for a thermos jug full of the powerful brew, and hid it in his cell until after he came back from the movies. This was just so he could drink it later on by himself without sharing it with his partner. The moonshine was potent! But the wing officer had seen him when he left the bottle in his cell, and rolled down on him after he was gone and busted him for the wine—which meant that old Slick Joe would have to go to courtline the next day and get fifteen days in the hole. That was mandatory.

But Slick Joe wasn't going for that shit! Even though he had been busted fair and square, he wasn't man enough to take his own weight by himself, so he decided to get eleven hundred men involved in his own petty problems. He went and got his little partner, whom I'll call Righteous Pete (the same person Slick Joe was trying to hide the wine from), and told him that the wing officer had planted the wine in his cell to set him up for the bust.

Now Righteous Pete was an ornery little bastard who could fight as well as he wanted to, but nobody in his right mind would follow either one of these guys as far as the mess hall, even on the days they had chicken. So, together now, they went and got another wild nigger, whom I'll call Big Tom for this, and convinced him of the same lie that Slick Joe had conned Righteous Pete with. Now Big Tom was cool as long as he was sober, but they took him over to Four Wing to visit the little winemaker, and drunk he was a motherfucker!

I was up in the movies by this time watching the sex picture like everybody else was, with my eyes glued to the screen, trying to implant the vision of naked women in my mind until I could get back to my cell. Then I planned on making some passionate love to somebody's make-believe daughter. Suddenly, the auditorium doors flew open and in walked the ungodly three: Slick Joe, Righteous Pete, and Big Tom, all hooched up and drunker than hoot owls. Big Tom bent down and almost fell, but managed to pick up a chair and throw it point-blank through the movie screen.

"I'm tired of all you motherfucking cops always taking advantage of us!" he shouted in drunken defiance, as a ragged hole appeared where the chair had gone through the screen. The house lights came on. "And I'll be goddamned if I'm going to let you fuckin' rollers get away with it tonight!" he yelled.

"Right on, Lord!" Righteous Pete pushed Big Tom on. Tom turned to the audience.

"These goddamn crackers are trying to set this brother up," he shouted, pointing to Slick Joe—who was standing off to the side trying to melt inconspicuously into the floor.

The deadly silence that followed was frightening. A poignant hunger for violence hung heavily in the air. I could feel the tension that had lain dormant for all these months spring to life and begin to wiggle. Sparked into flame by the lethal fuel of an inebriated fool. My God! Eleven hundred men cramped up into close quarters. This is what I had been waiting for—a riot! It would begin just as it was doing now, with fear that slowly built up into a frenzy, which would inevitably breed savage courage where none had previously existed. I felt the Hurricane beating on my chest, chafing at his chains to be set free.

Big Tom jumped up on the piano and reams of revolutionary toilet paper that he wouldn't have wiped his own ass with, had he been sober, began to spill from his mouth. If this thing wasn't so goddamn serious, I would gladly have stepped into my hip boots just to keep the dukey out of my pockets. The shit was really getting deep! Cops were all over the joint, but the inmates were now openly brandishing their shanks, daring the guards to move, and those who hadn't brought their knives to the movies were easing out of the auditorium to go and get them. A blanket of fear had settled in, the frenzy would be next, and then the mob courage.

I don't know what made me do what I did next. Maybe it was only because Attica had just jumped off three months earlier and I knew that if the State Police of New Jersey were to come into

Rahway with their guns, they would make the New York police look like juvenile delinquents and the forty-three deaths in Attica like a window-smashing spree. Maybe it was because I was scared. Maybe it was because Fred Hogan's shadow had influenced my life and pumped a little hope back into it again. Maybe I didn't like the reason this thing was being started in the first place. Or maybe I had just been an undercover punk all along, and it took this to bring out the sissy in me. However it was, I decided to get the drunken nigger out of the auditorium, hoping to slow this thing down.

Tom was a big, black, husky rascal, perhaps twice my size, but I had pulled him out of a few tight corners a time or two, and he usually listened to me whenever I had something to say. Just the Sunday before I had stopped him from whupping a worthless cop's ass, although I should have let him kill the punk. But Big Tom had just won a reversal of his ten-year conviction in federal court, and this prejudiced bastard just wasn't worth the extra time. So I had talked Big Tom out of it, and this time was no different. After I rapped with him for two or three minutes, he climbed down from the piano and started walking out of the auditorium with me. But then the unexpected happened. Smilin' Sam Buck Savage arrived on the scene, and that was the catalyst which tipped the delicate balance in the room.

"Awright! Awright," he said, pushing his way through the crowd like gangbusters, his shirt sleeves rolled up as though he was going to whup somebody's ass or something. "Let's break this shit up, men! You can't win!"

Those words were his third mistake. Three strikes and out.

Oooooh, man! I thought, what's wrong with this motherfucker? —telling a prison full of born losers that they couldn't win. Jesus fucking Christ! That was like waving a red flag in the face of a charging bull. Even Big Tom, drunk as he was, wheeled around on him after that brainy salvo.

"Yeah, we can win, motherfucker!" Big Tom spat at Buck Savage, ignoring me completely. "Because we got you, and you're the one who started all this shit in the first place! And we're gonna tear this goddamn place down, now, sho 'nuff!" he said.

"Why don't you wise up, Tom?" The superintendent was pursuing his stupidity ruthlessly. "You know that you guys can't win! All I have to do is to push a button, and the state police will be here in two minutes."

"Why don't you button up your motherfucking lip!" I snapped at Buck Savage myself, now, and tried to get Tom's attention again. Things here were getting out of control.

"Don't even listen to him, Tom. Talk to me," I said. "Rubin. *I'm* talking to you!"

But it was already too late. Tom had broken away from me and jumped up on the stage. The inmates crowded around at the bottom of the platform, and the cops eased over to the doors, getting ready to get out of there. Just like any sensible person would have done. But the superintendent, either too brave or too goddamn stupid to know what he was getting into, followed the crowd to the foot of the stage. He was surrounded by a sea of shanks, clubs, baseball bats and iron pipes, and his life was hanging there by a little thread—but he had too much contempt for these guys to know it. I went up on the stage with Tom. I wasn't about to get shanked in that crowd.

"We gonna tear this motherfucker down!" Big Tom shouted.

And the inmates agreed: "Right on, brother!"

"We gonna stop these creeps from fuckin' with us!" he said.

And the crowd cheered again: "That's right, Lord!"

But I couldn't agree. I was torn between four different kinds of allegiances: to the inmates, because I had to continue living with them; to Fred Hogan, because he believed in me when no one else would; to my wife and daughter, for sticking with me for so long, and now I might have a shot to be back with them again; and to myself, for knowing the difference between right and wrong. Had this been for any one of the million-and-one valid instances of racism and brutality that normally pollute the insides of any jail, this would have been my Mecca here tonight—I would have gotten to them all! But it wasn't; it was about some goddamn wine. So I decided to make one more effort at this peacemaking shit, and then I was getting the fuck out of there—if I could. The superintendent's attitude seemed to be a growing cancer in the inmates' bloodstreams.

Big Tom was the only strong man who was doing any talking, but he was no leader, just a roughneck, and I felt certain that if I could somehow get rid of him, it might give somebody else a chance to take over and ask why. Because the other strong men in the jail, those who pulled some kind of weight with the inmates, were just laying back in the bin to see what would happen. So I challenged Big Tom; he was the leader for the moment.

"Tom," I said, and the auditorium got quiet, "if you just want to fight somebody tonight, then I'll fight you. Up here on the stage. Just me and you. There's no sense getting everybody involved in this stupid shit."

"No! No! No!" the crowd chanted, shouting me down. "We ain't going for that!"

"Then I can't help you," I told them, "because this is wrong. But I won't hurt you either," I said, "because if I stayed, that's exactly what I would do. So I'm leaving."

And half the auditorium walked out with me.

The moment I left the stage, Big Tom grabbed Smilin' Sam Buck Savage and the revolution was on. The rest of the inmates vamped down on him and lit his stupid ass up. He was stabbed, kicked, beat over the back with a fire extinguisher, had a chair broke over his head, and ended up as the first superintendent in New Jersey prison history to be taken hostage in a riot. Six guards were also beaten and seized.

At the initial outburst, most of the inmates in the auditorium who hadn't left when I did now broke for the exits. The wing cops thought it was a full-scale assault and got in the wind with their shirttails smoking, leaving the doors wide open. When the would-be revolutionaries realized that the jail was theirs for the taking, they immediately began tearing ass. One guard found himself trapped up on the top floor in Four Wing, and when he was confronted with a bunch of inmates with shanks in their hands, had no other recourse but to give up his keys. The keys fit the locked boxes of the whole wing. So all the doors were swung open, and the bewildered inmates stuck their heads out. When they saw that the prison was being controlled by other prisoners, tired war cries began ringing out from tier to tier.

"Right on, baby!" "Let's tear this rotten motherfucker down!" "Kill the pigs, and power to the gorilla!"

But Big Tom, the gorilla, was stretched out in a cell, drunk.

The inmates tore the prison down, too! Then they turned their energies against one another, burning up people's cells, drinking up all the homemade brew they could find, robbing each other's personal belongings, jumping guys, looking for the stool pigeons, fucking them in the ass, degrading young boys, old men, anybody who didn't run with a pack. This was the mob courage that I was talking about.

The isolation unit on the top floor of One Wing was the last stronghold to be conquered. A band of staggering marauders, armed with sledgehammers and damn near drowned in tomato wine, ripped out a five-hundred-pound steel door, took another guard hostage, and released the prisoners held in solitary confinement. Among them was Alfred (Qayyum) Ravenal—a bad motherfucker! They released him for need of a leader.

This brother was a born warrior, known for his honesty and lack of jive. He was cunning as a fox, deadly as a coiled pit viper, and a man who didn't play the radio, didn't drink, didn't cuss, and didn't smoke. It took him only five minutes to see what was going down; that is, the condition of the "revolutionaries." So he backed off, sat down in a corner of the auditorium, and called anyone who approached him about taking over a goddamn fool. After this the rebelling inmates split up into little groups, each faction with their own thoughts on how to handle the situation.

Once the authorities accepted the rebellion as a legitimate riot, they turned off the heat and water—which left the prison cold and dry in the winter. The entrance door to Three Wing was a self-locking affair, and one of the guards had the foresight to slam it after I had gotten in. But he trapped the wing officer in there too. The same situation prevailed in Two Wing. Thus, the only two wings involved were One Wing and Four Wing, and they were connected by the auditorium, so the traffic between the two cell blocks was left unhampered. On a number of occasions, a band of drunken inmates tried to break down the Three Wing door to add the wing officer to their growing list of hostages, but the beginning of the wing was located only a few feet away from the rotunda, which is the Center, and a steady barrage of tear gas drove them scurrying back to Four Wing time and time again.

But we happened to have a veteran of prison riots locked in Three Wing, and the moment that the action started, he went around telling the guys to fill up their buckets with water before it was cut off. There were those who disregarded his advice, nonetheless, and, of course, they suffered miserably for it later on. Tear gas and smoke repeatedly burned everybody's eyes. There was no getting away from it. Gas hung in the air like smothering clouds of fog.

It was a time for sharing too: each inmate had to help the other, and there were many surprising examples of this concern for others shown. But we had a lot of creeps, too, so it was mostly an "Up your ass, buddy! I'm looking out for number one" action.

All night long the radios blared, and guys crowded around them hungry for news. Some goddamn revolution, I thought. No food. No water. No heat. And we had to get the latest from WCBS in New York to find out what was happening to us in New Jersey. Goddamn! No wonder the crackers had our black asses in slavery for so motherfuckin' long. Niggers couldn't even die right. A bunch of stupid sons of bitches!

I sat there in my cell all night just cussing the drunken niggers and Buck Savage out for having placed me in this unforgivable position. For five long years I'd been trying to avoid just this kind of situation, trying to fight my way back into court before the prison authorities could conjure up such an excuse as this to wipe me off the face of the planet. I hated this prison as much as it hated me for resisting to conform to its degenerate ways. I didn't need this penitentiary's kind of rehabilitation, which only meant giving up my manhood, anyhow. I had never been debilitated. I had never committed any crime. The crimes were committed against me. I was the victim of all the shit!

Yet, the fact remains that there are some things that one cannot allow to be done to himself, in or out of jail, regardless of the consequences—not without resistance or retaliation of some sort, anyway, not without losing part of his integrity, not without feeling ashamed and incomplete for the rest of his life. And being dehumanized, brutalized, and finally killed in snakepits like Rahway are just a few of those things, to my way of thinking. So I sat there all through the night lovingly caressing a twelve-inch shank.

Thanksgiving morning loomed dark and dreary with rain, startlingly reminiscent of the day back in September when Attica was stormed. At 7:45 a.m. the news came over the air that shotgun-bearing state troopers were massing outside of the prison, lining up four abreast at the front door and getting ready to come into Rahway to put down the rebellion by armed force. Vivid pictures of inmates being slaughtered like cattle flashed luridly in my mind. Anybody with any sense knew that once those trigger-happy law-and-order freaks crashed into the prison, a whole lot of black butts would be shitting for their last time.

One word from the governor, who, the radio said, was sitting 150 yards away in the Woodbridge State School, and the Grim

Reaper would have swept through the hallways of Rahway State Prison like Teddy Roosevelt taking San Juan Hill. I was one steaming mad black motherfucker, because I knew that my life wasn't worth a smell of rotten wolf pussy or two dead flies. If there was some kind of list being passed around of whom to get, of the inmates who were definitely slated for the graveyard, as there had been in other riots in New Jersey, I knew that my name would be at the very top. There was no doubt in my mind about that. When the state troopers rolled in here smoking, I'd be shot so full of lead that they wouldn't even bother to bury me—just stake out a claim and sell my body for the mineral rights.

John Artis was in Four Wing, and he couldn't help but be smack in the middle of all the shit. He was disturbed at what was going on though, and he came to the Three Wing door, through dense clouds of tear gas, to call for me. When I got there he told me about the condition of Buck Savage, saying that the man was hurt bad and in need of some medical attention—quick. But the revolutionaries would only give him an inmate nurse named James C. Garrett, who was already locked in Four Wing. Garrett was sewing up the warden's wounds with cotton thread and a common sewing needle, all he had available. John wanted to know if he should try to get Buck Savage out of there, but I told him to cool it, and if it came to that I'd come out myself.

By this time all the tough guys had started to wake up cold sober. All the wine was gone, the peanut butter and jelly stashes were depleted, and the big-time Mao Tse-tungs were reduced to smoking cigarette butts. The dry peanut butter had made them thirsty, but there wasn't any water to drink, and the freezing temperatures had long ago invaded their weary bones. Their hearts were weary, too. One group of inmates found Big Tom laying in a cell, huddled under a pile of rags, sleeping off his tomato high. The whole cell stunk of mildewed fruit wine from where he had thrown up during the night.

"Wake up, Tom!" they called, shaking their leader up out of his drunken stupor. "Get yourself together, man! The state troopers are outside. They're getting ready to come in here, and we want to know what to do with your hostages!"

Big Tom grunted, looked out from underneath the coats and rags he'd piled on top of himself during the night to keep warm, then sat up and wiped the sleep from his eyes. He was trembling from the cold and the after-effects of a terrible hangover. (Tomato wine was good going down, but the next day it was a mother-fucker!) His lips were cracked from the lack of water, and his eyes were bloodshot from the hooch. He sat there so long with his eyes closed and his mouth shut that the inmates thought he had gone back to sleep. They shook him again.

"Wake up, Tom!"

"Huh?" he said, finally getting himself together. "Whose hostages? Whatcha talkin' about, man?"

"We're talking about hostages, motherfucker," one inmate hissed. "The warden and them other six guards we got locked up on three tier—that's what we're talking about!"

"Oooh, Lord!" Tom exclaimed, definitely sober now. He was shaking like a leaf, and it wasn't from the hooch or the cold, either. "What have ya'll done did!" he moaned. "Ya'll gonna take me hostage, too?"

Black people, as a rule, are fearless enough after a fashion, whenever they really have to be. But the terror of sure death always hangs over them, the reality of certain destruction, and not idle threats. It was this way with the majority of the inmates.

"Not ya'll, you winehead nigger, you!" the inmate shouted in rage. "This is *your* revolution, motherfucker! And the cops are getting ready to kill us all. For you! So get your black ass out there and tell us what to do! We're ready to go with it!"

"Oooooh, Lord, not me," Big Tom moaned pathetically. "I don't want to die!" he said. The only thing missing was the "Robert E. Lee" rolling around the bend of the Mississippi River, a bale of cotton for the tough nigger to sit on, and Old Black Joe would have been reborn. The group of inmates dug it, too, and just walked away shaking their heads, leaving their illustrious generalissimo pissing in his pants and scratching his nappy head. He had placed the lives of eleven hundred men in jeopardy for a quart of tomato wine. Goddamn!

So for all intents and purposes, the Rahway rebellion was now over. Fortunately, however, there were a few good dudes who managed to salvage a rosebud out of the pile of shit: they presented a hastily formed list of grievances to the authorities, which wasn't hard to do, considering, and a short time later, Vukcevich and the six guards were released. It was kept comparatively quiet, but all this was due to a black guard named Mr. Eddie Mullins, who was held as a hostage at one point himself but was released on his word of honor to get the inmates' side of the story out to the news media to prevent another Attica. This he did, and kept his word, but he lost his job because of it.

Shortly after seven o'clock that night, the blaring loudspeakers inside the prison politely asked the inmates to return to their cells, and a team of community people were allowed inside the jail to oversee this movement, guaranteeing no reprisals while makeshift repairs were performed on the broken locks. But let me tell you something: a whole lot of would-be bad motherfuckers in this prison sighed with ecstatic relief when they saw the state troopers appear at the end of the tiers, unarmed. It was a miracle that nobody had been killed—then.

But just as surely as if the ungodly three had placed a gun to Qayyum Ravenal's head and pulled the trigger themselves, they killed one of the best men in the state of New Jersey, maybe even the world. Once the disturbance was quelled, forty-one inmates were shipped out to the Vroom Building, to the Trenton State Hospital for the criminally insane. Alfred Ravenal was one of those to go, even though he had nothing to do with the riot (he had been the one who released the black officer to get to the press) and had been released from solitary confinement through no fault of his own. But the administration was afraid of him, so they sent him away. Months later he escaped with four others and was killed in a shoot-out with the state police in Pennsylvania. A state trooper was also killed.

On the morning following the Thanksgiving Day Rebellion, Fred Hogan rushed to the penitentiary to see me. With him was the Public Defender of New Jersey, a Mr. Stanley Van Ness, Arthur Penn, and many others from that office who were to assist the inmates who had any criminal charges lodged against them for their participation in the riot. Hogan and Van Ness had been waiting outside the prison all night long at the request of the governor.

When I was introduced to Stanley Van Ness that morning, I was surprised that he was so young, because I had heard so much about him. But what startled me the most was to find myself talking to another black man! Mr. Van Ness had accepted my case on the strength of Fred Hogan's new "evidence." And hope galore abounded within me.

From that day on, Fred Hogan was assigned to Rahway State Prison as the resident father-confessor for society's forgotten other half and assumed the unpopular position as liaison between the frightened inmates and the still prickling administration. He brought in teams of lawyers every day, coordinated their workloads, and held his own interviews all day and far into the night, talking to anybody with a problem. His relentless driving energy soon freed many a poor prisoner who'd been abandoned by his shyster lawyer to languish in jail for the lack of hard cold cash, and at the same time he continued to work steadily on my own case.

The man was simply inexhaustible, and Rahway's miserable administration was smarting under the weight of his tireless efforts. He was burdening them too quickly with meaningful change, and they despised him for that; the deep wounds from the riot were still festering. They considered him a poacher on their sacred territory, stealing their bread and butter, because the inmates respected Hogan more than anyone else in the jail. So the administration started throwing stumbling blocks in his path: two dirt-farming sergeants who had no business working around men in the first place, always made it their business to harass him unnecessarily, and finally Smilin' Sam Buck Savage himself—still crippled and out on sick leave—banished Fred from the institution. He claimed that Hogan had carried a letter out of the institution from me to my manager's wife (who was on my mailing list anyway), when in fact I had mailed the letter to Hogan from the prison as a letter of introduction to her.

Before Fred was exiled, however, and to the chagrin of my enemies, I know, he completed his job to perfection. He left behind a helluva footprint pointing in the right direction for penal reform in New Jersey. But that wasn't all he did. He opened up several blocked avenues on which I could continue to work towards gaining my release. The publication of this book is just one of those avenues. Fred also encouraged an attorney, Michael B. Blacker— who played a major role in abolishing the death penalty in New Jersey before it had been decided by the United States Supreme Court—to help research my case and draw up the legal arguments to submit to a federal court.

But since the time of Fred's ouster, Rahway State Prison has moved persistently backward rather than forward, in terms of what it was before the Thanksgiving Day Rebellion. It has deteriorated from being the most progressive penal institution in the state of New Jersey to the most repressive. There was no such thing as racism in Rahway before the riot, between the inmates or the cops, but it's more deeply rooted here now than in any prison in the country. And it's growing worse with every passing day, because now this racism is being directed against our minds as well as our physical selves. There was no brutality before, but now it's a common sight, because cowards, when finally placed in a position of strength, bear the most malice toward the cowardice in others, feeding their own tired egos at the expense of those they're suppose to be helping. Before the Thanksgiving Day orgy, there were men walking around inside of this institution, but there aren't too many here now—only stool pigeons, punks, drug addicts, institutionalized freaks, religious cop-outs, and whatchamacallits running around with braided hair, tight pants, and high-heeled shoes hollering, "Right on, Brother! Power to the people!"

The riot did absolutely nothing to inform the community outside of the real horrors of this prison life. Regardless of how misdirected it was, it was valid, and what the administration here fails to understand is that it might not be the same way the next time—and *there will be a next time*. There always will be a next time, à la Attica, West Virginia, Oklahoma, Holmesburg, or Leavenworth. As long as there are frustrated men and women jammed into prisons like sardines in a can, with their backs pressed against the wall, there will definitely be a next time. But to satisfy the pigheaded demands of the people around us on the outside, reinforced concrete and steel are lavishly meted out around the world and transformed into high walls and modern cell blocks designed to meet the comfort of yet another generation of criminals. Maybe they will be some of your sons and daughters. Governments are willing to spend millions of their taxpayers' hard-earned dollars to rebuild or reinforce obsolete prisons, but they're not willing to stop for a minute to listen to the simple problems that make the spending of all this money so goddamn necessary! And when they do spend, it's seldom in the right places. Take, for example, our own Buck Savage building fences inside the jail instead of trying to improve the meals and the medical and educational facilities.

Since the Thanksgiving Day Rebellion at Rahway, inmates throughout New Jersey have been clamoring for some authentic rehabilitation, begging the public for their help, appealing to them to please listen to their troubles and pains, and still they've received nothing but false promises. Yet, at the same time, the public has given the prison authorities more money to buy more shotguns and more riot gear, and more electric eyes to sit out in the hallways of their cesspool penitentiaries on display, doing absolutely nothing.

Rahway, like most other prisons in this country, is once more teetering on the brink of a disaster similar to Thanksgiving Day's—only ten times more deadly—because there are those of us still here who found ourselves trapped in the middle of that last joke, and we won't be caught flatfooted again. Though our elected officials have loudly claimed to be more aware today than ever of what it means to a man and his family to be locked away for long periods of time in a debilitating jungle of concrete and steel bars, I have yet to hear anything from out there but apathetic silence. When some unfortunate mother's sons, fathers, husbands, and brothers cried out in Attica for peace and understanding, the community around them bared their fangs and slaughtered every nigger in sight, even killed some of their own, and then turned to the rest of the world and lied in the name of law and order.

Now I'm coming to you. This book is my life's blood spilled out on the fifteen rounds of these pages. The sixteenth round is still being fought, and there's much more at stake here than a mere boxing title, or a big fat juicy purse.

This fight isn't sanctioned by the World Boxing Association, nor is it governed by the Marquess of Queensberry's fair rules. The weapons are not padded boxing gloves, left hooks, or knockout punches. This is a brand-new game, with one-sided rules to control the most important fight of my career. There won't be any glaring lights, cheering crowds, or well-wishers awaiting me at the end of this final round, if I lose it; only steel bars, stone walls, mind-bending games, mental anguish, and near insanity. And you know I'm not exaggerating.

I come to you in the only manner left open to me. I've tried the courts, exhausted my life's earnings, and tortured my two loved ones with little grains and tidbits of hope that may never materialize. Now the only chance I have is in appealing directly to you, the people, and showing you the wrongs that have yet to be righted—the injustice that has been done to me. For the first time in my entire existence I'm saying that I need some help. Otherwise, there will be no more tomorrow for me: no more freedom, no more injustice, no more State Prison; no more Mae Thelma, no more Theodora, no more Rubin—no more Carter. Only the Hurricane.

And after him, there is no more.

PRIZE FIGHTING RECORD

Rubin (Hurricane) Carter

Born in Clifton, New Jersey, on May 6, 1937. Height 5 feet 8 inches. Engaged in 56 amateur bouts. Had 36 KOs, won 15 decisions, and lost 5. No draws.

1961	SEPTEMBER 22	Pike Reed, Annapolis	W	4
	OCTOBER 11	Joey Cooper, Reading	KO	2
	OCTOBER 24	Frank Nelson, Philadelphia	KO	1
	NOVEMBER 17	Herschell Jacobs, Totowa	W	4
1962	JANUARY 19	Herschell Jacobs, Totowa	L	6
	FEBRUARY 14	Tommy Settles, Union City	KO	1
	FEBRUARY 28	Felix Santiago, Union City	KO	1
	MARCH 16	Jimmy McMillan, Jersey City	KO	3
	APRIL 16	Johnny Tucker, New York	KO	1
	APRIL 30	Walter Daniels, New York	KO	2
	MAY 21	Sugar Boy Nando, New York	KO	3
	JUNE 23	Ernie Burford, New York	L	8
	AUGUST 4	Ernie Burford, New York	KO	2
	OCTOBER 5	Mel Collins, Jersey City	KO	5
	OCTOBER 27	Florentino Fernandez, New York	KO	1
	DECEMBER 22	Holly Mims, New York	KO	10
1963	FEBRUARY 2	Gomeo Brennan, New York	W	10
	MARCH 30	José Gonzalez, New York	KO by	6
	MAY 25	George Benton, New York	W	10
	SEPTEMBER 14	Farid Salim, Pittsburgh	W	10
	OCTOBER 25	Joey Archer, New York	L	10
	DECEMBER 20	Emile Griffith, Pittsburgh	KO	1

1964	FEBRUARY 28	Jimmy Ellis, New York	W	10
	JUNE 24	Clarence James, Los Angeles	KO	1
	DECEMBER 14	Joey Giardello, Philadelphia	L	15
		(*for Middleweight title*)		
1965	FEBRUARY 12	Luis Rodriguez, New York	L	10
	FEBRUARY 22	Fabio Bettini, Paris	KO	10
	MARCH 9	Harry Scott, London	KO	9
	APRIL 20	Harry Scott, London	L	10
	APRIL 30	Johnny Torres, Paterson	KO	8
	MAY 20	Dick Tiger, New York	L	10
	JULY 14	Fate Davis, Akron	KO	1
	AUGUST 26	Luis Rodriguez, Los Angeles	L	10
	SEPTEMBER 18	Joe Ngidi, Johannesburg	KO	2
1966	JANUARY 8	Wilbert Skeeter McClure, Chicago	W	10
	JANUARY 18	Johnny Morris, Pittsburgh	L	10
	JANUARY 25	Stan Harrington, Honolulu	L	10
	FEBRUARY 27	Ernie Burford, Johannesburg	KO	8
	*MARCH 8	Wilbert Skeeter McClure, Toledo	D	10
	AUGUST 6	Rocky Rivero, Rosario	L	10

From *The Ring Encyclopedia*, 1967 edition.
* Commission changed decision to a draw, due to incorrect score card.